Theology, Music and Time

Theology, Music and Time aims to show how music can enrich
and advance theology, extending our wisdom about God and
God's ways with the world. Instead of asking: what can
theology do for music?, it asks: what can music do for
theology? Jeremy Begbie argues that music's engagement
with time gives the theologian invaluable resources for
understanding how it is that God enables us to live 'peaceably'
with time as a dimension of the created world. Without
assuming any specialist knowledge of music, he explores
a wide range of musical phenomena – rhythm, metre,
resolution, repetition, improvisation – and through them
opens up some of the central themes of the Christian faith –
creation, salvation, eschatology, time and eternity, eucharist,
election and ecclesiology. In so doing, he shows that music can
not only refresh theology with new models, but also release it
from damaging habits of thought which have hampered its
work in the past.

JEREMY S. BEGBIE is Vice Principal of Ridley Hall,
Cambridge. He teaches systematic theology at Ridley Hall and
in Cambridge University. He is Director of 'Theology Through
the Arts', Centre for Advanced Religious and Theological
Studies, Faculty of Divinity, University of Cambridge. Jeremy
Begbie is a professionally trained musician, and has performed
extensively as a pianist, oboist and conductor. In addition, he
is an ordained minister in the Church of England and is a
member of the Doctrine Commission of the Church of
England. He is author of *Music in God's Purposes* (1989) and
Voicing Creation's Praise (1991), as well as many articles.

Cambridge Studies in Christian Doctrine

Edited by
Professor COLIN GUNTON, *King's College London*
Professor DANIEL W. HARDY, *University of Cambridge*

Cambridge Studies in Christian Doctrine is an important series
which aims to engage critically with the traditional doctrines of
Christianity, and at the same time to locate and make sense of
them within a secular context. Without losing sight of the
authority of scripture and the traditions of the church, the books
in this series subject pertinent dogmas and credal statements
to careful scrutiny, analysing them in light of the insights of both
church and society, and thereby practise theology in the
fullest sense of the word.

Titles published in the series

1. Self and Salvation: Being Transformed
   DAVID F. FORD

2. Realist Christian Theology in a Postmodern Age
   SUE PATTERSON

3. Trinity and Truth
   BRUCE D. MARSHALL

4. Theology, Music and Time
   JEREMY S. BEGBIE

5. The Bible, Theology, and Faith: A Study of Abraham and Jesus
   R. W. L. MOBERLY

6. Bound to Sin: Abuse, Holocaust and the Christian Doctrine of Sin
   ALISTAIR McFADYEN

7. Church, World and the Christian Life: Practical-Prophetic Ecclesiology
   NICHOLAS M. HEALY

8. Theology and the Dialogue of Religions
   MICHAEL BARNES SJ

Titles forthcoming in the series

A Political Theology of Nature
PETER SCOTT

Remythologizing Theology: Divine Action and Authorship
KEVIN J. VANHOOZER

Theology, Music and Time

Jeremy S. Begbie

PUBLISHED BY THE PRESS SYNDICATE OF THE UNIVERSITY OF CAMBRIDGE
The Pitt Building, Trumpington Street, Cambridge, United Kingdom

CAMBRIDGE UNIVERSITY PRESS
The Edinburgh Building, Cambridge CB2 2RU, UK
40 West 20th Street, New York, NY 10011–4211, USA
477 Williamstown Road, Port Melbourne, VIC 3207, Australia
Ruiz de Alarcón, 13, 28014 Madrid, Spain
Dock House, The Waterfront, Cape Town 8001, South Africa

http://www.cambridge.org

First published 2000
Reprinted 2001, 2002

Printed in the United Kingdom at the University Press, Cambridge

Typeface TEFFLexicon 9/13 pt   *System* QuarkXPress®   [SE]

A catalogue record for this book is available from the British Library

Library of Congress Cataloguing in Publication data

Begbie, Jeremy
Music, theology, and time / Jeremy S. Begbie.
    p.   cm.
Includes bibliographical references and index.
ISBN 0 521 44464 0 (hardback) – ISBN 0 521 78568 5 (paperback)
1. Music – Religious aspects. 2. Theology. I. Title.
ML3921.B44 2000
261.5'78–dc21   99-051389

ISBN 0 521 44464 0   hardback
ISBN 0 521 78568 5   paperback

To *Helen, Mark, Heather and Emma*

Contents

Musical examples

List of figures

Acknowledgements

An enterprise like this does not see the light of day without a large network of support, going back many years. I owe an immense debt of gratitude to one of my first teachers, Colin Kingsley of Edinburgh University, whose academic interests combined with high standards of performance provided an inspiration which has never waned, and to James Torrance, who many years ago introduced me to the limitless intellectual wonder of the Christian faith.

The Principal, Graham Cray, and the staff and students of Ridley Hall, Cambridge have shown much encouragement as this book has gradually taken shape. I am deeply grateful for dialogue with ordinands and graduate students at Ridley, and with many members of the University of Cambridge. David Ford has been a model of encouragement from the moment the idea for this book was first conceived. In numerous ways, his irrepressible intellectual enthusiasm has stretched me far beyond the predictable and commonplace. My thanks are also due to Daniel Hardy, whose extraordinary multi-disciplinary instincts have enabled me to reach much further with 'theology through music' than I initially thought possible. Over many years, Colin Gunton has provided both intellectual food and musical insight. Alan Torrance's support, musical acumen and theological rigour have proved enormously important. Steven Guthrie has read much of the text and offered penetrating insights and sound advice, and my colleague at Ridley Hall, Michael Thompson, provided very helpful comments on the biblical sections. I am also very grateful for many illuminating conversations with Richard Bauckham, Maggi Dawn, John De Gruchy, Robert Duerr, Malcolm Guite, Trevor Hart, Simon Heathfield, Roger Lundin, James MacMillan, Stephen May, Ann Nickson, Micheal O'Siadhail, John Polkinghorne, Tiffany Robinson,

Andrew Rumsey, Chris Russell, Luci Shaw, Janet Martin Soskice, Dal Schindell, Paul Spicer, Nigel Swinford, Stephen Sykes, John Tavener, Anthony Thiselton, Rowan Williams and Tom Wright.

Much of what follows arose from my experience teaching outside the UK. I have greatly benefited from discussions with friends, scholars, musicians and many artists at Regent College, Vancouver; Fuller Seminary, Pasadena; Wheaton College, Illinois; Calvin College, Michigan; as well as at the universities of Yale, Stanford, Berkeley, Edinburgh, London and Cape Town. A large part of the text was completed while on sabbatical leave in 1995 at the Center for Theological Inquiry in Princeton – I greatly appreciate the considerable help I received from the scholars and staff there.

This book is one of the main outcomes of a project entitled 'Theology Through the Arts' which I have directed at the Centre for Advanced Religious and Theological Studies in the Faculty of Divinity, University of Cambridge. I could never have finished without the enthusiasm, insight and sheer hard work of my colleagues in that project, Fiona Bond and more recently Ally Barrett, together with the invaluable research assistance of Catherine Price. I am indebted also to Andrew Pearson, who patiently assembled the musical examples, and to Michelle Arnold, who compiled the indexes. The British and Foreign Bible Society have provided substantial funding for 'Theology Through the Arts' – without their support I would never have had time to complete this work, and I am immensely grateful to them.

Cambridge University Press has provided three editors over the years to nag me – Alex Wright, Ruth Parr and Kevin Taylor. Their patience and dedication have been exemplary, and Lucy Carolan has been superlative with the copy-editing.

Inevitably, families contribute an enormous amount to this kind of publication, and bear much of the hidden cost. My gratitude extends to my loyal parents, whose love for learning and wide range of interests have proved so influential upon me. And the largest debt of thanks must go to my forbearing wife, Rachel, and to my children, Helen, Mark, Heather and Emma, to whom this book is warmly dedicated.

I
_____

Introduction

Introduction

My guiding conviction in this book is that music can serve to enrich and advance theology, extending our wisdom about God, God's relation to us and to the world at large. I hope to show this with particular attention to that dimension of the world we call 'time'.

In the twentieth century, the corridors of theology were not generally alive with the sound of music. Music has received virtually no sustained treatment in contemporary systematic theology. Much has been written about the bearing of literature upon theological disciplines (especially biblical hermeneutics), and the same goes for the visual arts. There have been some courageous forays into theology by musicologists,[1] but apart from a few notable exceptions, twentieth-century theologians paid scant attention to the potential of music to explore theological themes.[2]

---

1. E.g. Mellers (1981, 1983); Chafe (1991).
2. Bonhoeffer's enticing discussion of polyphony is an exception (Bonhoeffer 1972, 302). David Ford's engaging treatment of 'polyphonic' living draws upon Bonhoeffer's work (Ford 1999, ch. 10). Hans Urs von Balthasar's *Truth is Symphonic* (von Balthasar 1987) and J. Pelikan's *Bach Among the Theologians* (Pelikan 1986a) are other exceptions. Dorothy Sayers sought to expound trinitarian doctrine through an extended analogy of artistic making (Sayers 1941), although both the doctrine of the Trinity she advocates and the model of creativity she employs are, I believe, highly problematic. David Cunningham reflects on polyphony as a contribution to theology, especially as it embodies difference without exclusion, unity without homogeneity (Cunningham 1998, 127ff.). But he does not discuss any particular music at length, or how the distinctive features of sound-perception challenge the 'zero-sum game' which he rightly sees as endemic in much theology (the more active God is in the world the less active we can be). Francis Watson's recent and curiously over-sceptical article on theology and music does not address in any sustained way the possibilities of music advancing theology (Watson 1998). Barth's treatment of Mozart will be discussed later.
   There have been modern theologians who, without treating music at length, have nevertheless pursued theology in a musical manner. The American theologian Jonathan Edwards is a prime example – I am very grateful to Dr Gerald McDermott of Roanoke College, Salem, Virginia, for pointing this out to me. Cf. Jenson (1988), 20, 35f., 42, 47ff., 169, 182, 195. Mention should also be made of Friedrich Schleiermacher's *Christmas Eve*

In some respects this is puzzling, given not only the supposedly limitless interests of theology, but also the universality of music in all cultures, the unprecedented availability and ubiquity of music in so-called 'postmodern' culture, the persistence of music in the worship of the Church, the strong traditions of theological engagement with music in past centuries, the intense interest shown in music by many philosophers past and present, the growing literature on the politics, sociology and psychology of music, the recent emergence of ethnomusicology, and the intriguing deployment of musical metaphors by natural scientists. In the chapters which follow, we shall be touching upon some reasons for this theological neglect. Undoubtedly, one of them is the difficulty of speaking about music in ways which do justice to its appeal and which genuinely shed new light upon it. As George Steiner observes: 'In the face of music, the wonders of language are also its frustrations.'[3] Another reason is the opacity of the process of musical communication: it is clear *that* music is one of the most powerful communicative media we have, but *how* it communicates and *what* it communicates are anything but clear.

Whatever the reasons, this almost complete theological disregard of music is regrettable. For, as I hope to show, when theology is done with musicians as conversation partners, music is found to have considerable power to generate fresh and fruitful resources for the theological task. Jacques Attali, in his remarkable (if eccentric) book *Noise*, declares that 'Music is more than an object of study: it is a way of perceiving the world. My intention is ... not only to theorise *about* music, but to theorise *through* music.'[4] Attali's principal interests are in the socio-economic aspects of music but his words prompt the question: what would it mean to theologise not simply *about* music but *through* music? This book is a preliminary attempt to answer that question.

footnote 2. (*cont.*)
(Schleiermacher 1967). In a number of writings, Jon Michael Spencer has argued that 'theomusicology' should be recognised as a legitimate discipline (see e.g. Spencer 1991, 1994); theomusicology being 'a musicological method for theologizing about the sacred, the secular, and the profane, principally incorporating thought and method borrowed from anthropology, sociology, psychology, and philosophy' (Spencer 1991, 3). Among the differences between Spencer's approach and ours are that his focus is generally more cultural and anthropological, there is relatively little analytic attention to musical sounds and their interrelation, and theologically his purview is much wider than the Christological and trinitarian perspective of this book (his concern being with religion on a very broad scale).
   In relation to biblical interpretation, Frances Young's book *The Art of Performance* is an illuminating essay, utilising musical models to understand the hermeneutical process (Young 1990). Nicholas Lash and Stephen Barton develop similar lines of thought (Lash 1986; Barton 1997, ch. 2, and more fully in a later article, 1999).   3. Steiner (1997), 65.
   4. Attali (1985), 4.

My main aim, therefore, is not to offer a 'systematic theology of music', an account of music which situates it within a particular doctrinal environment. This kind of enterprise has a legitimate and necessary place in the music–theology conversation.[5] But this book is rather different. Without pretending that we can ever operate in a theological vacuum – we shall underline this in the final chapter – our primary purpose here is to enquire as to the ways in which music can benefit theology. The reader is invited to engage with music in such a way that central doctrinal loci are explored, interpreted, re-conceived and articulated. It will be found that unfamiliar themes are opened up, familiar topics exposed and negotiated in fresh and telling ways, obscure matters – resistant to some modes of understanding – are clarified, and distortions of theological truth avoided and even corrected. In this way, we seek to make a small but I hope significant contribution to the re-vitalising of Christian theology for the future. Not surprisingly, this can be a profoundly disturbing business, for many of theology's most cherished habits will be questioned and shaken.[6]

It is important to stress that when music advances theology in this way, it does so first and foremost by *enacting* theological wisdom. We shall be arguing that music is best construed primarily as a set of practices, actions involving the integration of many facets of our make-up. Music is fundamentally about making and receiving sounds, and this book is designed to show some of the theological fruit which can emerge from examining carefully what is involved in this making and reception. Obviously, then, the written form of this book is inadequate: ideally we need not only an enclosed CD but live music of some sort. But being restricted to written words need not worry us unduly, provided we bear in mind throughout that when we speak of music we speak chiefly of something made and heard – sung, played, performed, listened to – and it is to the complexities of this making and hearing that we seek to be true in what follows. (It is no accident that the major musical impetus for this book has come not from reading books about music but from my experience of giving concerts, music teaching, conducting orchestras

---

5. See Begbie (1989, 1991b).

6. My project here is parallel in many ways to that of Kathleen Marie Higgins in her fine study *The Music of Our Lives* (Higgins 1991). She sets out to show how music can further *ethical* reflection, noting that music's ethical dimension has been largely lost sight of in both musical and philosophical thought. In addition to what she says about ethics, I am very sympathetic to Higgins' general approach to music, marked as it is by a desire to overcome the damaging isolation of music from wider networks of thought and practice, while still doing justice to its distinctiveness.

and choirs, improvising with others, as well as talking to numerous musicians.)

Some of the limits I have set myself need to be made clear. Theologically, my main focus will be on the benefit of music for 'systematic theology' (sometimes also described as 'Christian doctrine', 'dogmatic theology' or 'constructive theology'), that branch of theology concerned with the doctrinal loci which give the Christian faith its characteristic shape and coherence – e.g. creation, Trinity, incarnation and so forth.

Many gain their main theological benefit from music by listening to settings of biblical texts, such as Bach's *St Matthew Passion* or Handel's *Messiah*; others from the setting of liturgical texts such as Mozart's Masses; others from musicals such as *Jesus Christ Superstar*; others from songs which tackle theological matters less directly (those of U2 or Van Morrison, for example); others from music which has no overt theological intent but which has come to have powerful theological associations. In this study I largely leave to one side music strongly tied to words, texts, narratives, liturgy and other particular associations. I concentrate on music in its more abstract genres not because I believe it to be intrinsically superior or because I believe music can or should be sealed off from everything extra-musical, but because such music is best at throwing into relief the peculiar properties of musical sounds I wish to highlight and the distinctive way in which they operate.[7]

I have chosen to concentrate on one major dimension of music, its temporality. Music is, of course, a temporal art. But beneath this apparently straightforward assertion lie many layers of significance. When we ask *how* music is temporal, we are confronted by an enormous range of temporal processes. We are also struck by how much can be learned about time through music. In the words of Victor Zuckerkandl: 'there is hardly a phenomenon that can tell us more about time and temporality than can music'.[8] Music offers a particular form of participation in the world's temporality and in so doing, we contend, it has a distinctive capacity to elicit something of the nature of this temporality and our involvement with it (as well as to question many misleading assumptions about it). Here we try to show how the experience of music can serve to open up features of a distinctively *theological* account of created temporality, redeemed by God

7. The one major exception I have allowed myself is John Tavener's music (chapter 5), much of which sets Christian texts. I make the exception because the music powerfully highlights key issues with regard to time and eternity, because it is so overtly theological in intent and because it currently enjoys immense popularity.   8. Zuckerkandl (1956), 152.

in Jesus Christ, and what it means to live in and with time as redeemed creatures.

For reasons of space, I have decided to concentrate principally on the kind of music that will be best known to readers, namely Western 'tonal' music. This musical tradition emerged towards the end of the seventeenth century and has been predominant ever since in European culture and in cultures primarily shaped by modern Europe. It is the tradition of Beethoven and Bach, as well as the Spice Girls and Michael Jackson. To restrict ourselves in this way does not commit us to a cultural hegemony which automatically exalts this music to a position of superiority above all others. Nor should it be taken to imply any particular value-judgements about types of music outside Western tonality. In any case, Western tonal music itself has unclear boundaries; it can share many features with traditions normally regarded as non-Western. (If 'tonal' is taken in a very broad sense to refer to any music with fixed reference pitches – tones within a piece which act as stabilisers – then virtually all music can be considered 'tonal', since such tonal stabilisers are extremely common in music worldwide.[9]) Nor do I want to suggest that this music is necessarily better equipped than any other for tackling questions of time and temporality. And I am not discounting other forms of music as fruitful for theology; different types of music have different theological capabilities.

No particular musical expertise is required to read this book. To be sure, we need to give music a certain amount of 'room' so that it is allowed to bring to the surface those aspects of Christian truth with which it is especially qualified to deal, and this entails some musical analysis. The sections in a contrasting (sans serif) typeface are designed for those who can read music and are accustomed to some of the basic vocabulary of musicology, and the footnotes do occasionally contain some technical terms. But these are intended only to support the main text, which should be comprehensible on its own to those who do not read music and are unfamiliar with its theoretical discourse.

In the first chapter, some markers are set down in musical aesthetics as guidelines for the material which follows. Chapter 2 outlines some of the main characteristics of the temporality of Western tonal music. This paves the way for the specifically theological matters which are addressed in the rest of the book. Four chapters relate the findings of chapters 1 and 2 to various theological fields: the reality and goodness of the world's

---

9. Sloboda (1993), 253ff.

temporality, created and redeemed in Christ (chapter 3); eschatology (with special attention to musical resolution) (chapter 4); time and God's eternity (with particular reference to the music of John Tavener) (chapter 5); and eucharistic theology (explored through musical repetition) (chapter 6). The next three chapters examine one particular musical practice – improvisation. We focus on its intriguing interplay of constraint and contingency, opening out a major theme in theological anthropology, namely human freedom (chapters 7 and 8). Election and ecclesial ethics are then explored through the dynamics of improvisatory gift-exchange (chapter 9). I close with some brief reflections on the ways in which music functions in this book, and some of the wider implications of our study for theology in the future (chapter 10).

I am aware that many composers and many forms of music which could throw light on issues of theology and time are not mentioned. Likewise, many areas of doctrine which could have been drawn into the discussion are left to one side. But my desire is not to be comprehensive, either musically or theologically, but to demonstrate possibilities in a few specific areas in order that others can extend the discussion further afield. Despite the limitations, my hope is that at the very least the reader will conclude that music, so often thought to be at best half-articulate and at worst corrupting, has significant potential to help us discover, understand and expound theological truth, to the advantage of theology and the deepening of our knowledge of God.

1

_____

Practising music

Any theologian who wants to learn from the world of music is going to have to ask some basic questions about what this remarkable practice we call 'music' actually is.[1] And if there is one thing we should stress from the start it is just that, that when we speak of music we speak of a practice or, better, a multiplicity of practices.

We can keep the principal practices in mind as we proceed, even if their edges are unclear and they often overlap. At the most basic level, there are two interlocking and mutually informative procedures: those which engender music – *music-making*, and those of perception – *music-hearing*, and under 'hearing' I mean to include all the faculties associated with musical reception, not only the ears. We may speak of music-making as the intentional bringing into being of temporally organised patterns of pitched sounds. For these sound-patterns to be called music, clearly, someone must be able to hear them not just as patterns of sounds but as patterns of 'tones'[2] to which the term 'music' can be appropriately applied: 'A person is making music when he intentionally produces certain sounds which he believes *could* be heard as music by some (extant) persons.'[3]

Music-making and hearing are properly considered the foundational realities of music. And throughout this book we shall be stressing that these practices entail a peculiarly intense involvement with *time*, with the world's temporality. By contrast, our culture has schooled many of us into thinking of music as basically about written 'works', which can be understood, to a large extent at any rate, apart from their temporal constitution

1. The word 'music' can in fact speak of a huge range of phenomena. It is a term without clear and widely accepted semantic boundaries, and this is especially so if one thinks globally. See Sparshott (1987), 43ff.
2. In this book I shall use 'tone' to denote any discrete pitched sound that is recognised as musical.   3. Wolterstorff (1987), 116.

or situation. In the Western tonal tradition, musical works, so under-stood, have come to occupy a very prominent place. Much modern musi-cology has revolved around the study of works, treated as if they were self-contained objects, with no intrinsic connection to the circumstances of their production or reception, and as if they were best understood in terms of their structural features (as written down in a score), rather than their acoustical and physical characteristics as experienced.[4] But, as many scholars have stressed, this objectification of the musical work is highly questionable.[5] People were making and hearing music long before works were conceived, written or performed. Moreover, when we look carefully at what is designated by the term 'work', we soon find that it is highly arti-ficial to imagine we are dealing merely with sound-patterns abstracted from actions. Nicholas Wolterstorff writes of an imaginary society whose music-making and hearing develops through stages, from the emergence of various musical genre concepts, through the establishing of rules for music-making, and repeated acts of music-making which follow the same rules, through to the emergence of works.[6] Whatever the historical accu-racy of his account, it serves to remind us that the concept of a work is not foundational but has emerged from a variety of activities. Wolterstorff goes on to argue that what we now choose to call a 'work' entails a com-plex interplay between a 'performance-kind' (types of performance); a set of correctness and completeness rules (rules of correctness specify what constitutes a correct playing or singing, rules of completeness specify what constitutes a complete playing or singing); a set of sounds and (usu-ally) ways of making sounds such that the rules specify those as the ones to be exemplified.[7] To insist that a work of music consists entirely of sound-patterns, or of sound-patterns heard in a certain way, or sound-patterns codified in a score, is artificial and inadequate – for it also con-sists of actions, and this means actions which can only properly be understood as temporally constituted and situated.

But we need to fill out these sketchy preliminary remarks. Without pretending that this book is a substantial treatise in musical aesthetics, and without attempting to provide a sustained case for any aesthetic stance (huge aesthetic issues will be side-stepped and giant questions

4. The rise of so-called 'autonomous', non-functional music, the development of the conviction that this kind of music is a paradigm for all music, and the emergence of sophisticated forms of notation – these are among the factors associated with this characteristically modern conception of a 'work'.
5. See e.g. the discussions by Cook (1998b) and Higgins (1991), among many others.
6. Wolterstorff (1987), 117ff.   7. Ibid., 120.

begged), I need at least to map some of the routes through the musical-aesthetic jungle with which I feel most content, even if I cannot justify here adequately why I choose these routes and not others.

Unnecessary polarisations

The way in which music 'means' has been an issue of perennial fascination and debate. Two broad tendencies in music theory may be distinguished. We may speak of *extrinsic* theories of musical meaning which pivot on what is believed to be music's capacity to relate in some manner to some extra-musical/non-musical object or objects or states of affairs (e.g. emotions, ideas, physical objects, events etc.); and *intrinsic* theories which lay the principal stress on the relationships between the constituent elements of music itself.[8] The history of musical aesthetics 'may well impress us as a kind of pendulum, swinging between these two conceptions, across a whole spectrum of intermediary nuances'.[9] But there seems little to be gained by polarising these as competing and mutually exclusive. For, as even common sense would seem to indicate, music generates meaning *both* through its own intrinsic relations *and* through its extra-musical connections.[10] It is hard to give any satisfactory account of musical meaning which rigorously excludes one or the other.

Music's referential limitations

Certainly, music of itself does not in any very obvious way 'point' with precision and reliability to particular extra-musical entities. The inadequacy of certain linguistic theories of reference when applied to music has long been recognised. The sound-patterns of music do not normally 'refer' beyond themselves with consistency and clarity to the world of specific objects, events, ideas etc. Music can provide virtually nothing in the way of propositions or assertions. Peter Kivy comments: 'even the simplest narration seems to require a propositional content beyond that of music to convey. Music cannot say that Jack and Jill went up the hill. It cannot say Mary had a little lamb, and the failure must lie in the inability

---

8. The latter type will tend to align with structuralist semantics, and is sometimes brought under the umbrella of 'formalism', although this term is notoriously polyvalent and perhaps should now be dropped altogether from the discussion.   **9.** Nattiez (1990), 110.
10. 'If there is an *essential being* of music defined from a semiological vantage point, I would locate that being in the *instability* of the two fundamental modes of musical referring' (ibid., 118).

of music to express the appropriate propositional content even of such limiting cases of narration.'[11] Attempts to account for musical meaning in terms of representation, in the manner of, say, a representational painting, are no less problematic. Music's capacities in this respect are extremely limited, and the pleasure derived from musical experience does not seem to arise to any large extent from its representative powers.[12]

This is not to deny that music has been and can be employed quite deliberately to refer specifically to extra-musical phenomena (as with the depiction of bird-song in the second movement of Beethoven's *Pastoral* symphony). It can be ordered in such a way as to correspond to some kind of atmospheric or pictorial reality (as in Debussy's *La Mer* or Musorgsky's *Pictures at An Exhibition*). It can be made to interact with extra-musical narrative or sequence of events (as in Richard Strauss's *Till Eulenspiegel* or Paul Dukas' *The Sorcerer's Apprentice*). A musical phrase or passage may be employed to indicate a character or event in, say, a music-drama of some sort (as so often in Wagner). Units of music, from motifs to whole pieces, can come to acquire an instantly recognisable significance. Composers for television, film and video rely heavily on these kinds of connections. But in these instances, what we hear would still be formally justified even if the connections were unknown or ignored. (The fact that the same tone-patterns can be employed successfully in radically different contexts strengthens the point.) The principal reason for this will become clear as we proceed: musical tones become meaningful, not fundamentally because of their relation to anything to which they might of themselves 'point' – not even other tones – but because they are *dynamically and intrinsically interrelated* to preceding and coming sounds. This is not an accidental feature of music derived from our present mode of interest in music; it would appear to belong to the heart of the way music turns sounds into tones. This feature of music is crucial to the main concerns of this book.

Music's interconnectedness

Nevertheless, we should be careful not to jump to the conclusion that musical meaning is best considered as locked up in its own autonomous zone, as if the rationality of music were somehow wholly intra-musical. The ideology of musical autonomy, the cult of what Kivy calls 'music alone',[13] has had a long and distinguished run for its money, even though

---

11. Kivy (1984), 159.   12. S. Davies (1994), ch. 2; Scruton (1997), ch. 5.   13. Kivy (1990).

its hold may have loosened considerably in the last few decades.[14] Indeed, just because music is relatively weak in consistent referral, it is generally freer than, say, language to interact with its contexts in the generation of meaning. Musical sounds relate to extra-musical phenomena and experience in a wide variety of ways, not only extrinsically by convention and ascription, but intrinsically by virtue of the properties of sounds, and of sound-producing and sound-receiving entities. 'Pure music,' Nicholas Cook reminds us, 'is an aesthetician's (and music theorist's) fiction'.[15] Or, as I sometimes say to my students, 'there is more to music than meets the ear'.

In this book, our particular interest is in music's temporality. One way in which music becomes meaningful for us is through the interplay between its temporal processes and a vast range of temporal processes which shape our lives in the world – from the rhythm of breathing to the coming and going of day and night. It will be our contention that this interplay can be of considerable interest to the theologian. But with this general point in mind, more specific connections between the musical and extra-musical need to be noted. I mention only four.

First, in musicology it has become commonplace to emphasise the *social and cultural embeddedness of musical practices*. It is not sound-patterns alone which mean but people who mean through producing and receiving sound-patterns in relation to each other. The *bête noire* here is 'essentialism': treating music as if it were an asocial, acultural (and ahistorical) phenomenon, with no intrinsic ties to contingent, shared human interests.[16] Music always, to some extent, embodies social and cultural reality – no matter how individualistically produced, no matter how autonomous with respect to intended function, now matter how intertwined with the circumstances of a particular composer.

14. See e.g. Cook (1998b), Higgins (1991), Norris (1989), Hargreaves and North (1997). Theories of the 'self-containedness' of music are members of a larger family of theories which promote the view that 'genuine art must forgo all attachments to language, meaning, and content in order to enjoy autonomous self-referentiality' (Thomas 1995, 6). Cf. Begbie (1991b), 193ff., 215ff.   **15.** Cook (1998a), 92.

16. This takes us to the heart of what is sometimes called the 'New' musicology – a name coined by Lawrence Kramer in 1990. Nicholas Cook (who believes this musicology is now 'mainstream') writes: 'Central to it is the rejection of music's claim to be autonomous of the world around it, and in particular to provide direct, unmediated access to absolute values of truth and beauty. This is on two grounds: first, that there are no such things as absolute values (all values are socially constructed), and second that there can be no such thing as unmediated access; our concepts, beliefs, and prior experiences are implicated in all our perceptions. The claim that there are absolute values which can be directly known is therefore an ideological one, with music being enlisted to its service. A musicology that is 'critical' in the sense of critical theory, that aims above all to expose ideology, must then demonstrate that music is replete with social and political meaning'. (Cook 1998b, 117).

Among other things, this means recognising the enormous variety of social roles music can play – establishing cohesion between people, arousing emotion, expressing grief, praising a deity, putting to sleep, and so on. Listening to music for its own sake – 'disinterested' aesthetic contemplation in a hushed concert-hall, for example – is only *one* of the uses to which music can be put. To insist on it as the *sine qua non* of true music is restrictive and distorting.[17]

In this study, at various points some of the links between musical practices and wider socio-cultural realities will be traced. However, it needs to be said that the links are often extremely hard to trace with any precision. Most promising are attempts to discover correspondences or parallels between the structures of music and the formal structural characteristics of social and cultural practices, but the waters here are very muddy, and we have to admit that some commonly quoted accounts of music in relation to cultural concerns have been very tenuous. Furthermore, it is wise to resist a social reductionism which would seek to account for music exclusively in terms of socio-cultural determinants, or which would forget that different kinds of music may be socially and culturally conditioned to different degrees.[18]

17. I argue this in relation to the arts in general, in Begbie (1991b), 186ff. One of the most useful discussions of the social situatedness of music is provided by Nicholas Wolterstorff, who argues, drawing especially on Alasdair MacIntyre, that musical practices are intrinsically 'social practices' (Wolterstorff 1987).

18. This should make us cautious about the more unguarded claims made for the 'New' musicology. A significant stream of 'ideological criticism' would seek to construe music fundamentally (and, sometimes it would seem, solely) as the product of power relations in a particular society. Cf. e.g. Ballantine (1984); McClary (1991); L. Kramer (1990, 1995). Accordingly, 'the critic must assume the role of undeceiver, enabling us to perceive truly what has been enchanted, mystified, and hallowed in the interests of power' (Scruton 1997, 428). This can veer perilously close to treating music-makers and music-hearers as little more than ciphers of group interests. While a piece of music may indeed reflect, endorse and reinforce the social conditions (including the power relations) in which it is made, it may also question, extend and even reject them. Sometimes it may come close to transcending them altogether. Indeed, the ideological dimensions may be what is least interesting about a piece of music. Similarly with hearing music: the way a person hears music may be markedly out of line with his/her society's dominant habits. In addition, a rush to trace social meanings and power-plots in music will risk overlooking the configurations of sounds themselves and their own particular character. It is interesting to observe how a prominent musicologist like Nicholas Cook can react strongly against the notion of musical works as autonomous, asocial and ahistorical but then fail to find any convincing way out of a vicious vortex of social and cultural constructivism (Cook 1998b). He insists that music 'is *not* a phenomenon of the natural world but a human construction' (131), without considering the possibility that it might be, in very profound senses, both. He attacks the idea of 'private consciousness' as a bourgeois social construction (128f.), but the same could be said of his conviction that 'human consciousness [is] something that is irreducibly public' (128), a belief which he thinks can pull us back from the abyss of extreme relativism, saving us from a 'pessimism' about understanding music and using it as a means of personal and social transformation. What is missing here is any rooting of

Second, music-making and hearing arise from *an engagement with the distinctive configurations of the physical world we inhabit*. The entities of the extra-human physical world vibrate in certain ways and produce certain kinds of sound waves in accordance with their constitution. This very obvious point has in fact frequently been forgotten, but can be used to open up large fields of theological import, not least in relation to time.

Third, musical practice is inescapably *bodily*, another matter of theological potential, as we shall see. Our own physical, physiological and neurological make-up mediates and shapes the production and experience of sound to a very high degree.

Fourth, it has long been recognised that music has very strong connections with our *emotional life*. Vast intellectual energy has been invested in trying to trace the links. While it is going too far to claim that musical meaning lies purely and entirely in its emotional content – this is another kind of reductionism we need to avoid – music does seem able to 'express' emotion in remarkably powerful ways. Theories which identify this expressive content with the composer's emotions or with the emotion evoked in hearers will inevitably falter.[19] Some would argue that there is a

musical sounds in features of the extra-human physical world and universal features of the human constitution, features which can work *along with* social and cultural shaping.

We might add that to over-play the socio-cultural card will likely result in the matter of *aesthetic value* being dissolved too quickly into matters of social utility or function. There is a justifiable attack on the elevation of the notion of the 'aesthetic' and associated concepts of 'high' and 'fine' art etc. But much less justifiable is the intensification of the critique such that the entire concept of aesthetic value is treated, for example, as a particular moment or phase in the development of Enlightenment bourgeois culture, to be accounted for solely in terms of that culture's economic infrastructure. It is disingenuous to put such historical or cultural limitations on the concept of the aesthetic – both as an object and as a mode of perception. The examples of something akin to both, *outside* modern bourgeois culture, are legion. See Scruton (1997), 474ff. It is probably wiser to argue that there is an irreducible dimension of reality which we term 'aesthetic', exemplified in various qualities, qualities which have always been valued to some extent; that music, as with any art, can possess these qualities; that there is an associated posture or attitude with respect to these qualities; and that at various times and places in the history of musical practice the aesthetic and its corresponding attitude have been elevated to a place of considerable importance, and this for a variety of reasons. On these matters, see Begbie (1991b), 186–232.

19. It is fallacious to attribute the emotional content of a piece of music to the artist who created it, as if it were our task to recover the content of the artist's emotional state when he or she was composing. Thousands of pieces bear little or no resemblance to the composer's emotional condition at the time of composition. It is also fallacious to identify expressive content with an emotion evoked. A work may express grief without our feeling grief. A similar point should be made about emotional associations – music may come to have strong emotional associations for us, but we would be misguided if we identified its expressive content with such associations.

Mention should be made here of Deryck Cooke's classic *tour de force* entitled *The Language of Music* (1959). The author proposes and defends the thesis that music is a 'language of the emotions'. He argues that a musical lexicon can be devised which assigns emotive resemblance between musical patterns and emotional patterns in the mind. Emotions are essentially states of mind which music in some way resembles: to say that music expresses an emotion is simply to draw attention to the resemblance.[20] Although it cannot be denied that there will be correspondences between the temporal patterns of emotional experience and the temporal patterns of music, there are weaknesses in this kind of account. In addition to presupposing too readily that emotions are best construed as mental states, resemblance theories of this sort trade on the main drawback of representational theories of music, the notion that essential to the understanding of music is the hearing, in addition to the sounds, of some kind of discrete referent which claims our intrinsic interest – in this case, an emotion or emotional pattern. It is far from obvious that this is what happens. Even in cases where a composer may deliberately draw our attention to emotional states – for instance, through a title or other associated texts – it is normally quite possible for the music to be intelligible without attending to the texts or their reference. Moreover, and perhaps most importantly, the most interesting question about

footnote **19** (*cont.*)
meanings to basic terms of musical vocabulary, even if such meanings are not rigidly fixed. In Western music since 1400, Cooke points to numerous correlations between emotions and particular patterns of melodies, rhythms and harmonies which have been used to convey these emotions. Such evidence suggests that music is a means of communicating moods and feelings. The sheer number of musical figurations which Cooke identifies in similar expressive contexts, across a wide historical spread of music, is impressive. Nonetheless, the weaknesses of his case are considerable, most of them hinging on the weight he is prepared to put on the music–language comparison – he too quickly assumes linguistic principles are operating in music, he underplays the malleability and context-dependent character of musical expression, he places too much stress on music as a means of emotional communication, he pays little attention to large-scale musical form, and it is not clear whether he believes expressiveness to be a property of the music or an emotional state to which it refers. For discussions of Cooke, see S. Davies (1994), 25f.; Scruton (1997), 203ff.; Begbie (1991b), 243ff.; Zuckerkandl (1960).
20. The classic account is offered by Susanne Langer, who speaks of an analogy of dynamic structure between emotion and music, and argues that music is an iconic symbol of mental states. Music conveys not the content of specific feelings but the *form* of feelings (Langer 1953). For her, music is an example of 'presentational' symbolism. A presentational symbol does not symbolise by means of fixed units of meaning as in the case of language or discursive symbolism. The elements of a presentational symbol are understood only through the meaning of the whole symbol as its elements interrelate with each other. A presentational symbol is a dynamic instrument of discovery and clarification rather than a purveyor of static references; it does not so much assert as articulate (Langer 1957, ch. 4). A piece of music, Langer believes, is a non-linguistic presentational symbol. It symbolises human feelings, not by ostensive denotation, but through possessing the same temporal structure as some segment or segments of emotional life. The dynamic structure of a musical work and the form in which emotions are experienced can resemble each other in their patterns of motion and rest, tension and release, fulfilment, excitation, sudden change, etc. Music, and indeed all art, 'is the creation of forms symbolic of human feeling' (Langer 1953, 40). For extended criticism of Langer, see S. Davies (1994), 123–34.

music and emotion is bypassed and left unexplained: what emotional
benefit do we gain by listening to music, especially by repeated hearing?
Models of similarity or resemblance by themselves tend to be too static,
allowing little room for what would seem to be a complex interaction
between our emotional life and music.

Roger Scruton has suggested a promising way of understanding emotional expression through music, and it links with important concerns in
this book.[21] He challenges the view that emotions are to be located solely
in some inner or 'subjective' life, the conditions of which are then exter-
nalised through music. Though emotions may have an 'inner' aspect,
they are publicly recognisable states of an organism, displayed in desires,
beliefs and actions. Further, they implicate the whole personality and are
intrinsically bound up with our relation to other people. Emotions
become what they essentially are through their public expression –
they are formed and amended through dialogue with others. Hence the
expression of an emotion is also to some extent the creating of an emotion, and this is one of the ways in which a human subject comes to self-
awareness and maturity. Normally, though emotions may include
feelings, they are also motives to actions – we act _out of_ fear, joy, sadness, or
whatever. Emotions are also intentional states: they are _of_ or _about_ an
object, and the most immediate object of an emotion is a thought – about
an external object or about the subject who has the emotion. (Fear
involves the thought that something threatens me, joy the thought there
is something which is good, beautiful, or whatever.)

Building on this, Scruton outlines an account of emotional engagement hinging on the notion of 'sympathetic response'. These responses
are quite complex in structure but the heart of the matter is clear enough:
if you are afraid of death, and I, observing your fear, come to share in it
while not being afraid for myself, then my fear is a sympathetic response.
Sympathetic responses are aroused more fully by fictional situations than
non-fictional ones, for in the latter, our interests are at stake and this
clouds our sympathies. In the world of fiction, our feelings are free from
the urge to intervene, to do something with or towards somebody, for
there are no concrete 'others' to be the objects of sympathy. Through the
exercise of our emotions in this way, we can be educated – our emotional
life can be stretched, widened, deepened. Sympathetic response is not
merely a matter of 'inner' feeling but also of action and gesture – I

21. Scruton (1997), 346–64.

comfort a bereaved friend, I put a hand on his shoulder. But in the fictional world we have action and gesture without objects, sympathy without any concrete person or situation in view. Among the most remarkable of such gestures-without-objects, according to Scruton, is dancing – when I 'move with' another, I find meaning in the appearance of the other's gestures, and respond accordingly with movements of my own, without seeking to change his predicament or share his burden. Dancing is not necessarily an aesthetic response, but it has a tendency in that direction, to involve responding to movement for its own sake. Our emotional response to musical sounds, claims Scruton, is fundamentally a sympathetic response of a similar kind, a response which does not *require* a precise object of sympathy or interest, whether a human subject or a situation perceived through the eyes of a subject.[22] It is a kind of latent dancing, internalised movement, a 'dancing to', or 'moving with' the sounds, even if the actual movement may be only subliminal and not overt. Gesture, in other words, is the (often invisible) intermediary between music and emotion. We are led into a kind of 'gravitational field' which draws us in, we participate in a process, a journey in and through sound. As far as the emotions are concerned, through sympathetic response they are *exercised* – and we must exercise our sympathies if they are to be alive at all. Moreover, we are emotionally *educated* – our emotional life is enriched, deepened, and perhaps even re-formed. Hearing music can mean 'the reordering of our sympathies'. Scruton remarks: 'The great triumphs of music . . . involve this synthesis, whereby a musical structure, moving according to its own logic, compels our feelings to move along with it, and so leads us to rehearse a feeling at which we would not otherwise arrive.'[23] Music can therefore not only reflect an emotional disposition already experienced – this is what resemblance theories latch on to – but can also enrich, nuance and even re-shape our emotion, affecting subsequent emotional experience. This would in part account for music being so emotionally beneficial and why we can derive pleasure again and again from the same piece. We can be emotionally exercised and educated.

Whatever questions we might ask about Scruton's account (and clearly much more could be said about the specific links between music and emotion), it chimes in with many of the theological strands which will appear

22. When words, images and other media are linked to music (and to some extent, *all* music has such links), these other media can serve to provide the 'formal objects' of the emotions embodied in the music. See Cook (1998a), 94.   23. Scruton (1997), 359.

in this book – musical experience as embodied action, participating in a dynamic field, and so forth. In particular, we shall argue that music can 'take our time' and give it back to us, enriched, re-ordered in some manner, and that its capacity in this respect can be of considerable theological interest. Through Scruton's notion of 'sympathetic response', we can begin to see something of what this temporal shaping might entail as far as our emotional life is concerned.

Music's distinctiveness

I have been arguing that to concede music's limitations when it comes to consistent and precise reference does not entail regarding musical meaning as entirely immanent. Musical meaning is realised through the interplay between its processes and a host of extra-musical processes and activities.

All this being said, however, two points need to be registered. First, much of the music we consider in this book will be examined from very restricted and limited perspectives. We will often bracket out specific aspects of pieces of music in order to press certain points pertinent to our theological concerns. We are not undertaking a theoretical overview of musical experience, or a comprehensive hermeneutics of music, or a theological hermeneutics on the basis of which we can provide secure 'readings' of the 'theological meaning' of this or that music. My aim is to focus on *one* main aspect of the realisation of musical meaning, the making and hearing of music in relation to time, and bring our findings into conversation with theology. Provided we are alert to the restricted scope of this exercise and to the rich contexts and many webs of meaning in which musical practices are involved, I propose that this is still a legitimate and instructive exercise.

Second, and this is the main burden of this section, for all its interconnectedness, music is marked by a unique and irreducible integrity, its own ways of working. Defenders of musical 'autonomy' are often quite properly reacting to a purely instrumentalist attitude to music, whereby it is seen as a mere tool, simply a function of forces outside it. This is to be resisted. Musical actions are indeed socially and culturally embedded, but there are forms of sociality and culture peculiar to music because of the particular ways in which discrete pitched sounds can be used by people in relation to each other. Music does indeed engage with the physical world we inhabit, but in its own way. Bodily make-up is indeed deeply implicated in music, but in a distinctive way. Music does indeed invite a sympathetic emotional response, but it does so in a particular manner. Music has an *irreducible* role to play in coming to terms with the world, in exploring and negotiating the constraints of our environment and the networks of relationships with others, and thus in forming human identity. This has ramifications for many disciplines, not least for theology: music has its own distinctive contribution to make to theology precisely because it is a distinctive human practice.[24]

My concern in this book is to explore only one main feature of this distinctiveness, namely music's temporality and its theological potential. To pave the way, I propose to make some comments about music in relation to language. It is popularly claimed that music is a language, even a 'universal language' which can speak across boundaries of class and race. There are undoubtedly strong links between music and language.[25] They are certainly not exclusive zones. Music is enjoyed in a world mediated through language. It cannot escape the effects of language, even when it is not governed by texts or providing the setting for words. Verbal interpretation of music often plays a constitutive role in the music of Western culture. Virtually all language has musical aspects to it, some language can be highly musical – poetry being the most obvious example – and most music has linguistic aspects.

Nonetheless, care needs to be taken not to press the correspondences too far and subsume music too quickly under linguistic categories. In the tradition stemming from Saussure, a distinction is drawn between the 'signifier' – the amalgam of sounds recognised through the structure of the language (and by people with language competence) as meaningful in

24. Here I concur with Wayne Bowman when he writes: 'I believe that appreciation of the uniquely and distinctly musical is of crucial significance to music students, and that addressing such concerns is among music philosophy's most fundamental obligations' (Bowman 1998, 3). With a particular interest in cultural theory, Shepherd and Wicke write: 'it can be argued that *no* aspect of music is capable of being understood independently of the wider gamut of social and cultural processes (social and cultural processes, it should be remembered, which include *as part of themselves* processes typically thought of as "musical"). Yet, *because* of this, it is possible that there are *aspects* of social and cultural processes which are revealed *uniquely* through their musical articulation. The *necessity* of referring to the wider gamut of social and cultural processes in order to explain "the musical" does not in other words amount to a *sufficiency*. There are aspects of affect and meaning *in culture* that can only be accessed through an understanding of the specific qualities of the signifying practices of music as a cultural form: that is, its sounds' (Shepherd and Wicke 1997, 33f). What we are attempting here in theology in many ways runs parallel to what Shepherd and Wicke are attempting in cultural theory.
25. For especially useful discussions of the music–language relation, see S. Davies (1994), ch. 1; Scruton (1997), ch. 7; Sloboda (1993), ch. 2; Norton (1984), 65–71; C. Brown (1987), ch. 9; Shepherd and Wicke (1997).

their differences, and the 'signified' – the mental concept traditionally associated through the structure of the language with that amalgam of sounds.[26] The relationship between the two, it is said, is *arbitrary* – there is nothing inherently 'tree-like' about the signifier 'tree', despite the relationship between the two being heavily conventionalised in habitual language use. Through this fundamentally arbitrary functioning and its consequent ability to disengage (to a certain extent) thought from reality, language has enabled people to develop remarkable skills to negotiate the world.

In the light of what we have said about musical reference, a model stressing the arbitrary connection between signified and signifier would, *prima facie*, appear attractive to music theorists. It has found much favour, especially in some French poststructuralism. Sounds in music are taken to signify in the same way as sounds in language, the key difference being that music does not possess the capacity to denote (with any consistent precision) objects, events and linguistically encodable ideas. How, then, can it be meaningful? The commonest answer is that music occasions a ground of physiological and affective stimulation which is subsequently taken into the order of language. The connection between sounds and the processes of signification is as arbitrary as in the case of language. But because musical sounds are not as heavily freighted with conventional correlations between signifiers and signifieds as they are in language, musical sounds can float even more freely in their relationship to signifying processes. Music can be seen as completely polysemic, in Roland Barthes's words, a 'field of *signifying* and not a system of signs'.[27] And this in turn leans towards the conclusion (not always articulated) that music is *no more* than the product of process and forces external to it. The *only* limitations to the construction of meaning in the case of music

26. Saussure (1966). The 'signifier' is not the sounds of a word considered in and of themselves, but the psychological image of the sounds constituted in the experience of the individual, the sensory 'sound-image'. The 'signified', correspondingly, is not the object/idea/event or whatever as it exists in the 'real' world; it is the mental *concept* linked by convention with the signifier. 'The linguistic sign,' says Saussure, 'unites not a thing and a name, but a concept and a sound-image' (ibid., 66).

27. Barthes (1977), 308. Music 'takes us to the limits of the system of signs', claims Julia Kristeva. It is 'a system of differences that is not a system that means something, as is the case with most of the structures of verbal language'. It has 'trans-linguistic status'; it is an "empty" sign' (Kristeva 1989, 309). Put another way, it is a 'code' – a system of entities (pitches, dynamics, rhythms, etc.) which are manipulated entirely according to culturally determined conventions. It is not surprising, then, that some who are sympathetic to this line of thinking will suggest that music stands for that 'nothingness and being' said to mark the subject before entry into language; it is assigned to the realm of the 'pre-symbolic', the 'pre-discursive' and unconscious.

come from the social and cultural environments in which it is prac-tised.[28]

Such accounts have been subjected to telling criticism by, among oth-ers, John Shepherd and Peter Wicke.[29] Among other things, they argue that insufficient attention is being paid to music's central feature – its sounds. The inherent characteristics of the sounds used in language are not necessarily implicated in the meanings they generate. But it is far from obvious that the same can be said of music, where the medium of sound appears to operate in a rather different manner.[30] In music, strong distinc-tions between sounds on the one hand and signifier and signified on the other are much more difficult to draw. Musical sounds acting as a medium become materially involved in the process of creating meaning. The work of the linguist Bierwisch and the musicologist Knepler, among others, points strongly to the conclusion that 'The visceral realities of sounds as "signifiers" in music are *themselves* of relevance, materially, culturally and subjectively.'[31] Bierwisch observes that 'a [musical] sound pattern which is supposed to show excitement has to be excited. On the other hand, the sentence, "He is excited" contains neither more nor less excitement than the sentence, "He is not excited", although it is saying the opposite.'[32]

The main reason for this divergence between music and language lies in the different ways in which the constituent components of language and music relate to each other. In hearing both language and music, reco-gnising meaning depends on recognising the relatedness of its constitu-ent entities. In the case of language, meaning is generated through relations of *difference*, amounting sometimes to *exclusion*, even *repulsion* and *opposition*. Only in this way can objects, concepts, entities or whatever be adequately negotiated.[33] In music, however, while phenomena such as

---

28. In Kristeva's words, 'the musical code is organised by the *arbitrary* and *cultural* (imposed within the frameworks of a certain civilisation) difference between various local values' (Kristeva 1989, 309).
29. Shepherd and Wicke (1997). It may well be that the ease with which music theory polarises between 'extrinsic' and 'intrinsic' approaches owes something to this over-reliance on certain forms of language-theory.
30. Shepherd and Wicke are here using 'medium' in the sense of an entity with its own particular structure, but which cannot be thought of as an 'agency' of meaning construction (ibid., 116ff).   **31.** Shepherd and Wicke (1997), 114.
32. Bierwisch (1979), 62.
33. For Saussure, language is a *system* or *structure* of interdependent terms. Every signifier that carries meaning does so by virtue of its being part of a system. Meaning is generated by relations of *difference* between component elements of the system. For instance, in a sub-system of colour-words, 'turquoise' derives its meaning from its difference from its immediate neighbours 'blue' and 'green', rather than from pointing to, say, the turquoiseness of a lake.

opposition may be present, structure is built primarily on relations of *likeness, attraction* or '*equivalence*'. This is one of the reasons for the far greater preponderance of repetition in music – with the associated practices of variation and transformation – something we shall deal with at length in chapter 6.[34] Music *depends* to a very high degree on the likeness and attraction between its sounds.

Closely related to this is the way in which music, because the order of sound is so inherent to its being and meaning, enables a distinctive experience of space and time. Speaking of the 'attraction' between musical elements, Shepherd and Wicke write:

> Each phase or charging is distinct and different from every other phase or charging, but *only* by virtue of the collectivity of all other actual chargings that constitute a musical event *as* they are gathered up and their complex relatedness *from the unique perspective of each musical moment* released as the actual charging of the passing present. It is for this reason that, in being deployed in the common-sense spatiotemporal framework of the everyday world … *the sounds of music move to supplant that framework in creating their own.* Sounds and their framework become synonymous.[35]

To make this clearer, let us focus for a few moments on music and space. One of the characteristic features of the perception of sound is that it can be severed in our perception from its material source. Objects do not 'have' sounds in the sense that they have 'secondary qualities' (like colours), such that the perception of the quality is inseparable from perception of the object. I can perceive a sound without perceiving its source, but I cannot see the colour red without seeing a red object of some sort. Of course, we know that sounds are produced by vibrating physical bodies. But it would be a mistake to *identify* what we *hear* with those vibrating bodies; the 'phenomenal reality of sound' – the object of our aural attention – cannot be identified with the source of sound. Likewise, we know that sounds are heard because of vibrations of air which reach the organs of the ear. But the phenomenal reality of sound cannot strictly be identified with these waves.[36]

---

34. This stress on equivalence as basic to music is associated with analytical techniques developed by Ruwet (following Jakobson), and drawn out at some length in the work of Middleton (1990).   **35.** Shepherd and Wicke (1997), 138.

36. The case is argued at length by Roger Scruton (Scruton 1997, ch. 1). The 'phenomenal reality of sound' (Scruton's phrase) is not reducible to physical analysis, but neither is it merely 'appearance' with no extra-mental correlates. Scruton believes that sounds have the same kind of reality for us as rainbows or smells. They are what he calls 'secondary objects', objects which can bear properties, about which there are objective truths, and about which we may mistaken. We may hesitate to call them physical objects, but neither are they purely mental.

This feature of sound-perception, in which our attention to sound can be severed from attention to objects and entities, is exploited in music. In hearing music it is not necessary to seek information about the causes of the sounds, nor do we have to identify a referent or referents. Sound is employed largely in a way which opens up a spatiality which does not depend on the discrete location and mutual exclusion of entities. In the world I see, an entity cannot be in two places at the same time, and two things cannot occupy the same place at the same time. Visual experience and discrete location become inseparable – seeing this lamp 'here' means I cannot see it 'over there'. But in aural experience, although a sound may have a discrete material source whose discrete location I can identify ('the trumpet is on the left, not on the right'), the sound I hear is not dependent on attention to that 'place'. It surrounds me, it fills the whole of my aural 'space'. I do not hear a sound 'there' but 'not there' – what I hear occupies the whole of my aural space.

This opens up a space which is not that of discrete location, but, for want of a better word, the space of 'omni-presence'. And when more than one sound is present, occupying the same space while remaining audibly distinct, we may speak of a space not of mutual exclusion but of 'inter-penetration'. Sounds do not have to 'cut each other off' or obscure each other, in the manner of visually perceived objects. The tones of a chord can be heard sounding *through* each other. In the acoustic realm, in other words, there is no neat distinction between a place and its occupant. This is tellingly expressed by John Hull as he reflects on the experience of going blind and coming to terms with what his ears were telling him. Deprived of sight, he asks:

> What is the world of sound? I have been spending some time out of doors trying to respond to the special nature of the acoustic world . . . The tangible world sets up only as many points of reality as can be touched by the body, and this seems to be restricted to *one problem at a time*. I can explore the splinters on the park bench with the tip of my finger but I cannot, *at the same time*, concentrate upon exploring the pebbles with my big toe . . . *The world revealed by sound is so different* . . . On Holy Saturday I sat in Cannon Hill Park while the children were playing . . . The footsteps came from both sides. They met, mingled, separated again. From the next bench, there was the rustle of a newspaper and the murmur of conversation . . . I heard the steady, deep roar of the through traffic, the buses and the trucks . . . [The acoustic world] *stays the same whichever way I turn my head*. This is not true of the perceptible [i.e. visually perceptible] world. It changes as I

turn my head. New things come into view. The view looking that way is quite different from the view looking this way. It is not like that with sound ... This is a world which I cannot shut out, which goes on all around me, and which gets on with its own life ... *Acoustic space is a world of revelation.*[37]

The capacity of sound to open up this spatiality is of course present in language inasmuch as language is spoken and heard, but it is not harnessed except insofar as language veers towards the condition of music. The sounds of language can be deployed in the commonsense spatio-temporal framework of the everyday world without being affected by (or affecting) that framework. In this case, the character of the sounds deployed have no intrinsic connection with the spatio-temporal characteristics of the phenomena evoked by the language.[38]

In the case of music, we find that sounds and spatial framework (and temporal framework, as we shall see) are completely intertwined. Because music depends supremely on the interrelationship-through-attraction of sounds, it exploits the 'omnipresent' and 'interpenetrating' quality of sound-experience.[39] Music directly 'pulls the strings', so to speak, of the spatial framework in which it is deployed – no neat divide marks off occupant and place in musical experience. We only need think of a three-tone major chord, which we hear as three distinct, mutually enhancing (not mutually exclusive) sounds, but together occupying the same aural space. The sound is rich and enjoyable, even more so in polyphony when different melodies can interweave and enhance each other. (Contrast the confusion of three people speaking simultaneously.)

We should be careful not to jump immediately to the conclusion that the spatiality of sound and music is of a totally different order to the 'real world' in which we live, and thus assign it to some 'inner' and sealed-off zone of mental experience, or to an utterly other world beyond the material world we inhabit from day to day.[40] It may well be that music, precisely through its emancipation of aural attention from particular identifiable objects, makes possible an apprehension of space as an inherent dimension of the physical world, a function of the way the physical entities involved in music are intrinsically related to one another, in such a way that writing its 'space' off as 'unreal' in some manner is unwise.

---

37. Hull (1990), 62ff. My italics.
38. Language may, of course, invoke the sonic characteristics of the 'external' physical world – through devices like onomatopoeia – but this is relatively rare and not necessary to the successful functioning of language.   39. Shepherd and Wicke (1997), 125ff.
40. See Zuckerkandl (1956), chs. 14–20.

Indeed, there are possible links here with conceptions of space in modern physical science.[41]

In any case, the theological usefulness of this sonic, musical understanding of space is considerable and far-ranging. The co-presence of the Son of God and humanity in Christ obviously comes to mind, as does the way we conceive the Trinity.[42] But what relevance has this for us, concerned as we are with time? First, I shall be suggesting that, as with space, the temporality experienced through music is not best construed as an empty hopper 'into which' notes are 'inserted' and then 'related' in order to make music. *Time is intrinsically bound up with music's sounds; musical sounds 'pulls the strings' of the temporality 'in which' they occur.* Auditory time, like auditory space, can only be articulated through auditory events internally related (in and through time) by attraction. Shepherd and Wicke put it baldly: 'Auditory events *are* auditory time and space.'[43] Second, what we have only indicated about space, physicality and the 'real world' will receive very much more discussion with respect to time. Much well-meaning talk about music's supposed 'spirituality' and its theological significance has been built on the questionable notion that music affords an entirely different kind of temporality to that which pervades our day-to-day, non-musical experience of the physical world.

One last matter is worth stressing here, concerning the distinctiveness of music in relation to language, which we have touched upon in passing. Musical involvement with the physical world is highly dependent on the mediation of the body. More than that, the way the body is involved in music belongs to the distinctiveness of musical experience.

> Sound . . . is the only major medium of communication that can vibrate perceptibly within the body. The sound of the human voice could not be amplified and projected were it not for chambers and

41. See below, p. 67, n. 99. On this matter, I remain unconvinced by Scruton, who I believe overstates his observation about the severance of the phenomenal reality of sound from physical objects (Scruton 1997, 5f). He takes the distinction between place and occupant to be 'fundamental' to the concept of space – 'real' space as opposed to the 'phenomenal' space of tones. He contrasts this 'real' space with time (times are not occupied or filled by the things that occur in them). He concludes that music presents us 'with the nature not of space but of time', time, that is, 'spread out' as if in space. In musical experience, we transfer to the temporal order 'the sense of freedom which characterises our experience of the spatial order. That is why we inevitably use spatial metaphors of music – 'high', 'low', etc. (ibid., 74f). But why posit such a sharp divide between 'phenomenal' and 'real' space (and presume the latter is determined entirely by what is visually plausible)? And why distinguish between space and time in this way, when receptacle conceptions of *both* space and time are highly dubious? Here I find Zuckerkandl much more persuasive (see n. 40 above), resisting the temptation to assume that auditory space is some kind of lesser reality in comparison with the supposed authentic space of visual experience.
42. See Gunton (1997c), 111ff.   43. Shepherd and Wicke (1997), 135.

resonators of air inside the human body (the lungs, the sinus passages, the mouth) that vibrate in sympathy with the frequencies of the vocal cords . . . the human experience of sound involves, in addition to the sympathetic vibration of the eardrums, the sympathetic vibration of the resonators of the body. Sound, shaped and resonating with the properties of the internal and external configurations, textures and movements of the objects of the external world, can thus be *felt* in addition to being heard . . . Sound . . . enters the body and is in the body.[44]

This bodiliness of sound-experience is harnessed intensively in music. To speak of the distinctive use of sound in music in which its inherent characteristics are directly implicated in musical meaning, and to speak of the distinctive kind of spatiality and temporality opened up through it, is to speak of musical sound as received *through the body*, and, as with all sound, this means very much more than through the ears. (Even a deaf person – for example, the percussionist Evelyn Glennie – can perform highly intricate music by sensing floor vibrations through her feet.) The dispositions and configurations of bodies and their movements are not incidental to musical experience but enter into the fundamental dynamics of musical production and reception, something often sidelined in European musical traditions.[45]

The point needs to be pressed with respect to the relationship between music and language. Shepherd and Wicke maintain that there has been a tendency in poststructuralist thought, for example, to overlook not only the power and directness but also the distinctiveness of the bodily mediation of sound in music: to treat the body as if it had no distinctive potential for signification which might stand independently alongside language, as if it merely provided the material ground and pathways for emotional and affective states, achieving potential for significance only when language is used. Again, the problem would appear to be a hegemony of language when accounting for music, and a consequent failure to allow that the body as mediator of musical sound itself might contain possibilities for signification which could operate in their own particularity along with those of language. This renders questionable the construal

---

44. Ibid., 127. My italics.

45. The elaboration of musical notation and of highly complex compositional techniques 'has encouraged a focus on the structural rather than the kinematic properties of music . . . At the same time, as this music has been performed mainly in church, court or concert hall, a social proscription against overt movements by listeners has long been in effect' (Shove and Repp 1995, 64).

of the body as merely 'pre-linguistic' or 'sub-linguistic', and the same goes for music.[46]

None of what we have said about music and language ought to be taken as implying that comparisons between the two are in every respect redundant and unfruitful. Nonetheless, theories of musical meaning based on linguistic analogies are notoriously hard to advance convincingly. And we would suggest that this is in part due to the fact that there are aspects of music-making and music-hearing which cannot be reduced to the conditions of language.

In this chapter, by way of prefacing the main material of the book, I have attempted to make clear my stance with regard to some of the vexed question of musical aesthetics, while acknowledging that space forbids extensive argument. Music, I have contended, is chiefly an activity or set of temporal activities, the two most fundamental being music-making – the intentional creation of temporally organised patterns of pitched sounds – and music-hearing, or reception. Although music is notoriously weak in affording reliable, referential precision, its meaning depends on a multitude of connections with extra-musical phenomena and human experience – it is socially and culturally embedded, it entails interaction with the configurations of the physical world, it is ineluctably bodily, and it has particularly strong connections with our emotional life. All of these connections will be revisited in the chapters which ensue. Nevertheless, music operates in irreducibly distinct ways. We brought to the fore the ways in which music, because of the manner in which it deploys sound, 'pulls the strings', as it were, of spatio-temporality and noted how this can be obscured if we try to accommodate music too quickly under the categories of language. It is now our task to explore more deeply music's temporality.

46. According to Shepherd and Wicke, it is a weakness of Jacques Lacan that the role of the body is underplayed in his account of how subjects are socially constituted through language. He lacks a grasp of the crucial relation between the material character of the signifier and the material character of the body. 'The world of the material is in this way rendered neutral and inconsequential, a ground for inscription rather than a medium for construction'(Shepherd and Wicke 1997, 74). Kristeva fares better, perceiving more clearly the link between sound and body, and the role of the body 'in the formation and maintenance of identity' (ibid.). However, she does not extend this insight sufficiently, Shepherd and Wicke contend. Both Lacan and Kristeva fail to loosen 'the tyranny of language' (97) in such a way as to allow appropriate 'conceptual space' for music (85). Shepherd and Wicke also believe that Roland Barthes, while taking very seriously the relation between music and the body, represents little advance on this matter (Shepherd and Wicke 1997, 891ff).

2

Music's time

Einstein's eldest son once recalled: 'Whenever [Einstein] felt that he had come to the end of the road or into a difficult situation in his work, he would take refuge in music, and that would usually resolve all his difficulties.'[1]

What must the world be like, what must I be like, if between me and the world the phenomenon of music can occur?[2]

VICTOR ZUCKERKANDL

[If music] is the most contemplative of the arts, it is *not* because it takes us into the timeless but because it obliges us to rethink time.[3]

ROWAN WILLIAMS

Music is a temporal art through and through. Inevitably, if we are asking about what we might learn theologically from music's temporality, we cannot avoid asking questions about what we might mean by 'time'.

Time, of course, has been a topic of perennial fascination to humankind, and perhaps never more than in the last hundred years or so, when it has been subject to sophisticated treatment in various fields – scientific, cultural, philosophical, literary as well as musical. The character of time has proved stubbornly resistant to comprehensive explanation or description. Philosophical treatments quickly lead to multiple perplexities due to the radical elusiveness of the subject in question. As Alasdair Heron observes, a large part of the problem is that 'reflection upon time by those who are themselves in and of time cannot extricate itself from the inevitable limitations imposed upon it by its own condition'.[4] We

---

1. Quoted in Clark (1973), 115.   2. Zuckerkandl (1956), 7.   3. R. Williams (1989), 248.
4. Heron (1979), 2. Augustine famously gave expression to the dilemma posed by time's dogged 'thereness' and its intellectual elusiveness: 'I confess to you, Lord, that I still do not

cannot step outside of time and subject it to the kind of description and analysis appropriate to, say, physical objects.[5] Whatever our final estimate of Immanuel Kant's account of time, there is no going back behind him in at least two respects. First, time is a fundamental and necessary condition of the possibility of any experience, thought or knowledge. 'The substance of every human act is the particular way it joins the poles of time, the particular way it rhymes remembrance and anticipation into lived present meaning.'[6] Time is our destiny because our lives are lived in the knowledge that we are directed towards death. Time is, in a sense, our necessity because there can be no un-knowing, re-living or un-living. Time is central to human change but also to stability: claiming that something is stable is to claim continuity of identity through time. Time is basic to human order, for without temporal order there can be no order in our lives at all. In short, time is profoundly implicated in every aspect of our existence. Second, our own conceptions of time are constructs in the strictest sense, objectifications of what we cannot adequately or correctly objectify.[7] Hence we should guard against 'any vaulting ambition in the matter of the description, let alone definition, of time'.[8]

Theologians have not been absent from the intellectual wrestling over the character of time. Many of the most intractable problems of theology are at root about the status of time, especially in relation to divine eternity. Crucial to this book is the conviction that music, although not providing a magic wand to dispel all the mists of confusion, can offer considerable assistance in the process of exploring temporality, as well as clarifying, interpreting and re-conceptualising its character. In particular, I am claiming that music can offer positive assistance to a theological approach to time, and it can do this first and foremost by providing a particular kind of temporal experience: music is 'lived through' in a time-intensive involvement with time-embedded realities.

footnote 4 (*cont.*)
know what time is, and I further confess to you, Lord, that as I say this I know myself to be conditioned by time. For a long period already I have been speaking about time, and that long period can only be an interval of time. So how do I know this, when I do not know what time is?' (*Confessions*, XI:25.32).
5. If we are to talk of 'time', we must not allow this to generate the belief that time itself is a substantive, self-subsistent reality amenable to examination. 'Time' is the form of that which is temporal. Accordingly, though we shall often use 'time' for the sake of convenience, it should be borne in mind that 'temporal' and 'temporality' – which we shall also employ – are less misleading words.   **6.** Jenson (1991), 1.   **7.** Heron (1979), 2.
8. Ibid., 6.

Music and time: general comments

To prepare the ground for our discussion of musical temporality, some remarks of a fairly general nature need to be made. The most important I have just anticipated. It is that *the production and reception of music deeply implicates physical realities and these realities are themselves time-laden.*

The supposition here is that time is an intrinsic condition of the universe, ingrained in its fabric, not ontologically dependent on human perception and action. To say the least, this is a contested assumption and no doubt will continue to be so. Even if it is accepted in some form, its meaning and ramifications will be much disputed. As we have said, acute difficulties arise from the inescapable reality of our own time-embeddedness.

There is a formidable thicket of debate in the natural sciences concerning the reality of time. Some have argued that because in relativity theory there is no unequivocal meaning to the simultaneity of events – different observers assess the simultaneity of separated events differently – there can be no unequivocal concept of time, and this in turn renders the concept of 'the future' or 'the past' highly questionable.[9] In reply, it needs to be said that these assessments of simultaneity accord different kinds of 'nowness' only to *past* events. They are retrospective judgements. The distinction between past and future is by no means erased on the basis of these findings, however problematic speaking of *the* past or *the* future may be. And while it is true that special relativity gives no special significance to any particular reference frame, this is not the case when general relativity is applied to a universe of our particular type, in other words a basically homogeneous one in which there is a preferred frame of reference (when microwave background is at rest).[10] More recent challenges come from quantum cosmology. Most famously, Stephen Hawking's fusion of relativity theory and quantum mechanics questions the postulation of an initial singularity from which the spacetime manifold emerged, and would have us suppose the universe we can observe, with its time (the time of spacetime in relativity theory), has arisen from another purely spatial, atemporal condition, so that what we call 'real' time is not fundamental but an epiphenomenon of 'imaginary' time. However,

9. The contention is that there is no universal 'now', no unambiguous temporal slice constituting a global physical 'present' which separates 'the' future from 'the' past; hence we cannot make unequivocal distinctions between present, past and future. The most that can be affirmed is the existence of an infinite collection of possible definitions of time which relate to inertial reference frames.
10. Polkinghorne (1995), 2f.; P. C. W. Davies (1995), 128f.; Isham and Polkinghorne (1993).

this is not an argument for the subjectivisation of time (as in: 'it's all in the imagination'), nor is it a rejection of the idea that the universe is finite; rather it is a denial that the universe's finitude is bounded by a clear singularity.[11] Of course, there is no question of *demonstrating* from the natural sciences that time is inherent to the universe, but at the very least we can say that conclusions drawn on the basis of relativistic and quantum mechanical evidence need not lead inexorably to the view that the human experience of temporality *cannot* correspond to a temporal ordering of the universe we inhabit.

Undoubtedly, a danger here is the common tendency to polarise views of time into a spurious either/or: an absolutising of time on the one hand and an idealising or subjectivising of time on the other.[12] An example of the former would be to speak of time as some kind of entity which exists prior to and independently of the existence of things and events, not only antecedent to humanity but antecedent to the entire physical world. The view is usually associated with Isaac Newton, for whom 'absolute' space and time form a vast envelope which contains all that goes on in the universe, conditioning events and our knowledge of them, independent of all that it embraces, infinite and homogenous, and by reference to which all our knowledge of the universe is derived and explicated.[13] Time and space are thus in a sense independent of what they 'contain'. On the other side lie approaches which claim that tensed statements are expressive not of any aspect of reality beyond the person or persons who utter them but only of an inescapable mode of perceiving, thinking and speaking about reality. One of the most oft-cited exponents of this tradition is Kant, whose subtle theory proposes that time and temporal relations are a matter of the way events as they appear to us are organised in the field of phenomena; they are forms which govern the possibility of cognition and pertain only to the manner in which the mind organises the manifold of sense-data.[14] Others have propounded more socially oriented versions of a similar thesis centring on the social construction of time.

Without sufficient space to argue an adequate case here, there is good reason to suppose that neither side of the polarity need be chosen.

11. Hawking (1988). An interesting debate around Hawking has developed, which some theologians have joined. Firm conclusions are very hard to establish. See e.g. P. C. W. Davies (1995), chs. 7 and 8; Wilkinson (1993); Stannard (1993), 42ff.
12. See Braine (1988), 41ff.
13. Newton formulated his famous definition at the beginning of the *Principia*: 'Absolute, true and mathematical time, of itself, and from its own nature, flows equably without relation to anything external' (Newton 1962, 7).   14. Kant (1996), 85–94.

Certainly, while Newton's idea of an absolute time has run into major difficulties, not only in the natural sciences but also in philosophy and theology,[15] this need not commit us to a subjectivisation of time.[16] As yet there is no overwhelming incentive to abandon the common-sensical, stubborn and persistent idea that our temporal apprehension corresponds in some way to a temporality intrinsic to the universe. There are very good grounds for supposing that the most adequate ways of conceiving temporality lie along the path of viewing it as a function of the way things and events are intrinsically interrelated. This path is, of course, a broad one, marked by fierce controversy – the relation between the time 'given' to the world and our experience of time is anything but the simple one-to-one correspondence of naive realism. And we cannot ignore the fact that the time of the universe as disclosed by natural science is highly mysterious, complex and manifold.

I have slightly laboured this general point about the time-ladenness of the universe because it links so closely with one of the chief concerns in this book: to show that music's temporality is most likely to be misrepresented if conceived in radically constructivist terms. It is more appropriately viewed as arising from an interaction with the time-embeddedness of the physical world.[17]

At first blush, this might seem an odd claim to make about music. For music, some will be inclined to say, is primarily about ordering, not exploring. It is chiefly about fashioning a new temporality. Many people will testify to music's ability to give us a temporal experience in radical contrast to extra-musical times (chronological time, astronomical time, clock time, or whatever). Indeed, some believe that music's greatest gift to Christianity is its ability to offer a measure of escape from the times which

15. See e.g. T. F. Torrance (1969, 1976).
16. Even Paul Davies – who repeatedly stresses the multiplicity of time and the contribution of the perceiving subject in the apprehension of time – can remark: 'as a human being, I find it impossible to relinquish the sensation of flowing time and a moving present moment. It is something so basic to my experience of the world that I am repelled by the claim that it is only an illusion or misperception' (P. C. W. Davies 1995, 275).
17. It is one of the weaknesses of what is probably the most comprehensive treatment of musical time available, Jonathan Kramer's *The Time of Music* (1988), that the author seems equivocal about whether or not there can be a temporality which is anything more than human construction. He writes: 'I do not wish to deny absolute time totally' (5), and claims that he is 'interested in the *interaction* between musical and absolute time' (3). But in addition he asserts, not only that 'absolute time' is 'little more than a social convention agreed to for practical reasons' (5) and that it is 'primarily subjective' (161), but also that 'time does not exist apart from experience' (3)! At the end of the book, confusingly, he defines absolute time as 'objective time, the time that is shared by most people in a given society and by physical processes' (452).

command our lives. Music, so to speak, is 'time-out'. Sometimes this is taken further: music's most important theological possibility is said to lie in the way it can suggest or approximate to a time*less* condition. (The twentieth century saw many attempts to achieve this in music through a variety of compositional techniques, some of which we examine later.) More specifically, it has been claimed that music can evoke the timelessness of eternity. This in turn is sometimes allied to an appeal to what is perceived to be music's extreme immateriality. Music, we are told, is the most 'spiritual' (i.e. non-physical) of the arts. Compared to, say, a painting, it is marked by a high degree of impermanence and insubstantiality, and has very limited referential powers; this means it is not nearly so tightly bound to the physical world as many of the other arts. This freedom from physicality, so the argument runs, is one of music's greatest theological virtues.[18]

Much of this book is designed to question and challenge this drift of thinking, a drift which derives its momentum from a cluster of overplayed half-truths. I shall argue that many of music's most instructive lessons for theology arise because *in and through its 'making'* it has the capacity for an intense and respectful engagement with 'given' temporalities integral to the world (human and non-human), and that to take this seriously entails taking with equal seriousness the intrinsic physicality and materiality of musical practices.

Of course, it must be recognised that music, does, in a sense, create its own time(s). Most of us have listened to music and become unaware of, or radically miscalculated, the time measured by the clock on the wall.[19] Thomas Clifton says 'There is a distinction between the time which a piece *takes* and the time which a piece presents or *evokes*.'[20] Our sense of duration in musical experience can differ markedly from our time-sense in other spheres, as numerous psychological studies have confirmed.[21] We do indeed experience a structuring of time with its own distinctive integrity. But it would be unwise to assume that this is best interpreted as the realisation of a temporality without intrinsic relation to extra-musical temporality, human and non-human. Most of the music we shall

18. This group of ideas, often encountered in discussions of theology and music, forms the heart of the theology of music advanced by the Congregationalist P. T. Forsyth, who in many respects takes his cues from Hegel's aesthetics. For an exposition and critique, see Begbie (1995).
19. 'Clock-time' can be defined as time measured by agreed criteria taken from the physical world; it forms the consensus according to which appointments are made, trains run, prison sentences are served, and so on. It might also be termed 'public time'.
20. Clifton (1983), 81.   21. See J. Kramer (1988), ch. 11.

examine derives a large part of its power from the *interaction* between its time(s) and the complex of extra-musical times which permeate its production and reception, and it does this, we shall argue, in ways which can be theologically enlightening.

Some other aspects of musical temporality also need to be registered at this stage. *Different pieces of music are temporal in different ways.* Such phenomena as coherence, continuity, fulfilment, the rhyming of past and future through the present are manifest in a diversity of ways depending on the composer, style, period, performance and so on. Even within Western tonal music, temporal process in music encompasses an enormous range of possibilities.

Within a piece of music there is usually *a multiplicity of temporal continua, operating concurrently*. By this I mean not only that there can be several kinds of event occurring concurrently. I mean that we can find different kinds of temporal succession, which intersect, interpenetrate and enhance one another as the music unfolds. So, for example, some pieces are thoroughly directional at one level but have little directionality at another. Strong ending gestures can come 'too soon' (and perhaps repeatedly) such that what is heard immediately after these 'endings' is music whose destination has already been experienced, establishing an alternative temporal continuum to the dominant underlying one. In these cases we hear distinct, though mutually interanimating, temporal strata. We will bring out some of the theological overtones of such multiple continua in due course. And there is an even more basic way in which music consists of different temporal continua – it is structured through metrical waves. We shall discover in due course how crucial this is for understanding musical temporality and its theological potential.

Further, as we have already underlined, *those who make music and those who hear or listen to it are time-involved creatures.* As physical creatures we inhabit the *multiple temporal continua of the physical world*. Barbara Adam chides social theorists who ignore the temporalities beyond those which are socially constructed, or who set 'social time' sharply against the 'natural' times of the universe and our bodies.[22] Oppositions between monolithic categories – subjective time vs. absolute time, social vs. natural time and so on – are to be resisted. 'It is not either winter or December, or hibernation time for the tortoise, or one o'clock, or time for Christmas dinner. It is planetary time, biological time, clock and calendar time,

22. Adam (1990), ch. 3.

natural and social time all at once.'[23] Music interacts with a plurality of temporal patterns, including *those processes which mark our own constitution as bodily, physical creatures,* many of which are closely bound up with extra-human temporal phenomena. A significant quantity of research into musical rhythms shows that the human neuro-physiological 'clock' against which periodic processes and temporal experiences are measured is intricate in the extreme, integrating many different temporal configurations associated with different bodily activities.[24] Our sense of time is radically affected by the innumerable biological clocks beating away with their own distinctive rhythms – the large-scale rhythms or macrocycles with their ebb and flow (e.g. sleep and digestion), within those the smaller-scale kinetic rhythms controlled by the central nervous system (e.g. heartbeat, breathing, pulse), and within those the very brief subliminal rhythms of the brain's electrical impulses along neural pathways. Music intertwines with all of these in ways we are only just beginning to understand.[25] And interlaced with these factors are a host of *social and cultural determinants* which affect the quality of temporal experience and hence the way music is practised, experienced and theorised. It would, of course, be naive to posit a single 'time-sense' in even the most homogeneous and stable of social groupings. Nevertheless, much has been written about certain broad perceptions of temporality characteristic of various social and cultural groupings, some of which we will allude to in what follows. In addition, the historical situatedness of musicology – in whatever form – needs to be borne in mind. Most musicologists have a tendency to assume that their insights alone carry some kind of stamp of universal applicability which transcends the particularities of history. But all theorising about music is inevitably affected by the patterns of thought,

---

23. Ibid., 16.   **24.** See Middleton (1990), 226f.

25. In an important essay on musical motion by Patrick Shove and Bruno Repp, the authors argue that 'natural motion' of the performer and listener (bodily movement) is intrinsic to the musical experience (whether or not a great deal of bodily movement actually takes place), a fact all too often forgotten in music theory and, indeed, by composers: 'An aesthetically satisfying performance is presumably one whose expressive microstructure satisfies basic constraints of biological motion while also being responsive to the structural and stylistic requirements of the composition. Much music composed in this century encourages only primitive forms of motion or inhibits natural motion altogether. Many twentieth-century composers focus on sound qualities or on abstract tonal patterns, and performers of their compositions often neglect whatever kinematic potential the music may have. The absence of natural motion information may be a significant factor limiting the appreciation of such music by audiences. While compositional techniques and sound materials are subject to continuous change and exploration . . . *the laws of biological motion can only be accepted, negated or violated.* If more new music and its performers took these laws into account, the size of the audiences might increase correspondingly'(Shove and Repp 1995, 78f). My italics.

outlooks, dispositions and so forth of the particular social and cultural contexts in which it is practised.

Music's time

We turn now to examine more closely some major features of music's temporality. Here I draw extensively on the work of the musicologist Victor Zuckerkandl, a figure strangely neglected in musical aesthetics.[26] Zuckerkandl seems to have been aware of the theological resonances of his work, especially its anti-reductionism. While not following him in every respect, I attempt to trace some of these theological resonances, modulating and amplifying them in dialogue with other musicologists and with theologians.

Tension and resolution

We are limiting ourselves in this book chiefly to Western music organised according to the 'tonal' system. This system came to fruition towards the end of the seventeenth century and has since pervaded European culture and cultures predominantly influenced by modern Europe. It extends far beyond the 'art music' tradition, being common to virtually all 'popular music'.[27] Tonal music operates to a large degree according to teleological

---

26. Zuckerkandl (1956, 1959, 1973). His book *The Sense of Music* (1959) serves as a good introduction to the main shape of his thought. Shepherd and Wicke are the only writers I have found to appreciate the importance of Zuckerkandl's work for our understanding of the experience of sound, time and space (Shepherd and Wicke 1997, 122f., 129ff., 141, 150ff., 159f). Berleant helpfully points to the ways in which Zuckerkandl can assist us in getting beyond overly constructivist accounts of musical creativity (Berleant 1987). Kathleen Marie Higgins outlines an approach to music very consonant with Zuckerkandl's, mentioning Zuckerkandl in passing (Higgins 1991, especially 33f., 167f). The music critic Edward Rothstein, in a book on the links between music and mathematics, draws on Zuckerkandl in passing, rightly commenting that Zuckerkandl's books are 'unassuming volumes, almost elementary, but there is a subtle power in the notions they introduce' (Rothstein 1995, 100). Rochberg (1984) makes perceptive (albeit brief) use of Zuckerkandl in his discussion of musical time and space (100ff.). In his recent wide-ranging aesthetics of music, Roger Scruton mentions Zuckerkandl (Scruton 1997, viii, 49, 52ff., 301n., 419f.) but allows him little room in the overall argument. Lippman grants Zuckerkandl a slot in his survey of musical aesthetics (1992, 455–61) but his treatment is very shallow.

27. It is sometimes claimed in music history courses that tonal music in the West suffered a major disintegration around the end of the nineteenth century – especially through Wagner and Schoenberg – leading to a bewildering myriad of twentieth-century 'atonal' experimentations. Tonality is thus said to have effectively died in the West around 1910. This kind of narrative, quite apart from its tendency to over-simplify grossly the work of the composers cited, is, to say the least, culturally blind. While it can safely be said that in the twentieth century, in the 'art music' stream, tonal music by no means exercised the determinative role it once did, this is untrue of the vast majority of music practised in that century. For a perceptive, albeit slightly cynical treatment of tonality in relation to Western culture, tracing some of the factors which led to the emergence of the 'tonality simplified' music of the nineteenth and twentieth centuries, see Norton (1984), ch. 10. Norton points

principles. Typically it possesses an integral relational order which in its large-scale and small-scale organisation is sensed as directional, driving towards rest and closure, often (but not always) leading to some kind of goal or 'gathering together' of the whole temporal process. We sense 'it is going somewhere'. This teleological dynamic is generated primarily through the twin elements of tension and resolution. Configurations of tension and resolution work in many different ways and at many different levels, potentially engaging every parameter of music.

I am using the word 'tension' in a very wide sense to describe the character of any musical event which arouses in us a sense of anticipation, that matters cannot be left as they are. The tension may arise through some kind of conflict or antagonism between two or more musical elements. But this is not necessarily so. All that is necessary is the generation of a sense of incompleteness, implying a later closure.[28] 'Resolution' is consequently also understood in a broad sense as the character of a musical event which dissipates tension. It is worth noting that the term 'tension' can refer to a process of intensification or to the place at which it occurs; likewise 'resolution' can denote the process of tension-release, or a place where tension-release takes place.[29]

To speak of 'tension' clearly presupposes an equilibrium subsequent

footnote 27 (cont.)
out that this music 'easily accounts for *all* the popular music of the last two centuries . . . There is no form of popular music in the modern industrialised world that exists outside the province of mass tonal consciousness. It is the tonality of the church, school, office, parade, convention, cafeteria, workplace, airport, airplane, automobile, truck, tractor, lounge, lobby, bar, gym, brothel, bank, and elevator. Afraid of being without it while on foot, humans are strapping it to their bodies in order to walk to it, run to it, work to it, and relax in it. It is everywhere. *It is music and it writes the songs*' (271). My italics.

28. Leonard Meyer wants to speak of 'implication' established by the demand for closure. 'An implicative relationship is one in which an event – be it a motive, a phrase, and so on – is patterned in such a way that reasonable inferences can be made both about its connections with preceding events and about how the event itself might be continued and perhaps reach closure and stability. By "reasonable inferences" I mean those which a competent, experienced listener – one familiar with and sensitive to the particular style – might make' (Meyer 1973, 110). I am content to use the language of implication, provided we are aware of its drawbacks, especially as deployed by Meyer. See below, p. 100, n. 2. For our purposes, we can leave the notion of 'incompleteness' fairly broad, and we need not enter the tangle of questions which inevitably arises about who decides what is incomplete and in what circumstances. It is worth adding that tension (in our sense) is not equivalent to dissonance, if dissonance refers to what emerges through a combination of two or more simultaneous notes which together are regarded as inherently unstable regardless of musical context. (There has been, of course, much disagreement about precisely when a combination of notes is to be regarded as inherently unstable, but we cannot enter that debate here.) All dissonances are tensions but not all tensions are dissonances.

29. The latter can take place at virtually any stage in a piece, including that juncture in a large tonal piece when there is a substantial 'return to the tonic' (e.g. the beginning of the recapitulation in a sonata movement) – what I shall call the 'return', or the very last tone or chord – the 'goal'. The place may not be a 'point'; it might be played out over a significant duration.

to which a tension is situated and sensed as such, even if the equilibrium is not actually sounded. The most pervasive basic temporal structure of tonal music might thus best be described as 'equilibrium–tension–resolution'.[30] To see this more clearly, we need to go into the temporal engine room of music and examine metre.

Rhythm as motion in the dynamic field of metre

Temporality in music is principally manifest through rhythm, more precisely, through rhythm interacting with *metre*. Metre is a configuration of beats[31] permeating a piece of music. In notated music it is usually written in the form of a 'time-signature' (2/4, 3/4, etc.) at the start of the piece. It is metre which makes us tap our feet and dance in step. It is metre which a conductor conveys to an orchestra.

Metre is sometimes wrongly aligned with inflexible form and dull regularity, in contrast to rhythm which is thought to be interesting and vital. In fact, metre is constituted not by a series of equally accented beats but by what is best represented as a wave of strong and weak beats. It is not so

30. In musicology, the theorist who naturally comes to mind in this regard is the German analyst Heinrich Schenker (1868–1935), a figure whose impact has been considerable though his proposals are by no means uncontested. It was Schenker's purpose to lay bare the 'organic coherence' of tonal pieces with particular attention to the way in which they moulded the dynamic of tension and resolution, a 'leaving behind' and 'return to' balance. He argued that this dynamic is structured in co-existing layers or levels of organisation. The notes we hear are in effect a transformation of an underlying primal form (*Ursatz*) of equilibrium–tension–resolution. Tonal pieces derive from a tiny class of *Ursätze*. What the ear immediately perceives is 'foreground' (the surface organisation), the *Ursatz* is the background, and the generation of the former from the latter takes place through the 'middle ground' (which may itself consist of multiple planes). To listen with understanding is to relate foreground to background by the same route whereby the composer derived it (although normally neither composer nor listener performs this process consciously). Crucial to this scheme is the distinction between 'structure' and 'prolongation' – between deep structural events and the prolongation of these events at the foreground level.

While it is beyond our scope to delineate all the differences between Schenker's approach and our own, some of the chief weaknesses of Schenkerian analysis need to be borne in mind. Most of them derive from pushing good points too far – what Scruton calls the 'astonishing ambition' of his proposals (Scruton 1997, 419). First, it is extremely hard to demonstrate the derivation of all tonal pieces from the small group of *Ursätze* proposed by Schenker, or that the *Ursatz* in each case does have the generative function accorded to it. Second, his theory has a relatively limited application: almost exclusively to tonal pieces between roughly 1680 and 1860. Third, Schenker says remarkably little about rhythm, which (we argue here) when seen in relation to metre, is fundamental to tonal music's temporality. This is not to deny the usefulness of Schenkerian analysis, especially in the harmonic field and as an instrument of small-scale analysis, in highlighting an interaction between a latent (and audible) structure and its prolongation. For introductions to Schenker, see Forte and Gilbert (1982); for critique, see Narmour (1977), Norton (1984), 35ff., and Scruton (1997), 313ff., 416ff.

31. Here I follow (broadly) Kramer's understanding of 'beat', 'accent' and 'pulse' (J. Kramer 1988, 97f). A beat is not, strictly speaking, heard, only intuited – it is without duration, and metrical accents are applied to beats. A pulse is a heard sound – pulses have duration, and rhythmic accents are applied to them.

much the goose step as the conductor's arms, or Fred Astaire's feet. Metre collates its beats into groups called bars, each bar containing a certain number of beats – in a waltz, three beats per bar. As anyone who has danced a waltz knows, the beats vary in intensity or degree of accentuation. The first beat – the downbeat – is always strongest, the other two weak. This creates a wave of equilibrium–tension–resolution in which each beat is dynamically related to the others. In a three-beat bar, the weak second beat 'moves away' from the first, and the weak third moves away from the second and 'towards' the end of the wave, which becomes the strong first beat (downbeat) of the next bar, the equilibrium of the next sequence of tension and resolution in the next bar, and so on (Figure 2.1).

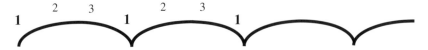

Figure 2.1 Metrical waves on one level

In the following waltz by Chopin, the metre is articulated clearly by the left hand:

Example 2.1 F. Chopin, Waltz in A flat major, op. 34, bars 17–22

Zuckerkandl speaks of 'intensification' and 'polarity' in metre – a force that augments and accumulates energy, and a force that closes and resolves.[32] Again, the two basic elements are tension and resolution; the first beat sets up a tension which reaches its highest point after the second beat and is resolved through the third, leading to the first beat of the next bar.

Metre is felt first and foremost through rhythm. It is important, however to distinguish the two. Metre is a patterned succession of beats;

32. Zuckerkandl (1956), 174ff. Beats within a bar, says Joel Lester, 'both recede from the preceding downbeat and also lead toward the following downbeat' (Lester 1986, 163). Christopher Hasty writes that 'It is the directed movement away from one moment and toward another which constitutes metre' (Hasty 1981, 188).

rhythm refers to the variegated pattern of durations given in a succession of tones. Rhythm is always articulated in tones. (A ballroom dancer dances chiefly not to rhythm but to metre.) Thus, strictly speaking, we don't hear metre directly, we hear tones which make up rhythmic patterns, and the metre is implied and sensed through the rhythm of tones. Rhythm and metre may coincide very closely, but they can be out of step, sometimes quite radically.[33]

Though metre is sensed with peculiar directedness through rhythm, it can be articulated by any parameter of music – including pitch change, tone duration, harmonic change, textural change, the entrance of a new voice, change of tempo, new register, contour change and dynamics.[34] In fact, all parameters of music potentially contribute to the delineation of metric accents, and thus to metrical waves.

Rhythmic patterns, then, 'ride' the metrical waves, and in so doing, reveal the shape of the waves.

> In this Chopin waltz above (Example 2.1), the rhythm of the right hand's melody 'rides' the metre articulated by the left hand.

Rhythm is always rhythm-over-metre. Zuckerkandl's metaphorically rich prose may have its moments of exaggeration, but it is worth quoting nonetheless:

> The wave is the metre; rhythm arises from the different arrangements of the tones on the wave. The greatest possible latitude is accorded to the nature and manner of these arrangements. The tones may be distributed over the measure regularly or irregularly; may fill the measure in rapid succession or leave it empty for long stretches; at one place crowd close together, at another spread thin; may follow the pattern of the measure with their accents or run contrary to it. This freedom of distribution and arrangement makes it possible for the tones to give the constant basic form of the wave a changing, perpetually different profile. In accordance with the will of the tones, the wave will display contours now soft and rounded, now sharp and jagged; will beat softly and calmly or with ever-increasing impact; will heave, topple, break against resistances. This playing with the wave by the tones, this shaping of the substance of the wave; the conjunction and opposition of two components, their mutual tension and continuous adjustment to each other – this, in music, we experience as rhythm.[35]

But matters are more interesting than this. For metre does not work on one level alone. The successive downbeats of each bar are themselves differently accented. Together they constitute another wave at another

---

33. On the complex relation between metrical and rhythmic accent, see the extended discussion in J. Kramer (1988), 81ff.   34. Ibid., 108ff.   35. Zuckerkandl (1956), 172.

level, itself a wave of equilibrium, tension and resolution. The wave
shown in Figure 2.2 arches over a 'hyperbar'.[36] The same dynamic is

'hyperbar'

Figure 2.2 Bars and hyperbars

repeated at a further level: the downbeats of hyperbars become new beats
in another metrical wave (a higher hyperbar). And so on. The process is
extended in still higher hyperbars, the lower waves giving rise to ever
higher waves (Figure 2.3).

Figure 2.3 Metrical matrix

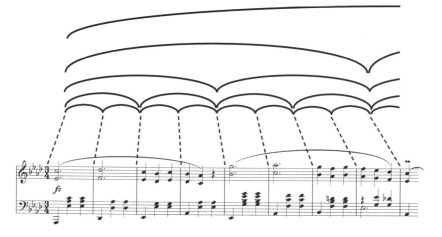

Example 2.2 F. Chopin, Waltz in A flat major, op. 34, bars 17–24

36. The American term is 'hypermeasure'.

In Example 2.2, the four-bar hyperbars are marked out by slurs. It is worth noting that slurs and phrasing do not always line up with metric waves so closely.

Metre, then, lends to tonal music a multi-layered texture of superordinate and subordinate waves, in which the wave of one layer is in turn a phase of the next higher layer and so on.[37] This applies also to large-scale musical forms – whole pieces and movements can be understood as waves of intensification and polarity, away-from and back-to, tension and resolution (even though, of course, they may not be consciously intuited or spoken about in these terms).[38]

The diagram (Figure 2.3) might suggest a certain tidiness and predictability. But even in the simplest pieces there is usually metrical irregularity of some sort. So, for example, at one level there may be a succession of waves of different lengths; the waves can overlap, conflict, fragment, be left 'hanging' in the air and so on. These irregularities are often 'balanced out' in various ways at higher levels, but this leaves virtually limitless room for novelty and unpredictability at lower levels.[39]

There is, then, a movement towards closure at one or more levels, and, just because of this repeated closure, a concurrent forward thrust at another level.

In the temporal component of music, then, we have to deal with a two-faced force, not to say a two-minded force. So far as it is responsible for the organisation of the individual bar, it is perpetually intent upon closing a cycle, reaching a goal; it wills the finite. On the other hand, with its renewed, ever more insistent 'On! Once again!' which hammers out measure after measure [i.e. bar after bar], it is a striving without end that accepts no limit, a willing of the infinite.[40]

37. Zuckerkandl (1956), 151–80; (1959), 97–139; J. Kramer (1988), ch. 4.
38. For a fine treatment of our perception of large-scale forms, see J. Kramer (1988), ch. 11, and his robust defence of the reality of large-scale metrical perception in 116ff. The claim is not that at every second metrical waves can be intuited. The opening of Beethoven's *Pathétique* Sonata, for example, starts with a long, held chord – and that is all we hear; it is only as the piece advances that we begin to intuit metrical waves. (Even here, it could be argued, during that first chord sounding, we expect another musical event, and insofar as we do, we are experiencing the 'reaching' forward of a wave, even if not a hierarchy of waves. Zuckerkandl makes much of this (Zuckerkandl 1956, 248ff.), but probably overplays his point, and certainly pushes his metaphysics too far.)
39. Some of the complexities of the 'balancing out' of irregularity in musical perception are treated by Kramer in J. Kramer (1988), 349ff. See below, pp. 89ff.
40. Zuckerkandl (1956), 176. David Greene can speak of classical pieces in sonata-allegro form as follows: 'all of them involve the interaction of two elements: balance and forward thrust. Both elements pervade every level of sonata structures. The most obvious and perhaps the most important example is the paired phrases which occur in every Classic sonata.' In this case, the cadence heard as closing the second phrase is also heard as closing

This works downwards as well: beats can be divided into smaller and smaller values, smaller and smaller waves of intensification and polarity. Moreover, not only can this process be articulated by any parameter of music, the parameters interact with each other so that what occurs between levels within one – the concurrence of resolution and tension – can also occur (and typically does occur) between parameters. Closure in one parameter – say, harmony – may run along with an opening or tension-inducing process in another – say, timbre. In fact, this is extremely common, for musical continuity usually depends on preventing simultaneous closure in all parameters.[41]

Musical time is thus not essentially about a line split into equal parts but about waves of tension and resolution. The succession of beat to beat is never mere advance along a straight line, but a variegated wave. When I ask a musician to play 'in time' I do not want her to play according to strict mathematical regularity – that is usually dull. I want her to reveal the metrical wave(s). Every piano teacher knows that pupils who play like human metronomes win no prizes. Variations from mathematical equality in a performance do not disturb us nearly as much as distortions of the metrical waves. The composer Johannes Brahms wrote:

> The metronome has no value . . . for myself I have never believed that my blood and a mechanical instrument go well together.[42]

It is Zuckerkandl's proposal that this metrical wave-order is best construed as a dynamic field. Every beat in every bar or hyperbar, and thus every tone, will have its own, unique 'dynamic quality',[43] a directional impulse, depending on its situation in the hierarchy of metrical waves. Accordingly, Zuckerkandl can define rhythm as 'motion in the dynamic field of metre'. It is important to understand that for Zuckerkandl, musical metre is not born in the beats themselves but, so to speak, in what happens 'in between' the beats. The beats are not like beads sliding down a time-line, or balls sliding down a tube of time, but are intrinsically interrelated through time.[44]

footnote **40.** (*cont.*)
the first. The cadence ending the first closes the first but carries 'elements of forward motion' across the cadence to the second. Moreover the pair (not just the second phrase) 'pushes into the next section of the music' (Greene 1982, 20).
41. See Meyer (1973), 81ff. It is worth noting that rhythm also operates hierarchically, usually only partly coinciding with metre, creating even in the simplest piece a temporal matrix of considerable richness and complexity. But here we confine ourselves to looking at the more fundamental phenomenon of metre.   **42.** As quoted in Campling (1997), 96.
43. Zuckerkandl (1956), ch. 1 *et passim*.   **44.** Ibid., 180ff.

Melody as motion in the dynamic field of key

Metre, or (better) rhythm-over-metre, is fundamental to musical tempo-rality. Less fundamental but also crucial to the temporality of tonal music is harmony, and this takes us into a discussion of the second field, that of key (alternatively the 'tonal' or 'harmonic' field).

Consider a melody. A melody is made up of a series of tones. These tones possess a dynamic quality not just in relation to metre, but with respect to other tones within the context of a 'key'. A key is a system of tones-in-relation which, when arranged according to pitch, form a 'scale'. Not all tones in the scale are of equal status; each tone 'knows its place', so to speak, in relation to the others. Most important, there is always a grav-itation towards the first tone of the scale – the 'tonic'. The tonic consti-tutes the dynamic centre of the field. Depending on what the tones are doing in relation to this tonic-centred field, they gain dynamic qualities. There will be tones which are involved in intensification and those involved in resolution.

For example, melodies quite often conclude with what is called a per-fect cadence – one type of which takes the form of two tones, each set over a chord (Example 2.3).

Example 2.3 Perfect cadence

The first tone has a 'pointing beyond' quality, an incompleteness directed towards its completion (on the tonic). The second tone is the res-olution of the former, and it too has a dynamic quality related to the pre-vious tone, this time of attraction, a quality of 'pulling in'.

This kind of harmonic tension and resolution, when expanded, gives rise to one of the commonest large-scale structural forms of tonal music: the establishment of a 'home' around the tonic, a move away from the tonic towards a point or period of tension (usually perceived as being 'dis-tant' from the starting-point), followed by a drive back towards the starting-point. Again, a wave of equilibrium–tension–resolution. Many popular songs exemplify the pattern (Example 2.4).

Example 2.4 George Gershwin, 'I got rhythm', bars 29–62

> In pieces such as this, the fact that we gain a sense of
> 'home–away–home again' is because the bass tones at any particular
> point in the music and the chords constructed upon them are related
> dynamically to the most important tone (the tonic), chord and key – in
> this case, B flat. The tones and chords acquire a dynamic quality
> according to their situation in this field. The whole middle section of bars
> 45–52 ('Old Man Trouble . . .') is heard as being 'away' because the
> music shifts from B flat through D⁷(45), G(47), C⁷(49) and F⁷(52); bars
> 51–2 leading to the 'return' to home at 53 (B flat).
>
> These processes work hierarchically. In this piece, there is the large-
> scale harmonic process I have just mentioned, but embedded within are
> many smaller processes of the same kind. For example, bars 37–40,
> harmonically speaking, constitute a small-scale equilibrium–tension–
> resolution running from B flat through Cm⁷, B flat⁶, Cm⁷, and back
> to B flat (41). Something similar can be said of bars 41–4.

Zuckerkandl argues that the dynamic quality of tones within this harmonic field, although inextricably mediated through physical realities,
cannot be explained by considering tones solely as physical events, as
acoustical phenomena. A note can be registered on an oscilloscope, but
not its dynamic quality. The dynamic quality of tones is a function of their
inter-relatedness.

So a key, like the metrical matrix, acts as a dynamic field. It is in relation to this field, Zuckerkandl avers, that we can best understand *melodic
motion*. We speak of a melody 'going' 'up' and 'down', and of tones 'moving'. What can we possibly mean? In fact, we are asking two things. First,
how can we speak of melodies 'rising' and 'falling', of some tones being
'higher' than others, when there seems to be no frame relative to which
tones move? Second, how can we speak of continuity in music when all we
seem to have is a succession of separate tones? Motion implies the movement of an entity which retains some kind of identity from one moment
to the next, from one place to another. But musical tones appear and disappear.

The answer to both questions depends on grasping the dynamic quality of tones in relation to key. When we hear those two tones of the
cadence cited above, we do not simply hear two different tones but two
tones related, the first reaching towards the other, the other attracting the
first. The dynamic quality of each is not a matter of pitch, as if there were
some perceivable spatial background against which tones move 'up' and
'down'. There *is* a 'background' against which tones 'move', but it is the

dynamic field of a key. Our sense of melodic motion is not pitch-dependent but relies on the place of tones in relation to this dynamic field.[45]

What, then, of the second question, musical continuity?[46] Much the same considerations apply. The theory which claims that the mind 'fills the gaps' between tones, much as one fills in the gaps between frames of a film, is highly misleading. A melody does not present us with the 'illusion' of motion; if it did, the ideal of musical continuity would be a wailing siren. But no one is claiming this, for this destroys the notion of melody: tones are no longer allowed their own discreteness and thus they cannot attain their characteristic dynamic quality. Tones in a dynamic field do not need to be psychologically 'stitched up' to make sense; they are *already* internally related by virtue of the field of key. The use of silence in music can testify to this – silences often function as an element in music just as important as any tone; in such cases there is no question of the silences interrupting musical motion. The concert pianist Arthur Schnabel once said:

> The notes I handle no better than many pianists. But the pauses between the notes – ah, that is where the art resides.[47]

In hearing or listening to music we are always 'between the tones, on the way from tone to tone; our hearing does not remain with the tone, it reaches through it and beyond it'.[48] The motion we hear is 'pure betweenness, pure passing over'. In sum, if rhythm is motion in the

45. I do not find Scruton's arguments against Zuckerkandl on this score convincing (Scruton 1997, 52ff.). He complains that Zuckerkandl does not explain our experience of musical movement in atonal music, such as, for example, Schoenberg's *Erwartung,* where there is a strong sense of motion yet without tonal harmony. And he comments that Zuckerkandl exaggerates his case when speaking of tensions within the diatonic scale. 'We can hear a melody move from B to C, without hearing a tension in B that is resolved in C' (54). The concept of a dynamic quality or property, says Scruton, does little to clarify the concept of musical motion. In reply, it needs to be said, first, that Zuckerkandl is only concerned with the intuition of musical movement in tonal music which operates through keys, not providing a comprehensive theory of such movement. (Even so, melody can still operate with tension and resolution without the field of harmony which developed from the seventeenth century onwards. Melodies and phrases have nearly always been fixed to notes which stand out as 'points of arrival and departure' or 'stations on the way' – this applies to much music which is not tonal in the fullest sense of operating with keys, from Gregorian chant to thousands of folk-melodies. In other words, we should not assume that 'tonal motion' in Zuckerkandl is confined exclusively to the modern Western tonal tradition, though to demonstrate and qualify this would take us too far afield.) Second, regarding tensions in the diatonic scale, Zuckerkandl makes very clear that the tensions are heard as such only when individual notes are perceived by the hearer against the context of a harmonic background; to point to two notes out of context in the way Scruton does is to miss the point.   46. Zuckerkandl (1956), 117–41.

47. Quoted in Campling (1997), 96. The main theme of the last movement of Beethoven's *Eroica* Symphony consists largely of silences. 'The difference between musical and acoustical events can hardly be better captured than by this example, of a musical event which continues after the silence has ceased' (Scruton 1997, 49).

48. Zuckerkandl (1956), 137.

dynamic field of metre, melody is motion in the dynamic field of a key. Tonal music is born of the interaction between these two dynamic fields, an interaction as complex as it is profound. And these fields operate through two main tendencies – tension and resolution: 'the tendency that drives on, accumulates, [which] is responsible for augmentation' and 'the tendency that closes, establishes symmetries, equalises every weight by a counterweight'.[49]

Though music's engagement with time is most directly intuited through metre and rhythm, both metre and key are intrinsically time-laden fields.[50] We do not have to adopt Zuckerkandl's somewhat over-ambitious metaphysics of time to appreciate that the kind of conception of time we are dealing with here, whatever else we say about it, is not that of an empty container or the channel down which tones roll, but an inherent function of the way musical tones interrelate. 'Music is temporal art not in the barren and empty sense that its tones succeed one another 'in time'; it is temporal art in the concrete sense that it enlists the flux of time as a force to serve its ends.'[51] The use of 'force' here and elsewhere by Zuckerkandl is curious and highly speculative, and his assertion that 'Music is temporal art in the special sense that in it *time reveals itself* to experience' needs treating with caution.[52] But none of this should be allowed to obscure his more solidly based and valuable insights. Musical tones, he is saying, as distinct from mere notes or sounds, are not essentially discrete entities which happen to be situated in some kind of container of time, but are intrinsically interrelated by and through time. A single tone, to state the obvious, cannot have anything akin to the meaning of a single word; tones will mean next to nothing apart from their dynamic interplay, and even when considered together, their meaning emerges primarily through this dynamic interaction, not because the tones, either individually or collectively, 'point' us to something.[53] Moreover, it is clear that Zuckerkandl is claiming that in sharing in

49. Ibid., 180.

50. Although he is by no means clear on the matter, it seems that Zuckerkandl is wanting to say that metre is most directly and closely intertwined with the world's temporality. The dynamic quality of tones in the harmonic field is, ultimately, harnessed to serve metre.

51. Ibid., 181.   52. Ibid., 200. My italics.

53. In line with this, in a fascinating article, Arnold Berleant proposes that instead of understanding the creative process as the musician fitting tones into pre-made packages (forms, in other words, such as fugue, sonata, passacaglia, etc.) it is wiser 'to think of the composer as an artist who possesses special sensitivity to *the dynamic pressures of sounds*. All musical materials have distinctive traits and thus generate their own individual ways of being developed' (Berleant 1987, 247).

music's temporality we share *to some extent at least* in the temporality or temporalities integral to the physical world.

Comments

Although we have only been able to sketch the main contours of Zuckerkandl's thesis, some fairly obvious objections to it need to be addressed.

Instead of speaking of a dynamic field, would it not be simpler to say that after frequent hearing of certain tone-sequences, we automatically attach certain expectations to them, and then quite naturally project feelings of tension and release, dissatisfaction and satisfaction, into the notes and call them 'dynamic qualities'?[54] Is it not the case that our responses are dependent on the music we have heard, and thus on purely social and cultural determinants? Someone schooled solely in, say, Indonesian music will not react to tonal music in the same way as a white teenager in Manchester. Any attempt to 'objectify' any aspect of music is likely to be expression of Western cultural hegemony. Attractive as it is, the difficulty with this line of argument is that it begs the question of why particular tone-patterns and practices become firmly established in the first place. An enormous debate lurks in the background here concerning the extent to which the development of a tradition such as Western tonality is grounded in universal dynamic features of the physical world, including universally shared characteristics of our own human make-up (e.g. the operation of the brain and nervous system), and the extent to which it can be accounted for in terms of particular individual and socio-cultural contingencies: individual preference, local customs and conventions, as well as broader cultural norms, etc.[55] Increasingly, it is being seen that this is not a simple matter of either/or. Two comments should be made. First, to concede that certain patterns of tones and rhythms are person/context/culture-specific does not itself imply anything about the rooting of these patterns in factors which transcend such particularities. To recognise that not all people share the same or similar expectations when hearing tonal music does not of itself inform us that such expectations are entirely constructive or conventional. Second, despite huge individual and cultural variation in music-making and music-perception, it is widely accepted that certain 'constants' do frequently reappear in the music of

---

54. Zuckerkandl calls this 'associationism' (1956), 41–52. He is by no means at his strongest in rebutting this objection. He can assume far too narrow a version of the relevant arguments (especially at 45f.).
55. On these and related issues see Nattiez (1990), 62ff.; Sloboda (1985), ch. 7.

almost all cultures – strategies, forms, intervals ('stable' and 'unstable') etc. And, moreover, a plausible case can be made for holding that the basis of at least some of these dynamic 'universals' and of our response to them lies not only in a constitution shared by all human beings but also in extra-human phenomena such as the harmonic series (on which tonal music's dynamic field of harmony is in part dependent) and the patterned movements and configurations of the natural world (with which the dynamic field of metre is almost certainly linked).[56] In other words, it is certainly not far-fetched to suppose that when we experience musical temporality we are experiencing not only what is distinctive and peculiar to particular people, and to social or cultural groups, but are also engaging with temporalities in which we all share to some extent. We are not, of course, in the realm of knock-down proofs here, but the assumption that our reactions to music's temporality can be accounted for solely in terms of particular human contingencies would often appear to owe more to the fashions of constructivism than to the evidence at hand.

A similar objection, concerning metre in particular, might be propounded along the following lines. Music tends to generate certain sympathetic movements in the hearer – we tap our fingers, sway our head, or whatever – and even if we are not always as overt as this, there are internal bodily sensations of pressure and tension aroused by music (muscular contractions, changes in blood pressure etc.). It is these motions of our own body we are perceiving and sensing directly when we hear music. Why project back into the music 'dynamic qualities' which are no more than our own bodily sensations? Clearly, large commitments about the relation of our bodies to the extra-human world and the inherent dynamism (or otherwise) of that world are playing a part in this kind of objection, some of which we tackle elsewhere in this book. But here we can at least say that the question needs to be thrown back into the objector's court. Granted that musical stimuli do indeed give rise to bodily kinetic impulses, why assume that the temporality of the former *is no more than* a projection of the latter? Why assume *a priori* that the physical entities beyond ourselves which are implicated in music cannot have their own

---

56. The literature on this is vast and burgeoning, but see e.g. Nattiez (1990), 62ff.; Blacking (1973), 108f., 112; Sloboda (1985), 253ff.; and, more boldly, Scruton (1997), ch. 9. George Steiner writes: 'the immediacy of our perceptions of harmony and of discord would seem to correspond not only to our readings of inner states of personal being, but also to that of the social contract and, ultimately, of the cosmos' (Steiner 1989, 196). With rather less mystique, Shepherd and Wicke argue for the generalisability of Zuckerkandl's arguments beyond the tradition of Western functional tonality (Shepherd and Wicke 1997, 150ff).

intrinsic temporality which might at least be *part* of what we experience through music, especially in the light of evidence (alluded to in the last paragraph) that all music *to some extent* would seem to be grounded in the dynamics of the world quite apart from human construction and making?

Related to this, however, is a more substantial objection, this time appealing to the power of memory and anticipation. Could not the dynamic relationship we think we sense between, say, two tones in a melody be seen as entirely a product of the mind's powers? The mind stores the past tone and sets it next to the present one; it is only natural for the mind to continue the process into the future, anticipating what will be, and then (confusingly) ascribing to the tone itself the dynamic quality of anticipation. The memory collates melodic tones and sets them in sequence, and this is why we 'perceive' continuity, not because of any intrinsic interconnectedness among the tones. Though the music is given 'bit by bit' in our consciousness, part stands next to part in the mind and the mind constructs the relations between them. Something similar could be said of metre.

The problem with this is that, as just expressed, it relies on construing musical hearing as if it were like analysing a musical score, where formal structures are set out and understood linearly and spatially. There is a wealth of data which would lead us to suppose that most musical perception is rather different: we do not sense tones on a time-line and view them, as it were, from a distance; we sense a dynamic 'from the inside' of the relatedness of tones.[57] Certainly, there is evidence of a 'chunking' process: we seem to gather musical information into manageable units which can be held in the short-term memory, constituting a kind of psychological 'present' of about eight to ten seconds (the average length of a phrase) which forms the object of our focal attention. But there is little to support the idea that musical experience necessarily (or even commonly) involves abstracting oneself from this 'present', surveying retrospectively past events as if on an extended straight line and from that anticipating prospectively a series of future musical events. Indeed, this kind of remembering and foretelling would actually *destroy* the experience of both metre and melody. We attend to what is present/ed to us, a present dynamically and internally related to what has been heard and what is yet to be heard. Hearing a melody is a hearing with the melody, not a hearing of a present

57. See e.g. J. Kramer (1988), 328ff.

with a simultaneous focal attention to particular past events and particular anticipated events. In music, 'time is not a mere formality, [it] flows not outside thought, but is consubstantial with the tones themselves, with the particular melody they form. *Here one thinks not in time but with time; indeed one thinks time itself in the form of tones*'.[58] The expectation I feel on hearing a tone is not directed towards any particular mental happening which I represent to myself in my consciousness. The state of expectation in music does not involve simultaneously imagining the future event which will satisfy the expectation. The enjoyment is not in the expectation *of some event* but in *pure expectation*.[59] This is why we can enjoy the surprise in Haydn's 'Surprise' symphony over and over again.[60] (There are, of course, pieces which involve direct quotation of past and future music, and we shall return to these later.[61]) Zuckerkandl undoubtedly presses some of the metaphors too far, but on the matter of the musical 'present' he is worth quoting:

> This is a present from which not *I*, thanks to my particular powers, look backward into the past and forward into the future, but which *itself* thus looks backward and forward. These particular powers of remembering and foreknowing, then, are not required in order that

58. Zuckerkandl (1973), 303. My italics.
59. Hepburn (1976) argues that Zuckerkandl is working with over-simplified notions of memory and anticipation, according to which they are concerned (respectively) with recalling past events and imagining future ones (161f.). It may indeed be the case that Zuckerkandl is not careful enough with his use of the words 'memory' and 'anticipation', and, as Hepburn hints, Zuckerkandl may indeed allow his metaphors to run beyond their usefulness. But none of this substantially affects Zuckerkandl's claim that musical perception does not appear to involve in any central or essential way a 'synoptic' view of a work. (Moreover, it is not at all clear that Hepburn has understood Zuckerkandl's account of the interpenetration of the temporal modes in musical perception.)
60. The same could be said of large-scale musical form (Zuckerkandl 1956, 235ff.; 1973, ch. 13). It seems that many people do and can perceive large-scale form as they listen to music (see J. Kramer 1988, ch. 11) but there is little reason to believe that this entails 'standing back' and mentally setting part against part to measure them. More plausible is the view that *we sense in the dynamic of the music itself different phases of the metrical wave(s) pervading the music* – it is *these* which we intuit as 'balanced' or 'unbalanced.' Balance in musical form is not equivalent to exact durational symmetry according to clock-time. See J. Kramer (1988), 112ff. Opposition to the view that we can perceive large-scale structure often rests on the assumption that in order for us to do this we would have to 'measure' time-lengths according to some regular clock and compare them in the mind's eye in some kind of synoptic gaze. Charles Rosen puts the matter well: 'In too much writing on music, a work appears like a large system of inter-relationships in which the order, the intensity, and, above all, the direction of the relations are of secondary, and even negligible, consideration. Too often, the music could be played backward without affecting the analysis in any significant way. This is to treat music as a spatial art. Yet the movement from past to future is more significant in music than the movement from left to right in a picture ... There must be a constant interaction between the individual motif and the direction of the piece – the intensity and proportions of its gradual unfolding' (Rosen 1971, 40f).
61. See below, pp. 111ff.

future things and past things shall *not be nothing*. The past is not extinguished, but not because a memory stores it; it is not extinguished because *time itself stores it*, or, better put, because the being of time is a storing of itself; the future is not an impenetrable wall, but not because a foreknowledge or forefeeling anticipates time; it is not impenetrable because time always anticipates itself, because the being of time is an anticipating itself.[62]

Of course, it could still be said that even if we reject a picture of memory and anticipation as necessarily involving some kind of conscious focus on past and future events, it might still be that our mind's memory and anticipation in some way constructs the sense of time-embeddedness we ascribe to tones. But again the points made in relation to the earlier two objections are apt. There is much to indicate that not only the temporality of our biological and physiological characteristics but the temporality of processes in the physical world at large have an essential part to play in our experience of musical temporality. It is surely wise to resist the kind of picture of the mind which seems tacit in this objection, namely as an essentially disembodied organ, set apart from physical process, which can do no other than project its (utterly unique?) temporality into musical phenomena.

If all this has any cogency, then it is clear that what might broadly be termed 'subjectivist' or 'constructivist' theories of music are thrown sharply into question – those which would seek to explain musical practices solely in terms of the activities and projections of the composer, performer, listener, hearer, culture or whatever. One of music's distinctions would seem to be that its time-intensiveness is connected not only to socially and culturally contingent temporalities, and not only to the temporalities of intellectual construction, and not only to the temporalities of our bodies, but to the temporalities of the physical world at large in which all these temporalities participate. If this is so, music is a thoroughly *this*-worldly art: 'If our world is a temporal world, if temporality is one of its bases . . . then music is anything but superterrestial; it is peculiarly terrestial, of this world.'[63] The question which sets the agenda of Zuckerkandl's first study *Sound and Symbol* points us to a broad vision of music's significance: 'What must the world be like, what must I be like, if between me and the world the phenomenon of music can occur?'[64] Music's

---

62. Zuckerkandl (1956), 228.   63. Ibid., 152.
64. Ibid., 7. There are undoubtedly connections between what I am attempting in this study and Paul Ricoeur's subtle and ambitious project in *Time and Narrative*. Ricoeur makes much of the dichotomy between a 'phenomenological' account of time – anticipated in

impermanence and insubstantiality (it employs physical realities which
have a very short endurance) together with its relatively weak and unstable referential powers should not lead us to conclude that it is best regarded as the least 'worldly' or physical of the arts, but rather that it is
especially free to offer a peculiarly intense experience of the temporality
not only of human existence but of the world we indwell as physical creatures.

It is worth mentioning in passing that one of the reasons for a common
neglect of the time-embedded character of musical experience is that certain habits of thought have become deeply ingrained in musical acade-
mia, especially a heavy dependence on the examination of a written score.
An extreme statement of the ethos can be found in Schoenberg's claim
that 'Music need not be performed any more than books need to be read
aloud, for its logic is perfectly represented on the printed page.'[65] Nicholas Cook has written at length about the process of turning a temporal
experience into what he calls an 'imaginary object' in Western musical
culture.[66] In a similar vein Kathleen Marie Higgins, in her study of music
and ethics, criticises the repeated tendency of musical aesthetics to equate
'structure' with 'notatable structure' and to 'screen out' or ignore much
that is essential to musical experience, especially 'the fact that we experience music as temporally, dynamically *alive*'.[67]

What time is it?

We have sketched in barest outline one way of understanding some of the
principal temporal determinants of tonal music. Some qualifications are
necessary before we draw the strands together. First, it would take us
beyond our scope to delineate the similarities and differences between the
temporality of music and other art-forms. But we should be wary both of

footnote 64. (*cont.*)
Augustine, and associated especially with Husserl and Heidegger; and a 'physical' account,
seen in Aristotle, with its stress on the link between time and movement through space.
Both are inadequate – the first to the temporality of the natural order, the second to the
temporality of human experience. The true mediation between them is the humanised
time of *narrative*, whether fictional or historical. Narrative orders scattered sequential
experiences and events into a coherent structure of human time. 'The world unfolded by
every narrative work is always a temporal world . . . Time becomes human time to the
extent that it is organised after the manner of a narrative; narrative, in turn, is meaningful
to the extent that it portrays the features of temporal experience' (Ricoeur 1984, 3).
65. As quoted in Newlin (1980), 164.
66. Cook (1998b), 72. Cook's fascinating study *Music, Imagination and Culture* (1990) engages
with just these issues at length.   67. Higgins (1991), 48; cf. ch. 2, *passim*.

assuming that music's temporality has nothing in common with that of other temporal arts, and of supposing that music has no unique temporal capacities. To claim that all we have said about musical temporality could also apply to literature, for example, is clearly not convincing. Though there may be likenesses, there are many dissimilarities: to cite an obvious one, the many-layered temporal waves are integral to music in a way which they are not in literature, even if something like them can be found in the latter art-form. Second, it is worth repeating that in this book I am not assuming or claiming that Western tonal music, arranged metrically, is privileged above all others with respect to our engagement with time. Third, in speaking of time or temporality we are not in an area where unassailable arguments or proofs are appropriate. My purpose here is to show how music might advance our wisdom about time (and, in due course, a theological approach to time), not provide irrefutable and total-ising theories.

Nevertheless, from what we have observed so far, a number of tentative and general remarks may be made about the kind of temporality music appears to exhibit and the significance of this for wider concerns about time.

A false polarity

First of all, music's temporality is not easily assimilated to either the 'sub-jectivist/idealist' or the 'absolutist' approaches to time we noted above.[68] Obviously, music is intimately bound up with the times we fashion and shape, but we have been suggesting that its temporality cannot be accounted for solely in terms of human imposition, formation or con-struction. Similarly, there is an implicit challenge to those who would objectivise time into some kind of inert receptacle which is simply 'there' irrespective of concrete things, people, and so forth, a mere frame or mode of extension into which musical events are installed. The kind of picture which emerges, if we are to speak pictorially, is not of atemporal entities or discrete 'substances' 'moving' through a volume or channel of time, but rather of successive tones and metrical beats internally and dynamically related through time, of time as a function of the intercon-nectedness of tones and beats:

> the character of the relatedness of auditory events in music can no more be thought of as a consequences of the 'placing' of notes *in*

musical time and musical space (that is, notes placed in the pre-existing, empty hopper of musical time and musical space which then lends definition to their relatedness) than can individual auditory events in material reality be thought of as being 'placed' and 'related' in auditory time and space.[69]

Theologically, this is both significant and suggestive, as we shall see.

Straight lines?

It should be clear by now that to construe music's temporality in strictly linear and homogeneous terms is misleading. Concepts of time dependent on the notion of a singular and continuous one-dimensional line stretching from the past into the future have, together with a cluster of related assumptions and practices, played a prominent (if complex) part in modernity.[70] Many have urged that from a theological perspective such concepts are highly problematic. Some commentators have been quick to align tonal music with these linearities. This is understandable. Tonal music is generally an asymmetrical process. In its large-scale constitution a tonal piece can reach forward to an ultimate resolution, and its constitutive events are explicitly oriented to succeeding musical events.[71]

---

69. Shepherd and Wicke (1997), 135.

70. 'The explanation offered by contemporary European culture – which, during the last two centuries, has increasingly marginalised other explanations – is that which constructs a uniform, abstract, unilinear law of time applying to all events, and according to which all "times" can be compared and regulated' (Berger 1984, 9f).

71. A vigorous debate has arisen about whether or not we can speak of an intrinsic temporal directionality in physical processes – the so-called 'arrow of time'. In the physical sciences, the issue is not so much about time *per se* as the reversibility or otherwise of physical processes. Newtonian dynamics provided no basis for the irreversibility of physical process; Newtonian equations are indifferent with regard to temporal orientation. There are those who claim that none of the major theories of physics – from classical mechanics to quantum field theory – provide evidence for the 'arrow of time'. The psychological arrow of time can be described as an illusion or an 'emergent property', not found in nature but arising in, say, biology, or perhaps psychology. Others believe that physical processes are time-asymmetrical in some cases, that certain theories in physics provide at least partial evidence of time's arrow. Classical thermodynamics introduced a macroscopic arrow of time, suggesting a cosmos of increasing entropy (entropy being, roughly, a measure of disorder), but it is not clear how and if this relates to the whole universe. More recently some have argued that non-linear, non-equilibrium thermodynamics indicates that time's arrow may be fundamental at a microscopic level (Prigogine 1980, and Prigogine and Stengers 1984), but this has by no means been universally accepted. Some also point to the biological sciences as offering grounds for an evolutionary arrow of time, in this case working towards increased order rather than disorder – what Paul Davies calls the 'optimistic arrow of time'. The debate, now significantly stimulated by the writings of Hawking, continues. (See e.g. P. C. W. Davies 1995, chs. 9–12.) Music does not of course prove or demonstrate the world to be of a 'directional' character, but it is arguable that it can do much to assist us in clarifying, articulating and embodying something of such a temporality.

And yet, without denying that tonal music has arisen in the context of modernity and has often reflected some of its temporal configurations (including what some would regard as its more harmful configurations), it cannot – at least in its fundamental ways of operating – be easily pressed into linear modes. In this respect, we shall argue, it can be of considerable theological usefulness, not least in releasing us from conceptualities which have done more harm than good.

Pinpointing some of the differences between linear and musical temporality will serve to open up some of the main trajectories of the book.

First, most obviously, music is structured through layers of waves of intensification and release. *Directionality is one thing; one-dimensional linearity is another.*[72] This distinction will be crucial to much of the theological discussion which follows.

Closely connected with this, second, it is fair to say that much of modernity has favoured a time which can be conceptualised in primarily *quantitative* terms. A time-line becomes divided up and measured in units. The propensity to speak and think in this way is encouraged by the invention of mechanical clocks (quantifying duration with precision), the advent of 'standard time', the development of calendars, and so on, as well as the economic quantification of time (as in 'time is money').[73] We have seen that music's temporality is not of this character. It is not that the quantitative dimension is absent – far from it – but it by no means dominates. We shall allude to this a number of times.

Third, various brands of *progressivism* have arisen, according to which, for example, history is construed as advancing cumulatively along a time-line towards a goal which gathers the temporal process together. Some tonal music follows this pattern, but by no means all: for example, most song-type compositions (which make up the bulk of popular music) do

---

72. Kramer, in his major study of musical time, is keen to use the term 'linear' of much tonal music, and sets up a basic polarity between linearity and nonlinearity (J. Kramer 1988, 20ff.). Linearity is 'the determination of some characteristic(s) of music in accordance with implications that arise from earlier events of the piece' – a 'characteristic' being a concrete detail (e.g. a note or interval), or a larger unit (e.g. phrase), or the duration of a section, the nature of a passage, or a subjective mood, or indeed, anything in or about a piece of music. Nonlinearity is 'the determination of some characteristic(s) of music in accordance with implications that arise from principles or tendencies governing an entire piece or section' (20). Kramer's definition of linearity is indeed applicable to most tonal music and helpful as far as it goes. But for the reasons we outline here, the misunderstandings which easily attach to the word 'linear' make its usefulness very limited.   73. See e.g. Adam (1990), Landes (1983).

not proceed towards such a 'collecting' goal. We pick up these matters again in chapter 4.[74]

Fourth, this last feature of linear models has in turn frequently *masked or downplayed the role of discontinuity* as pervasive and potentially beneficial to historical process. In much tonal music, unpredictable interruptions, 'indirect routes' and ruptures are an inherent and enriching part of the process.[75] Sometimes implications are never picked up at all, and implications can be established which are discarded and not taken up until much later. Single-line models find it hard to do justice to such possibilities. We bring this into play with theology at a number of points in what follows.

Fifth, related to this, linear metaphors have often had the effect of *minimising the place of radical and qualitative novelty*, encouraging a view of the future as proceeding inexorably from the past through the present, governed (in at least some currents of modernity) by a deistic 'God', or by the laws of Newtonian mechanics, or sometimes by both. This can have the effect of curbing due recognition of the place of contingency and intrinsic unpredictability. There is little room for acknowledging that past and future are experienced as qualitatively (not just quantitatively) different.[76] (It is paradoxical, though perhaps understandable, that a time-line model often used to bolster directionality can easily undermine it through stressing uniformity.) This relates to many of the points we shall make in our chapters on improvisation.

Sixth, the stress on homogeneity and continuity in linearity can have a marked effect on the way we understand *transience*. On the one hand, an over-reliance on linear models of time will tend to mean that *transience is masked or suppressed*, especially biological death. The notion of an inexorable and inevitable line of progress has sometimes engendered the illusion of immortality, not least in modernity. The accompanying assumption is that transience is something intrinsically and necessarily negative which needs to be hidden or denied in some manner. On the

74. Jürgen Moltmann has advanced a substantial theological critique of the assumptions driving modernity's historical progressivisms (Moltmann 1996, part I.). Drawing especially on Jewish writers such as Benjamin and Rosenzweig, he mounts a heavy attack on conceptions of time as an undifferentiated linear sequence of cause and effect; this is done against those who would transpose eschatology into time (e.g. secular millenarianism), and against those who would transpose eschatology into eternity (e.g. the early Barth, Bultmann). Cf. Bauckham (1999), an essay from which I have benefited enormously in this part of the book.   75. J. Kramer (1988), 21, 25–32.

76. That is, on the homogeneous view, the future is different from the past only in the quantity of clock-time which keeps them apart, i.e. they simply describe events which occur at different 'time-points'.

other hand, linear models can have the effect of *intensifying the experience of transience as negative and destructive*: when we lose what is good and valuable, happy meals, enriching conversations, joyful relationships cut short by tragedy. Wonderful things and events, or the enjoyable present moment, are conceived as retreating down the time-line, slipping into the increasingly distant and irrecoverable past. Here temporal closeness and distance are seen as quantitative or quasi-spatial apartness – *x* calendar months in the past, *y* months in the future. Matters are rendered rather different, however, when brought into play with music. Music does not mask its transience: musical continuity depends to a very high degree on transience, on the coming into being and dying of tones. In this way and only in this way are the dynamic qualities of tones sensed. And yet music can be gloriously ordered and enriching. The tones which die to give way to others are related, not externally by being placed on a straight line but internally by virtue of waves of tension and resolution, such that the tones' past, present and future are, in some sense, interwoven. Music, in other words, subverts the assumption that transience is necessarily harmful, that fleetingness is intrinsically irrational. That music can demonstrate and embody in sound a positive transience will be one of our main points in chapter 3. By the same token, even where transience is very obviously destructive, music, through its interweaving of the temporal modes, enacts its own kind of challenge to the notion that past events are necessarily and irretrievably 'distant'. This comes very close to something which might be called 'redeemed' time, and which we explore in chapter 5.[77]

77. It needs to be said that I am not proposing that what music is offering here is the chance for theology simply to substitute one visual model (a line) with another (musical wave patterns). Three points are in order. First, the visual image of multi-levelled waves is illuminating in some respects but inadequate and even potentially misleading in others. It could well be misunderstood, for example, as endorsing a version of the 'myth of passage', in which musical events be understood as 'moving along' its lines, or else a surge of the 'present moment' doing likewise (see below, pp. 63ff). It might wrongly suggest a neat and closed temporality – the diagram does little to evoke contingency, which is crucial for both music and a theology which takes the non-determinist character of the world seriously. Second, music opens up concepts of temporality which defy visualisation – the interweaving of the temporal modes, for example. Third, basic to this study is the conviction that music offers *more* than fresh and more fruitful conceptualities of time, it offers a concrete instantiation of a form of participation in the world's temporality: a temporal experience, involving all of our faculties, which can open up the character of the world's temporality in a distinctive and telling way (as well as undermine some of our most cherished and potentially misleading assumptions about it), and, more fundamentally, which can open up something of what is involved in a distinctively Christian participation in the temporality of the world created and redeemed in Christ. Any visual model we employ must seek to be true to this experience.

Temporal modes interpenetrating

We need to say a little more about this 'interweaving of the temporal modes' in music before concluding the chapter. Music effectively challenges two major forms of linear conceptuality. The first is one in which future events and things get their brief chance at being present before passing away down the time-line into an ever-receding distance. The second is one in which the present is conceived as a sort of 'swell' travelling down a line of events and things, the event and things riding over the swell before becoming ever more distant in the past.

It should be clear by now, even though we have only spoken about the first, that musical temporality cannot be accommodated easily into either of these models. We recall the wave-patterns of metre. If we are in the second phase of a two-beat wave, because of the hierarchical nature of metrical waves, in every instant of the existence of 'two', the 'one' is also, in a sense, contained as the partner; 'two' is the symmetrical completion of 'one'. Similarly, in a succession of waves, because of the multi-levelled interconnected matrix, 'the first wave lives on in the second, the first and second together in the third, the first three in the fourth, and so on and on'.[78] We are not dealing with past musical events that are lost forever. The same applies to melody. Certainly, in a melody the demand for completion in the first tone is a demand satisfied only by the replacement of the tone with another tone; what is lacking succeeds and replaces the tone. The tone must give way to the next tone in order to be complete, it does not simply add the next tone to itself, it ceases to sound. Yet, this tone is not thereby gone for ever, for the second tone is precisely the completion of the first, internally connected to the first. The same applies to its future orientation. The present of 'one' is charged with its future. In a melodic succession of tones there is a 'carrying from' and a 'reaching beyond' sensed through each present: 'past and future are given with and in the present and are experienced with and in the present; hearing a melody is hearing, having heard, and being about to hear, all at once'.[79] We are meeting phenomena which are hard to account for within a straightforward linear model, with its tendency to divide past, present and future into three mutually exclusive modes: 'To a great extent the problems posed by the old concept of time arise from the fact that it distinguished three mutually exclusive elements, whereas only the picture of a constant interaction and intertwining of these elements is adequate to the actual

78. Zuckerkandl (1956), 175.   79. Ibid., 235.

process.'[80] The present is no longer the 'saddle' between the two abysses of past and future, but rather that 'in which 'now', 'not yet', and 'no more' are given together, in the most intimate interpenetration'.[81]

We can amplify this by reference to a lively and pertinent debate in the philosophy of time, that surrounding the so-called 'myth of passage.'[82] The dispute concerns the status of tense. It has been claimed by some that only 'presentness' can be understood to be a property of a thing which impacts its nature. We cannot say the same of 'futurity', for the future is not yet; nor of 'pastness', for the past is no longer. An entity cannot have the property of being future or past. It only 'is' in the present. So, for Augustine, 'Everything past now does not exist, everything future does not yet exist, therefore nothing past and nothing future exists.'[83] Genuine existence is existence in the 'infinitesimal pulse of the present' (D. C. Williams).[84]

In this tradition, the kind of scheme which emerges is that of things or events moving down a time line, or of the present moment doing the same.[85] In other words, it is a conception of things moving in time or time itself moving. Strictly speaking, *only what is present can be said to 'exist'*.[86] Past and future are not given to our experience now in any other way than in our memory and expectation, whereas the present is there not only *in* the mind but *for* the mind. We cannot speak meaningfully of things which no longer exist as existing now except in memory, nor of things not yet existing as existing now except in expectation. Past and future are given *in* our experience (in our minds) but not *to* our experience. So existence necessarily carries the predicate of temporal presentness. This is a

80. Ibid., 228.
81. Ibid., 227f. For further support, see Shepherd and Wicke (1997), 129ff.
82. On this, see among others D. C. Williams (1951); Padgett (1992), ch. 5; A. J. Torrance (1997b). I am deeply indebted in this whole section to Professor Alan Torrance of St Andrews University for his writing and many conversations on these themes.
83. Augustine, *De diversis quaestionibus 83*, q. 17; as quoted in Leftow (1991), 84. see also *Confessions*, XI:15.18. In his *Confessions*, XI:20.26, Augustine writes: 'neither future nor past exists, and it is inexact language to speak of three times – past, present and future. Perhaps it would be exact to say: there are three times, a present of things past, a present of things present, a present of things to come.'
84. D. C. Williams (1951), 458. Williams, it should be noted, is arguing *against* this tradition.
85. Augustine speaks of things and events moving from future through present to past, and also of time proceeding from the future through present to the past. See e.g., *Confessions*, XI:27.35: 'Where is the short syllable with which I am making my measurement? Where is the long which I am measuring? Both have sounded; they have flown away; they belong to the past'; XI:21.27: '[Time] must come out of the future, pass by the present, and go into the past; so it comes from what as yet does not exist, passes through that which lacks extension, and goes into that which is now non-existent.'
86. Alan Torrance describes this as 'temporal solipsism' (A. J. Torrance 1997a, 24).

vision of the exclusive reality of the present moment (albeit a durationless present), of the equivalence of 'what is' (the case) and 'what is' (now), at least from the human point of view.

Alan Torrance has written at some length about the consequences of this manner of thinking for the theology of creation, especially the misleading assimilation of *creatio ex nihilo* to a supposedly temporal *creatio originalis* and the consequent relegation of Christology to a position secondary to (because temporally 'distant' from) original creation.[87] We shall allude to some of the other theological drawbacks as we proceed. At this stage we should note that, unavoidable as 'passage' language may be ('heading towards a crisis', 'time flying', 'Time, like an ever-rolling stream, / Bears all its sons away', etc.), care needs to be taken as to how far we ontologise time accordingly. Ironically, despite the apparent ontological magnification of the present, in this view there is a tendency towards the disappearance of the present, for in order to retain its status as not future or past (and therefore existent) the present must be without duration. This, of course, leaves us wondering what sense can be made of that which is designated by the word 'present' which exists with no duration; is it any more intelligible than an entity with zero breadth and length? Augustine himself felt the strain of this acutely, and it is at least arguable that his presuppositions about existence and temporal presence do not ease the strain. Part of what makes Augustine so intriguing to read is that he so openly displays his struggle to give validity to the present:

> Take the two tenses, past and future. How can they 'be' when the past is not now present and the future is not yet present? Yet if the present were always present, it would not pass into the past: it would not be time but eternity. If then, in order to be time at all, the present is so made that it passes into the past, how can we say that this present also 'is'? The cause of its being is that it will cease to be. So indeed we cannot truly say that time exists except in the sense that it tends towards non-existence.[88]

Such is the tension between Augustine's implicit hypostatisation of the present as if it were a 'part' of time and his belief that 'the present has no extension'.[89] The former trades on the belief (which he shared with most ancient philosophy) that time is an infinitely divisible continuum, and therefore, logically, the division of an extended entity will always result

87. A. J. Torrance (1997b).   88. *Confessions*, XI:14.17.
89. Ibid., XI:15.20. Cf. O'Daly (1987), 154ff.

in extended entities – there is always 'something' else to divide. But against this lies his other strong conviction that the 'present' is without extension: it must be extensionless if it is to retain its character of existing 'now' and not in the future or past.[90]

In any case, the tradition which Augustine at this point represents has been subject to considerable critique on philosophical grounds.[91] In particular, D. C. Williams argues that to speak of things moving 'in time' or time itself as moving is simply confusing – it is the 'myth of passage'.[92] The claim that we advance through time or time flows past us commits us to an infinite number of 'times'.[93] As an alternative, Williams proposes a view of the realm of existence as 'a manifold of occurrences', a 'spatio-temporal volume . . . chockablock with things and events',[94] not a three-dimensional reality moving 'through' time, but a 'four-dimensional fabric' (three of space and one of time). Things do not move in time alone; they 'move' with respect to spacetime, the 'movement' consisting only in being at different times in different places. Temporal passage is not an 'extra'; it is the mere happening of things, their strung-alongness in the spacetime manifold. Time 'moves' only in the sense in which a landscape 'recedes into the West'.[95] And we proceed through time only in the sense that a fence proceeds across a farm.[96]

According to opponents of the 'myth of passage' view, a key weakness

---

90. Augustine's way of addressing this problem, as we shall see in the next chapter, is to say that we attend to impressions left in the mind by things which pass from the future – in expectation, through to the past – known in memory. Inasmuch as, through attention, that which is to be passes towards the state in which it is to be no more, we can say that the mind's attention persists. This, however, by no means alleviates the difficulties. See below, pp. 75ff.

91. Amidst the myriad of literature we point to D. C. Williams (1951), Smart (1972, 1980), Black (1962).

92. Newton's famous definition of time clearly assumes the myth of passage: 'Absolute, true and mathematical time, of itself and from its own nature, flows equably without relation to anything external.' Whitrow asks: 'what is meant by saying that "time flows equably" or uniformly? This would seem to imply that there is something which controls the rate of flow of time so that it always goes at the same speed. If, however, time exists "without relation to anything external", what meaning can be attached to saying that its rate of flow is not uniform? If no meaning can be attached even to the possibility of non-uniform flow, what is the point of stipulating that its flow is "equable"? (Whitrow 1988, 129).

93. All movement is in relation to a time. If we say that time moves, this must be with respect to another 'hypertime', and since this hypertime presumably moves, it can only do so with respect to another, and so on. Similarly, if I say that I move through time, that is to commit myself to an infinite series of meta-times. If I ask: 'at what rate do I move through time? Minutes per . . . ?', the blank can only be filled with some temporal term – say, 'minute'. But this 'meta-minute' to which my motion is now being referred, can only make sense against some further 'minute', and so on *ad infinitum*.

94. D. C. Williams (1951), 457.   95. Ibid., 463.   96. Ibid.

is to suppose that presentness, futurity or pastness are discrete properties like 'red' or 'hard' which can be ascribed to things or events irrespective of the spatio-temporal location of the person who makes such an ascription. It makes no more sense to speak of an entity possessing 'presentness' than it does to speak of something that is spatially present possessing 'hereness.' Likewise, it is confusing to speak of events changing with respect to pastness, presentness or futurity. 'Past', 'present' and future' relate to their own utterance. To say 'X is present' is to say 'X is simultaneous with this utterance.' To say 'X is future' is to say it is later than this utterance. There is no need to exalt the temporal (indexical) present any more than the spatial present. Nor need we accept the thesis that events move from a state of unreality (in the future), to reality (the present moment) and then into unreality (the past). Things and events that don't exist now should not be thought of as not existing at all; they exist somewhere (or 'somewhen'?) else in the spacetime manifold. In short, in stating the temporal relationships between things and events in the manifold, we have said all there is to say about their temporal character.

It might be thought this approach leads inexorably to a homogeneous and reversible view of temporal process. But there is nothing about this manifold account of spacetime which denies directionality, only the propriety of relating this directionality to some 'time-scale' external to and independent of entities and occurrences. Nor is it to deny change: to take account of change, we can say that events differ from one another in various ways, and that, in the case of a thing, one spatial cross-section of it is different from an earlier one.[97] Nor need we eradicate the language of past, present and future provided we are cautious about what we invest in these terms. Nor does Williams' view necessarily commit us to a deterministic 'block-universe' conception of spacetime, according to which the cosmos is conceived as a closed system – a 'petrified *fait accompli*',[98] whose future is not open but simply waiting for us to meet it. To speak of future or past things and occurrences existing in the manifold does not inevitably entail positing tight, necessary and closed causal relationships between them. And there is nothing in this view which excludes the contingency of the creation upon God, nor the possibility of God interacting in an intentional and immediate way with the spacetime continuum.

Williams *may* offer a way forward. Far more argument and qualification would be needed. These matters are minefields of controversy and a

97. Smart (1972), 128.   98. D. C. Williams (1951), 469.

certain tentativeness is both wise and necessary. My proposal here is relatively modest: that if the 'myth of passage' tradition in addition to being philosophically weak is also theologically problematic (and its weaknesses will become more apparent as we proceed), musical practice in effect constitutes its own critique, rendering dubious the reification of some presumed aspects of temporality from certain conceptions of temporal linearity and passage, and this critique takes place not theoretically – the *aporias* of time cannot be so resolved – but first and foremost through concrete enactment in sound. We have seen enough to suppose that it is not only inadequate but misleading to invest very much in the notion of music 'moving through time'. Its temporality is part of what it is, not the environment 'in which' it happens. Similarly, a philosophy of time which accords an exclusive ontological privileging of temporal presence rendering past and future non-existent to human experience will be relatively hard to sustain when brought into rigorous engagement with the phenomena of musical practices. For it would seem that the 'reality' we experience at any one 'moment' in music cannot be exhausted by those phenomena which can be said to exist 'now'. We are not given an evaporating present but a present through which the past is directed towards the future, or – to put it another way – with phenomena which in their physicality are intrinsically and very closely bound to earlier and later musical occurrences.[99]

This chapter has been concerned with delineating some of the chief characteristics of music's temporality. While fully recognising that music does to an extent 'create' its own kind of temporality, I have been suggesting that this occurs through an intense involvement with a complex of times in which its production and reception are embedded. I have been resisting the assumption that music will yield its most instructive lessons for theology through some supposedly heightened ability to extract us from temporality and/or from the physical world. It can arguably reveal much more when we recognise its capacity for intense and respectful engagement with the temporality integral to the world

99. This finds striking parallels in some reflections on music offered by the philosopher of science Milic Capek (Capek 1961, 1991). Capek has urged that in the exploration and the articulation of the character of spacetime in relativistic and post-relativistic physics, music can be a highly effective model, scoring over other models in many respects, especially visually based ones. The fact that his reflections can be cited with strong approval by the biological scientist Arthur Peacocke (Peacocke 1980), who himself advocates greater use of musical models in the natural sciences, is significant.

(human and non-human), and its thoroughly physical and material character. We explored some of the main features of tonal music – in particular, rhythm as motion in the field of metre, and melody as motion in the field of key. Tonal music exhibits not the temporality of a single straight line but that of a multi-levelled matrix of waves of tension and resolution, in which the temporal modes interweave within an overall directionality. With the material of this chapter in mind, we can now move on to deal more directly with theological matters.

II

In God's good time

3

In God's good time

At the centre of the debates about the metaphors for time, whether
mathematical, physical, or philosophical, are questions about whether
time is a threat or gift.[1]

STEPHEN HAPPEL

Any theological account of time in the Christian tradition is sooner
or later going to have to reckon with those Christological affirmations of
the New Testament which relate the totality of created existence to what
has taken place in the person of Jesus Christ. If in Christ 'all things' have
found their fulfilment, then, presumably, the same is to be said of time as
an integral dimension of the created order. The one 'through whom' all
things were created (Col. 1:17), is 'the firstborn of all creation . . . the beginning, the firstborn from the dead' (Col. 1:15, 18), the one in whom God
'gathered up' all things (Eph. 1:10f.), 'the first and the last, and the living
one' (Rev. 1:17–18.). Christ's time and history, his incarnate life, death and
resurrection, are thus properly conceived as central and decisive for all
time and history. In this chapter, drawing on material from the last two
chapters, we explore through music two important corollaries of this,
namely that due weight should be given, first, to the reality of time as
intrinsic to God's creation and, second, to the essentially positive character of time as part of God's 'good ordering' of the world.

At home with time

A number of writers have remarked upon a peculiar paradox confronting
us at the turn of the millennium: we have witnessed vast leaps in our

---

1. Happel (1993), 134.

conceptual understanding of time and space in the physical sciences but have generally found ourselves singularly inept at coming to terms in any integrated way with either. 'Whatever the integration of space and time in science, in modern life there is at once cultural stagnation and febrile change, a restless movement from place to place, experience to experience, revealing little evidence of a serene dwelling in the body and on the good earth.'[2] A range of studies have attempted to chart the ways in which our contemporary unease with time is manifest and some of the contributory factors involved. To state the obvious, being 'pressured by time' is a pervasive feature of contemporary life in the West. 'It is because our days are too full and because they move too fast that we seem never quite to catch up with ourselves.'[3] Even if there are many who appear to be *under*-pressurised – the unemployed, the disadvantaged, the prematurely retired – it is likely that 'The internal drives and external mechanisms that produce the time-scarce condition are the selfsame ones that produce its opposite.'[4]

One of the ways in which our uneasiness with time is most apparent is in what might broadly be termed *time-control*. Human beings have always tried to control time by attempting to decelerate transience, to postpone the entropic processes of decay. Through language, artefacts, technology and institutions we have striven to arrest our 'running down' by seeking now that 'good place permanent' (R. S. Thomas). Much of human history bears witness to the massive threat which death poses to all moral, social and individual value, and the multitude of ways in which it becomes something to be held at bay, averted, avoided, cheated, controlled or refused, and it is probably fair to say that 'The dominant modern response to the relentless approach of death is massive denial.'[5]

But especially characteristic of Western industrial life is another form of control, associated with the conjunction of industrialisation and the development of calendars and clocks. A fairly extensive quantity of writing in the area has appeared, much of it extending Marx's conception of industrial time.[6] Even a cursory glance at Western contemporary (especially urban) life indicates that the largest part of it is strictly timed. Delamont and Galton argue that daily time-structuring through schedules and timetables is one of the features which distinguishes school, work and institutional life from the routine of those on holiday or the

---

2. Gunton (1993), 77.   3. Banks (1983), 25.   4. Ibid., 35.   5. Weigert (1981), 235.
6. E.g. Giddens (1995); Hohn (1984); Adam (1990), ch. 5.

unemployed.[7] But even those on vacation or at home are inescapably influenced by the opening hours of banks, shops and so on, by their own habits and those of people around them. 'Whether we are affected in a primary or secondary way, we cannot escape the clock time that structures and times our daily lives.'[8] Disputes about duration, intervals, sequencing, synchronisation and pace are common to a degree which contrasts markedly with pre-industrial societies: 'Where before the capacity of a person to work a piece of land in one day would be the determinant of the measure, now 'man-hours' are calculated on the basis of universally applicable units of clock time.'[9] In other words, a process of de-contextualisation has taken place: 'the cycles of work and relaxation, which formerly accompanied the nature- and task-bound rhythms, attain their own metric dynamic and gradually become indifferent towards traditional contexts of meaning and significance'.[10] This is correlated by some interpreters with the pressure towards turning labour-time into a quantity that helps to mediate exchange, a commodity to be bought and sold. Hence 'industrial time' has become a resource with both a use and an exchange value, and as such, forms an intrinsic part of societies where social interaction and exchanges have become independent of context and content, and where time-structuring is based on standardised, fixed units. Time is fragmented into different strata or areas – family time, leisure time, market time etc. – and what links them all is chronological, calendar and clock-time, which is treated as 'real' time, time *per se*. Moreover, by reifying clock-time in this manner – as something we can use, spend, allocate or fill – it can become a significant means of the exercise of power (and domination) over others. David Harvey writes that 'in money economies in general, and in capitalist society in particular, the intersecting command of money, time, and space forms a substantial nexus of social power that we cannot afford to ignore'.[11]

Harvey is perhaps best known for his treatment of the postmodern sensibility. He chooses to read postmodernism as a wide-ranging cluster of phenomena constructed against the background of 'time-space compression'.[12] The history of capitalism has been characterised by a speed-up in the pace of life, while so overcoming spatial barriers that the world sometimes seems to collapse inwards upon us: 'As space appears to shrink to a "global village" of telecommunications and a "spaceship earth" of

---

7. Delamont and Galton (1986).   8. Adam (1990), 107.   9. Ibid., 112.
10. Hohn (1984), 150.   11. Harvey (1990b), 226.
12. Harvey (1990a), 11f.; (1990b), especially chs. 12–18.

economic and ecological interdependencies . . . and as time horizons shorten to the point where the present is all there is (the world of the schizophrenic), so we have to learn how to cope with an overwhelming sense of *compression* of our spatial and temporal worlds.'[13] This, claims Harvey, has had a widespread and disorienting impact upon political-economic practices, the balance of class power, and social and cultural life. In similar fashion John Michon writes of 'several more or less independent times, one for each of the major activities: family life, work, community activities, and the public arena as it is reflected in the news media. Connecting these times into one global time scale may be quite difficult and exceed people's cognitive capacity.'[14] The rate of change and the sheer amount of information now available exceeds our capacity to process and respond. The 'regional resistances' of postmodernity – Lyotard's 'local determinisms', Fish's communities of interpretation, Frampton's 'critical regionalism' – could be read as examples of attempts to re-instate space or spaces amidst compression. With regard to time, the postmodern disorientation includes an intense privileging and isolation of the 'present', supposedly singular and discontinuous with its past and future, and with all other times. Hence the postmodern discomfort with narratives, the evasion of a sense of duration (as in rock video), the multiple dislocations and 'time-foldbacks' in postmodern film and novels. Despite the playful and celebratory way in which such phenomena are sometimes lauded (refusing the stifling closures of modernity) there is much to suggest that elements of an intractable sterility and even destructiveness are also at work, extending rather than healing the malaise of modernity. As I shall suggest later, it may well be against this background that part of the current popularity of the music of Tavener (and perhaps Gorecki and Pärt) can be understood – a counteractive to both modernism's tyranny of clock-time and postmodernism's fragmentation and multiplicity of times.

Whatever conclusions are drawn from the sociology of time, there is enough to indicate that for a variety of reasons, a 'serene dwelling in the body and on the good earth', and with it an enriching and positive indwelling of time, are rarities in industrial and post-industrial societies. In this chapter, using music as a dialogue-partner, we shall try to delineate some of the specifically theological issues which may be involved: what-

---

13. Harvey (1990b), 240. Whether or not all the features of postmodern dissipation and surface-fixation can be traced to the intensification of capitalist practice is questionable, to say the least.   14. Michon (1985), 40f.

ever the web of circumstances which have led to current practices, theological factors have not been absent. But before that, we trace some patterns from antiquity.

Patterns from antiquity

What kind of reality has time? Of course, to deny any existence to time is virtually impossible and radically counter-intuitive. On that, most are agreed. But the character of its reality and how its reality may be best construed have been matters of perennial argument. Despite notable and important exceptions, it is generally accepted that the philosophical ethos of antiquity was marked by a large degree of hesitation about time's reality and the things and events of the temporal world. Among the more pointed examples is the Presocratic Parmenides of Elea, for whom the sheer fleetingness, change and decay of the world throw a question mark against the reality and significance of the temporal world accessible and presented to sense perception. The endlessly shifting character of sense experience is a theme taken up by Plato in a rather different but not entirely dissimilar manner. Departing from conceptions which would see *chronos* as an island of time surrounded by a boundless and undifferentiated *apeiron*, he grounds *chronos* in *aion*, conceiving *aion* as the unmoving mode of being of the Ideas in which past, present and future coincide in one. From one point of view, *aion* is definitely not timeless, being characterised by simultaneity, the embracing of past, present and future – it possesses the structure, though not the movement, of time. Nevertheless, *chronos*, the form of the world of the senses, is still only the image and reflection of *aion*,[15] and we are left distinctly unclear as to the value and validity of the temporal world, except insofar as it reflects eternity.[16]

As is well known, a sense of disjunction between time and eternity allied to a sense of the relative ontological inferiority and devaluing of the former was intensified with the Neoplatonists. But it is to Augustine that we give more sustained attention here, to his many-sided conception of time which had such a sizeable impact on the development of medieval and modern thought, and which is set forth most fully in an extended, highly rhetorical, and problem-driven argument in the eleventh book of the *Confessions*. It is foolish to charge Augustine with 'subjectivising' or

---

15. *Timaeus*, 37.
16. The variety of interpretations of Plato's dialogue *Timaeus* itself witnesses to this ambiguity.

'psychologising' time – as some have done[17] – but there is a more serious common charge, which although possible to exaggerate, is nevertheless not without force, namely that even in his mature writings we find rather too strong a link between temporality, unreality and fallenness, in which respect he echoes the Platonic and Neoplatonic traditions he knew so well.

It is in the context of a meditation on the relation between time and eternity that Augustine famously asks: *quid est ergo tempus?* – 'What then is time? Provided that no one asks me, I know. If I want to explain it to an inquirer, I do not know.'[18] Especially notable is the radical *contrast* Augustine perceives between, on the one hand, the created, transient temporal order which is never still, in which we experience the acute dispersal of past, present and future events, and on the other hand, eternity, which is still and free from any such dispersal. The diversity of temporality is painfully at odds with the oneness of the everlasting, as is its ontological lack and deficiency in comparison with the fullness of divine being.[19]

If Gerard O'Daly and others are correct, behind Augustine's question 'what then is time?' lies not the search for a definition of time but the question: 'how can we measure time?' given the experience of the non-appearance of the future, the disappearance of the past, and therefore the apparent non-existence of both.[20] Before something begins we cannot measure the time it is going to take, for it has not yet come to be. Nor can we measure it after it has happened, for then it is no more. Only the present, it would seem, exists. Here Augustine assumes the infinite divisibility of the temporal continuum: there are no 'time-atoms', irreducibly small units of time. From this he concludes that, despite its being extensionless and having no duration,[21] only the present *is*, in the sense of 'exists now'.[22] The past and future do not exist in the specialised sense of existing now.

How, then, can we measure time – and everyday language and experience pushes us into believing that we do – if time's very existence is so

17. That there is an irreducible 'objective' aspect of time for Augustine is rightly stressed by many. See e.g. Milbank (1990), 426; Wetzel (1990), 32ff. Whatever the contrary tendencies in Augustine, given his conviction that the world was created not before time nor in time but *with* time, it would have been impossible for him to assert that time has no existence independent of the human mind.   **18.** *Confessions*, XI:14.17.
19. See Ricoeur's extended discussion of the time/eternity contrast in Augustine; Ricoeur (1984), 22ff.
20. O'Daly (1977). Cf. Rist (1994), 81f., and Ricoeur (1984), 7. Torrance Kirby draws attention to the wider background of the discussion, namely the integrity of *praise* in relation to time. In particular, how can speech with its words which sound and pass away be fit for the praise of the eternal One, who is without any transience? See Kirby (1997).   **21.** XI:15.20.
22. XI:17.22–XI:20.26.

problematic? Augustine's response is to say that the past and future are present in the mind, in memory and expectation respectively. As we have seen, he writes of a three-fold present: 'neither future nor past exists, and it is inexact language to speak of three times – past, present and future. Perhaps it would be exact to say: there are three times, a present of things past, a present of things present, a present of things to come.'[23] The answer to the question 'how can we measure time?' is: in the mind.[24] We compare memories of time-stretches. And the measure of time in this way is the measure of duration.[25] It is not that we measure time as it passes, for only the present is actually given to our experience from beyond ourselves. Nor can we assess the length of any process while it is going on, only after it is over or we have ceased to perceive it. It is not the processes we measure but the effect or 'impression (*affectio*)' which the perceptions leave behind like footprints.[26]

Corresponding to the three-fold present there is a three-fold activity of the mind. An impression or sense-image is left in the mind by things as they pass from future to past. The mind performs three functions with respect to these impressions, those of expectation, attention and memory.[27] Things are not present to us in their futurity and pastness; past and future are 'there' for the mind *as* they appear in the mind's essential presentness. 'Some such different times do exist in the mind, and nowhere else that I can see. The presence of past things is memory, the presence of present things is direct apprehension, the presence of future things is expectation.'[28] In this way, Augustine can make at least some sense of the notion of a present without extension. Inasmuch as the present passes, it lacks extension, it is reduced to a point, 'it passes in a flash'. 'Yet,' he continues, 'attention is continuous, and it is through this that what will be present progresses towards being absent.'[29] Inasmuch as it is *through* the mind's present attention that what is to be passes towards the state in which it is to be no more, we can say that the mind's attention persists.

Augustine intertwines this line of argument with another – concerning the *distentio animi* – which, Paul Ricoeur contends, paves the way for a tradition in the philosophy of time extending to Husserl, Heidegger and Merleau-Ponty.[30] The *distentio animi* – distension of the mind[31] – refers to the 'stretching out' of the mind in relation to past and future. According to Ricoeur this aligns with Augustine's conception of the three-fold

---

23. XI:20.26.   24. XI:27.36.   25. XI:21.27; XI:23.30.
26. XI:27.36; for the footprints metaphor, see also XI:18.23.   27. XI:28.37.   28. XI:20.26.
29. XI:28.37.   30. Ricoeur (1984), 16.   31. XI:26.33; XI:29.39.

present, known in memory, attention and expectation. This *distentio* is conceived as the three-fold present, and the three-fold present as *distentio*. The *distentio* consists in the non-coincidence of the mind's three modes of action. They are in discord. As we attend to impressions, expectation and memory pull in opposite directions: in the process of reciting a psalm, 'the scope of the action which I am performing is divided between the two faculties of memory and expectation, the one looking back to the past which I have already recited, the other looking forward to the part which I have still to recite'.[32] Augustine notes that this *distentio* is experienced not only in an activity such as the recitation of a psalm, but also in longer actions, our entire lives, and the total history of humankind.[33] The supreme 'enigma' Augustine exposes (to use Ricoeur's word) is that the more the mind engages in its three-fold activity, the more acutely *distentio* is felt: discordance emerges 'again and again out of the very concordance of the intentions of expectation, attention, and memory.'[34] The more the mind works in memory, attention and expectation, the more it is felt to be pulled asunder.

We have already spoken of some of the disputable aspects of this kind of account of time from a philosophical point of view in our discussion of the 'myth of passage' debate.[35] He, we concentrate on two issues of an explicitly theological nature which inevitably arise.

What kind of reality has time?

The first concerns the status of time as conferred by God and intrinsic to the created order, a matter central to Augustine's struggle, and much discussed in Augustine's day.[36] As part of a lengthy analysis, Brian Leftow contends that Augustine was affected by a basic conviction of Neoplatonic metaphysics, that 'true' existence is immutable existence: 'Nobody has true being, pure being, real being except one who does not change.'[37]

> For that exists in the highest sense of the word which continues always the same, which is throughout like itself, which cannot in any part be

---

32. XI:28.38.   33. Ibid.
34. Ricoeur (1984), 21. This lines up with Wetzel's argument that *distentio* has two main senses in the *Confessions,* not only the negative sense I have spoken about, the *distentio* of scattering, 'coming apart', but also the more positive *distentio* of measured time, when the mind is stretched but in such a way that it encompasses or holds the times together (Wetzel 1992, 35ff).   35. See above, pp. 63ff.   36. Sorabji (1983), 7–32.
37. Leftow (1991), 73.

corrupted or changed, which is not subject to time, which admits of no variation in its present as compared with its former condition. This is existence in its truest sense.[38]

In the *Confessions*, Augustine addresses God:

> And I viewed the other things below you, and I saw that neither can they be said absolutely to be or absolutely not to be. They are because they come from you. But they are not, because they are not what you are. That which truly is is that which unchangeably abides.[39]

By the same token, changeable objects are less truly said to be. This accords temporal existence with a status between highest-degree existence and non-existence. Timeless existence is more genuinely existence than temporal, timeless entities exist more genuinely than temporal ones. This is of a piece with Augustine's conviction that – from the human point of view at any rate – genuine existence is present existence. For Augustine, 'is' necessarily means 'is now'. Timeless beings are more genuinely existing than temporal beings, for they are more genuinely present, untainted with past or future.[40]

It is important not to fall into an easy misunderstanding of Augustine at this point. Paul Helm argues that Augustine is 'not offering a reductionist approach to the past or future . . . that they are respectively constructed out of memories or expectations. He is, rather, offering both a metaphysical and an epistemological thesis about what time is from the standpoint of a creature, and how present, past and future are to be known from such a standpoint.'[41] Helm urges that for Augustine, 'exists' is an 'elliptical expression', requiring to be completed either by reference to God or to creatures. For a time to be real, that time must be related to someone's metaphysical situation (human or divine). According to the standpoint of the creature, only things present can be said to exist; hence when Augustine writes that 'the past now has no existence and the future is not yet',[42] he is speaking of time as experienced from our perspective. However, all moments are present to God (in a similar way), not temporally present – for God is not subject to time – but eternally present to God's mind. The times which are at present future to us exist for God; the future is real to God (though not as future), but it is not present to us now. Likewise the times which are past to us are not now present or real to us, but they are eternally present and real to God.[43] This underlines the danger of

---

38. *De Mor. Manich.*, c. i.   39. *Confessions*, VII:11.17.   40. See Leftow (1991), 84.
41. Helm (1997), 41.   42. *Confessions*, XI:15.18.   43. Helm (1997), 36–46.

superficially dismissing Augustine as a subjectiviser of time. As Wetzel correctly points out, Augustine is acutely aware not just of the difficulty of measuring time, but of his life 'coming apart' in time. Augustine is neither assuming nor arguing for the subjectivity of time.[44]

That said, the question still remains whether Augustine can provide an adequate account of past, present and future dimensions *even from the perspective of the creature* – we have, in effect, posed this question already in the last chapter – and, more importantly, whether our own temporal experience is grounded sufficiently, or is seen as participating adequately and fully enough, in the temporality which God has conferred upon created reality. What would seem to be required is a more pointed stress on Augustine's own doctrine of *creatio ex nihilo*, according to which the cosmos, the entirety of all that is not God, is regarded as possessing its own full but distinct reality, directly contingent upon God, and as created not before time or in time but *with* time.[45] Following this through would entail stressing that the entire spatio-temporal nexus is the product of creation out of nothing, and refusing any conception of creation as taking place 'before', 'in' or 'through' time. Moreover, I would suggest there would need to be a more concentrated orientation towards the earthly economy of salvation – more particularly, a view of temporality with (a) an uncompromising focus on the engagement of the Son of God (through whom all things were created) with spatio-temporal reality, enacted in the history of Jesus Christ, and (b) an equally uncompromising stress on the work of the Spirit as the one who directs created reality towards its fulfilment, which includes the fulfilment of temporality as a dimension of created being.[46]

It is here that some of our observations about music in the last chapter come into their own. Music does not of course prove this or that theological stance, but it can serve to free us from some of the assumptions which hinder or obscure the theology of creation to which we are alluding, primarily by enacting different possibilities in sound. For music, we have seen, by virtue of the very way it operates, seems to offer a temporal adventure in which time is experienced not as an absolute receptacle or inert background (and certainly not as merely a mental or cultural construct), but as an inherent aspect of the interrelationship between the physical entities involved in the production and reception of sound.

44. Wetzel (1992), 34.
45. *Confessions*, XI:12.14–XI:13.15; XI:30.40; cf. *De genesis contra Manichaeos*, I:2.3; *City of God*, XI:6.   46. Gunton (1993), 54ff.; (1998), 73ff.

How good is time?

We turn to our second issue in connection with Augustine, time's goodness. Here a trinitarian account of creation – one which affirms the direct involvement of God the Son, the mediator of creation, with material historicity in a human life, and the Spirit as the one who gives shape and temporal orientation to creation – effectively forbids us to treat temporality as fundamentally problematic or evil. And again, music has much to offer.

Even Augustine's most ardent supporters recognise an ambivalence in Augustine in this respect. And his treatment of music brings this to the surface. Of course, it needs to be borne in mind that musical practice in Augustine's day was largely in the form of a single melodic line, sung or played, its metre and rhythm strongly allied to speech. (Augustine can hardly be blamed for not appreciating the potential of tonal music for theology!) Nevertheless, what he says about music is highly instructive, for his positive regard for it is not principally based on what it could achieve *qua* temporal art but in what it could effect with regard to that which is not constrained by the temporal order.

This is clear in his relatively early work, *De Musica*, which mediated a modified form of the aesthetic thought of Plato and Plotinus and was to have a huge influence on subsequent medieval aesthetics. *De Musica* is restricted to the study of metre and rhythm, and these can apply as much to poetry as to what we would call music. Rhythmics and metrics are understood as a way of discerning the mathematical proportions which pervade the universe. Music, as the science of measurements, engages with the proportions which characterise the whole of reality. Audible music makes accessible to the ear these proportions or 'numbers'. But Augustine's prime interest is not in musical performance. Rather, music finds its ideal form in the intellectual knowledge of the numerical character of the universe.[47] The climax of the work, the sixth book, in effect consists of a re-statement of the Platonic belief that mathematical principles are the chief clue to the providential ordering of the world, and that musical theory accustoms the mind to grasp immaterial reality. The

47. Henry Chadwick speaks of the Platonic tradition, in which Augustine in this respect stands, as regarding musical theory 'not so much as a route to the better appreciation of the latest composition in the Lydian mode but rather to the mathematical design and order pervading the universe' (Chadwick 1994, 208). He adds, perhaps too strongly: 'The theory of music is akin to metaphysics, and the fact that it has something to do with sound is, for ancient theorists, almost an embarrassment' (Ibid.).

entire cosmos is an assemblage of all the relations that it encompasses; in Catherine Pickstock's words, 'One might say that the totality of reality is not one big note, but instead, as Augustine says, a poem or song (*carmen*), and so, in other words, the total series of numerical interactions.'[48] Book VI traces out the grades of the various numbers in poetic metres according to a hierarchy. The numbers of music derive from the unchanging order of 'eternal numbers' which themselves proceed from God. Guided by the hand of divine providence, the mind is privileged to rise from the lowest to the highest numbers and to God, the fount of numerical beauty.

Accordingly, the purpose of *De Musica* is to bring the soul to a recognition of its fallen state and promote its return to God, to move from the world of sense to the world of intelligibility. The soul is fallen from the restful contemplation of eternal truth, into the busy-ness of temporal activity. Because of the fall, we are ordered by the tapestry of time, 'sewn into' the order of spatio-temporality. We have become so many individual 'words', each forming part of the poem of the temporal whole but unable to perceive the harmony and beauty of the connected work. By immersion in temporal sequence, we have lost that purview of the whole temporal series we possessed prior to the fall.[49] But reason possesses continuing insight into the higher, beautiful, unchanging order of numbers – this is the ground of its ability to pass judgement upon the lower, 'imitations' of the temporal world. Music enables us to delight in the numbers of reason rather than the numbers of sense. It can assist the soul's ascent under the trace of God from the realm of sense to the eternal, realm of perfect number, and thus to God: 'the presiding thrust of [*De Musica*] is this ascent from the realm of sense and authority to the higher world directly accessible to the eye of reason'.[50] And music is in a very strong position to do this because no other art is equally independent of at least four of the five senses, and thus so strongly controlled by mathematical axioms.

The extent to which this 'ascent' entails leaving behind the sensible, material order is not entirely clear. In any case, by the time we reach the *Confessions* a more positive attitude to the created order, materiality and temporality is evident.[51] Nevertheless, the basic outlines of his approach

---

48. Pickstock (1999), 247.   **49.** *De Musica*, VI:11.30–2.   **50.** O'Connell (1978), 69.
51. Harrison (1992), 270ff., *et passim*. It is Harrison's contention that even in Augustine's early thought there were decisive breaks with the 'spiritualising' Manichaeist and

to time and music are by no means dissimilar. *Distentio* – in its sense of dispersal, the experience of time as sundering – gives rise to the mind's longing to find its original unity. As such, *distentio* becomes synonymous with the dispersal into the many, the life of the old Adam. It is the gift of God to 're-collect' the distracted/distended person, bringing him back from the distracting world of the temporal into that unity from which he fell. To show that the mind has not entirely lost its ability to apprehend unity amidst temporal multiplicity, Ambrose's hymn *Deus creator omnium* makes an appearance as it did in *De Musica*,[52] along with the recitation of a poem[53] and a psalm.[54] The poem is the first to be mentioned in order to underline the difficulty of measuring temporal extension: we speak of elements of a poem as 'long' but only in relation to other elements, there is no certain measure of time through this method. The hymn, however – here treated as poetry only – is introduced to show how measurement is possible through memory. The argument is taken further with regard to the psalm. The future is now included: a 'long future' is a 'long expectation of the future'. The mind both anticipates what is to come and holds in memory what has been. This leads immediately into a recognition of the purpose of God to 'gather' us, freeing us from distraction:

> see how my life is a distension in several directions. 'Your right hand upheld me' (Ps. 17:36; 62:9) in my Lord, the Son of man who is mediator between you the One and us the many, who live in a multiplicity of distractions by many things; so 'I might apprehend him in whom also I am apprehended' (Phil. 3:12–14), and leaving behind the old days I might be gathered to follow the One . . . I am scattered in times whose order I do not understand. The storms of incoherent events tear to pieces my thoughts, the inmost entrails of my soul, until that day when, purified and molten by the fire of your love, I flow together to merge into you.[55]

The recitation of a psalm, though so obviously in time and subject to the distractions of the temporal order, is thus used to illustrate the way in

---

Neoplatonist strands of his thinking. This more positive evaluation of the created, temporal order flowers in his later thought and to a degree not always appreciated by commentators.
52. XI:27.35; cf. XI:12.32; X:34.52; and *De Musica*, VI:2.2. In *De Musica* he argues that we remember past syllables and hold them in the memory until we have a grasp of the entire word over a stretch of time; VI:8.21.   **53.** XI:26.33.   **54.** XI:28.38.
55. XI:29.39.

which the mind's descent into diversity has not entirely effaced its ability to grasp that Unity from which all things proceed. Insofar as the mind achieves some ordering power over time,[56] it approximates, albeit very weakly, to the perspective and character of eternity.

It should be remembered that in these passages Augustine is thinking only of the music of spoken words, not the music of singing or instruments. How far what we would understand as specifically musical characteristics contribute to this 're-collection' is not possible to say with confidence.[57] At any rate, insofar as music is the bearer of metre and rhythm, and as such, mediated by the activity of the mind, offers a 'time-bridging' glimpse of the unified order of eternity,[58] there is implicit here a relatively positive account of music. This is backed up in other places in the *Confessions*.[59] However, even when he has in view not only words but the music of voice and instrument, it is clear that the primary theological value of music is not in what it might offer in terms of embodying good temporal order, but in its capacity to empower the mind, despite its agonising *distentio*, to apprehend the unified order of eternity.[60]

For all the qualifications we have noted, it is hard to ignore the signs of the ancient tendency to run together temporality and fallenness, and especially significant for us is the way in which music is deployed in this context: what is valuable about music is discovered and known insofar as we abstract from the temporal relations of physical realities patterns which reflect in some measure the order of eternity. Despite its considerable subtlety and fascination, for this vision to be advanced as offering a

---

56. This is the positive sense of *distentio animi* – see above, n. 34.

57. Augustine could speak in rhapsodic terms about the tears he shed 'at the songs of the Church' (*Confessions*, x:33.50). As a young man he found music a major source of consolation. He is probably speaking of himself when he writes that there are 'many for whom happiness consists in the music of voices and strings, and who count themselves miserable when music is lacking to their lives' (*De Libero Arbitrio Voluntatis*, ii:13.35). In his maturity, he never lost his conviction that Plato was right to speak of a 'hidden affinity' between music and the soul. This enthusiasm is nevertheless tempered by a fear of idolatry and of being tugged away from God by the pleasures of music (x:33.49–50). Chadwick offers a three-word summary of Augustine's view of music in Church: 'Indispensable but dangerous' (Chadwick 1994, 208).

58. Commenting on Augustine, Pannenberg writes: 'the fact of the time-bridging present and duration in the life of creatures gives us a remote inkling of eternity and a form of participation in it' (Pannenberg 1991, 409).

59. See e.g. x:34.53: 'my God and my glory . . . I say a hymn of praise to you and offer praise to him who offered sacrifice for me. For the beautiful objects designed by artists' souls and realised by skilled hands come from that beauty which is higher than souls; after that beauty my soul sighs day and night' (Ps. 1:2).   **60.** See O'Connell (1978), ch. 8 *et passim*.

way forward for the theological deployment of music today would be, I suggest, dubious.[61] The conception of music's temporality which emerged in the last chapter offers a different, and we would contend, more fruitful way ahead. For it would seem that music is capable of demonstrating that such a strong link between time and fallenness need not be assumed, and that there is no necessity to distance ourselves from the mutable multiplicity of the temporal world in order to experience beneficial and enriching order. This can be expanded under four headings.

Change and order

First and most obvious, music demonstrates that there can be ordered change, that change need not imply chaos. Not only are its constituent entities marked by a high degree of impermanence and insubstantiality, its capacity for precise and stable reference is very limited, making its bonds with enduring and substantial entities or states of affairs relatively weak. And yet it is experienced as ordered and beneficial. There may be more than a grain of truth in Zuckerkandl's provocative contention that 'All fundamental opposition to music . . . is rooted in the same concern: that music may hold the threat of chaos.' Music, he believes, can undermine 'the dogma that order is possible only in the enduring, the immutably fixed, the substantial'. It presents us with 'the unprecedented spectacle of an order in what is wholly flux, of a building without matter'.[62] Music shows

---

61. In a bold and intriguing essay, Catherine Pickstock mounts a vigorous commendation of Augustine's *De Musica* and the tradition it represents, in the context of a wider appeal for the restoration of the Western (Platonic/Christian) theological tradition and its vision of a cosmos informed by sacred *logos* (Pickstock 1999). She argues, among other things, that Augustine holds time and space in a proper balance under transcendence. Both in his conception of music and in later polyphony we find a co-articulation of time and space, a structured flow within a context of a belief in creation out of nothing (which guarantees order), and this constitutes the best possible expression of the 'eternal music'. Augustine, she believes, offers great promise for healing, for example, some of the subjectivist–objectivist dichotomies so characteristic of the modern 'refractions' of this ancient tradition. Augustine's notion of music as the measure of the soul–body proportion, opens a non-dualist perspective on reality: 'in music, uniquely, there is in a beautiful phrase at once an objectively expressible proportion, and subjective selection and appreciation of this proportion as beautiful. Meaning, therefore, is seen to be the *world's* meaning, and yet, at the same time, our *own* meaning' (Pickstock 1999, 269). This essay reached me just before submitting this text, and space forbids doing justice to the argument. However, we can note that while sympathetic to her estimation of those traditions she contrasts with Augustine, and while wanting to endorse much in the musical theological cosmology she advocates, Pickstock's confidence in Augustine and in medieval polyphony seems to me excessive. The ambivalences and ambiguities in Augustine seem to me much more marked and significant than she appears to allow.
62. Zuckerkandl (1956), 241f.

us in a particularly potent way that dynamic order is possible, that there can be ordered being and becoming, form and vitality, structure and dynamics, flux and articulation. For something to be subject to persistent change need not imply disorder.

Taking time

Second, music also challenges the assumption that because something takes time to be what it is, it is thereby of deficient value or goodness compared to that which is not subject to created time. It is part of the being of creation (and its constituent elements) to be temporal. The created world takes time to be. Music presents us with a concrete demonstration of the inseparability of time and created reality, of the truth that it need not be seen as a vice of creation that it can only reach its fulfilment, its perfection, through time. It shows us in an intense way that 'taking time' can be good, profitable and enriching. (It might be objected that this is also true of other temporal arts, literature for example. Quite so. But we should remind ourselves that music's engagement with time, for the reasons outlined at some length in the previous chapters, is peculiarly intimate, which makes its capacity to embody enriching temporal process especially strong.)

We can go further. Not only will we be encouraged to re-discover the truth that creation as a whole and the constituent elements of creation take time to be what they are, and that this need not necessarily be a mark of fallenness, we will also be reminded that *different entities take different times to be*: 'While all begin and end in some way, there is a different time-span for each, which will vary somewhat according to the local provision of needs and the use made of their "capacity for finitude"'.[63] Pleading for recognition by the social sciences of the multiplicity of non-human time-scales, Barbara Adam insists that 'Far from being incessant, undifferentiated flux depending on humans to get together and structure them, natural processes have an inherent rhythmic time-structure. If they did not have time embedded in them, a time proper to them which is demarcated by beginnings and endings, much of human and animal waiting would not exist.'[64]

Recognising that duration is not itself a mark of fallenness makes possible a positive assessment of *patience* and *waiting*:

63. Hardy (1996), 158.   64. Adam (1990), 121.

> The essential temporality of everyday life means that humans
> experience not only the passing of time, but also the necessity to wait
> until one temporal process has run its course in order for another to
> begin. All humans wait, and in the fullest sense of the term, only
> humans wait. Waiting is an experience based on the interpretation and
> understanding of the temporal structures of events and human
> desires.[65]

The performance and enjoyment of music can teach us a constructive
waiting and patience, a waiting which need not be empty or resigned
but felicitous and abundant. To state the obvious, because music takes
or demands our time, it cannot be rushed. It schools us in the art of
patience. Certainly, we can play or sing the piece faster, but this is possible only to a very limited degree before it becomes incoherent. We
can, given today's technology, 'cut and paste' music in ways unimagin-
able to our forebears: we can hop from track to track on the CD, flip
from one rock number to another, buy highlights of a three-hour opera.
But few would claim they hear a work in its integrity by doing this. As
Rowan Williams puts it, music says to us 'There are things you will
learn only by passing through this process, by being caught up in this
series of relations and transformations.'[66] Music requires my time, my
flesh and blood, my thought and action for its performance and reception. Music asks for my patience, my trust that there is something
worth waiting for. And it does this without promising some particular
visible thing or idea or principle we can take away with us when the
music is over, something which shows us that it was 'worth the wait'.
Music itself is not the bearer of detachable commodities, timeless truths
or abstract principles or visions (though it has often been yoked to
these). And yet, even without a neatly packaged reward or 'take-away'
value, the waiting which music demands, by catching us up in its interrelations, is experienced as anything but pointless or vain. Music can
teach us a kind of patience which stretches and enlarges, deepens us in
the very waiting.[67]

---

65. Weigert (1981), 227.   66. R. Williams (1994), 247.
67. Speaking against the tendency to think that music is there to 'wash over' us, the
composer James MacMillan has said: '[Music] needs us to sacrifice something of ourselves
to meet it, and it's very difficult sometimes to do that, especially [in] the whole culture
we're in. Sacrifice and self-sacrifice – certainly sacrificing *your time* – is not valued any more'
(as quoted in Jaffé (1999), 28; my italics).

Something of this kind of patience and waiting can, it would seem, be learned in the midst of tragedy and trauma. I have already quoted John Hull in another context. He has written of his negotiation of time after going blind. Not only did everything have to be done more slowly, his attitude to time had to undergo a significant shift:

> For me, as a blind person, *time is simply the medium of my activities. It is that inexorable context within which I do what must be done.* For example, the reason why I do not seem to be in a hurry as I go around a building is not that I have less to do than my colleagues, but I am simply unable to hurry . . . The measured pace, the calm concentration, the continual recollection of exactly how far one has come and how far is still to go, the pause at each marked spot to make sure that one is orientated, all this must be conducted at the same controlled pace.[68]

Time could not be regarded as something 'out of which' things had to be wrenched:

> When I had sight, I would have worked with feverish haste, correcting forty footnotes in a single morning. Now, I am happy if, with the help of a sighted reader, by the end of the morning I have corrected ten . . . The simplicity, the careful planning, the long-term preparation, the deliberateness with which the blind person must live, all this means that he cannot take advantage of time by suddenly harvesting a whole lot of it.[69]

In contrast to 'time-compression', Hull remarks that:

> When you have a lot of time, you experience time-inflation . . . *You are no longer fighting against the clock* but against the task. You no longer think of the time it takes. You only think of what you have to do. It cannot be done any faster. *Time, against which you previously fought, becomes simply the stream of consciousness within which you act.*[70]

The links between this and our comments above on musical time should be clear by now, especially the inadequacy of conceiving time as a framework 'against' which – and the word 'against' is significant – activities are performed.

The kind of patience we are speaking of here can be viewed from

68. Hull (1990), 60. My italics.   69. Ibid.   70. Ibid., 61. My italics.

another perspective. Rowan Williams contends that music can function as a 'moral event': it can remind us we are not in control of the world, that we do not have the overview, that we are in the narrative of the world's history and never above it. Music 'tells us what we are and what we are not, creatures, not gods, creators only when we remember that we are not the Creator, and so are able to manage the labour and attention and expectancy that belongs to art.'[71] In short, we are liberated from the destructive illusion that we are supposed to be God.

Different time-structures

Third, not only different durations, there are different time-structures appropriate to different created entities: different rates at which things happen, different concentrations of activities at different periods, and so forth. Plants and animals possess different rates of change and flourish at different points relative to their birth and death. People 'reach their peak' at different stages. The fact that there are such differences need not be seen in all cases as a sign of corruption; rather, they are part of the diversity God bestows on his creation, intrinsically bound up with the constitution of entities themselves and intended for good. As such, they demand our respect and gratitude.

Music is highly instructive in this regard because coming to terms with music means continually coming to terms with this kind of temporal differentiation. In even the simplest song we find different temporal configurations operating concurrently: each having a place within the musical ecology.

Metrical structures provide good examples. We have seen that metrical accents form hierarchical patterns. At different levels, however, we may well find different configurations of metrical waves. The opening of the first movement of Haydn's Piano Sonata no. 61 in D (Example 3.1) provides a case in point, where there is metrical irregularity (an extra hypermetric 'beat' within a hyperbar at two different levels) in the opening bars. The fact that these irregularities are regularised at higher levels does not alter the fact that crucial to the interest and success of this piece is the distinctive integrity of each metrical level, in this case demarcated by specific irregularities.

71. R. Williams (1994), 249.

Example 3.1 Haydn, Piano Sonata no. 61 in D major, first movement, bars 1–21

To begin with, at the level of the bar, the metric beats in this piece are simply twin beats, strong-weak. At the two-bar level, there are hyperbars of two beats each, strong-weak (the bars are grouped in twos). However, when we reach bars 17–19 we are confronted with a *three*-beat hyperbar (a stretched two-beat hyperbar): the cadence leading to D major is delayed. Here we have a wave of tension and resolution spread out over three beats. At the four-bar level, bars 1–4 form a two-beat hyperbar, but this is followed by a *three*-beat hyperbar (5–10); then a two-beat hyperbar (11–14) is answered by a two-beat hyperbar (15–19) with an *extended second beat*. At the next level up, however, these irregularities disappear in the two-beat hyperbars of 1–10 and 11–19.

Limited duration

The fourth area where music can challenge a distrust of temporality concerns the temporal limits or boundaries imposed by finitude. Awareness of our limited life-span is a common theme in the Bible, often accompanied by an acute sense of the brevity of life – a person's days are swifter than a weaver's shuttle (Job 7:6), they are like a fleeting shadow (Job 14:2), a handbreadth (Ps. 39:5). The link between transience and a sense of futility runs deep in many cultures, including our own. The universe is, of course, replete with beginnings and endings, formation and de-formation, births and deaths. With so much death, it is not surprising that we find a common reversion to the language of futility, hopelessness, emptiness, as if transience were intrinsically resistant to rationality. The second law of thermodynamics would seem to encourage this; in closed systems there is a flow of available energy in the direction of increasing disorder and randomness, of increasing unavailability for further useful work or organisation. The decay of our body and its tissues is a forcible reminder of this. 'We owe a death to entropy.'[72]

> Time doth transfix the flourish set on youth
> And delves the parallels in beauty's brow,
> Feeds on the rarities of nature's truth,
> And nothing stands but for his scythe to mow.[73]
> SHAKESPEARE, SONNET 60

Yet the second law, strictly speaking, applies only to closed systems. In open systems there is also 'negentropy', the negation of disorder, the use of available energy to build order and organisation, such as the human

72. Bowker (1991b), 218.   73. Shakespeare (1978), 70.

body or minerals in the earth. And this is only possible through death. Our very existence is only possible through the destruction of stars millions of years ago. In John Bowker's words, 'it is because the universe is so finely tuned to produce life, *but only through the process of death*, that death receives from life the highest possible tribute and value . . . it is not possible to have life on any other terms than those of death; but where you *do* have death, there immediately you have the possibility of life'.[74] Christian hope speaks of a life through death which is fuller than this life, a life given by God, this life transformed into the life of the 'age to come'. Moreover, if we are to think on a cosmic scale, even if in purely physical terms the universe is heading either for some kind of heat death or for death by a giant implosion – and things seem fairly evenly balanced between the two at present – Christian hope speaks of the cosmos transformed into the new heaven and new earth.

Music offers an extremely vivid and particular embodiment of fruitful transience. In the last chapter we have already touched upon this.[75] Music depends heavily for its meaning on finitude at every level. Tones give way to tones. Music is constantly dying, giving way. The next tone in the plainsong melody can only come if the last one is not sung. Musical continuity emerges from transience, from the coming into being and dying of tones, for in this way and only in this way can their dynamic qualities be sensed. The fact that music never solidifies or coagulates to form a thing or substance is critical to its intelligibility. Of course, it will be said that all the arts are insubstantial to the extent that they involve physical realities which are temporarily constituted and bound to disintegrate: even the best preserved painting will ultimately crumble. But music relies with a peculiar intensity on transience for its very functioning. Even poetry and fiction – which also turn on the coming into being and dying of words – possess the capacity to designate or refer in various ways to enduring things, people, ideas, states of affairs or whatever. And such references, though they do not of course exhaust the semantics of literature, normally constitute an intrinsic part of its meaning. But, as we have stressed several times, this is rarely the case with music.

Music, then, is one of the least substantial art forms, especially prone to the supposed destructive effects of time, implicated and intertwined with finitude to a very high degree. And yet, because of the internal relatedness of its tones in and through time (rather than simply being a string

---

74. Bowker (1991b), 218, 220.   75. See above, pp. 6off.

of discrete, intermittent sounds), because of its interweaving of the temporal modes, music *in and through its very transience* can be ordered, glorious and enhancing, the very opposite of futile and senseless.

To be sure, as we noted earlier, there is a destructive kind of transience, when we lose what is good and beneficial. Death has become enmeshed in the corruption which has afflicted all things. There is death unleashed by evil, death which is cruel and tragically premature. Even here, music's interweaving of the temporal modes embodies its own kind of challenge to the notion of irretrievable loss – we will pick this up in a later chapter. The point we are establishing now is more limited and modest, but nonetheless significant: that music, by its very constitution, can serve to release us from the assumption that limited duration is of necessity problematic, that we can only discover authentic meaning in the unbounded and unlimited.

Put more positively and theologically, music can serve as a means of discovering afresh and articulating the theological truth that limited duration can be beneficial, and as such, an expression of divine generosity. Karl Barth expounds the matter in a section entitled 'Allotted Time' in the *Church Dogmatics*.[76] Permeating Barth's discussion is a conviction that all that is said about time is related to the grace of the triune God, a matter we signalled at the outset of this chapter. He writes: 'there is no such thing as absolute time, no immutable law of time . . . There is no time in itself, rivalling God and imposing conditions on him. There is no god called Chronos.'[77] Time is divinely *created* – there is no other time. More specifically, created time is to be related to the time of Jesus Christ, and Christ's temporality is inseparable from his history as Jesus of Nazareth. Here is a limited, restricted life among us, bound by birth and death. Nevertheless, in his resurrection he is inaugurated as the 'Lord of time' so as not to be bound by our succession of beginning, duration, and end; his time begins but exists before its beginning, has duration but in such a way that his present includes his past and future, and ends but in such a way that the time after its end is that of his renewed presence.[78] It is notable that for Barth, God's direct engagement with spatio-temporal reality and its redemption in Jesus Christ confirms time as unambiguously real, to God and to us: 'The many philosophical theories of time which deny its reality and regard it as a mere form or abstraction or figment of the imagination can only be finally abandoned when we consider that

76. Barth (1960a), 553–72.   77. Ibid., 456.   78. Ibid., 437–511.

God himself once took time and thus treated it as something real.'[79] Thus we find Barth stressing that time is intrinsic to created being, established with ('co-created' with) all particular things, as a form of all reality distinct from God.[80] Moreover, time is no neutral backcloth, still less some kind of necessary evil or imposition on God, but rather good gift, conferred by God for benefit.

With this in mind, Barth urges that the limited duration of human life is fundamentally beneficial and advantageous. Would not unlimited, endless time be a more appropriate environment for us through which to relate to God than a life bound by birth and death? Barth replies that God's eternity is not endless time (God not being subject to some kind of time-line), that unlimited time would not guarantee the fulfilment of relationship with God (only unrestricted opportunity), and, moreover, with unlimited time, we would never actually reach our fulfilment (we would be condemned to perpetual yearning).[81] More positively, 'allotted' life must be related to the God of Jesus Christ: this trustworthy God has allotted us all the time we need to fulfil our destiny. Crucially, however, the boundaries of birth and death, beginning and end, are marks of our dependence on God's grace: 'at the very point where we emerge from non-existence and return to non-existence, we are confronted in a particular way by the gracious God'.[82] Here we encounter a God beyond our possibilities and making. Had we unlimited lives we might still be able to live by the grace of God, 'But it would not be natural or obvious. [We] would be blinded by the illusion that [we] can rely on many other things as well as God.'[83] That we are bounded by non-being at our beginning testifies that we come not from nothing but from God. That we are bounded at our end by death – considered as a mark of finitude – is also testimony that our life is a gift from God. Implicit in our finitude is an invitation and direction to throw ourselves upon the divine graciousness, 'to give him alone [our] trust and full obedience, and in so doing to fulfil [our] determination and satisfy [our] craving for duration and perfection'.[84]

Arguably, much of this could also be applied to the non-human order. The scientific debate on what kind of 'beginning' and 'ending' is proper to the universe and the way in which these terms themselves have to be qualified, is not our concern here. The central point is that we are speaking of a finite universe bounded by non-being, utterly contingent and owing its

79. Ibid., 455f.   80. Ibid., 438.   81. Ibid., 558–62.   82. Ibid., 568.
83. Ibid., 569.   84. Ibid., 569f.

being wholly to the Creator, its finitude and contingency testifying to divine grace. This, I submit, is the light in which Barth's famous adulation of Mozart's music as a 'parable of the Kingdom' should be set.[85] Why did Barth believe this composer deserved a central place in theology, 'especially in the doctrine of creation and also in eschatology'?[86] Why was he so certain that when the angels praise God they play only Bach, but that together *en famille* they play Mozart and God listens with special pleasure?[87] A large part of the answer seems to be that for Barth, Mozart's music embodies and gives voice to the authentic praise of a finite, limited creation. (To spend too long arguing about whether or not Barth is actually right about Mozart risks missing the force of this theological point.[88]) In the *Church Dogmatics* the fulsome eulogy on Mozart appears in the middle of a discussion of the 'shadowside (*Schattenseite*)' or negative aspect of the universe.[89] Here Barth is not entirely precise as to what this 'shadowside' is, but comparison with a later passage[90] makes it probable that he is thinking of finitude and all its effects (including death), the quality of having been created out of nothing and therefore always being on the verge of collapsing back into non-existence. Barth is especially keen to distinguish the shadowside from genuine evil (*das Nichtige*); to fail to do this both masks the destructive nature of evil and might suggest that finitude is itself evil. The shadowside is the expression of God's 'positive will, election and activity'.[91] Mozart's music is presented in this context as articulating the praise of creation in all its aspects, it sings the praise of the cosmos in its 'total goodness', *including* its shadowside. The music does indeed contain its 'No' but this is the 'No' of the shadowside, not evil.[92] What does it matter if Mozart died in misery like an 'unknown soldier', Barth asks, 'when a life is permitted simply and unpretentiously, and therefore serenely, authentically and impressively, to express the good creation of God, *which also includes the limitation and end of man*?'[93] Mozart heard the harmony of creation in which 'the shadow is not darkness, deficiency is not defeat, sadness cannot become despair, trouble cannot degenerate into tragedy and infinite melancholy is not ultimately forced to claim undisputed sway'.[94] Mozart even acknowledges the limit of death. But he heard the negative only in and with the positive: the overriding impression and

85. Barth (1986), 57.   86. Barth (1960b), 298.   87. Barth (1986), 23.
88. For the same reason, we should not be distracted by Barth's indefensible remarks about other composers (see Busch 1976, 362f., 401).   89. Barth (1960b), 297ff.
90. Ibid., 349f.   91. Ibid., 350.   92. Ibid., 297ff.
93. Ibid., 298f. My italics.   94. Ibid., 298.

impact of the music, as Barth hears it, is God's almighty 'Yes' to creation. Here creation praises God *in its very finitude* and thus shows what authentic praise truly is. Confirming this, later Barth speaks of the difference between shadowside and *das Nichtige* – when the creature 'crosses the frontier' of finitude, 'nothingness achieves its actuality in the created world'.[95] This is just what Mozart's music does not do. It does not try to be divine. Nor does Mozart. He does not obtrude himself in some 'mania for self-expression'.[96] Nor does he try to force a 'message' on the listener.[97] He does not '*will* to proclaim the praise of God. He just does it – precisely in that humility in which he himself is, so to speak, only the instrument with which he allows us to hear what he hears: what surges at him from God's creation, what rises in him, and must proceed from him.'[98] 'He simply offered himself as the agent by which little bits of horn, metal and catgut could serve as the voices of creation.'[99] This is what gives Mozart's music its 'freedom', its effortless and light quality.[100] It is the freedom of creation liberated to praise God in and through its God-given temporal limitations.

We might add that it is here that the role of silence within, preceding and succeeding music is seen to be highly instructive. Augustine touched upon this in his correlation of music and cosmic order in *De Musica*. Just as musical rhythm is exemplified cosmically, so also is the silence within music – the interlude or rest. As Catherine Pickstock explains, 'The alternation of sound and silence in music is seen by Augustine as a manifestation of the alternation of coming into being and non-being which must characterise a universe created out of nothing.'[101] 'Nothing' is given a profound ontological place, for musical silences are not mere void but enter into the proportional ordering of music. Likewise 'nothingness' is intrinsic to the order of the cosmos, the fact that things are continuously coming to be and ceasing to be: 'it is when human creatures fail to confess this nothingness, when their life in time is without pauses, that this order is denied and a greater nothingness of disharmony ensues'.[102] In other words, humanity forgets that life is utterly and completely contingent upon the plenitude of God. Augustine here appears to see a link between the artistic possibility of creating something authentically new, the perpetual 'coming to be' of things, and the emergence of finite reality as a whole from nothing. This 'point' of nullity is not only the edge of finitude but also a participation in the fullness of God; in other words, the uni-

95. Ibid., 350.   96. Ibid., 298.   97. Barth (1986), 37.   98. Ibid., 38.
99. Barth (1960b), 298.   100. Barth (1986), 47ff.   101. Pickstock (1999), 247.
102. Ibid., 247.

verse is suspended between nothingness and the infinity of God – music can exemplify and embody just this suspension.

Amidst a culture which, for a complex cluster of reasons has found itself with a certain malaise with regard to time, music, we have found, can be highly significant in coming to terms with and challenging some of the theological currents associated with this malaise, and it does this principally by embodying alternatives. Much has been said in other contexts about the propensity of the Christian tradition to treat the temporal order with insufficient ontological seriousness, and to assume a necessary bond between temporality and fallenness. Not very much, however, has been said about the ability of music to provide a means of exploring and counteracting both tendencies – hence the substance of this chapter. The Christian faith, above all because of its commitment to the Son's assumption of creaturely reality (including time) in Jesus Christ and the Spirit's direction of all temporal things to their eschatological fulfilment, announces that our experience of temporality corresponds to a dimension of created reality, conferred by the Creator. Music, I have tried to argue, entails practices in which time is experienced not as an inert container (or merely as a human construct) but as an intrinsic dimension of physical entities and events. More than this, the Christian faith affirms that this temporality is a gift, and that consequently it is neither neutral nor inherently threatening. Consequently our interaction with temporality need not be characterised by struggle, competition, intrusion or invasion; nor need it be marked by retreat, evasion or escape. Music, in this context, has the potential to demonstrate that these two broad options do not exhaust the possibilities. It can provide a concrete means of establishing and experiencing a more contented 'living peaceably' with time than our contemporary existence seems able to offer. To cite Rowan Williams again: 'What we learn, in music as in the contemplative faith of which music is a part and also a symbol, is what it is to work *with* the [temporal] grain of things, to work in the stream of God's wisdom.'[103] In all this, we have not only been uncovering the potential of music to generate fresh means of advancing doctrinal understanding, but likely uncovering some of the reasons why music has so persistently been drawn into the purposes of God in the life of the Church.

---

103. R. Williams (1994), 250.

4

Resolution and salvation

The word of promise . . . always creates an interval of tension between the uttering and the redeeming of the promise. In so doing it provides man with a peculiar area of freedom to obey or disobey, to be hopeful or resigned.[1]

JÜRGEN MOLTMANN

In this chapter we aim to 'think together' musical process and some major themes in eschatology. Whatever else 'eschatology' may mean, it bespeaks a future-directedness in the Christian faith, an orientation towards a fulfilment of the purposes for which God has brought all things into being. Seen from the point of view of salvation, this orientation is intensified, for now it focuses on a resolution of the corruptions and dis-locations of the world.

The ground for this chapter has already been laid in chapter 2. There we found that music was characterised by a teleological dynamic, marked by multi-levelled patterns of equilibrium, tension and resolution. Crea-tion–fall–redemption may well come to mind in this connection, a huge metrical wave occasioned by the crises of evil and sin, within which are nested a multitude of smaller waves of divine activity at different levels. In the New Testament, the pattern is probably enshrined most memor-ably in the so-called parable of the prodigal son (Lk. 15:11–32). It is perhaps not surprising that the kind of music we are considering germinated and grew within a predominantly Christian setting. (Considerable care, how-ever, is needed when making this kind of correlation. There are subtle varieties of directionality both in Christian thought and in tonal music.

1. Moltmann (1967), 104.

And the theme of displacement from 'home' and subsequent 'arrival' has been rehearsed in the literature, drama and music of many cultures not directly affected by the Christian story of salvation. Nevertheless, that major theological factors have been involved in tonal music's history would be hard to deny.)

Our explorations in this chapter traverse five broad areas of eschatology, all concerning the salvific process of resolution, and all intimately interrelated: delay and patience, fulfilment and hope, the prefiguring of final resolution, the delay of the parousia, and the character of the final resolution.

Delay and patience

Extremely common in the Bible is a sense among the writers of delay, that things are being in some manner held back, whether the final fulfilment of God's intentions or the more proximate small-scale fulfilments. This sense is often intensified by the memory of some past fulfilment, when God acted in a relatively unambiguous way. The conviction that this is not merely a human perception but that delay can in some manner be directly put into effect by God is also a frequent theme (e.g. Joel 2:13; Is. 42:14; Rom. 8:20; 2 Pet. 3:9).

Through its layered patterns of tension and resolution, music relies for much of its effect on generating a sense of the incompleteness of the present, that not all is now given. Theologically, the dynamic of promise and fulfilment is an obvious correlate of this. A tension is aroused, promoting a reaching forward to its release in some form of fulfilment. So the Christian tradition speaks of an open-endedness in the Scriptures prior to Christ's appearance, an enormous metrical wave spanning the centuries, in a continual (though varied) state of tension. And in New Testament faith we also find a sense of the inconclusiveness of what is presently offered to experience: 'For the creation waits with eager longing . . .' (Romans 8:19ff.). This impression of incompleteness is intensified when the expected fulfilment is delayed, either entirely or in part. Musicians are adept at generating expectations which are deliberately deferred through a myriad of devices: diversions, digressions, pauses and so forth. Indeed, some analysts have laid huge stress on the extension of resolution and consequent 'deferred gratification' as among the most critical determinants of musical structure, especially in Western tonal music since the eighteenth century.[2] This kind of delay occurs especially towards the end of sections of music, both because deferral is most effective when a specific closure is in view and also because the clearer and more predictable the mode of continuation, the more the need for heightened interest. But wherever it happens, from the small-scale phrase all the way up to the shaping of an entire piece, maintaining the 'not yet' of resolution through delayed gratification is generally reckoned to be one of the crucial skills to be learned by any composer. Be it a rock song or symphony, ballet score or ballad, a huge amount depends on learning to fashion the dynamic space between tensions and delayed resolutions in ways that are coherent enough to sustain expectation and yet interesting enough to sustain attention. Leroy Ostransky, in *The Anatomy of Jazz*, observes:

> What distinguishes superior creative musicians from the mediocre ones of all periods is the manner in which they create resolutions, and to create resolutions it is necessary to set up irresolutions . . . Poor and mediocre jazzmen . . . often do not understand that the quality of their jazz will depend not on any resolution, however elaborate, but rather on the inherent intricacy of the irresolution.[3]

2. By far the most important scholar in this connection is Leonard B. Meyer. Adopting an information-theoretical approach, and focusing especially on tension and release, Meyer believed that musical processes appeal directly to the logic and flux of mental and psychological processes (Meyer 1970). Striving to resolve ambiguity and to bring order to the disorderly are fundamental human needs or tendencies. Affect in music is generated through setting up patterns of expectations, gratifications and frustrations. So long as a musical work fulfils a listener's expectations immediately, it conveys no information. When an expectation is temporarily inhibited, however, a response is produced which can be affective (a feeling) or intellectual (a thought). A fulfilment which follows a deferral is more satisfying than immediate gratification. Meyer argues that the 'best' music in the 'classical' tradition works according to 'deferred gratification' (Meyer 1959). In Meyer's later, more cautious work (1973), in what would seem to be an effort to give his theories a less subjective leaning, he shifts significantly away from the notion of 'creating expectations' to that of implication: a musical event is said to imply another by rendering it more or less probable. Closure happens when that which has been rendered increasingly probable over a time-span actually happens. Melody, harmony and rhythm work to build up patterns of diminishing and increasing probabilities, frustrating and finally fulfilling our musical expectations.
    The overlaps between this and our interests in this chapter are considerable. However, the weaknesses of Meyer's claims need to be borne in mind. There is an over-reliance on linguistic analogies. His understanding of affect has been challenged, not least his belief that affect is dependent on the blocking of a tendency. One would think, following Meyer's model, that the better one knows a musical work the less information it conveys and the less interesting it becomes – but this is by no means always the case. Further, there are problems in speaking of implication and probability as if we were dealing with scientific inference. And Meyer's model of psychological response has been criticised as too mechanistic, paying scant attention to the hearer's situation and cultural background. Also, the limited scope of his thesis needs to be remembered – at best, this is an account of how some musical passages (mainly in the eighteenth- and nineteenth-century tonal tradition) appear to operate, and are heard as more interesting (or more dull) than others. For careful critiques, see Bowman (1998), 166–95, and S. Davies (1994), 27ff.
3. Ostrensky (1960), 83.

John Coltrane's 'A Love Supreme' builds towards a postponed and greatly desired climax, frequently evading release at expected points. Richard Wagner depends on delayed gratification to a very high degree. But perhaps the most influential and skilful of them all in this respect was Beethoven. In much of his music, a sense of delay is engendered through conflict, sometimes momentous struggle. It is as if victory can only be granted at great cost, and the victory is all the more impressive because of the prior battle. The architecture of his Fifth Symphony is a good example of this pattern. But he can also suspend resolution in less dramatic ways, as in the first movement of his String Quartet, op. 59, no. 1. One of the notable peculiarities of this piece is the lack of a sense of equilibrium at the opening. It is as if we left home before the piece began: we are already projected towards a future. The unsettledness of the first section of the movement is created by carefully controlled harmonic and metric ambiguity, leaving a sizeable legacy to be resolved (Example 4.1). The opening chord is highly ambiguous with regard to key.[4] The instability is heightened by placing the root position of the tonic chord on the weakest beat of the first bar and mid-way through bar 3, and by avoiding a statement of the theme over a root-position tonic. There is metrical imbalance created by six and a half bars of tonic followed by eleven and a half bars of dominant; in other words, a bias towards a weak metrical 'beat', if we take the bars 1–18 as a large hyperbar. Within the opening sequence, therefore, there is both considerable tension between harmony and metre.

As Kramer puts it: 'We may not understand all the implications of the unusual opening when we first hear it, but we are struck by its strangeness and we wait for an 'explanation.'[5] And how does the explanation/resolution come? In a movement of this sort, it is customary for the first main resolution to appear at the 'recapitulation', often about two-thirds of the way through the piece, when the home key (the tonic) reappears and the opening material is repeated. But Beethoven can hardly do this, given all the unsteadiness and ambivalence of the opening. What he writes instead is a dispersed reprise, spread out over different stages. The key is restored, but not fully (bar 242); then the melody is restored in the tonic, but over a not-yet centralised key (254); then the tonic note is restored, but offset against a new insecurity in the harmony (279); then a very brief glimpse of the key is given in unadorned simplicity; then the key is properly established (307), and

---

4. Interestingly, exactly the same three notes create an even more intense and stretched-out ambiguity at the opening of the Adagietto of Mahler's Fifth Symphony; the delay tactics here are eloquently described by Bernstein (1976), 197ff.   5. J. Kramer (1988), 26.

Example 4.1 Beethoven, String Quartet no. 7 in F major, op. 59, no. 1, bars 1–21

eventually, after further delay, the melody appears in the context of its own (now secure) key (348). Moreover, when the melody eventually appears in its fully stabilised form, the metric ambiguity of the opening is also resolved, in that from 348 onwards, dominant and tonic receive roughly equal duration.

The return of the tonic, therefore, is spread out, dissipated over five timepoints. Delay is added to delay: there is the delay which has preceded the return, and the return itself is delayed, at least in part. And, we should add, this is not a continuous progressive resolution, a gradual 'explanation' – for in some cases the resolutions come and go.

I spoke in the last chapter in fairly general terms about the ability of music to school us in the art of patience. We are now speaking of patience associated with the resolution of tension. Kathleen Marie Higgins has recently drawn attention to this aspect of musical experience, in writing of the ways music can illuminate tensions in our ethical experience. Though she does not mention patience explicitly, this particular virtue seems to be close to the surface of her thinking.[6] 'Musical experience,' she writes, 'can be described as *enjoying* tension.'[7] She observes that 'The dominant approach of philosophical ethics emphasises final resolution over the appreciation of tensions in process. But this is to treat the tensions of everyday life as *negatively problematic*, not even as a means to an end . . . Tension is seen as something to be rejected, reduced, or, ideally, eliminated. The resolution of a moral dilemma is considered most ideal when it affords escape from tension and absolves the ethicist or agent from any need for further thought.'[8] Higgins notes how much ethical discourse resorts to static models when dealing with complex ethical situations, and these 'tend either to promote unrealistic expectations or to arouse the belief that one's situation is hopeless'.[9] Believing that 'well-handled maintenance of tensions is ethically desirable', even 'essential to living a balanced, happy life', she contends that music 'presents tensions, not as obstructions, but as themselves vehicles to the achievement of resolution'.[10] She goes on to say that what is at issue is learning through music 'the possibility of *graceful navigation within a texture of external and internal tensions*'[11] and, by extension, developing capacities which can affect other areas of our lives:

Learning to hear passing dissonances in counterpoint, for instance, made me more attentive to (and thus in greater control of) subtle

6. Higgins (1991), 164ff.   7. Ibid., 165.   8. Ibid., 166. My italics.   9. Ibid., 167.
10. Ibid.   11. Ibid., 168. My italics.

dissonances arising in other areas of experience. (The most conspicuous example is writing.) More generally, the 'inner dancing' involved in listening naturally suggests 'moving well' in life. Similarly, the organic development of a theme evident in symphonic music, or the culmination of a tension toward climax in a jazz solo, are images of motional possibilities that are akin to configurations that arise in practical life ... The symphonic development of a theme brings to mind the possibility that I can take a longer view of my relationship to any particular project, that perhaps I am making progress even when my particular hours of effort seem ungratifying. Or when a project is moving comfortably forward, music of admirable complexity can suggest the possibility of organisation on multiple, often subtle levels.[12]

It is not hard to move from these general ethical reflections to theological ethics, where we often find the same tendency to fall back on models which either raise impossibly high expectations or encourage despair in the present – everything is focused on hope for a speedy and singular resolution, unrelated in any integral way with tension, or else we give up hope of experiencing any resolution at all. Music opens up a much more theological vision of a 'meantime' which calls us into a 'graceful' – grace-inspired and grace-filled – 'navigation' of a 'texture' of tensions. This is a meantime created by deferred gratification, a delay of that day when nothing shall separate us from the love of God in Christ (Rom. 8:35–9). The meantime entails patience: 'if we hope for what we do not see, we wait for it with patience' (Rom. 8:25). Far from being empty or pernicious, however, this meantime is potentially rich, enlarging. Christ's resurrection has anticipated the general resurrection on the 'last day' and through the Spirit we have a foretaste of that resurrection age here and now (Rom. 8:9–11). This is the same Spirit who is active deep within creation and the Church, struggling to bring about in the world what has already been achieved in Christ (Rom. 8:17–30). The Spirit enlarges us in the very waiting, within and through the apparently circuitous, mysterious and painful process of deferred fulfilment: 'we suffer with [Christ] so that we may also be glorified with him.' (Rom. 8:17) In the New Testament, patience is often associated with growth in steadfastness and faith through perseverance in the midst of opposition (see e.g. Heb. 11).[13] Moreover, human patience can be very closely linked to God's own forgiving patience. God's

12. Ibid., 169. Higgins relates her work to moves she observes in ethics from 'quandary ethics' – characterised by a preoccupation with moral dilemmas, crisis situations – towards character or virtue ethics (MacIntyre, Nussbaum) – concerned with the development of virtuous day-to-day living (ibid., 191ff).   13. Falkenroth and Brown (1978), 764–76.

refusal to bring things quickly to a close does not indicate inertia or aban-donment (or compliance or indulgence) but is full of his passion for the world's salvation (2 Pet. 3:9; cf. Rom. 2:4, 3:25). And this bears on the kind of patient forgiveness we are to show to others: witness the way divine and human patience are brought together powerfully in the parable of the unforgiving servant (Matt. 18:21–35). Patience is one of the marks of authentic love (1 Cor. 13:4).

Of course, delay can at times be anything but enriching – the psalmist cries out of an experience of enervating delay: 'How long?' Lament and protest are common biblical responses to delay, as they are today. And in speaking positively about delay, we should avoid any tendency to read inevitability or non-contingency into the world's evil, such that delay is accorded a place in some 'necessary', inexorably unfolding plan.[14] None-theless there is a patience proper to Christian faith in which *something new is learned* of incalculable *value*, which cannot be learned in any other way. Music introduces us to just this kind of dynamic, this enriching mean-time, in which we are made to cultivate a kind of patience which subverts the belief that delay must inevitably be void or harmful ('negatively prob-lematic'). It can do so with a distinct potency, given, as we have seen, its intense involvement with a temporal dynamic that interweaves the tem-poral modes in a multi-levelled matrix.

It is worth noting in passing that much of the music currently employed in Christian worship deploys remarkably little in the way of delayed gratification. Admittedly, a congregation must be able to grasp quickly new hymns and songs if music is to enable and release their wor-ship, but as I have argued elsewhere,[15] rather too often goals are reached directly and predictably with a minimum of the kind of delay of which we have been speaking. Could we be witnessing here a musical articulation of the tendency in some quarters of the Church to insist on immediate

---

14. If the contingency of the world is to be taken seriously, as genuinely other to God, even though this otherness is properly understood as grounded in the otherness 'internal' to the triune God, it cannot be understood as a mere replication of divine difference. Rowan Williams, in conversation with John Milbank, pleads that we take with equal seriousness both the fact that it takes time for the world's good to be enacted (in contest with other goods) and the contingency of that enactment, not least the contingency of evil. The positing of difference 'outside' the divine life, he writes, 'is not a *repetition* of divine generation; it is the making of a world whose good will take time to realise, whose good is to emerge from uncontrolled circumstance – not by divine enactment in a direct sense, but by a kind of interaction of divine and contingent causality, entailing a divine responsiveness such as the doctrine of the Trinity ... authorises, in letting us think both a divine giving and a divine receiving ... The Fall is not necessary, logically or ontologically, but ... its story can be "retrieved" as one outworking of what creation (logically) cannot but make possible if it really is *other* to God' (R. Williams 1992, 322).   15. Begbie (1991a).

rewards and not to come to terms with the (potentially positive) realities of frustration and disappointment? One of the most significant challenges for any composer for worship today is to offer music which can reflect the conviction that intrinsic to salvation is a process of learning in which we are led towards goals by paths which are not easy, straightforward or expected. (We shall return to these matters when we speak more overtly of cross and resurrection in chapter 5.)

Promise and fulfilment

Musical delay is, of course, intertwined with much larger temporal patterns, of the sort we were uncovering in chapter 2. We return now to these basic metrical wave-formations to open up another area of eschatology.

We saw that within each bar, a pattern of beats is created which takes the form of a wave of intensification and resolution. This is played out in a hierarchy of levels. Waves on one level generate larger and larger waves above. Resolution at one level increases tension on higher levels. In Figure 4.1, the downbeat '1' serves to heighten tension two levels above, and on the level above that, and so on; similarly with the downbeat '2' three levels above, and on the level above that, and so on. Every downbeat constitutes an upbeat or upbeats somewhere higher up. Likewise, the process of 'closing' a wave (A) concurrently generates an increase of tension on the level above, and on the next level up, and so on. The double closure (B) of the two lowest waves in the diagram will increase tension on the level above, and so on further up. This is the process into which we are drawn whenever we listen to metrical music. Fulfilments, far from lessening hope for resolution, serve to heighten it. Provisional closures function

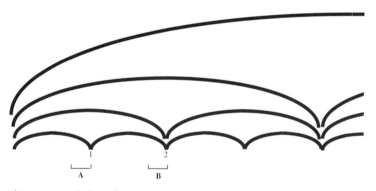

Figure 4.1 Metrical matrix

both to 'ease' tension and at the same time to intensify, and this is because both closure and forward impetus are maintained through multiple levels of tension and resolution.

The power of delayed gratification in music depends on just this duality: resolution is delayed on one level (or levels) while being effected on another (or others). This is sometimes achieved through (unexpectedly) setting up higher, longer-term waves; sometimes through the 'stretching' of one or more of the waves. Whatever its form, it involves the ability both to resolve and to increase tension concurrently. (To thwart *every* implication towards closure on *every* level would be impossible. The music would have to stop, or at least become so unintelligible that we would lose patience, surrender our trust. Even in pieces where the delay may be extreme, there will be some gratification on at least one level.)

The crucial point to note is this: however complex the process gets, *one level's return is always another's advance*. However strong closure may be at any one level, *there will always be levels in relation to which closure generates an increase in tension, giving rise to a stronger reaching out for resolution*. Each fulfilment constitutes an increase in the demand for fulfilment at a higher level. Every return closes *and* opens, completes *and* extends, resolves *and* intensifies. (Further, it will be obvious that resolution takes place not only on one level but on many – in Figure 4.1, the closing process of B takes place on the two lowest levels. The more levels resolution involves, the greater the sense of an immanent final closure.)

While not assuming a uniform systematic of promise-fulfilment in the Bible, frequently we are presented with fulfilments of divine promises such that 'each fulfilment in the past becomes promise for the future'.[16] A fulfilment – a 'downbeat' or closing process – resolves something of the tension generated by the initial promise, and of the tension created by previous fulfilments. But each fulfilment also gives rise to a further tension demanding completion, a tension not only of the same power at the same level (the next wave), but of greater and accumulating power at

---

16. Goldingay (1990), 117. Of course, it could be objected that the setting up of a 'tension' is one thing, a promise another: a promise is surely not a 'tension', and in any case, in music it is rare to find anything closely resembling a specific promise directed towards a very specific end. But we are understanding 'tension' in music in a wide sense, to denote that which generates a sense of incompleteness in the present (see above, p. 38), and this could certainly include a promise. Furthermore, in the Bible there is frequently a discrepancy or tension between promise and its context. At times this can be very acute: for example, when what is promised may radically call in question the situation in which the promise is uttered (as with the prophetic promise of return in the midst of Israel's exile). (Much is made of this by, for example, Moltmann. See Moltmann 1967, 103f.)

upper levels. In this way, hope is intensified, re-charged, a more potent 'reaching out' engendered.

In the history narrated in Scripture, this extra reaching for fulfilment arises in part because fulfilments are experienced as in some way inadequate to expectation. Every fulfilment is partial and provisional, and therefore a partial *non*-fulfilment. And yet, far from diminishing hope, we find that successive fulfilments increase the hope both in power and content. Deeply ingrained in the biblical testimony is a sense, sometimes acute, of the absence of an adequate fulfilment of what has been promised, a lack or deficiency which impels the people of God to reach forward and strain more fervently for what is to come.[17] In many cases this higher level of hope is 'marked out' through a drawing out or an enlargement of the original promise. With each repeated fulfilment, the promise is elaborated or augmented in some fashion, sometimes in highly surprising (though consistent) ways. 'As successive hopes find fulfilment, a tradition of "effective history", or "history of effects" (*Wirkungsgeschichte*) emerges in which horizons of promise become enlarged and filled with new content.'[18] Each downbeat brings an expectation and hope for *more*, so expanding the content and range of the original promise.

The hope can also be intensified when each fulfilment is seen as a partial realisation of what will eventually occur in its fullness. Every resolution in a piece of music is in some manner a partial realisation of the final resolution. Indeed, in much music the last major resolution is specifically anticipated in advance (a phenomenon we shall return to below).

We can expand on this by turning to one substantial area of Old Testament theology. For David Clines, the Pentateuch as a whole 'receives its impetus' from the patriarchal promise declared in Gen. 12:1–3, which contains three main themes or elements: posterity, divine–human relationship, and land. Clines claims that the Pentateuch's 'central conceptual content' is 'divine promise awaiting fulfilment',[19] such that 'the interval between the promise and its redemption is one of tension'.[20] 'The theme of the Pentateuch is the partial fulfilment – which implies also the partial non-fulfilment – of the promise to or blessing of the patriarchs.'[21] Fulfilments carry forward (and sometimes explicitly reiterate) the original promise at another level: 'the partial fulfilments of the triple promise that

17. The degree to which fulfilments actually failed to meet up to precisely what was promised need not concern us here; the point is that they were invariably experienced as in some sense inadequate to expectation.
18. Thiselton (1995), 150f., paraphrasing Pannenberg.
19. Clines (1994), 111. Clines draws on the work of others, notably Zimmerli's treatment of promise and fulfilment (1963, 1971).   20. Clines (1994).   21. Ibid., 29.

occur within the Pentateuch have an anticipatory as well as a conclusive function'.[22] Both their inadequacy and the fact that they are partial realisations of the end engender a reaching out towards a final conclusion. Furthermore – moving one level up in the theological metrical waves – Clines demonstrates that the patriarchal promise is a reaffirmation of the primal divine intentions for humanity (as expounded in Genesis 1–11).[23] He also stresses that the Pentateuch as a whole narrates a movement towards a goal yet to be realised. Its incompleteness is intrinsic to its meaning.[24]

For the Christian, the most important Scriptural promise–fulfilment pattern is Christologically determined. In the New Testament the coming of Jesus is presented as the completion of multiple implications inherent in the promissory story of Israel (without the assumption that there have been no prior fulfilments!). But this very conclusion in Christ, climactic and utterly decisive as it may be, also brings with it an intensification and an enrichment of the promise originally made to Abraham. The first Christians are impelled towards a yet more fervent longing for a yet more glorious future. Again, this arises both because of a sense of the fulfilment's provisionality – the world has not yet reached its intended end – and a sense that *in him* the end has already arrived – Jesus Christ is raised as the first fruits of those who have died (1 Cor. 15:20).[25] Moreover, through the Spirit there can be many provisional fulfilments of the new promise set in motion by Christ (on the lowest level, as it were), without effacing belief in a terminating fulfilment at the eschaton, and without effacing the decisiveness of the fulfilment in Christ. To know Christ by means of the Spirit outpoured is to know the 'first fruits' of the life to come (Rom. 8:23).

Much of this finds expression in the Epistle to the Hebrews, written to a community tempted to fall away from its eschatological calling, and imbued with a theology of promise (see especially 6:13–18). Few texts in the

22. Ibid., 117.   23. Ibid., 61ff.   24. Ibid., 110f. The dynamic is of course considerably richer than I can indicate here, not least because in the Pentateuch not only are we presented with repeated fulfilments, the patriarchal promise *itself* is repeated (and amplified).

25. The convolutions of Romans 9–11, to take one of many examples, can usefully be read in this manner. Faced with the agonising problem of the rejection of the Messiah by the Jews, Paul attempts to wrench his hearers away from understanding the historical outworking of the promise to Abraham on one level alone. To claim that the unbelieving Jews are necessarily excluded from the fulfilment of God's promises in Christ is to fail to see that the rejection of Jesus by the Jews has meant that (on a higher level) the Gospel has gone to the Gentiles, that this fulfilment in turn means that (on a higher level still) the Gospel can return to the Jews – and that all of these fulfilments therefore carry *forward* the original over-arching promise to Abraham to form one people without racial exclusion, inclusive of Gentile and Jew (the final fulfilment). I return to this passage in chapter 9; see below, pp. 255ff.

New Testament stress with such vigour Christ's perfect and complete sacrificial offering, once-and-for-all (*ephapax*) (7:27), culminating in his ascension and eternal priesthood. This is in contrast to the unfinished character
of Jewish priesthood of which Christ is the decisive completion. All the
same, Old Testament texts about journeying and waiting are appropriated
to remind the readers that they have not yet achieved eschatological finality and perfection, the divine closing cadence, the 'rest' only provisionally
fulfilled prior to Christ (3:7–4:11). As Graham Hughes points out in his
study *Hebrews and Hermeneutics*, 'Jesus' exaltation is a *final and definitive
form of the promise* [given to Abraham].'[26] And Jesus' exaltation is also an
anticipation of the final goal which the Christian community will enjoy.
Continually 'looking to Jesus' now, to the pioneer and perfecter of our
faith (12:2), *is* therefore to 'venture forth', to press forward in faith, living
'in between' both the promise and fulfilment enacted in him.

Matters are hugely more elaborate than we have space to set out here.
In both music and in scriptural renderings of promises and fulfilments,
we are dealing with interweaving trajectories, overlapping short-term
promises, interruptions and so on. But enough has been said to show
something of the theological potential of music's metrical hierarchy. It is
arguable that eschatology which has clung to single-levelled, single-line
models of temporality has done little to help us grasp these dynamics of
promise and fulfilment. It has encouraged, for example, assumptions
that the resolution of promise (or prophecy) must be found in a singular,
punctiliar, concentrated, and unambiguous happening (or highly compressed cluster of happenings), in the absence of which we are forced to
pronounce the original promise unfulfilled, void or at least severely problematic. (We recall that music played 'on the flat', with no attention to the
'larger' waves, is usually stultifying.) What is needed is an exposition and
exploration of the multi-levelled character of divine promise and fulfilment, one that is true to its rich integrity. Music, with its repeated and
concurrent generation and dissolution of tension on different levels, provides an extraordinarily helpful way of clarifying conceptually, and
apprehending through sound, how it is possible for resolutions not to
lessen but to heighten hope, for God's intention to be disclosed through
the 'in-tension' of promissory waves. Music's very rationality challenges
the assumption that time must be conceived in one-level linear terms
(and, we might add, it equally challenges what is often wrongly thought
to be the only other option, so-called 'cyclical' time).

26. Hughes (1979), 53. My italics.

Final resolutions prefigured

As I have said above, the hopeful dynamic of Christian faith is carried forward not simply by what we do *not* possess but by what we *are* given now of the future. Many of the partial fulfilments of biblical promise and prophecy are regarded not simply as incomplete fulfilments of earlier implications but as foretastes of the end to come. This 'pre-figuring' aspect of eschatology can be explored tellingly through music. In chapter 2, we observed that in hearing or listening to music, because of its metrical wave structure we are always '*between* the tones, *on the way* from tone to tone; our hearing does not remain with the tone, it reaches through and beyond it'.[27] There is a sense in which the musical present is charged with its future. This, I went on to say, does not entail positing a mental act whereby we present to our consciousness now some particular future musical event; rather, though the possible futures are by no means unlimited, we enjoy the dynamism of expectation itself: 'I experience futurity as that toward which the present is directed and always remains directed.'[28] This means that we should be wary of making *too* direct a jump from music to biblical and theological fulfilment patterns. Music offers the dynamic of hopefulness without always directing our explicit attention to specific goals. Biblical hope, on the other hand, though exhibiting this dynamic of hopefulness, is also normally quite explicitly directing attention to happenings of varying degrees of specificity.

Nevertheless, music is capable of bringing specific and particular futures to our awareness through anticipation.[29] As we have seen, every closure is intrinsically related in and through time to every other closure (including the final closure), not only because of its interconnectedness with the others through many layers of metre, but also because of its characteristic shape and positioning with respect to the metrical waves. More overt still, a cadence which closes, say, the first section of a work may be identical to the cadence which eventually brings the whole piece to a conclusion.

Here we can cite two instructive examples of prefigured endings. The first is from Mozart at his wittiest. In the third movement of his 'Jupiter' Symphony no. 41 in C major (1788), immediately after the end of the minuet section we encounter a 'perfect cadence' – an unambiguous and universally recognisable gesture of closure in tonal music (Example 4.2).

27. Zuckerkandl (1956), 137. Cf. above, pp. 48ff.   28. Ibid., 233.
29. Likewise, it is capable of particular retrocipations, through repetition, a matter we shall deal with later in chapter 6.

Example 4.2 Mozart, Symphony no. 41 in C major, K. 551, 'Jupiter', third movement, bars 52–61

The crucial cadence is at (A).

Indeed, so redolent is this cadence with closure, if it were not for the reduced orchestration we might think it was a reiteration of the ending we have just heard. From the point of view of metre, there is nothing to suggest it is anything other than an ordinary cadence. Yet it turns out to be the beginning of an entirely new phrase (Example 4.3).

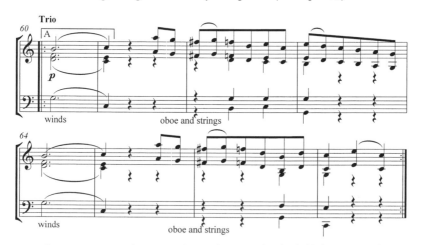

Example 4.3 Mozart, Symphony no. 41 in C major, K. 551, 'Jupiter', third movement, bars 60–7

What we recognise as an 'ending' constitutes a new start. Mozart is playing on the ambiguity between closing gesture and opening process.

Consider Luke's portrayal of the day of Pentecost in Acts 2: is this an ending or a beginning? The pouring out of the Spirit and its associated signs speak of the ending promised by Joel, the 'last days' so fervently awaited. God's cadence fills the air. Yet the atmosphere is also one of initiation: Peter's address makes clear that this was only the start of a fresh phase (or phrase?) during which it is to be made known 'to the house of Israel' that God has made the crucified Jesus 'both Lord and Christ' (36) and that they are to be baptised in his name (38). Mozart offers this dynamic in sound.

Not only that, the cadence becomes the chief ingredient out of which the next section of the music is elegantly woven (Example 4.4).

> The two-note cadence is repeated at a higher level, inverted, and repeated in sequence.

Example 4.4 Mozart, Symphony no. 41 in C major, K. 551, 'Jupiter', third movement, bars 68–87

An ending becomes the initiative and the material for a sequence of novel developments. The raising of Christ and the explosion of the Spirit are the end, the 'last days' upon us, and they initiate a series of extraordinary elaborations. And all this music takes place *in the midst* of the third movement: here Mozart introduces an atmosphere rife with fertile rumours of the end. God's 'new start' is presented in the midst of our history. It would seem that Mozart was something of a theologian of eschatology, in ways that perhaps not even Karl Barth fully appreciated.

In this example, to borrow Jonathan Kramer's distinction between 'product' and 'process', Mozart gives us an ending-profile or product without actually giving us an ending process. (In most tonal pieces, both are needed for closure.)[30] The humour of the passage turns on the ambiguity between closing product and opening process. But the cadence doesn't become *the* ending of the movement; and so it does not anticipate the final cadence in any exact way. However, this can happen, and it can happen in ways which have profound and far-reaching repercussions. Indeed, it can create a tension of such power that the whole character of a piece and the manner in which it is experienced are affected.

Consider, for example, Beethoven's last string quartet, op. 135.[31] It is basic to this book that music achieves much of its interest through an interaction between its temporality and the time(s) in which we live our lives from day to day. The musical and extra-musical temporalities may be very different. But what if there is also strong discrepancy *within* a piece of music? What if, for example, an end-time temporality is introduced in the midst of a relatively ordinary temporality? In the Old and New Testaments, the announcement of the 'end' and its proleptic arrival frequently contradict the context in which they are set, announcing and embodying a future contrary to the present reality, setting up a tension which has to be resolved in some manner. Isaiah's announcement to the Israelites in exile (Is. 40–55) is a case in point, as is the way in which Paul presents the Spirit as drawing us into the temporality of the new age, already established in Christ, a temporality which strains against that in which we now live. We live in the overlap of the two incongruous ages, the incongruity only being resolvable in the eschaton. This is what is played out in the first movement of this Beethoven quartet. Very near the opening (bar 10) a grand closing gesture appears, of the kind one would normally associate with the very end of a work (Example 4.5). This tenth bar

---

30. J. Kramer (1988), 143ff.   31. For full discussion, see ibid., 150–66.

Example 4.5 Beethoven, String Quartet in F major, op. 135, first movement, bars 1–12

has the gestural impact of a final cadence, a robust closure. Indeed, it is the cadence which will (with minor modifications) bring the movement to completion. So strong is its impact here that Jonathan Kramer, in the course of an extensive analysis of this movement, insists that 'In a certain sense . . . *it is the end*.'[32] Heard in what Kramer wants to call 'gestural time', 'the movement *actually* ends' in the tenth bar.[33] And this ending gesture is heard in a 'beginning' context – only ten bars from the start. Against what might be our inclination to say that the resurrection of Christ does not constitute an authentic ending, the New Testament is quite explicit: Christ's resurrection *concretely* anticipates *the* (final) resurrection of the new creation. Easter speaks of the establishment of a reality which is not simply anticipatory in the sense of shadow to substance, reflection to reality, but is a genuine instantiation of that which is to come.

As the music continues, we hear a present whose future (we might well presume) we have already experienced. The past is not merely past for us but lies before us, as does the past achievement of Jesus Christ. A few

32. Ibid., 150.   33. Ibid.

Example 4.6 Beethoven, String Quartet in F major, op. 135, first movement, bars 104–10

minutes later, the same grand closing gesture greets us again and then the piece continues to unfold (Example 4.6). The movement ends with the same cadence, only this time its ultimate finality underlined by small details of texture, harmony and timing (Example 4.7).

> The cadence receives fuller orchestration, subdominant harmony (bar 189), a pause (bar 191), and the addition of a third in the final chord (resolving the B flat of bar 192).

So the movement *ends three times* with essentially the same cadential gesture. Furthermore, in the middle of the movement these closing gestures are woven into the musical argument and become integral to a rich and prolific development. There is, in other words, an interplay of the temporalities with an acute incongruence between the time of the 'end' and the time in which there is a more straightforward unfolding of musical material. The two temporal continua collide, interact and are eventually woven together in the closing cadence.[34]

34. Meyer finds similar phenomena in Haydn's Symphony no. 97 in C major (Meyer 1973, 212f).

Example 4.7 Beethoven, String Quartet in F major, op. 135, first movement, bars 186–93

Perhaps there is a link between the temporal extremities of
Beethoven's late quartets and the extremity of his own impending death.
At any rate, the musicological fascination of these pieces derives in large
part from the way in which limits and parameters are transgressed,
deconstructed and reconstructed, not least with regard to temporality.[35]
Interestingly, Kramer makes the suggestion that music such as this might
be of considerable value in a culture which (as he interprets it) is disaf-
fected with certain alienating and imprisoning conceptions of linear
time, which rely excessively on simple and rigid patterns of cause and
effect, and which can easily lead to mechanistic notions of progress.[36]
Much of the music of late modernity and postmodernity has understand-
ably sought to dispense with goal-directed temporality altogether: as
with all the arts, music has been heavily implicated in the refusal and dis-
avowal of monolithic metanarratives. But movements such as the Beethoven so obviously break through the categories of singular linear

35. For a remarkable study of the radical implications for music and society of three of
these quartets (opp. 127, 130 and 132), drawing attention especially to the implicit
challenges to musical analysis, see Chua (1995).
36. J. Kramer (1988), 163ff. This links up with remarks we made earlier about the more
damaging aspects of temporal linearity. See above, pp. 58ff.

narrativity, yet while also being directional, without evoking temporal chaos. Beethoven, composing during a period of huge upheavals in conceptions of time, writes music which is goal-directed on every level, yet far from exhibiting a single-level linearity. If there is substance in Kramer's thesis, it is, to say the least, intriguing that this music's temporal processes are so akin to those of the eschatological, anticipatory character of salvation in Christ.

Music and the parousia

The main strands we have explored so far in this chapter can be usefully brought together by addressing a specific and controversial issue, very much alive in biblical studies and systematic theology: the final revelation or eschatological parousia of Christ.[37] Many discussions of the parousia have been conducted against the background of what has been called the 'problem of the delay', stemming from at least as far back as the work of Albert Schweitzer. Jesus, like most of his contemporaries, expected that the Kingdom of God would come within a very short time. So convinced was he of this that he went to his death to try to force God's hand, to install the Kingdom by fulfilling the Messianic woes of the 'last days'. Tragically misguided, he tried to halt the wheel of history but the wheel crushed him on the cross. For his followers, this left the huge problem of how to speak of a future Kingdom. Paul claimed that believers live both in the new age and the old age, looking forward to the day of final victory, which included the appearance of Christ. Paul's belief that this would happen within his own lifetime (or at least very soon) was mistaken, leaving the Church with a further crisis. We see signs of the Church adjusting to this crisis in the New Testament: in the Pastoral Epistles especially, Christianity is increasingly treated as very much at home in the world, in stark contrast to the earlier perspective in which the Church sits loose to the world because of its belief in an imminent end.

For a host of reasons this kind of account has fallen on very hard times among exegetes. Martin Hengel speaks of the 'problem of the delay' as a 'tired cliché'.[38] There are very few signs of a severe crisis or dismay over this issue in the early Church. Some adjustment of expectation can be

---

37. The New Testament does not use the terms 'second coming' or 'return' of Christ. It speaks of Christ's 'arrival', 'appearance', 'revelation' and 'presence'.
38. As quoted in Wright (1992), 462. See the balanced discussion by Cranfield (1982).

detected but there is little sign of widespread dismay or major embarrassment.[39] It is increasingly recognised that the whole matter needs to be set against its Jewish background.[40] For centuries the Jews had managed to combine the language of 'delay' and 'nearness' without embarrassment, even when the 'near' event did not happen as soon as desired or expected. An event spoken of as 'very near' could be thought of as in some sense delayed without abandoning or weakening the language of nearness or sense of imminence. Each partial fulfilment which did transpire could be seen as a limited realisation of what would eventually occur in its fullness. The original announcement could be amplified, re-interpreted, adapted and the hope accordingly strengthened. This 're-interpretation and adaptation of prophetic promises had always been a staple of Jewish religion, indeed a positive theological asset rather than a liability'.[41] Hence a sense of nearness, urgency and intense hope seems to have been able to accommodate the possibility and reality of delay. In much Jewish apocalyptic literature this is further borne out. We find impatience, a sense of exigency and hope: 'The promise of God's eschatological righteousness presses in upon the present, contradicting the evils of the present, arousing our hopes, motivating us to live towards it. Because the righteousness of God is at stake in this expectation it demands immediate fulfilment.'[42] But along with this, an attitude of patience is also recommended, a patience which acknowledges that God, in his freedom, *does* delay. There is, in other words, an appeal both to God's righteousness – God's justice will eventually prevail – and to God's sovereignty – his righteousness will prevail at his own appointed time. Neither element need be suppressed in favour of the other. In late Jewish apocalyptic, especially in the wake of the disastrous wars of AD 66–70 and 132–5, attempts were made to give meaning to the delay; most notably in the Apocalypse of Baruch, for example, where God, in his forbearance and patience, is said to restrain his wrath in order to give his people time to repent.[43]

These strands are all taken up in the New Testament in a way that is expressed summarily by Cranfield: 'history's most significant events have already taken place in the ministry, death, resurrection and ascension of Christ, so that what remains between his ascension and his parousia can only be a sort of epilogue, during the whole of which, *whether*

39. See e.g., Rowland (1985), 285ff.   40. See e.g., Bauckham (1980).
41. Bockmuehl (1994), 101.   42. Bauckham (1980), 9.
43. For fuller discussion of these and other relevant passages, see ibid., 4ff.

the actual length of time involved is short or long, the end presses upon the life and concerns of the believer as something urgently relevant to the present'.[44] The affirmation of the parousia's nearness did not entail affirming that the event *must* occur within a few decades (even though it would seem that some early Christians did believe this). In 2 Peter 3, for example, where the parousia is treated very directly, the language of imminence, urgency and expectation is retained alongside that of delay. In reply to the 'scoffers' who combined eschatological scepticism and ethical libertinism, the author is thoroughly in line with Jewish apocalyptic. We find a passion for God's righteousness (3:13), and an appeal to God's sovereignty: God is not 'late' or slow, the delay belongs to his purpose. And the positive purpose perceived behind the delay is spelt out: God's desire to bring his people to repentance (3:9). In the Apocalypse of John, imminent expectation of the parousia and allowance for its delay likewise belong together.[45] Similar patterns are evident in the Pauline corpus.[46]

These matters have received much attention in biblical scholarship and it is unnecessary to spell them out any further. What we want to stress here is that conceptualities of time which lean heavily on single-level linear models are of little help here – indeed, the tendency to conceive time in quantitative rather than qualitative terms has often exacerbated, perhaps in some cases even caused, some of the difficulties. New Testament language about nearness can too easily be read as pertaining to some particular period on a single time-line, and since the parousia did not arrive at a point within that period, it is assumed there must have been a serious 'crisis' or that a 'contradiction' arose which had to be explained away in some manner. What is needed here is not simply a refusal of crude linearity, but a search for more adequate models which can do justice to the experience of living within a dynamic directional field, a field in which

---

44. Cranfield (1982), 505. My italics.

45. The former is especially evident in the opening and closing sections of Revelation, and is strengthened by the strong conviction that Jesus has *already* won the eschatological battle with evil. See Bauckham (1980), 28ff.; (1993), 157ff.

46. In Paul's very early 1 Thessalonians for example, he urges his hearers to be ready and alert, because the coming of Christ will be unexpected, sudden. He seems to expect the parousia in his own lifetime. When he writes 2 Thessalonians, he tells the same hearers of things which have to happen before the end, but there is no relaxing of the urgency and expectation, or any suggestion that he is contradicting his earlier position. By the time he writes 2 Corinthians, Paul believes that he might well die before Christ's return but again, that does not diminish his sense of urgency and hope. For Paul the sense of nearness is intensified because of his belief that the end has already begun in Jesus and can be known through the Spirit's anticipatory work now.

things and events are intrinsically interrelated by virtue of sharing in waves of tension and fulfilment, in which anticipatory fulfilments generate wider and more intense hopes for the final fulfilment, and in which imminence and delay *can* therefore go together. Music offers not only this conceptuality but, more fundamentally, this temporal dynamic in sound. Indeed, because of its metrical matrix, *music actually depends for its very intelligibility on the enmeshing of nearness and delay,* to a degree unmatched by other art-forms.[47] As we have already seen, music's very rationality challenges the assumption that time must be conceived in one-level linear terms.

This would suggest that musical temporality may have much to offer when struggling with some of the more vexed passages which address the parousia. For example, Mark 13:26f. (and parallels) which speaks of the 'coming' of the Son of Man, has been taken by some to refer solely to the parousia at the end of time, while others insist that the reference is to the destruction of the temple in AD 70. If, as some would argue, we have assumed too easily that these are mutually exclusive options, and that the judgement on Jerusalem was being understood as a provisional and partial enactment of the final judgement, and that apocalyptic language here is being used to refer both to socio-political transformation within history and to cosmic transformation at the end of history, then it would seem that we need to be released from ways of thinking about temporality which obscure such an exegesis, and here the multi-levelled temporality of music would seem to come into its own.

In relation to the parousia, Jürgen Moltmann has been a strong opponent of linear conceptions of time. Indeed, he urges that it is highly misleading to speak of the parousia as an event 'in time', an event that 'will be'. By assimilating it to 'our time' in this way, locating it in our temporal future, we turn it into simply another transient event (albeit the last one). Everything that will be will one day be no more, but the parousia initiates eternity, the coming of Christ 'to all times simultaneously'. 'What *will come* according to the Christian expectation of the parousia brings the end of time and the beginning of eternal creation . . . the future of Christ also brings the end of becoming and the end of passing away.'[48] The parousia is related not merely to the future of being but to its present and past: 'As

---

47. In this connection it is striking that Revelation 6–11, in which the 'delay' motif in the letter is strongest, the literary structure keeps the reader in suspense through the repeated raising of expectation and subsequent frustration, in precisely the manner we have seen in music – 'deferred gratification'.   **48.** Moltmann (1990), 317.

the end of time, the parousia comes to all times simultaneously in a single instant.'[49]

But even if we take Moltmann's point, it needs qualifying, and here again music would seem to have much to contribute. There may well be a danger of quantitative time dominating all else, but the same could be said of qualitative time, so that the theological significance of historical 'distance', calendar time and delay is completely erased. Bultmann's tendency to pull past and future into the present 'eschatological moment' is a case in point. Even for Moltmann the parousia happens *both* 'in' time and 'to' time. It brings to an end the process of historical time while also transforming historical time.[50] Music, with its particularly stubborn and intense 'taking time', can serve to bring just this aspect of New Testament temporality to the fore, questioning the adequacy of speaking of a 'present' whose meaning is not intrinsically related to its distinct past and distinct future. To speak of the interweaving of the temporal modes is not to subsume all under the present, or to erase any sense of distance and delay.

Further, the awkward fact remains that there still *is* a fundamental 'delay problem' in both Old and New Testaments which will not be solved simply by abandoning linear concepts of time and insisting that the parousia transforms time.[51] Questions about 'sooner' or 'later' do not dissolve away so easily. For there is still the stubborn and radical contradiction between God's righteousness and the persistence of evil. Why

49. Ibid. The argument against the 'transposition of eschatology into time' (as Moltmann puts it) is elaborated, by no means always very clearly, in his book *The Coming of God* (1996), 6–13. Here Oscar Cullmann, along with Schweitzer and seventeenth-century 'prophetic theology', comes under fire (Moltmann 1996, 10ff). Attempting to mediate between Schweitzer and Bultmann – between the 'not yet' stress of the former and the 'now already' stress of the latter – Cullmann assumes linear time, arguing that this was central to the early Christian proclamation, and contends that since the coming of Christ we have been living in a new section of time, 'fulfilled but not yet completed'. Christians live between the 'now already' and the 'not yet'. The battle which decides the final victory has taken place but the day of victory is still to come. The 'delay of the parousia' was not for early Christians a disappointment, merely an 'error in perspective'. According to Moltmann, the weaknesses of this thesis are, first, that it fails to account for how we are to believe a decisive battle has taken place when the delay seems so long; second, the notion of linear time is 'not in fact biblical'; and third, it presupposes Enlightenment Deism, where God becomes the author of a master blueprint of salvation-history. The core of Moltmann's criticism is that this approach effectively destroys eschatology, swallowing it up in *chronos*, the power of transience. This is to rob the parousia of its non-transient, non-passing-away character. Christ, Moltmann insists, does not come 'in time' but comes to transform time.
50. Witness Moltmann's understandable refusal to join Bultmann and his associates in what Moltmann sees as an eternalising of the expectation of the parousia into a 'supratemporal' breaking in of eternity. This loses 'the real and futuristic expectation of the parousia' in the New Testament. See Moltmann (1990), 317f., and the section on the 'transposition of eschatology into eternity' in (1996), 13–22.   **51.** Bauckham (1999) 181f.

should the righteous God allow evil to flourish for so long? ('How long O Lord?') This is felt acutely in Jewish apocalyptic literature – innocent suffering cries out to God. The cry is not simply 'why should God delay?' but 'why should he allow a delay which includes evil and suffering?' The quandary is carried into the New Testament: there is a grinding dissension between the promise of a new world, already established in Christ, and ongoing evil which holds the world back from its fulfilment. Here the practical problem is not that of coping with an empty, dull interim but with an interim full of things which fly in the face of God's righteousness. Part of wresting some meaning out of this is to cultivate a certain kind of patience, something which we have already spoken about and in relation to which music undoubtedly can tell us much.[52] But this is anything but a complete 'answer', and certainly does not abolish the acuteness of the problem.

Resolution and overflow

For many, part of the agony of coping with the interim out of which the psalmist cries 'How long?' is a sense that God has in some sense 'run out' or come to the end of his resources. The rediscovery of God in such circumstances will likely bring a sense of divine inexhaustibility. One of the intriguing things about listening to a piece of music for the first time is that one never knows how many upper metrical waves are being generated. There is always, potentially, a higher wave. Moltmann speaks of an 'overspill' of divine promise which history cannot accommodate (however close the correspondence between the promise and its historical outcomes), an overspill which has its source in the limitlessness and uncontainability of God, 'the sheer inexhaustibility of the God of promise, who never exhausts himself in any historic reality but finally comes 'to rest' only in a reality that wholly corresponds to him.'[53] Compare Zuckerkandl:

> In the temporal component of music, then, we have to deal with a two-faced force, not to say a two-minded force. So far as it is responsible for the organisation of the individual [bar], it is perpetually intent upon closing a cycle, reaching a goal; it wills the finite. On the other hand, with its renewed, ever more insistent 'On! Once again!' which hammers out [bar] after [bar], it is a striving without end that accepts no limit, *a willing of the infinite*.[54]

---

52. See above, pp. 87ff., 99ff.   53. Moltmann (1967), 106.
54. Zuckerkandl (1956), 176. My italics.

Some might protest that the language of infinity here could be misleading, its theological attractiveness deceptive. Certainly, within the experience of a piece of music, there may well be a sense of 'potentially always more in store' – within history, there may well be a sense of the resourcefulness of God which may be taken to testify to his infinite inexhaustibility. But this 'potentially-always-more' feature of music cannot be used as a way of illuminating the ultimate participation of creation in God's life, the eschaton. For a piece of music ends. It *does* accept its limit. There *is* a 'highest' wave, and along with all the others it will 'fall' and converge on one point – the last note or chord – to be succeeded only by silence. While this may be helpful in understanding the contingency of creation on the plenitude of God,[55] it will not aid us when it comes to grasping what it means for all creation to find its ultimate fulfilment by being taken up into that abundant plenitude. Moreover, it might be said that the closures of tonal music are positively *unhelpful* in this respect, dangerous even, for they betray the more questionable aspects of modernity – its confidence in progress towards a goal marked by the ultimate purging of all unresolved implication and dissonance, the harmonisation of all conflict, a 'grand temporal consonance' (Kermode). By the same token, the break-up of tonality towards the end of the nineteenth century – the relinquishment (in Schoenberg, for example) of goal-directed, 'home-based' and 'home-oriented' music – attests to a widespread loss of confidence in historical closure, a profound suspicion (voiced repeatedly in postmodern texts) that even to speak of 'resolution' is to echo or extend the totalitarian impulse present in the worst of modernism, to smother difference in homogenising oneness, absorbing all distinctions in a quasi-mathematical point.

But, granted the limitations of music which arise from its finitude, can Zuckerkandl's language be swept aside quite so easily? We venture three comments.

In the first place, it is prudent to eschew postmodern generalisations about the history of tonal music which would render it as displaying *one* ending strategy or one principal group of strategies. In fact there are a marked variety of procedures, sometimes working against each other, and a wealth of further commentary could follow on the theological resonances of this heterogeneity.

Second, much tonal music makes its major return to 'home', its main

---

55. See above, pp. 96f.

restoration of equilibrium, some distance *before* the temporal end of the piece. This can leave the last section of the piece one in which its principal resolution is played out in music of considerable fecundity. In some symphonies, the last two or three minutes may properly be called resolution – the 'home key' is reiterated, celebrated even. If we are to seek musical analogues to the life of the world to come, there will be plenty of material in music to draw from which involves closures which are anything but lifeless, abstract points.

Third, and this extends the last point, even restricting ourselves to music's own endings, there is in fact a very pervasive feature of tonal music which lends it a very specific kind of openness, making hasty judgements about its supposed closed finality very dubious. It concerns the positioning of cadences (musical closures) relative to metrical and rhythmic accents. We recall that rhythm and metre are not identical: rhythm concerns temporal patterns of notes, metre concerns patterns of beats. Rhythmic accents underline notes within a rhythmic group (such as a phrase, or phrase pair, period, section or movement), and a rhythmic group often has a rhythmic accent near its end. Metrical accents mark the beginning of groups of beats. The point to underscore is this: *cadences* are normally *metrically weak* even though they may be (and usually are) *rhythmically strong*. They normally occur on the weak beat of a metrical wave – the beat which leads forward to the first beat of the next bar or hyperbar.[56] If we move up to the highest metrical level (the level of the piece as a whole) in many musical forms we discover that the final cadence of the piece is likewise metrically weak even though rhythmically strong. If we accept that metre is a prime structural determinant in music (some would say *the* prime determinant), we reach the intriguing conclusion: in cases such as these, *metrically speaking, the piece never finishes*. In a typical sonata movement – one of the classic forms of tonal music, and sometimes cited as the example *par excellence* of a modernist form which smothers all differences into all-embracing finality, the final cadence, metrically considered, reaches towards a further resolution (Figure 4.2). True, the strongest *rhythmic* accent is nearly always the structural cadence which occurs at (or very close to) the finish of the piece. But seen from the point of view of metre, things are different. The strongest metrical accent is at the point

---

56. See the painstaking analysis in J. Kramer (1988), 86ff. In most cases this is only so if one moves above the level of an individual bar. Within the bar in which a cadence occurs, the cadence is nearly always metrically accented – it comes on the first beat of the bar. But as soon as one moves to the next level (and all others) it is (often) metrically weak.

where the home key (the tonic) returns – the recapitulation – and this accent is not followed by a metrical accent of comparable strength. *The wave is not closed.*

exposition and development   recapitulation   close

Figure 4.2 Sonata form

> Jonathan Kramer makes a convincing case for regarding the strongest metrical accent to be at the return of the tonic – the recapitulation (J. Kramer 1988, 117ff). This return is also a rhythmic accent, since it includes an accent on a cadence. Here, significantly, is one of the places where metrical and rhythmic accents *do* coincide at a cadence. But the strongest rhythmic accent is at the close of the movement, for this is the end of a rhythmic 'group'. The return to the tonic after the development is a metrical arrival, and the most forceful metrical accent in the piece (prepared as it normally is by considerable activity focusing around the dominant). The closing cadence is not prepared for in anything like the same way (except in cases where there is an elaborate coda, as in, for example, the first movement of Beethoven's Seventh Symphony). The strong, accented metrical beat of the hyperbar (the return to the tonic) is followed by weak beats within the recapitulation, but there is not another first beat of comparable strength to complete the wave. Hence the entire movement can be described as a complete hyperbar followed by an incomplete one.

So, in the field of key, a cadence is a *closure* but in the field of metre it typically occurs *prior to closure* and *demands (metric) resolution*. In one sense, the music resolves; in another it strives ahead towards resolution. Over and over again in tonal music we have closures which are positioned in the metric matrix in such a way that they 'stretch forward' for further resolution. This lends the piece an incomplete character, an 'opening out'. We are given a tension which is not fully resolved, or which is only dissipated in the silence which follows the piece. The music is projected beyond the final cadence into the ensuing silence. Promise 'breaks out' of sound. The upshot is that far from being a model which needs to be treated with intense suspicion, or rejected as exhibiting a kind of closure which is inevitably tight and confining, we can say that sonata form – and with it,

many other forms in tonal music – is in fact highly apt to embody the kind
of openness characteristic of a properly theological eschatology, one
which can at least suggest the openness of created temporality to the inexhaustibility of God.

I have sought to give music room to do its own work amidst five major
areas of eschatology. I spoke of delay and patience: music is especially
qualified to form in us, not just the patience required when something
takes time, but the patience needed in the midst of delay. Delayed gratification is integral to the experience of salvation; it is also integral to music,
which leads us into a particular kind of beneficial and enriching 'meantime' in a manner which can be theologically instructive. In relation to
promise and fulfilment, music's metrical make-up elicits conceptualities
which release us from those which have so often obscured or even
besmirched our understanding of the trajectories of promise and fulfilment which weave through the Bible. We saw that the specific pre-
figuring of resolution in music can provide a way of exploring the
prefiguring of the eschaton in the coming of Christ and the giving of the
Spirit, again releasing us from crude linear models which cannot accommodate the tension and interplay between different temporalities.
Common misunderstandings of the parousia, we went on to see, are
circumvented and the whole field opened out in fresh ways when read
through musical experience, and the same can be said of the way we
understand resolution in relation to God's inexhaustible abundance.
Again, in all this, we have been discovering not only the potential of
music to generate invaluable resources for exploring particular doctrinal
areas, but also some of the reasons why music, under the grace of God,
appears to have been involved in the very salvific processes of which we
have been speaking, in the life, worship and witness of Christians.

5

Music, time and eternity

A God enthroned beyond time in timeless eternity would have to
renounce music . . . Are we to suppose that we mortals, in possessing
such a wonder as music, are more privileged than God? Rather, to save
music for him, we shall hold, with the Greeks, that God cannot go
behind time. Otherwise what would he be doing with all the choiring
angels?[1]

VICTOR ZUCKERKANDL

The whole purpose of sacred music must be to lead us to the threshold
of prayer or to the threshold of a true encounter with the living God.
An Ikon . . . is beyond art – a real presence that we venerate, looking
tenderly at us, helping us to pray, and lifting our minds and hearts
above this earth (where we are in exile for a short time) into Heaven,
our true 'Homeland'.[2]

JOHN TAVENER

To gain some clarity about the relationship between God's eternity
and created time is at once one of the most important and intractable
tasks of theology. In fact, we have been touching upon the matter repeatedly in the previous pages. Here my purpose is fairly modest: to show that
music has the capacity to play a valuable part in exposing and interpreting many of the most significant issues at stake, as well as advancing the
contemporary discussion of them.

Icons of eternity? – John Tavener

I want to begin by entering the sound-world of one composer whose music
brings questions of eternity and time very much to the fore. The spacious

---

1. Zuckerkandl (1956), 151.   2. Tavener, as quoted in Haydon (1995), 209.

and radiant compositions of John Tavener (b. 1944) have recently enjoyed huge popularity, especially since the premiere of *The Protecting Veil* in 1989 and the performance of his *Song for Athene* at Princess Diana's funeral service in 1997. The enthusiasm extends far beyond the devotees of 'classical music' – glowing reviews can be found in rock music magazines. In some ways, this success is an enigma. The lush harmonic extravagance of much of Tavener's music has, to say the least, not been prominent in the art-music tradition over the last few decades. More significantly, in a culture where it is often thought unwise for Christian composers to be very overt about their faith, Tavener is unashamedly open. Not only is his technique drawn to a large extent from the conventions and idioms of Orthodox church music, and not only does most of his music employ sacred texts, he often goes to great lengths to help the listener grasp its theological dimensions.[3]

Tavener provokes a variety of reactions. Some view his music as a route to eternity. The tenor Robert Tear has said: 'I really do think he's a great composer, responsible for a trend which is going to go right through art, where the spiritual quality will reassert itself.'[4] From the music-critical establishment, praise is not hard to find. Paul Driver wrote of his feelings at the end of the first performance of Tavener's monumental *The Apocalypse* (1993): 'It wasn't just relief that the ordeal of sitting was over, I believe, that gave one an alluring sense of the numinous at this point. Tavener's religious genius seemed nearly to achieve what Auden claimed poetry can never do: make something happen.'[5] Tavener himself believes that his music may well be tapping into a deep longing for the sacred in contemporary life, touching people at a level beyond and beneath emotion, will and intellect.[6] But he has his disparaging critics. Minds which thrive on aesthetic complexity distrust music so severely reduced and pared down. Is this anything more than an attempt to escape the buzzing, blooming confusion of post-industrial society's conflicting messages and communication systems? Robin Holloway, composer and lecturer, pronounces:

> I don't like it, I'm afraid. It's a lovely sound but it's so simple. What does it have to offer the musically literate? Every parameter has been drastically limited, so that what you have is ritual – repetitive simplicity. I think it's substitute religion, that's its appeal. At least Messiaen at his most vacant has a lot more content, gives the pure musician more to enjoy.[7]

3. He unashamedly calls his music 'liquid metaphysics'. See Begbie (1998), 20.
4. Quoted in Haydon (1995), 136.   5. Driver (1994), 21.
6. Ramsey (1989), 7. Tavener frequently alludes to Augustine's notion of the 'intellective organ of the heart'. See Begbie (1998), 18.   7. As quoted in Wood (1992), 19.

Others censure Tavener for his constant appropriation of religious themes. The composer John Bentley comments: 'I think he does a good line in ecstasy and makes some very nice noises . . . [But] I'm suspicious of ideas imported into music in this way.'[8]

Yet, despite the misgivings of some, as a critic recently reflected, 'on the evidence of recent record sales, Tavener's music, for all its religious demands, is beginning to rival that of Johann Strauss the Younger in popularity'.[9] And Tavener is no isolated phenomenon. The Polish composer Henryk Gorecki (b. 1933) and the Estonian Arvo Pärt (b. 1935) – the latter is someone to whom Tavener feels especially close – also write in a similar vein and are enjoying a vogue (as the 'holy minimalists') quite unparalleled by any other serious composers of the last forty years.

The most decisive twentieth-century influence on Tavener is the Russian composer Igor Stravinsky (1882–1971), himself a convert to Russian Orthodoxy. At the age of twelve, Tavener heard a broadcast of Stravinsky's *Canticum Sacrum* (1955). Its impact was considerable. The piece shows features which have become central to Tavener: a variety of textures; the coherence of the music with architecture (it was written specifically for St Mark's, Venice); palindrome (the final movement is a palindrome of the first)[10]; and the disciplined assimilation of a variety of styles (especially Byzantium, organum and Webern) into what Tavener calls a 'totally integrated synthesis'.[11] Perhaps most importantly, Stravinsky had drawn deep from the wells of ancient sacred music.

Tavener also owes much to the visionary sound-world and theological concerns of the French Roman Catholic Olivier Messiaen (1908–92). In Messiaen's music, he says, we find 'an impressive testimony of a sacred tradition in this century'.[12] The lusher side of Messiaen has greatly appealed to Tavener: 'In one sense,' he says, Messiaen 'stems from the saccharine school of nineteenth-century French organ music – half-way between the brothel and the Sacred Heart.'[13] But other elements of Messiaen were to have their impact: melodic arabesques, revolving harmonic patterns, a love of palindrome, and some currents in Roman Catholic mysticism. Tavener particularly underlines the impact of Messiaen on his own piece *In Alium* (written for a 1968 London Promenade concert).

The ghosts of Stravinsky and Messiaen can be sensed powerfully in a very dominant feature of Tavener's music – the construction of pieces

---

8. Ibid.   9. Driver (1994), 21.
10. A palindrome is the reversal of a musical sequence of some sort – e.g. ABC–CBA.
11. 'Sacred Music in the 20th Century', no page number.   12. Ibid.   13. Ibid.

around internally coherent blocks of musical material, connected only in very loose ways.

> This is evident in his early dramatic fantasy *The Whale* (1965–6), the work which put him on the musical map. Instead of a progressive dramatic unity, with evolving or organic development of motifs or themes, Tavener juxtaposes substantial blocks of music. Within the blocks, a sense of stasis predominates, especially in the supplicatory music, but also in the 'Storm' which is characterised not by wildness but by an ominous stillness.
>
> *Doxa* (1982) for double choir, exemplifies the same technique. The piece is in five massive blocks; the bass pedal notes, sung in each block by the first choir, together form the first five notes of a melody that constitutes the only material of the piece: the other voices of the first choir sing this melody (sometimes in retrograde) repeatedly at different speeds; the second choir follows in strict canon at a bar's distance. The details of the scheme are not as important as the sonorities of the five blocks, and, particularly, the silences between them.

One effect of this block construction is to quell the sense of goal-directed momentum. Sometimes, a sense of motionlessness seems to take over in a number of Tavener's early works, deriving from elements of the Catholicism which attracted him in the early 1970s. For example, drawing on the writings of St John of the Cross in *Coplas* (1970), there is a sustained attempt to still the perception of temporal motion.

> *Coplas* (1970) is scored for SATB soloists and sixteen–voice choir. The soloists share verses from St John of the Cross (1542–91) – 'an ecstasy experienced in high contemplation'. The singers in the choir are arranged in the shape of a cross and given homophonic music, softly passing the syllables of the 'Crucifixus' between them. Behind this are played pre-recorded extracts from the 'Crucifixus' of J. S. Bach's Mass in B minor. Towards the end, the live chorus drops out section by section, leaving only the taped music. In Tavener's words, Bach is allowed to 'put my music to sleep'.[14] The soloists chant a twelve-tone row derived from the opening notes of each vocal entry in the Bach movement.[15]

14. Ibid.
15. *Coplas* became the fifth and last movement of *Ultimos Ritos* (1972), an hour-long solemn meditation on the crucifixion and one's own death. Every note is derived from Bach's 'Crucifixus'. Intended for a large church or cathedral with at least six seconds reverberation, it employs a vast array of instrumental and choral forces: multiple choirs, nine trumpets, six recorders, organ, multiple brass and wind, strings and pre-recorded tape. Twelve-tone techniques and palindrome abound, but especially noteworthy are the striking sonorities, not least in the second movement in which twelve solo basses chant to the accompaniment of seven piccolo trumpets.

Undoubtedly the most momentous event in Tavener's musical and personal development was his conversion to Russian Orthodoxy in 1977. From now on, all his output becomes linked to this tradition (though by no means all of it is designed for liturgical use). Life-changing as it may have been, however, the shift to Orthodoxy did not entail radical discontinuity with his earlier work. Within the Orthodox world were musical streams which were already part of his lifeblood: shifting parallel chords, a sense of stasis, ornamented melody, the exploration of a building's acoustic, and a belief in the centrality of the human voice. These were all basic to Tavener by 1977, and after this date many of his early compositional devices were retained.

> For example, we find a general evasion of a developing musical argument, the widespread use of block structures, simple melodic and harmonic fragments in close proximity to or in combination with their inversions, the extensive use of stretto, retrograde motion and a host of symmetrical large-scale structures. One of his best-known works, *The Lamb* (1982), sung in churches and cathedrals all over the world, displays many of these features. (Its counterpart, *The Tyger* (1987) exhibits them all.)

It is not in the least puzzling, therefore, to find Tavener describing his move to Orthodoxy as 'a sensation of homecoming'.

Nevertheless, from 1977 a number of fresh emphases emerge. Two may be highlighted here. First, we find an increasing simplicity.[16] Comparing the sound-world of a work like *The Whale* (1965–6) with that of a recent piece like *Syvati* (1995) will quickly make the point, as will comparing the visual impact of a score from 1977 (Example 5.1) with one from 1987 (Example 5.2).

> During the late 1970s and early 1980s Tavener was still making use of twelve-tone rows, though not in a serial manner. Gradually the twelve-tone writing is superseded by techniques and chants derived from Orthodoxy.[17] (There was a similar critical turning-point in Arvo Pärt's career.) *Akhmatova: Requiem* (1979–80) demonstrates clearly the confrontation between twelve-tone writing and very simple tonal or modal material, within a symmetrical structure. The form of the piece as a whole is governed by a straightforward passacaglia-like usage of note-rows. There are insertions of orthodox prayers and chants from the

16. The beginning of a progression to extreme austerity was *Canticle of the Mother of God* (1977). This sets the Magnificat text, a solo soprano singing the Hebrew, the choir singing the Greek. Over a distant choral cushion, the soloist spins freewheeling, melismatic lines.
17. E.g. *Mandelion* (1981), for organ, coheres in relation to a twelve-note set derived from chant.

Orthodox Rite for the dead, and the influence of chant can be seen in
Tavener's own free writing.

Along with simpler scales and note-series, there is a gradual replacement
of the extrovert, leaping coloratura typical of the early seventies by the
small intervals and sustained singing characteristic of Orthodox chant.
The rhythmic palindromes of earlier years are often now set aside by the
rhythms of the Orthodox church. The tonal colour palette becomes more
restricted, much as an icon painter limits the range of colours.[18] More
important now than large instrumental or choral forces is evoking a sense
of 'space' and 'concept'. *The Protecting Veil* (1987) is designed to awaken an
ambience of cavernous space, but it is scored only for 'cello and string
orchestra. His *Ikon of Light* (1984) deals with an infinite concept (the
uncreated light of God) but the forces are small-scale: voices and string
trio.

> *Ikon of Light*, written for the Tallis Scholars, encapsulates most of the
> components of Tavener's mature style. Its overall plan is symmetrical –
> the first and second movements correspond to the sixth and seventh, the
> third to the fifth, and the fourth forms the centrepiece. The whole piece
> is steeped in large- and small-scale repetitions, and in long silences.

This scaling down is of enormous importance to Tavener. He is convinced
that complexity and evil are closely linked.[19] The simplifying process also
applies to the process of composition, which Tavener describes as 'an act
of repentance, stripping away of unessentials, ever more naked, ever more
simple . . . one might even say, ever more "*foolish*".'[20]

A second emphasis to emerge is an intensification of what we might
loosely call a contemplative ambience, in many cases achieved (at least in
part) through music of exceptional slowness. Such music is sometimes
dubbed 'iconic', a term Tavener is happy to use, for he speaks of his works
as 'icons of sound',[21] media through which eternity may in some manner
be brought to the ear. Tavener claims that his conversion to Orthodoxy
came through gazing at an icon.[22] 'The Ikon is the supreme example of
Christian art, and of Transcendence and Transfiguration.'[23] Many of his
titles reflect this: *Ikon of Light* (1984), *Ikon of St Cuthbert* (1986), and so forth.
In his large-scale work *We Shall See Him as He Is* (1990), virtually every
movement is given the title 'Ikon'. In the same vein, he has spoken of his
opera *Mary of Egypt* (1992) as a slow-moving icon.[24] His giant musical

18. The analogy is Tavener's (Garfield 1992, 18).   19. See Begbie (1998), 21.
20. 'The Sacred in Art', 88.   21. Garfield (1992), 17.   22. Ibid.
23. 'The Sacred in Art', 88.   24. Steinitz (1994).

Example 5.1 *Kyklike Kinesis* (p. 27), by John Tavener (1977)

Example 5.2 *God is With Us* (p. 1), by John Tavener (1987)

meditation on the Revelation to John, *The Apocalypse* (1993), is arranged as a series of 'Ikons'.

As already indicated, these two prominent marks of Tavener's mature work – its simplicity and its contemplative character – are achieved not only through devices he carried forward from his early pieces, but also through those of the Orthodox tradition, by far the most important of which is chant. One of the crucial musical experiences of his adult life was the discovery of Byzantine and Russian Znamenny chant,[25] and most of his works employ or adapt Orthodox chant to some extent, often with its chromatic and microtonal inflections. Along with chant goes the drone or *ison*, a long sustained note representing 'the eternal', sometimes lasting for an entire piece. Tavener speculates that the reason why some of his pieces have become so well accepted is that they are tapping into sounds which are rooted, ultimately, in eternity, in God. Chants and drones form a kind of 'umbilical cord' to the sacred[26] and music, he believes, should rediscover its sacred roots through chant. In addition to chants and drones Tavener also makes extensive use of *troparia*, short musical refrains, and hymns – the *kontakion* and later, the *kanon*.

Directionality, multiplicity, change and motion, beginnings and endings

We have already seen enough to be able to highlight features of Tavener's style which are very pertinent to conceptions of eternity and time. Either directly or indirectly, much of his work is concerned with an evocation of divine eternity (providing a 'window on God'[27]), and the eternity which is brought to sound appears to involve the avoidance, even the negation, of time: to be more precise, the restraint of directionality (as articulated through tension and resolution), multiplicity, change and motion, and the evasion of clearly defined beginnings and endings. We can look briefly at each of these in turn.

Undoubtedly, Tavener is writing music which in some respects coincides with the Western tonal tradition.

> Tavener can still employ, with modifications, major and minor chords, the twelve notes of the chromatic scale, conventional instruments associated

25. 'Sacred Music in the 20th Century', no page number.   26. Ibid.
27. Dunnett (1992), 20.

with tonal music, demarcated phrases, regular pulse, and hierarchical patterns of organisation. He has little time, now, for serialism, electronic music and the techniques often linked with 'atonality'.

But in other ways he stands apart from Western tonality. He has become increasingly dissatisfied with the trappings associated with tonal music – e.g. the symphony orchestra, concert halls, etc.[28] Not least, he eschews and subverts many of the artifices which give tonal music its characteristic *directionality* and goal-orientation.[29] He avoids patterns of irreversible tension and resolution. The kind of music which establishes a polemic, pursues conflict and reaches towards resolution holds little attraction for Tavener. (He tends to link this with what he sees as the baneful influence of the dominating ego of the 'humanist' tradition, which pervades Western musical life.[30]) Even on the small-scale level, implicatory tensions are kept to a minimum.[31] An extreme example is his relatively early piece *Celtic Requiem* (1969), which is, in essence, a twenty-minute elaboration of the chord of E flat major. In one of his more extreme pronouncements, Tavener declared: 'I dislike the way that *angst* got into music through

28. He laments the move of music from Church or temple into concert hall: 'the present-day concert-hall is an anomaly which must be annihilated if music is to survive. The Orthodox Church and her music presents that which is not human, but a [sic] divine and theanthropic: what is beyond yet among us' (Tavener 1997, no page number). At the same time he sees a positive side to the concert hall, for it enables sacred music to be heard in 'secular' settings.

29. After the first American performance of *The Protecting Veil* in New York, some attacked the piece for having 'lacked argument'. Geoffrey Haydon tells us that Tavener's stock answer to this kind of objection was to say that 'complaining about the absence of argument in John Tavener's music was as sensible as attacking Jane Austen's novels for failing to serve up violence. He also recommended a visit to a Russian Orthodox Church' (Haydon 1995, 268).

30. Tavener wants to understand composition in its ideal form not as the struggle of a composer with ideas, or with materials, but a process in which God is allowed maximum freedom and space. Indeed, it is a form of prayer. He sees this as consonant with what he calls 'The Sacred Tradition' and links it with his appropriation of Augustine's conception of the 'intellective organ of the heart'. He interprets this as making possible an apprehension in which we understand not by the mind, nor by the heart alone, 'but by the mind that has extinguished the ego, and descended into the heart'. Speaking of a period after serious illness, he reflects on the remarkable steady and unimpeded 'flow' of music from him: 'the "ego" or the "John Tavener" had been torn to shreds, and something other, something new, something that had always existed but heard for the first time was coming to birth' (Tavener 1997, no page number). This leads Tavener to make some extreme statements about other traditions in which, as he views it, the composer's ego, especially the composer's mind, obtrudes.

31. Interestingly, the music critic Paul Driver comments: 'For me, the best Tavener works are those in which his religious austerity and aesthetic fervour are held in electric tension; for instance, the spectacular Bach-inspired *Ultimos Ritos* of 1972 or the dramatically thrilling *Akhmatova: Requiem* of 1980. In his works of the past decade, however, *tension of any sort is largely eschewed*; the fervour is entirely religious; the austerity no longer a dramatic gesture but a pre-condition of the only kind of art that Tavener now recognises: icon-making' (Driver 1994, 21). My italics.

psychology at the turn of the century. I think the composer should deal with his *angst* in the composing room, not in the score.'[32]

Typical of his pieces are symmetrical structures; not *strictly* symmetrical structures – for that would mean the almost impossible reversal of every parameter of the music, including the attack and decay of notes – but structures in which symmetrical arrangement is pursued to a much greater extent than in most tonal music. His liking for relatively discrete blocks of internally uniform and self-contained material also testifies to the suppression of directionality. There is sometimes a directional flow connecting the blocks – one leading to, or pointing ahead towards another – but one often has the sense that the sections could be juxtaposed in any order. Even when sections are not self-contained, repetition or internal allusion is not usually functioning to resolve (or increase) tension.[33] There is sometimes climax-building – for example, through blocks of music, each of relatively uniform volume, repeated at different pitches and/or volumes – but this is very different from the implicatory dynamic which is so basic to Western tonality. Tavener's music is more akin to the increase and decrease of light intensity than the winding-up and release of a clock-spring.

The second restraint – that of *multiplicity* – we have already spoken about at length. It is one of the most notable marks of his music over the last twenty years. The third, however – the suppression of *change and motion* – requires further comment. The word 'stasis' is often used rather loosely to describe music of extreme stillness or repose. And the word

---

32. Quoted in Wood (1992), 18. There are pieces and passages which evoke tears and sorrow: the loss of his own mother is sensed in *Eis Thanaton* (1986). It was written in memory of her and consists of a setting of Andreas Kalvos' 'Ode to Death'. Tavener remarks on the effect of his serious illness in 1980: 'I am aware since then, of a greater simplicity and a more canonical and iconographical approach to my work' ('Sacred Music in the 20th Century', no page number). In an interview he explains that 'it was necessary to go through the experience I went through of nearly dying . . . in order for certain aspects of my life to become clear' (Garfield 1992, 32). It is significant that the text of *Akhmatova: Requiem* has strong political undertones of protest, but these are ignored by Tavener who chose the text primarily for its expressive qualities and because it was so adaptable to his liturgical sympathies. 'He was neither unaware of, nor unreceptive to, the element of protest in the poem, but his purpose in setting it was entirely spiritual' (Phillips 1983, 30).
33. Kramer calls such musical structure, following Stockhausen, 'moment form' (J. Kramer 1988, ch. 8). Stravinsky and Messiaen are the key characters in the wings here. Stravinsky's highly sophisticated *Symphonies of Wind Instruments* (1920) consists of mosaic-like self-contained sections presented in conjunction with more traditional goal-directed procedures. See J. Kramer (1988), ch. 9. Messiaen I speak about below. Karlheinz Stockhausen (b. 1928) – whose music and vision Tavener attacks as 'megalomaniac', betraying an 'aberrant spirituality' ('Sacred Music in the 20th Century', no page number) – can himself sometimes speak in similar ways to Tavener, though he has generally been motivated by a more oriental metaphysics.

'timelessness' is often yoked to it, along with 'eternity'. But it is important to be a little more precise. Total stasis, is, of course, impossible to achieve, whether in music or anywhere else. Music takes time to happen. It is normally understood as involving the succession of at least two notes. And as long as we are alive, we cannot freeze up our mental processes in any act of perception. Talk of stasis can only be shorthand for various degrees of *approximation* to the cessation of change and motion – in the music and/or in our perception of it. In Tavener's case this is most often pursued through music of a very slow tempo with a relatively uniform texture, and with an erasure (or near erasure) of regular pointed accent or pulse. The sense of changelessness and motionlessness is sometimes heightened indirectly through juxtaposing such music alongside strongly contrasting sections.[34]

Fourth, clearly delineated *beginnings and endings*, framed by strong opening and closing gestures, may be common in Western tonal music but are not in Tavener. Frequently the music emerges out of silence and drifts seamlessly back into silence, giving the impression of being in the midst of previously (and subsequently) unheard music. This too is often explicitly linked to the evocation of eternity. The fact that his beginnings are like processes and that his endings simply give way relates to his belief that the music of eternity sounds inaudibly 'before' the arrival of earthly sound and 'after' its cessation.

Parallels and forebears

Comparison with Tavener's mentor, Messiaen, is instructive here, especially since the latter's techniques were so strongly shaped by theological convictions. It was common for Messiaen to suspend the sense of time in music (except in those works which are based on birdsong in relation to nature), in order to express the idea of the 'eternal' – in which time does not exist – as distinct from the temporal.[35] Speaking of harmony, the manner in which Messiaen combines sounds, Robert Sherlaw Johnson explains that 'traditional symphonic procedure arose from a harmonic practice which depended on progression and on the tensions and relaxations created by the principle of dissonance and resolution'. This is not

---

34. It should be noted that not all of Tavener's music is characterised by slowness. There are some sections of his music, which swirl in a kind of rapture of motion (e.g. passages in *The Repentant Thief* (1990)). Yet even in cases like this, there will be little sense of progression and direction.   35. J. Kramer (1988), 214.

so in the case of Messiaen, which 'lends his music a static rather than dynamic quality, *his harmony existing in a state which is neither tension nor relaxation – the mood of the moment is captured and transfixed in a timelessness which is implied by the structure of the music itself*'.[36] Like Tavener, Messiaen wrote many works which deploy 'sectional' form, and he was strongly drawn to symmetrical structures. Moreover, '[i]nstead of a metre, which gives each moment in the bar a different significance and hence fosters a sense of orderly progression, Messiaen's music is most frequently tied to a pulse, which insists that all moments are the same, that the past, the present, and the future are identifiable. Sometimes the pulse is so slow that causal links are sufficiently distended not to be felt … But Messiaen's presto toccatas can be equally removed from any progressive experience of time: the race is around a circle joined by repetition (repetition of pulse, repetition of structural unit) in an ecstasy of stasis.'[37] There are important dissimilarities between Tavener and Messiaen. Messiaen's pursuit of simplicity is much less marked than Tavener, his rhythmic configurations are more often set over a clearly defined pulse and are generally more complex, the range of his musical sources is very much wider, and his output as a whole displays a greater variety of technique.[38] And, although it would be unwise to press too far the links between Messiaen's music and his vision of eternity, it would seem to be an eternity with much more room for movement than Tavener is prepared to allow. Nevertheless, the general posture towards created time, as far as it can be understood from his music and his own spoken and written reflections, bears more than a passing resemblance to that of Tavener. This is a decidedly negative attitude, especially inasmuch as time implies processes with direction.[39] And

36. Johnson (1989), 13. My italics.
37. Griffiths (1985b), 15f.
38. Indeed, one of the engaging aspects of Messiaen's work is the way in which he can combine strikingly different structural techniques – static block form and sonata form, for example – even within single pieces. See J. Kramer (1988), 213ff.; Johnson (1989), 22ff.
39. In the course of a description of his organ masterpiece *Méditations sur le mystère de la Sainte Trinité* (1969), Messiaen writes: 'Then comes eternity: God is eternal; he has neither beginning nor end nor succession. I treated this notion like a glittering flash of colour. God is immutable, which is to say, no change can occur in him' (Messiaen 1994, 126). His chamber piece *Quatuor pour la fin du Temps* (1940), bears the inscription: 'in homage to the Angel of the Apocalypse, who raises his hand heavenwards saying: "There will be no more Time."' (The reference is to Rev. 10:6.) Interestingly, the phrase 'end of time' has a double meaning for Messiaen: not only the end of created time in heaven, but the end of musical time based on the durational divisions of classical music (Johnson 1989, 61f). 'There is … no thrust from one movement into the next … the movements are comparatively indifferent as to order', thus undermining any large-scale sense of temporal succession. Supporting this, the work is in some parts 'more blatantly symmetrical than anything outside his own output' (Griffiths 1985b, 100, 101). There is also a dislocation of pulse and

his conception of the eschaton, the world's destiny in God's eternity, though not motionless, seems to be one which turns on the negation of time rather than, say, its fulfilment.

Further light can be thrown on Tavener by setting his work against the broader horizon of some other twentieth-century experiments in musical temporality. His propensity towards what we might call 'the spatialisation of time' is characteristic of a significant stream of composers, stretching back at least as far as Debussy and including such diverse figures as Mahler, Varèse, Stravinsky and Stockhausen. Musical space is constituted by pitch, timbre and volume – it is these elements which distinguish simultaneous musical phenomena.[40] In most music of the Western tonal tradition, these are subordinate to temporal patterns of tension and resolution. In Tavener, the spatial aspects of music become, or tend to become, ends in themselves. Sound is, at least to a considerable extent, explored for its own sake in relative independence from temporal factors. And much twentieth-century music travelled a similar path. Indeed, one way of reading the advent of 'atonal' music in the twentieth century is as a reversal of the dominant relationship between time and space to be found in most tonal music.

> In the art-music tradition, by the end of the nineteenth century, tonality, especially in the Germanic world, was in a state of exhaustion, 'burdened by an overextended harmonic vocabulary which was no longer solely dependent on simple triads and their functions or related melodic motions'.[41] 'Atonality' was already a living force in music by

the compression of history (a mixture of styles from different periods). The fifth and eighth movements directly concern eternity, the former a homage to Jesus as the eternal Word of God ('Louange à l'Éternité de Jésus') and the latter a homage to Jesus as Man, risen to immortality ('Louange à l'Immortalité de Jésus'). Both are extremely slow. The fifth movement is marked 'Infinitely slow' and involves the gradual removal of chromatic elements from a very simple fundamental pentatonic scale. Here the harmony is in essence very straightforward, and in most Western music that would mean one could well move faster (speed and harmonic complexity vary inversely in most tonal music). But here harmonic simplicity is combined with exceptional slowness. The long delay of the end is felt to be worth it, so to speak, because of the gradual disappearance of the chromatic disturbances of the opening. Messiaen's purpose here, according to Paul Griffiths, was 'to give the impression of changelessness while all the time there is change, to make an image of blessed eternity that is still intelligible to minds existing in the present world.' (ibid., 102). (In fact, Messiaen radically misreads Rev. 10:6, for the verse does not speak of the end of time. The vast majority of exegetes and translations understand it as saying: 'there will be no more time left before God completes his purposes'.)
40. We have already touched upon these matters in the introduction (see above, pp. 23ff). See Zuckerkandl (1956), 267–362; Morgan (1980); Rochberg (1984), 78–136. One important example of the spatialisation of musical time is notation, in which temporal sequence is presented on a two-dimensional surface which can be scanned in a similar way to a picture.
41. Rochberg (1984), 105.

1915 (though the term 'atonal' is highly problematic[42]). The twelve-tone method proposed by Arnold Schoenberg (1874–1951) was in part an attempt to solve the difficulties posed by the abandonment of tonality. Pitch relationships were organised according to non-hierarchical and non-functional harmonic principles. Even here, however, the musical phrase, related to metre, was not abandoned, though it became more supple and asymmetrical. Anton Webern (1883–1945), however, severely reduced the significance of phrases and metre: a tendency towards the 'single note', the loss of evident melodic shape and a penchant for structural symmetry led to music in which 'The beat and metre is . . . a frame, not a process – a frame on which to construct symmetries of pitch and rhythm.'[43] Now there is no 'moving from' and 'proceeding towards'. The metrical beat becomes merely a reference point: it assumes a mechanical function by means of which a structure can be temporally 'spread out'. In effect, Webern prepared the way for the emergence of pointillism and similar techniques, in which metre and recognisable phrases are abandoned altogether.[44]

As a result, 'a unique phenomenon occurred for the first time in music: sound, as concrete musical space, emerged as an independent structural force, no longer subject to periodicity; and duration, formerly embodied in the growth process of periodicity, emerged in a totally new role'.[45] In such music, time becomes no more than durational proportion, having no relation to metrical waves, or harmonic tension and resolution. Musical time, having first become separated from musical space, is, as it were, suppressed by it. To use Rochberg's categories, this is the music of 'space-time' as opposed to 'time-space':

> The prototype *time-space* generates dynamic architectural forms in which duration as passage shapes the course of the events in the musical discourse along a structurally continuous axis. The prototype *space-time* generates forms in which spatial projection, freed from the dynamism of rhythmic periodicity, occurs in unpredictable patterns, occupying a time structure which stands outside the propulsive influence of the beat and metric pulse. An essentially static structure is the end result, verified by aural perception.[46]

Numerous illustrations of this from the last hundred years could be cited.[47] To describe such music as 'timeless' would be inaccurate, for in

42. Norton (1984), 231f., 263.   43. Rochberg (1984), 111.
44. For a fuller account of these developments, see e.g. Norton (1984), chs. 10, 11.
45. Rochberg (1984), 105.   46. Ibid., 117. My italics.
47. See Morgan (1977, 1980); Rochberg (1984), 125ff.

many cases there are musical events of different durations, and events of different volume or timbre, and therefore at least the suggestion of temporal distinction between more and less significant events. However, the process can been taken to much further extremes, such that any impression of distinct past and distinct future is resolutely subdued. The entire essence of a piece may be one of near-unchanging consistency, in which no event is privileged over any other. Jonathan Kramer dubs this 'vertical time' music, in which, supposedly, past and future are denied in favour of an 'extended present'. Everything presses towards undifferentiated, equilibrial homogeneity. Vertical time music may be constituted by process as well as by stasis. Pieces such as Steve Reich's *Come Out* (1966) involve rapid internal motion: 'The result is a single present stretched out into an enormous duration, a potentially infinite "now" that nonetheless feels [or can feel] like an instant.'[48] The claim among some is that such pieces can induce in the sympathetic listener (one who does not attempt to project teleological order and succession into the music) a lack of awareness of any distinction between past, present and future; an 'eternal now' similar to that state achieved through the use of certain drugs.[49]

It may well be that some of this could be related to earlier observations we made about the theological aspects of modernity's unease with time. But here we are concerned with Tavener's location within this broad proclivity. He too shares an avoidance or suppression of directionality. Also characteristic is the exploration of musical space as intrinsically interesting in itself. This Tavener accomplishes through skilful manipulation of pitch-, timbre- and volume-differences. Spatial language can be prominent in Tavener's commentary on his own work. The drive towards simplicity and the suppression of change and motion contribute to a downplaying of time in favour of space. On the other hand, the suppression of temporal distinction is rarely taken to the extremes we find in 'vertical time' music. Further, most of Tavener's pieces will contain some kind of pulse (even if not metre), many are built around demarcated phrases, some contain hierarchical features, and some have very strong contrasts between constituent sections.

What distinguishes Tavener above all from most of the others in this stream is that the restraint of directionality, plurality, change and motion is carried out for specifically *theological* reasons. It has become common to

---

48. J. Kramer (1988), 55; see also 375–97. Other examples include Philip Glass's *Music in Twelve Parts* (1974), John Cage and Lejaren Hiller's *HPSCHD* (1969), and Iannis Xenakis' *Bohor I* (1962).   49. J. Kramer (1988), ch. 12.

claim that a composer's intention is at best irrelevant and at worst obstruc-
tive to musical analysis; as Tom Wright has put it, 'the road to hell is paved
with authorial intention'.[50] But the fact remains that since Tavener's conversion to Orthodoxy, virtually all of his music has issued directly from
this spiritual environment: quite literally every note he writes stems from
his aspiration to produce 'liquid metaphysics'. Without pretending that
his theological convictions can provide a total 'explanation' of his work, to
ignore them totally, in addition to being somewhat perverse, would be to
deny ourselves the opportunity which his music affords to open out crucial theological issues with respect to eternity and time.

Comments and questions

I am not competent to judge the extent to which Tavener is being faithful to
Orthodox theologies of time and eternity. But, in commenting on Tavener,
I do want to address two areas of theological concern. The first is to do with
this music's cultural context. I have already cited those, such as David Harvey, who would see temporal disorientation as crucial to the postmodern
sensibility, generated by 'time-space compression'.[51] If there is any force in
this, it may be that Tavener offers a kind of musical de-compression, an
aural 'space' amidst a temporally compressed culture, a stable place, in
which we are not shoved and driven from 'here' to 'there'. And in a society
overloaded with multiple and contradictory communication systems and
messages, he provides a simple space – unified and relatively undifferentiated. This, I believe, may well point to a significant factor behind the economic success of his music: our culture's inability to live peaceably with
time. And if so, while being cautious about the somewhat inflated claims
which he and others have made about this music tapping into the 'sacred'
in some privileged and direct way, we might nevertheless propose that one
of the benefits of this music is its provision of a cool cathedral, so to speak,
in a hot, rushed and overcrowded town. It offers a challenge and alternative
to the destructive, distracting and alienating busy-ness which is so much a
mark of our culture and, surely, far from what God intends.

The second area for comment concerns God's eternity and eternity's
relation to time. Here my remarks are more critical. As I have said a
number of times, music does not translate into anything like straightforward statements, theological or otherwise, capable of evaluation and

---

50. Wright (1992), 55.   **51.** See above, pp. 73f.

criticism. This makes doctrinal critique of music a hazardous business. There are indeed dangers, especially in the case of music, of leaning to heavily on 'authorial intention'.[52] Nonetheless, insofar as this music is presented (by Tavener and others) as offering a sonic approximation to eternity, it would appear to be an eternity construed largely in terms of the *negation of time*. The point can be expanded through asking some pointed questions, closely related to each other. First – and this links up especially with our discussion in chapter 3 – is there an adequate recognition that eternity, God's own life, has been made known decisively through *an engagement and interaction with the created world, in a history, climaxing in the history of Jesus Christ, in which God confirms the created goodness and reality of the world's temporality?* There seems more than a hint in Tavener of the idea that the more deeply we relate to God, the more we will need to abstract ourselves from time, develop an immunity to time's opportunities and threats. Is sufficient weight being given to the time-implicated character of God's self-giving, the embeddedness of salvation in trajectories of promise and fulfilment, waiting, patience, delay? Second, is there due attention to the conviction that God's eternity has been enacted through a human life which has embraced our *fallen humanity*, including the experiences of deprivation, fear, anxiety, hunger, loss, frustration and disappointment, and that these have themselves been drawn into, indeed, become the very material of salvation? In Tavener, the cool cathedral is in danger of bearing little relation to the sordid life on the streets. Third, is there sufficient concern for the way in which God's eternity has been opened up through a particular and ugly *death*? If the cross truly is the 'wisdom of God' (1 Cor. 1:18–25), the icon of Golgotha cannot be erased from any truly Christian conception of God's eternity and our participation in it. Indeed all conceptions of the eternity–time relationship must pass through the cross. To be fair, Tavener sees himself in a tradition which views Good Friday as integrally linked to Easter: 'It is symptomatic of Western tradition that it stops at the image of the murdered Man and few go beyond. Perhaps that image has done more evil because of the concentration for so many years on the murdered Man rather than on the Resurrected one . . . [In the Eastern tradition] we never speak of the

---

52. Even in the case of literary texts, 'authorial intention' needs to be nuanced with considerable care: see the subtle discussion of meaning as 'communicative action' in Vanhoozer (1998), especially ch. 5. Owing to music's relatively weak referential power (to which we have alluded a number of times), determining 'meaning' (in anything like Vanhoozer's carefully qualified sense) is a far harder and more complex business than in the case of most literary texts.

Crucifixion without the Resurrection.'[53] For Tavener, everything must come under the 'glow' of the resurrection.[54] But the issue is whether eternity is linked sufficiently to 'the descent into hell' such that there can be no talk of the former (and no resurrection) without the latter. Fourth, questions need to be asked of *the vision of the eschaton* suggested and evoked by Tavener. For it seems to sit uneasily alongside the New Testament vista of the re-creation of the temporal and fallen world, the final participation of created reality in the eternity of God. In *The Apocalypse* (1993), we are offered magnificent musical sound-images of the book of Revelation, but the piece ends on one simple, single note (the 'eternity note') which fades into silence. The eternity of Revelation is one of multiplicity, activity and abundance – the new earth and the new heaven, complete with heavenly city (Rev. 21, 22). Tavener's eschaton appears to entail a divine eternity of absolute simplicity, and the negation of temporality; the same cannot be said of the writer of Revelation. Nor can it easily be said of any other New Testament author for that matter. What is the congruence, for example, between Tavener's 'one note' and what the writer to the Ephesians describes as the 'gathering up' of all things in Christ (Eph. 1:10)? The problem here, I suggest, is not only Tavener's assumption about a necessary link between multiplicity and evil, but an eclipsing of the biblical stress on time as intrinsic to the goodness of creation and integral to the purposes of God for that same creation. (And even if it were claimed that God's eternity itself, considered apart from time and the eschaton, could be represented as one 'note', how could this be consonant with the irreducibly trinitarian character of God?)

Of course, no theologically inspired music can hope to cover the full gamut of the Christian faith, and certainly not single pieces. And, to repeat, Tavener's music does offer a welcome respite from the worst of fallen and alienating temporalities, and as far as it does this it is surely to be welcomed. But my point here is that, inasmuch as this is construed as a musico-theological vision, we find an evasion and even an obscuring of the belief that God's eternity has been made known and accessible through a redemption which has integrally involved created time.

Christ's time and ours

This discussion of Tavener has enabled us to clarify some of the crucial matters at stake in attempting to explicate the nature of God's eternity

---

53. Ramsey (1989), 7.   54. Begbie (1998), 20.

and eternity's relation to time. Is it possible for music to offer something more adequate to God's involvement with the temporal, created order, especially to the pivotal events of Good Friday and Easter?

Tavener is deeply pessimistic about Western tonality's theological possibilities. But, if our findings in the previous chapters are anything to go by, we need not be so suspicious. However, the potential of the tradition will only be properly seen when something of a theological reorientation takes place, specifically towards the divine sharing and reinstatement of our temporality in Jesus Christ.

This brings what has been implicit in much of the previous chapters to a head: created time, we are affirming, has in some sense been enfolded, judged, broken and re-fashioned in Jesus Christ, and our final destiny is nothing other than to participate fully in this redeemed temporality. Even the metrical wave picture we have been deploying falls badly short here. As with one-level linear models of time, it could lead us to overlook (a) the ontological decisiveness of Christ as the one in whose history the temporal world has 'once and for all' found its fulfilment in God's eternity, and therefore (b) the epistemological decisiveness of Christ for comprehending the character and significance of time and its relation to eternity. To lean too heavily on our wave model could lead us to treat Christ as merely 'another' event, another moment in a sequence of wave patterns. Christology would thus be in danger of becoming *determined by* prior conceptions of temporality rather than being *determinative of* all our thinking about temporality.

I have already suggested that the Christian conviction about the reality and goodness of time is grounded ultimately in the coming of the eternal Son in Jesus Christ. This has taken place not in a manner tangential to the world's temporality, nor through the insertion of a 'block' of eternity into our time (such as to 'push aside' our temporality), but through a respectful engagement with creation *including its temporality*, the temporality which was brought into being 'in' Christ, 'through' him and 'for' him (Col. 1:16).

Let us unfold this further, drawing upon what we have learned about music. The temporality in which music occurs is subject to a disruption between the temporal modes, past, present and future. It stands under the shadow of the fall and the promise of redemption. Though it has not been allowed to slip into sheer chaos and nothingness, created time has nevertheless become 'refracted time, time that has broken loose from God'.[55]

---

55. T. F. Torrance (1976), 97.

There is a myriad of ways in which this is experienced. We have already spoken of some of the modern and postmodern pathologies of time. As far as our past is concerned, perhaps the most basic experience of 'refracted time' is an acute awareness of the loss of what is good: destructive transience.[56] The past appears irrevocably behind us, gone for ever:

> For us the past is the time we leave and are in no longer. It was once ours. We had our life in it years ago or even this morning. In it we made our contribution to history. In it we were then ourselves. But we are so no longer. For, with all that filled or did not fill it, it has now eluded us and been taken from us. It has remained behind never to be restored.[57]

Our memory at best is limited in its powers of retention, so that 'even what we recall soon sinks back into oblivion'.[58] We can, of course, know a past which we wish would disappear but does not – the past which condemns and haunts, the tragedy of the past we long to forget but cannot. But the root difficulty here is still one of loss. The particular agony of the guilty memory, for example, resides in the permanent and increasing inaccessibility of the past event: it can never be grasped in order to be altered, lived again differently. Further, temporal refraction affects our future orientation: our future becomes apparently impenetrable, and thus engenders the fear that to step into the future is to step into a void. (The filling of the future in anticipation is a common but dangerous way of dealing with this, pouring energy into hopes which may well be dashed.) Furthermore, poised between future and past, as Augustine so agonisingly sensed, lies the seemingly durationless 'present', perilously insecure, midway between ungraspable past and unfathomable future. Something like this is arguably near the heart of many if not most pathologies of time – the temporal modes are experienced as alienated from one another, in contradiction and strife, they are not in mutual peace: 'beginning, middle and end are distinct and even opposed as past, present and future'.[59]

Such is the time in which music occurs. And such is the time Jesus of Nazareth shared: the Son of God inhabits this time with us as one of us, as part of God's determination to reconcile our time to his eternity.

We have seen that music is capable of offering an 'interpenetrating' temporality, in which, because of a complex hierarchy of waves of tension and resolution, we are given not an evaporating present but a present through which past is directed towards future, in which a past

---

56. See above, p. 93.   57. Barth (1960a), 512.   58. Ibid., 513.
59. Barth (1957), 608.

occurrence does not retreat into an ever-receding and unreal 'beyond', and in which future occurrences are not totally unknowable or unreal but can, in various ways, be intuited now. The 'reality' we experience at any one 'moment' in music is not exhausted by those phenomena which can be said to exist 'now'. Christian theology dares to speak of an inter-penetrating temporality made possible and accessible through what has happened on Good Friday and on Easter Day. Golgotha speaks of eterni-ty's submission to the 'ever-older' time, to the dis-integration of the temporal modes, ultimately to death. Here the past of Jesus and his future are threatened with non-being, in the abysmal, ruptured and silent 'present' of Holy Saturday. Here the old Adam dies. Here the old world dies. Here dissipated and corrupted finitude is taken into the heart of God. In the resurrection of the crucified Christ, a kind of tempo-rality is established in which the destructive alienation of fallen time is overcome, in which there is no growing old. To speak of the resurrection is to speak of an occurrence, *the* occurrence, whose newness does not pass away; here is an event which does not fall back into an ever more distant remoteness, which does not run into dark forgetfulness or some vacuity of permanently lost events. In contrast to all merely worldly innovations, novelties and revolutions, the resurrection is utterly free from fading decay. And in this respect the resurrection establishes and anticipates the time of the eschaton, the end-times, in which there is no temporal fragmentation and nothing ever becomes old but is always new. More than this, we are witnessing here the fulfilment not only of the hypostatic union between humanity and God but of the union between the whole creation and the Creator. The resurrection marks the climactic fulfilment of God's intentions for *all* creation. All times are thus limited and determined by their proximity to the time of the risen Christ.

The risen Christ's time is properly considered to be the most fully true and authentic time. Thus, as Jüngel reminds us, the resurrection radical-ises our understanding of the created world's temporality: 'The occur-rence of something unsurpassably new which does not grow old, but rather remains *new for all time*, is completely out of joint with the popular understanding of time.'[60] Insofar as we are speaking of the life of Christ as his eternal life, we cannot separate past, present and future abstractly, but must consider them first of all as mutually co-inhering in him in such a

60. Jüngel (1995), 53.

way that the alienation and disruption which is characteristic of fallen time is healed. This does not mean that the historicity of Christ's earthly life is now (to us) of no account, or not fully real – for the risen Christ is indissolubly connected to that particular history; his 'lordship' over time implicates and includes it. Yet he is not encapsulated or contained by it; he both negates its corruption and reconstitutes its goodness within the life of God.

But what of our participation, as fallen creatures, in Christ's time? As we have said a number of times, in musical experience, we can enjoy a temporality which is in some measure incongruous with the extra-musical time(s) which we inhabit in our day to day lives. Something is happening which at its best might be described as music 'taking' our time and 'returning it' to us re-shaped in some manner. To share in music is to find a temporality in which – at least to some extent – past, present and future have been made to interweave fruitfully.

This 'taking' and 'returning' process can happen not only *between* a piece of music and the temporalities in which it is experienced and known, it can also happen – and often does – *within* a piece of music. We saw a pointed example of this in Beethoven's last string quartet.[61] But there are hundreds of examples of music which, within its own textures, engages with much more fractured and dislocated temporalities, re-moulding and healing them. A recent one is James MacMillan's *The Confessions of Isobel Gowdie* (1990), where a sonic nightmare is progressively healed and transformed by, among other things, Gregorian chant. Now internationally acclaimed, MacMillan is one of the leading overtly Christian composers of our day. His aesthetic contrasts sharply with Tavener's, centring much more on the three days of crucifixion and resurrection. MacMillan feels compelled, primarily *for theological reasons*, to integrate conflict into his work: 'I think that a lot of so-called spiritual music can be a monodimensional experience without the sense of sacrifice . . . I am drawn by the sacrificial aspect of the great Christian narrative, and I seem to be going round and round in circles round the same three days in history. The fact is that if history had to be changed – if *we* had to be changed – then God had to interact with us in a severe way. You can't have the Resurrection without the Crucifixion . . . the best stories are ones which have resolutions of conflict, not just resolution.'[62]

The process of salvation can be conceived along just these lines, as an

---

61. See above, pp. 114ff.   62. As quoted in Mitchell (1999), 19.

ongoing healing of our time through participation in the temporality established in Jesus Christ. The Church might be said to inhabit two temporal continua, the broad continuum of 'this passing world' and that of the new aeon which has already overtaken us in Christ (Christ's ascension underlining for us now the fact that the two have by no means yet found their correspondence, except in Christ). And while we live in both times, our redemption turns on the ongoing transformation of our time(s) by Christ's time. This occurs through the Holy Spirit, who enables a sharing in Christ's time in the midst of the world's dysfunctional and distorted temporalities. To take part in the temporality of the risen Christ through the Spirit is to discover an interweaving of the temporal modes. We discover that we were loved 'then' also, our past is real in Christ's eyes and God's eyes (Ps. 139:16). Our past 'not only was real but is real. It is not lost. It has not escaped us or ceased to be. It is as genuinely ours as our being in the present and future.'[63] To share in the 'redeemed time' of the risen Christ through the Spirit means there can be a 'looking back' with thankfulness – 'Forget not all his benefits' (Ps. 103:2) – but this is not a wistful longing, nor an attempt to transport what was into the now, but an act of gratitude flowing from a sense that the benefits of the past, remembered now, anticipate the future.[64] And *the* 'benefit' is Christ's own death and his risen life among us mediated by the Spirit. Moreover, since Christ's temporality is the temporality of the *eschaton*, the temporality which will mark the new heaven and the new earth, accessible now through the Spirit, we may agree with Pannenberg that 'It is possible to see all time-bridging duration, and all experiences of it in the flux of time, as an anticipation of the eschatological future of a participation of creatures in the eternity of God.'[65]

Far from abstracting us *out of* time, the vision opened up by music in this way is one in which to be 'saved' is, among other things, to be given

---

63. Barth (1960a), 537.

64. 'This future [of the new age] was already the benefit of yesterday. By its very nature it cannot be a thing of yesterday . . . It cannot, then, be the object of a sorrowful looking backwards' (Barth 1957, 628).

65. Pannenberg (1991), 410. There is of course a negative aspect to all this. Christ, as the eschaton, is competent to judge our past, for he is the telos of creation in relation to whom all will find their true telos. To share in the time of the risen Christ is to enter a sphere of judgement, in which our distorted, sinful nature comes under condemnation, and this judgement entails the possibility of eternal loss at the eschaton. The eschaton, achieved through Good Friday and Easter, determines whether something has a temporal future or an eternal future. Music offers little help in explicating this, given its tendency towards 'binding' past, present and future, except in perhaps relatively trivial ways – themes and motifs are sometimes not repeated or taken up; and music is followed by silence (though, as we have seen, even this need not be seen simply as cessation and void).

new resources for living 'peaceably' *with* time. There are obvious links here with a fairly vigorous body of theological writing on human identity and vocation. In contrast to conceptions of human personhood which trade on notions of quasi-timeless 'essences', the importance of time and narrative for the formation of identity has been underlined and explored extensively by Paul Ricoeur, Hans Frei, George Lindbeck, Anthony Thiselton and others. Some of this is Christologically oriented to a high degree. For example, Thiselton, after a forceful argument against some postmodernist construals of the self, especially those which would advocate 'instantaneousness' as a privileged vantage point, and thus create 'insoluble problems about meaning, identity, self and God', concludes that '"*who we are*" *emerges in terms of God's larger purposes and promises for the world, society, for the church and for us*. This purposive anticipation of the future finds expression in our sense of *being called by God to a task within that frame*. We find our identity and meaning when we discover our *vocation*.'[66] Thiselton has also pointed to the ways in which this finds substantial exegetical support in the New Testament, for example in Hebrews and 1 Corinthians.[67] Here we would want to point to not only the potential of music to help us comprehend these temporalities through concrete demonstration and experience, but also its potential to be taken up into the process of shaping a mature Christian identity.[68]

Matters may be taken a stage further, albeit very tentatively, by linking these reflections with the trinitarian ontology of God. Karl Barth is one of a number who wish to link a vision of redemption as the integrating of past, present and future in Christ with the dynamic interrelatedness

---

66. Thiselton (1995), 151.
67. In the Epistle to the Hebrews, the paradigm of humanness is exhibited and fulfilled in Jesus Christ in a way which is irreducibly temporal. Christ is himself set in the context of an 'ongoing temporal narrative' in which promise and covenant (temporally grounded and understood) are prominent. The purposive history of the prophets, Moses and Joshua, the Psalmists, the heroes of the faith (now 'ahead' of us) provide the frame in which Jesus himself is presented. There is a contrast and narrative continuity between the 'prophets' who mediated revelation 'in various ways' (1:1) and Jesus who is the climax, the decisive and definitive revelation 'in these last days' (1:2). Hope is the 'anchor' (6:19), grounded in what God promised with an oath (6:17), and this stands in contrast to the tendency of human beings to 'drift' (2:1–4). Christ himself joins us in a frail, temporal pilgrimage. Human identity is forged in his own humanity, as one of us, suffering included (2:14ff.). Indeed, he learns obedience through suffering (5:8; 2:10). The ascended human Jesus, 'at the right hand of God', is the one who has journeyed with us. Hebrews' characteristic themes of 'entering in', 'approach', are, again, temporally grounded in the pilgrimage of Jesus. Consequently, patience and perseverance are demanded of us (11:1–39; 12:2), for this was the way of Jesus, our 'pioneer' or trail-blazer (2:10). Thiselton offers an illuminating exploration of these themes, along with an examination of similar ideas in 1 Corinthians (Thiselton 1998).   68. See Higgins (1991), *passim*.

of God's triunity.[69] Barth specifies the eternity of the triune God as 'pure duration', in which beginning, succession and end do not fall apart, in which there is no conflict between source, movement and goal, but rather mutual coinherence. Eternity, then, is 'a fluid conjunction of simultaneity and sequence'.[70] Temporal distinctions are not conceived as being absent from eternity, but rather as being present with a simultaneity that does not efface their sequence. What distinguishes eternity from time is 'the fact that there is in [God] no opposition or competition or conflict, but peace between origin, movement and goal, between present, past and future, between "not yet", "now" and "no more", between rest and movement, potentiality and actuality, whither and whence, here and there, this and that. In him all these things are *simul*, held together by the omnipotence of his knowing and willing, a totality without gap or rift, free from the threat of death under which time, our time, stands.'[71]

In this chapter, I have been setting out starting-points for discussion, not comprehensive theses. But they do, I believe, indicate substantial ways ahead for any who are concerned with the theology of time and eternity. While sympathetic to much in Tavener's music, and while certainly not

69. Barth (1957), 640. Barth refuses to define eternity apart from the particular temporality of Jesus. Only in and through Jesus Christ can the ontology of time be properly understood; there can be no general human temporality which takes ontological priority over that of Jesus Christ. 'Real time' is that time, revelation time, which God has for us, when the time of the world is turned back and reconciled to its Maker. To operate *a priori* with a supposedly neutral concept of 'created' time or 'human' time, or indeed a concept of 'fallen' time, is to risk reading the divine purposes for creation according to categories which have not been adequately shaped by and made consonant with God's bringing to fulfilment the created (temporal) order in Jesus Christ. It is a failure to grasp this methodological strategy which leads to so many misreadings of Barth; see Jenson (1969), 72; Hunsinger (1991), 15ff. The idea that in Barth's scheme, God's eternity either keeps him from making contact with time, or allows God to be temporal only by including a peculiar sort of time which is not ours, as Bruce Marshall has pointed out, trades upon a presumed opposition between time and eternity (not dissimilar to that presupposed by Tavener!). But in Barth's theology, 'As an attribute of his freedom, God's eternity is not his opposition to mundane time, but his transcendence of the opposition between time and timelessness.' The contact of God with our time 'signals neither its destruction nor his, but the conquest of our time's corrosive divisions' (Marshall 1993, 458).   **70.** Hunsinger (1991), 56.
71. Barth (1957), 612. Whatever questions we may ask of Barth, if this broad approach leads in the right direction, it would be unwise to insist that eternity is best conceived as mere timelessness, or as the polar opposite of created time. It would be equally unwise to insist that because the world is temporal, God *must* in some way also be temporal; that kind of argument (of which there are many versions) all too easily tends towards the projection of created time into God. Indeed, both lines of argument are in danger of projecting inappropriate qualities into God by short-circuiting the economy of salvation. The triune God through the work of Christ and the Spirit enacts a positive relation to time; this God is carrying all things, including their temporality, to their appointed end, a participation in his own life. Instead of speaking of God's being as non-temporal, or simply temporal, it may well be that something like 'more than temporal' offers a better way forward.

claiming it is devoid of theological value, I expressed some fundamental hesitations about its adequacy in opening up a vision of eternity and eternity's relation to created time, especially one which is faithful to the self-involvement of God with the world in Jesus Christ. There seems to be an avoidance, amounting almost to an obfuscation, of the belief that God's eternity has been made known and opened up through a time-intensive interaction with the created order, an interaction which turns on the three days of the crucifixion and resurrection. We suggested that other musical processes and our participation in them offer an impressive resource for opening up a view of time and eternity which is rather more adequate to the reality of God's participation and reinstatement of our temporality in Jesus Christ, the one by whom and through whom this temporality was created.

6

Repetition and Eucharist

> Our understanding of musical technique would have advanced much
> further if only someone had asked: Where, when, and how did music
> first develop its most striking and distinctive characteristic –
> repetition?[1]
>
> HEINRICH SCHENKER

The topic of repetition has attracted an enormous quantity of interest in the last few decades, especially in postmodern cultural theory. The
perceived tilt towards 'sameness' and homogenisation in some currents
of late modernity has raised critical questions about what constitutes an
'original' reality. It is said that with the proliferation of processes for the
replication of products, texts and information, we are witnessing a dimi-
nution in the authority of ideas of originality.[2] Music is sometimes alluded to in this discussion: of what does the 'original' consist when the vast
majority of music heard today is multiply processed by an increasingly
sophisticated technology of reproduction?[3]

Much of the material of this chapter was delivered as a paper at the Annual Conference of
The Society for the Study of Theology, at the University of Kent at Canterbury, 9 April 1997.
I am very grateful for the many comments I received there.
1. Heinrich Schenker, quoted in Kivy (1993), 327.
2. A stream of writers from Benjamin to Baudrillard. See e.g. Deleuze (1969), Derrida
(1976).
3. See Attali (1985) on the era of 'repetition'. For Attali, mass reproduction is in crisis.
Overproduction leads to a devolution, even a universalising, of cultural power among
users, because the enormous accessibility of music threatens all traditional 'uses' of music
and communicative codes. Music, all music, is just *there*. Unlike Adorno, Attali sees no
redemptive role for 'serious' music in this situation: in generating remote and inaccessible
works, it shares with popular music the definitive meaninglessness and silence of
repetition, confirming the end of music and of its role as a creator of sociality. For more
careful and nuanced discussions of the same issues, see Connor (1997), 165ff. and Middleton
(1990), especially chs. 2 and 3. For a balanced treatment of Attali himself, see Bowman
(1998), 334–52.

However, it is relatively rare to find attention given to repetitive processes *within* pieces of music. Even Theodor Adorno, who had so much to
say about the dangers of musical repetition in mass culture, devoted little
sustained work to repetitive processes within particular pieces and forms
of music.[4] It is this latter kind of repetition we examine in this chapter.

In doing so, we draw extensively upon material from previous chapters. The argument culminates with a discussion of the Eucharist, which
(perhaps not surprisingly) serves to pull together most of the major
strands of the foregoing pages.

Musical repetition

To state the obvious, every piece of music, to some extent, integrates 'sameness' with 'difference'. It must have sameness (similarity, association) in
order to have some kind of coherence, and difference in order to avoid complete monotony. Middleton posits a spectrum of musical structural types
between two poles, ranging from the 'monadic' – most nearly approached
by silence or by a single, unchanging, unending sound – to the 'infinite set'
– most nearly approached by pieces whose aim is that nothing be heard
twice. Absolute monadic sameness and absolute non-recurring difference
are, of course, impossible to achieve. Further, sameness and difference are
mutually dependent and can only be mediated through each other.[5]

What is striking about music is that relations of sameness would
appear to play a more crucial role than relations of difference. This is
something we have already noted in passing in chapter 1.[6] Music tends
towards the pole of absolute sameness, and this is borne out by the
extraordinary prominence of repetition in music compared to the other
arts. There are the more or less regular beats of metre. The 'repeat sign' on
a score can prescribe the reiteration of long stretches of music, note for
note. Even in music where there is a high level of unpredictability (for
example, in some of the melodies of Bach's unaccompanied Partitas) repetition of some sort usually plays a major and quite fundamental structural role. Repetition is the basis of musical forms in almost every period:
verse forms, 'formes fixes', the Burgundian chanson, rondo, sonata,
theme and variations, ground-bass/passacaglia, and many others.

In short, it would seem that in the vast majority of cases, 'music can never

---

4. Adorno tended to see the enjoyment of repetition as psychotic and infantile; Adorno
(1973), 160ff., esp. 178–81. On Adorno, see Paddison (1993), Witkin (1998), and, in relation to
popular music, Middleton (1990), ch. 2.   5. Middleton (1990), 183, 188f., 214ff.
6. See above, pp. 22f.

have enough of saying over again what has already been said'.[7] And in popular music, this is especially so.[8] As Peter Kivy observes, music 'from Bach to
Brahms, and before and beyond, consists to a large, although of course varying degree, in quite literal repetition of what has been heard before'.[9]

Repetition comes in different types. Some is recognised only with
increased familiarity with the piece. Some is concealed and never intended to be consciously heard as repetition at all. Some is quite unknown to
the creators of the music. Two broad types may be distinguished: 'immediate repetition' – when an entity is repeated straight away, and 'remote
repetition' (or 'return') – when the entity recurs after a significant period
of time.[10] Here we shall concern ourselves with immediate and remote
repetition when it involves the clear, patent, more or less literal reiteration of groups of notes.

For an extreme example, we can point to the first movement of
Beethoven's Sixth Symphony (*Pastoral*) where we find a section in which
essentially the same rhythmic motif is repeated incessantly. The opening
of the section is shown in Example 6.1. On this rhythm rides a melody

Example 6.1 Beethoven, Symphony no. 6 in F major, op. 68, first movement, bars 151–62

7. Zuckerkandl (1956), 213. Of course, there are numerous exceptions: e.g. twentieth-
century works which deliberately eschew repetition, some sacred texts where musical
organisation is secondary to liturgical significance, pieces so short or highly sectionalised
that repetition schemes are unnecessary.   **8.** Middleton (1990), 215ff., 267ff.
9. Kivy (1993), 328.
10. Meyer (1973), 49ff. An example of the former would be the Beethoven passage we
examine below (pp. 157ff.), and of the latter, recapitulation in sonata form.

which in basic shape remains the same throughout. No sooner are we finished with this section than another begins, virtually identical except for being at a different pitch. There is extensive repetition in rhythm, harmony and melody, on the micro- and macro-scale.

Why has this music claimed so much enjoyment? What is *novel* amidst the almost obsessive reiteration?[11] *Prima facie* it would seem that we *should* be thoroughly weary after only a few bars. Why are we prepared to put up with so much repetition? Parallels and analogies with other art-forms do not get us very far. Certainly, carpets and tapestries can contain extensive repetition. In architecture we find repetition of elements and sometimes entire formal complexes. But in these cases we have the simultaneous presence of many similar or identical elements. Although the perception of repetition may not be instantaneous – the eye and perhaps the body must move in order to apprehend it – the enjoyment depends in large part on being able to set part against part, to wander back and forth, to compare. In music the repetition itself is presented to us in a prescribed, irreversible, unbroken, sequence.[12]

In literature, repetition can play a crucial role. But it is only exceptionally taken to the extremes that we find in music. In a typical eighteenth-century symphony it is common for the entire first section of a movement (lasting, say, five minutes) to be repeated note for note. It is very rare for a novel, poem or play to do anything like this. Some twentieth-century literature can deploy repetitive strategies comparable to music. But in cases like this it is at least arguable that we are on the very edges of literature and bordering on music, which only makes us press again the question about repetitive procedures in music. As I said in chapter 1, notwithstanding the likenesses between music and language, we should not be blind to the marked differences. And this is one of them. In music, structure is built primarily on relations based not upon difference or contrast but on

11. That some have found this music dull is beside the point for the moment; the fact is that millions have found it a source of endless delight, without believing that Beethoven was experiencing some kind of 'off day'!
12. Kivy tries to argue that the model of a Persian carpet is capable of accommodating the pleasure of musical repeats (Kivy 1993, 349ff). He speaks of the enjoyment of tracing a repetitive pattern around a carpet. To circumnavigate a carpet completely until we are back where we started is 'a perfect visual analogue of experiencing the musical repeat . . . the border of my carpet is the exposition, repeated, of a visual sonata movement with two themes' (350). But this does not explain why musical repetition can afford such a high degree of interest. A crucial part of the interest in the case of the carpet depends upon being able to move back and forth, compare one motif or set of motifs with another. This does not apply to music, as Kivy himself acknowledges. We are under what he calls the 'military discipline' of the composer – the repeats are to be experienced in this sequence, in this continuous temporal order. Thus with Kivy we are still left wondering why musical repetition can occur on a vast scale without engendering sheer apathy.

attraction.[13] The bias towards repetition is one of the things which fore-grounds just this feature of music. This is borne out in an interesting way by a glance at the lively disputes in the eighteenth century over the aesthetic merits of the *da capo* aria. In this operatic form, the first section of the aria would often be linked to a leading emotion, the second to a contrasting or related emotion, and then the first section would be repeated. Many argued that this made little dramatic sense. Writing in 1755, a critic of Italian opera could protest:

> Words are to be treated in no other manner but according as the passion dictates; and when the sense of an air [i.e. an aria] is finished, the first part of it ought never to be sung over again, which is one of our modern innovations and quite repugnant to the natural process of our speech and passions, that are not accustomed to thus turn about and recoil upon themselves.[14]

At this stage in musical history, music and speech were much more close-ly intertwined than in the high classical period a few decades later. But the strain between the two is clearly being felt. When music later became considerably freer from the patterns of speech, we still find musical repeats being questioned from a literary standpoint. The composer Grétry could protest against large-scale repeats in sonatas:

> A sonata is a discourse. What would one think of a man who, after cutting his discourse in two, would repeat each half? . . . That is just about the effect repeats in music have on me.[15]

However, in both periods it was widely recognised that when considered purely from a *musical* point of view this kind of repetition of a whole sec-tion could make good sense. The fact that classical music persisted with sonata form, which relies heavily on large-scale repetition, only proved the point that, *pace* Grétry, musical repetition *cannot* find suitable parallels in linguistic discourse.[16]

How, then, is it that music can operate with such a high degree of repe-tition, that it can 'turn about and recoil' upon itself without inducing a paralysing boredom?

The commonest way of accounting for the pervasiveness of repetition

---

13. See above, pp. 22f.   **14.** As quoted in Kivy (1993), 334.
15. As quoted in Broyles (1980), 343.
16. In this connection we might also cite Wagner's well-known swipe at Beethoven for smuggling a repetition into his third *Leonore* overture for *Fidelio*. It seems that Beethoven wanted to present the 'argument' of the drama which followed. But instead of ending with an instrumental version of a chorus rejoicing (to match the opera), Beethoven rounded the overture off with a traditional recapitulation of its opening material, provoking Wagner's snarl that this 'distorts the idea of the work' and that 'the evil could have only been avoided by entirely giving up the repetition' (Wagner 1907, 245f).

in music is to point to music's deficiency in consistent, precise denotation. It cannot refer reliably and accurately to extra-musical phenomena, so it will tend to 'speak about itself' – what Richard Middleton calls 'introversive signification'.[17] In this light, a high measure of repetition is seen to be psychologically necessary if music is to make sense. The application of information-theory to musical cognition suggests that given music's lack of a specific and clear 'object' to which we can direct and concentrate our minds, and given our limited short-term memory, repetition becomes vital for imprinting the characteristic shape of music's features in the memory – motifs, phrases, or whatever – so that when they reappear after being absent, we have a sense of coherence and intelligible form.[18]

But intelligibility is one thing. The deeper and more pressing issue is: how can so much repetition be *interesting*?

Part of the answer undoubtedly lies in the *variation of musical parameters*. In the Beethoven piece we have mentioned, as the section unfolds, the rhythm of the repeated motif remains constant, but the shape of the melody alters slightly, the timbre changes through varied orchestration, the background harmony shifts, the volume swells and dies. This is a very common procedure in music: one parameter stays constant, the others are modified. And even when such modifications are not written down, often a performer will vary repeated material by ornamenting it, 'stretching' it in time, and so forth. Much improvised jazz works in this way.

Along with this observation, some might want to cut the Gordian knot and say that there is in fact no such thing as repetition in music because *the 'environment' of a repeated unit is always different*. In speaking of Chopin's Polonaise in A major, Edward Cone observes:

> This is a piece notable for the six-fold statement of its opening period, each time literally repeated: AABABA Trio, ABA – thus six A's in all. But the second A is already different from the first. The first was preceded by silence and followed by its repetition; the second is preceded by the first and followed by B. The third is now preceded and followed by B, and the fourth is preceded by B but followed by the Trio, and so on. My contention is that each statement is influenced by its position, by what precedes and what follows it, so that each is, in important respects, different from all the others ... In general, there is no such thing as true redundancy in music.[19]

In other words, each repeated unit is perceived as coming after and before music which is different from that which surrounded its earlier occur-

17. Middleton (1983), 236.   18. Barry (1990), 65ff.   19. Cone (1968), 46.

rence(s). The sounds may be duplicated but the music *as heard* is not. In some cases, this is undoubtedly part of the reason why musical repetition can claim our interest. In Schumann's *Arabesque*, when we hear the second appearance of the main theme (repeated note for note), we will likely hear it differently because of the musical interlude that has preceded it. To say 'it's just the same' would be to misunderstand.

However, though this may apply to 'remote' repetition, it says little about 'immediate' repetition, especially if this repetition is multiple (as in Beethoven's Sixth Symphony). It is hardly convincing to say that in a string of identical motifs, the fifth will hold our interest because it is surrounded by the fourth and sixth as distinct from, say, the third which is surrounded by the second and fourth!

These suggested explanations may account for part of the interest in musical repetition, but they are partial and secondary, and overlook a more fundamental factor. As might now be expected, it concerns the metrical waves (Figure 6.1). The nub of the matter is this: each repeated com-

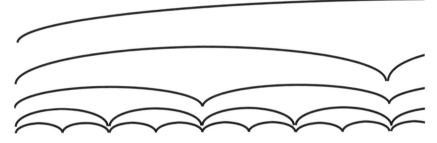

Figure 6.1 Metrical matrix

ponent of music will have a different dynamic quality because *each occurs in relation to a different configuration of metrical tensions and resolutions*. It is clear from what we have learned about metre that 'if we consider *every* level in the metric hierarchy, no two beats in a piece have *exactly* the same accentual quality'.[20] Draw a vertical line through the metrical matrix at any moment, and it will intersect the waves at particular points in their journeys of tension and resolution, giving that moment a certain dynamic quality. Draw a vertical line somewhere else and the waves will be intersected differently, giving that moment a different dynamic quality. It follows that every re-iterated note, motif or whatever is going to possess a different dynamic quality. The repetitions ride the waves in

20. J. Kramer (1988), 94.

different ways. *This* is where the fundamental novelty lies within tonal music – two occurrences of the same motif can be sensed as different because each relates to a different combination of metrical tensions and resolutions. Viewed from the point of view of metre, *everything is '"new"',* 'nothing can ever be the same', we are never 'back where we started'. This is why, as Berleant puts it, 'Repetition . . . becomes regeneration rather than reiteration.'[21]

Cone was right, up to a point. There is, in a sense, no such thing as redundancy in music. But much more critical than the 'horizontal' positioning of a repeated entity in relation to its predecessors and successors is its location with respect to the hierarchy of metrical waves.

In order that these differences in dynamic quality can be sensed, wave patterns have to be brought into relief, 'etched' by sound. There will need to be variation in some parameter of the music in order that the ever-different wave patterns can be heard. Hence those slight elements of variation we noted in the Beethoven example – the orchestration, harmony and volume changes. To say that these alterations satisfy our need for variety, staving off boredom, is to miss the heart of the matter. More fundamentally, they bring to our ear the patterns of tension and release in metrical waves.[22] We are left with a fascinating irony:

The tones do not alter for the sake of variety, that is in order to give the same thing an *appearance* of being different; on the contrary, *because what is apparently the same is basically always different,* the tones do not always want to remain the same.[23]

> To illustrate these ideas, we can return to the section we cited earlier from the first movement of Beethoven's *Pastoral* Symphony (Example 6.2).
>
> In bars 151–4, the same motif is played four times. But to what extent is it 'the same'? At the level of the first two-bar hyperbar (151–2), the first occurrence is metrically strong (a downbeat), the second weak (an upbeat). The first 'opens' and the second 'closes' the hyperbar. Likewise with the third and fourth – the third is strong, the fourth is weak. So 152 is not simply a repetition of 151, nor 154 simply a repetition of 153.
>
> But is not 153 simply a repetition of 151 (and 154 of 152)? No, because at the level of the next hyperbar (151–4), 151 is metrically strong and 153 metrically weak. Similarly, at the next hyperbar, 155–8 is the metrically weak answer to the metrically strong 151–4. The change in orchestration at bar 155 highlights this: it does not simply flavour the music with variety, it throws into relief a crucial aspect of the hyperbar

21. Berleant (1987), 247.   22. Zuckerkandl (1956), 220f.   23. Ibid., 222. My italics.

Example 6.2 Beethoven, Symphony no. 6 in F major, op. 68, first movement, bars 151–75

151–8. In a similar fashion the crescendo (151–75) is not simply there to keep things interesting, but to underline that the twenty-four-bar section it spans is the first 'intensifying' part of a vast metrical wave, 'peaking' at bar 175.

As if to add a further denial of any charge that these motifs are involved in 'mere repetition', Beethoven includes a *metrical ambiguity* in these twenty-four bars (Figure 6.2). There is a harmonic change (from B flat major to D major) at bar 163, which marks the beginning of the second part of a two-part wave (twelve bars of B flat, twelve of D). But there is an incongruence between this two-part structure and the orchestral texture. The orchestration is in *three* sections, each lasting four measures (four bars of Vl. I followed by four bars of Fl. and Vl. II). There is, then, a metrical wave articulated by the harmony, and another articulated by the instrumental arrangement.[24]

24. See Bernstein (1976), 181ff.

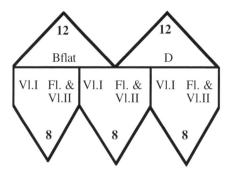

Figure 6.2 Beethoven, Symphony no. 6 in F major, op. 68, first movement, bars 151–74

What is true of the phrases and sections of music will also be true on the large- or macro-scale. The total course of a musical piece, after all, is only an extension of the same principles we have been outlining above. The overall construction of a piece will have its own metrical wave of tension and resolution, and the repetition we often find in large-scale construction will relate to that wave.

Music's bias towards repetition now makes much more sense. It is not enough to say that with weak and unstable referential capacities, music is forced to 'speak about itself'. More profoundly, repetition is a kind of 'natural state' of music because the very equality of repetitive units brings out with special clarity the inequality (wave patterns) of successive bars and hyperbars, the manifold differences within the metrical matrix. Music depends on repetition – in some form – to highlight the endlessly different hierarchy of metrical waves. Modifications in the tones, are, as it were, in danger of obscuring the shape of the metrical wave. Non-repetition will thus be the intrusion: 'Every new tonal statement in the course of a composition is . . . made *against* the will of an ever-present urge for repetition.'[25]

This bias of music towards repetition need not, then, be seen as the enemy of newness (in the sense of unprecedented, different from what has gone before); rather repetition serves to highlight the ever-new variegated metrical matrix which the music 'rides'. *Repetition, which might seem to be the enemy of novelty, can in fact promote it*, insofar as its identical repeated units are allowed to highlight the ever-different metrical network, and

25. Zuckerkandl (1956), 219.

insofar as at least one parameter of the music draws attention to its ever-different character.[26]

Eucharistic repetition

We are now going to take this discussion into an area where questions about repetition inevitably arise – liturgy, more particularly, the Eucharist. Most Churches repeatedly perform something akin to a liturgical pattern (even those who call themselves 'non-liturgical'!), and these repeated acts themselves often include a substantial amount of repetition (responses, litanies, sung refrains, etc.). Huge controversy has surrounded liturgical repetition. Very often, questions about power are close to the surface. The decision about who authorises repeated liturgies 'is among the most far-reaching decisions any church can make'.[27] The fear of imposed liturgical conformity can run very deep, as can the associated fear of mindless, 'vain repetition' (cf. Matt. 6:7).[28]

Many of the most pointed disagreements about liturgical repetition, deeply intertwined with questions of power, have been about eucharistic repetition, especially about the extent to which such repetition can be manipulative, about the relation between successive eucharistic celebrations, and about the links between each celebration and the unrepeatable work of Jesus Christ. I want to suggest that these debates have much to gain from a study of musical repetition.

A celebration of the Eucharist relates, or ought to relate, first and foremost to that temporality graciously given and generated by the activity of the triune God in and for the world, a temporality which, we have contended, can be usefully conceived as a multi-layered texture of metrical waves. At the lowest level, each downbeat could signify successive Eucharists; the highest wave the over-arching history of God's engagement with the cosmos; and a multitude of waves, interacting and overlapping, lie in between. Insofar as we are bound to Christ through the Spirit, each Eucharist enables us to participate in this abundant complexity of waves.

---

26. Nor, we should mention, need repetition be an enemy of newness in the sense of unpredictability – for the metrical matrix, as we have noted, is rarely regular and predictable at all levels. *Within the metrical matrix*, irregular waves can 'ride' the regular ones, thus highlighting their ever-changing character, and regular waves can 'ride' over these irregular ones, stabilising the structure at a higher level. See above, pp. 89ff.

27. Sykes (1996), 158, *et passim*.

28. Speaking of Matt. 6, Stephen Sykes remarks: 'It is ironic that the most frequently repeated prayer of all in the Christian tradition [the Lord's Prayer] should follow an injunction against vain repetition' (ibid., 160).

It is important to remember, however (presuming our discussion in the previous chapter is along the right lines), that to partake of Christ means not the negation of our created temporality, but its transforming and re-shaping. Likewise, every eucharistic celebration can be seen as a repeated opportunity for time-laden creatures to be incorporated into a temporal environment, established in Christ, in which past, present and future co-inhere, in such a way that our identities can be healed, recast and reformed.

With this in mind, what would a musical reading of the Eucharist look like? Let us imagine that we are speaking of a theme being stated and then repeatedly recurring, each recurrence interspersed with different, per-haps contrasting material.

First, *eucharistic repetition both stabilises and destabilises.* In chapter 4 I spoke of the way in which closures in the metrical matrix work both to ease tension on one at least one level and (concurrently) to intensify it on others.[29] Likewise, the repetition of a musical figure, section, movement or whatever can serve to increase tension, but also, concurrently, to effect resolution (Example 6.3).

Example 6.3 Beethoven, Symphony no. 6 in F major, op. 68, first movement, bars 151–5

The motif of bar 152 is identical to that of 151 (leaving aside for the moment the small increase of volume produced by the crescendo). Yet in 152 it promotes the closure of hyperbar 1 and in 151 it initiates tension. The same motif in two occurrences functions in a different way in each case.

Concurrent dual function can also be demonstrated easily. The third occurrence of the motif, in bar 153, serves to initiate a new wave (hyperbar 2) but also, at the next level up (hyperbar 3), to begin to 'balance' or equalise the strong metrical beat which initiated hyperbar 1. The one occurrence of the motif functions in two different ways.

Therefore, although it is often assumed that repetition is basically a stabil-ising practice, marking out secure points amidst life's flux, in metrical music, repetition can both stabilise *and destabilise.* It can both close the wave *and* provoke a desire for further fulfilment, and it can do both concurrently.

29. See above, pp. 106ff.

The repetition of the Eucharist stabilises. Here God regularly re-calls the Christian community to know again the transforming power of the cross – here the Church's generative and inexhaustible theme is heard and sung again, here 'the Lord's death' is proclaimed (1 Cor. 11:26). At every Eucharist, in being opened to Christ by the Spirit, we are opened to his past, bearing upon us. However, the very same eucharistic repetition also destabilises. To be opened out repeatedly to Christ's past is to be opened out to a future anticipated in him, and thus to experience a re-charging of God's promise of a new future. It is to be incorporated into a forward momentum of the Spirit which activates in us an increased longing – 'until he comes'. To speak of stabilising and destabilising here is *not* to speak of a dialectic of opposites set against each other, or of successive phases of a process (as if we *first* 'look back' and *then* 'look forward'); in music, the accumulated tension at an upper level is *generated by* the repeated 'return' at the lower level(s). Repeated stabilising *gives rise to* instability. To be regularly re-bound to Christ who was crucified and raised from the dead *is* to be drawn into a stronger hope for the world.

I have used the word 'destabilise' here primarily because of the way in which this aspect of the Eucharist is to be felt by the Church. Repeated eucharistic celebration will of course provide consolation, a rooting again in the forgiveness forged at the cross. But because it settles us *in Christ* crucified and risen, in whom the new humanity of the future has been given in our midst, the Eucharist will provoke unsettledness, in ourselves and in relation to our surrounding reality, an acute sense that we have not yet reached our 'rest' (Heb. 4). Christopher Rowland, writing of the Latin American Church's experience of poverty and oppression, speaks of every Eucharist as an anticipation of Christ's final judgement. In relation to some of the Pauline and Johannine eucharistic texts, he comments: 'One has very little sense here of a ritual occasion which was seen as the messianic banquet reserved only for the elect, cut off from the struggles and misdemeanours of ordinary life . . . the identity of the group is not allowed to mask either the costliness of participation in social terms or the activity of God in history . . . the Eucharist requires of us a *transformation of our present condition* pre-eminently in the case of the poor.'[30]

---

30. Rowland (1995), 207, 208. My italics. (For an impressive presentation of a similar dynamic in Old Testament worship, see Brueggemann 1988.) Even more fundamentally, the Eucharist destabilises *our very understanding* of 'our present condition' by positioning us in a temporality which is directed towards a new future promised in Christ. This prevents us from making our particular 'present situation' some fixed and immutable point of reference (for God as well as us!). See Thiselton's damaging critique of some pastoral

Second, *eucharistic repetition can 'go flat'*. We have seen that repeated musical units – phrases, motifs, or whatever – invite and retain interest chiefly because each repetition carries a different dynamic quality in relation to a hierarchy of waves, and that in music with a very large amount of repetition, variations of one sort or another are introduced to highlight or clarify this hierarchy so that we can sense these different dynamic qualities.

It is quite possible, however, for a composer or performer to fail in this respect. We need only listen to a beginner playing a piece of very repetitive music. It will often sound flat, mechanical and dull because he or she has not yet learned to feel, and turn into physical movement, those upper metrical levels. This helps us to see part of what might be involved in 'empty' repetition, 'ritualized' ritual (Mary Douglas). Christian history is replete with thousands of one-levelled eucharistic performances where each celebration is effectively flattened on to one level of significance, with little regard for the diverse layers of theological import involved. There is, for instance, a kind of eucharistic worship over-concerned with closure and completeness, which builds up no tension on any more elevated level than that of its own recurring (and fully resolved) performances. Here there is an exaggerated sense of stability, little sense of participating in a movement of divine longing beyond this particular act, of being caught up in a work of the Spirit (cf. Zuckerkandl's 'willing of the infinite'), little sense of being drawn into a larger, wider hope for the world. Eucharists of this kind, 'empty symbols of conformity' (Douglas), ensnared by their own single-level reiterations, quickly become inured against the anguish of the world. This is worship 'without bite of threat or gift'.[31]

Many Churches, out of a desire to avoid dull liturgy, make frantic efforts to 'make services more interesting', which often means trying to make each as different as possible from the last. Ironically this can lead to a strong sense of 'sameness'. A wiser strategy is to learn from the musician who has developed a heightened sensibility to many layers of metre. There may well be variation, but the variations, properly employed, will serve the purpose of marking out for the ear those upper waves. Whether or not we belong to a tradition which celebrates the Church's liturgical

footnote **30.** (*cont.*)
theology, especially its tendency to pivot theological understanding around 'the present situation' (Thiselton 1992, 604ff). Music reminds us, as we have seen, that our present is 'temporalised' from past and future. It may be that if more pastoral theologians took music seriously, some of these problems might not arise!   **31.** Brueggemann (1988), 45.

year, this practice is one way of enabling the Church to experience something of the multi-layered waves of salvation. As each Eucharist is known as occupying a different 'place' in the seasonal waves, it will be sensed differently.

Third, *eucharistic repetition does not efface the temporal integrity of the initial appearance of the theme, or of its repetitions.* The initial sounding of the theme is circumscribed and bounded. It begins and ends. It has its own completeness. A later repetition is not a prolongation or extension of the theme. Moreover, the subsequent repetition of the theme is not a matter of extracting the theme from its temporal relations and re-locating it, as if we could wrench it from 'that time' to 'this time'. It is embedded in a field of temporal contingencies – other notes, phrases, elaborations – which are intrinsic to its identity. Most important, it has a unique dynamic quality by virtue of its relation to a hierarchy of metrical waves. No later appearance of the theme will have this same quality. Identical repetition in the 'now' is impossible, not just because *we* are in a different temporal context, but because every musical event relates to a different hierarchical pattern of tension and resolution.

Eucharistic repetition is not a matter of prolongation, continuation or protraction. Nor is it a matter of extracting something from one time to another. The crucifixion of Jesus took place in relation to a specific combination of historical contingencies (captured in the phrase 'under Pontius Pilate'), and in a quite unique set of relations to different levels of God's salvific purposes. There can therefore be no attempt to extract that occurrence from its situatedness and 'make it happen again now'. This is the classic Protestant concern for the completeness and particularity of Christ's work.[32]

By the same token, every subsequent repetition of the theme will have *its* own temporal integrity, not only in relation to our own temporal context (and we shall deal with this shortly) but also in relation to the unique configuration of tensions and resolutions to which it relates in the metrical hierarchy. Similarly with every Eucharist in relation to the many-levelled purposes of God. Furthermore, in music where the repeated theme is elaborated, we will never hear the original theme in the same way after we have heard its elaborations. Every Eucharist relates not only directly in

---

32. Dr Markus Bockmuehl helpfully pointed out to me that 'remote' repetition of the kind we are considering might lead us to forget the revelational and soteriological uniqueness of Christ: the notes of the theme are, after all, still reiterated, however different their dynamic quality. This is undoubtedly a weakness of which we need to be aware.

an over-arching wave to the death and resurrection of Christ, but also, via its 'bottom-level' waves to every previous Eucharist. Our reception of any Eucharist will be shaped, sometimes quite radically, by our accumulated experience of previous celebrations.[33]

Fourth, *eucharistic repetition means improvising*. I have said that each appearance of the theme relates to our temporal context. Especially instructive here is musical improvisation (and I say much more about improvisation in the next three chapters). If I improvise in front of others on a well-known theme, I engage intensely with the particular constraints of the setting – the acoustic of the building, the number of people present, their expectations and experience, their audible response as the performance proceeds, and, not least, the music produced by other improvisers (if there are others). These elements are not accidental to the outcome but constitutive of it; they are incorporated into the improvisation in order that the improvisation can be, so to speak, 'true' and profoundly authentic to this time (and place). Most performance works like this. But the increased contingency of improvisation obliges the musician to work particularly hard at bringing alive the given (repeated) music in a way which 'hooks into' the unique occasion, the 'one off' combination of constraints, such that the theme is heard as fruitful in a new way for the present, and, implicitly, for the future. Fresh possibilities inherent in the theme are thereby brought to light. And in the process, the constraints are themselves enhanced, magnified, developed, enabled in some manner to be more fully themselves: players become more skilful, new features of the instrument come to light, we become more aware of the ambience of the setting, and so on.

John Calvin used to insist that although the Lord's Supper does not mean inviting Christ to share in our spatio-temporality but rather the ascended Christ inviting us to share in his, our space and time are nevertheless not effaced or escaped.[34] Far from it. In this occasion, our humanity, in union with Christ, with its history, is redeemed and enhanced in its particularity, brought nearer to its intended end and fruition. And this is

---

33. Rowan Williams, speaking of the Bible, writes: 'What we are dealing with is a text that has generated an enormous family of contrapuntal elaborations, variations, even inversions – rather like the simple theme given to Bach by Frederick the Great, that forms the core of [the *Musical Offering*]. When we have listened to the whole of that extraordinary work, we cannot simply hear the original notes picked out by the King of Prussia as if nothing had happened. We can't avoid saying now: "*This* can be the source of *that*" – and that is a fact of some importance about the simple base motif' (R. Williams 1989, 93f).
34. Calvin (1961), IV:17, especially pars. 10, 11, 12, 26.

the work of the Holy Spirit. The Spirit is *the* improviser *par excellence* in every eucharistic repetition.

Fifth, *eucharistic repetition depends on and enables a particular kind of inter-penetration of past, present and future.* We have said much about this in rela-tion to music, and by extension, in relation to our sharing in the 'redeemed time' of Christ. The Eucharist is the celebration of the Church at which this should be experienced most fully. A musical construal of the temporal character of eucharistic repetition can take more adequate account of both Jewish and Christian 'remembrance' (*anamnesis*) and the Eucharist's future anticipation than many eucharistic theologies. Robert Jenson has recently argued that ecumenical debates about the Eucharist between Catholics and Protestants have been corrupted by flawed assumptions about time and temporal occurrence which have impeded a proper understanding of the character of *anamnesis* and anticipation. The assumptions are by now familiar to us. A one-level linear view of time is often presupposed, in which events are seen as receding into ever greater remoteness in the memory unless preserved or held in some manner. 'In the Catholic interpretation, some events are left behind as time marches on and others are carried along by institutionalization' (i.e. the ecclesial institution tries to maintain continuity between Christ's finished work and every Eucharist).[35] 'In the Protestant interpretation, time goes on with or without the repetition of any one event; repetition, if it occurs, is occasioned *extrinsically*.'[36] In other words, God, or Christ (or the presi-dent?) must repeatedly break into time in order to make the past event live *now* in the Eucharist. And, as Jenson puts it, 'both interpretations seem to presuppose the mutual extrinsicality . . . of time and *events*. Events happen *in* time, by both interpretations, and may or may not be carried along *through* time.'[37] If Jenson is correct, it is noteworthy that music effectively subverts these two basic assumptions. Repetition in music is not a one-level succession of ever-receding events on a straight time-line but occurs only in a composite of metrical waves in relation to which musical events cannot be conceived as falling back into vacuity. And we have seen that time and musical events are intrinsically bound together: the events have their dynamic life in and through time.

This can be usefully expanded by reference to Jean-Luc Marion's treat-ment of the Eucharist in *God Without Being*. Marion is especially concerned to stress that eucharistic presence is not a function of the will, attention or

---

35. Jenson (1992), 110.   36. Ibid. My italics.   37. Ibid.

consciousness of the Church. (This is as much a Protestant error as Catholic!) The logical extension of this would be the belief that Christ's presence endures only for as long as the community is present; the Church's present becomes the unique and sole horizon of the eucharistic gift: 'presence is valid only in the present, and in the present of the community consciousness'.[38] Marion maintains that this clamping of eucharistic presence to 'the immediate consciousness of the collective self' is dependent on a conception of time in which there is an 'ontological overdetermination of a primacy of the present: the past finishes and the future begins as soon as the present begins or finishes. Their respective temporalities count only negatively, as a double nonpresent, even a double nontime.'[39] Countering this, Marion proposes that eucharistic presence be understood chiefly as gift, and according to the order of the gift the eucharistic present is temporalised from past and future, and only finally from the present. From the past it is temporalised as memorial (the present is understood as a today to which alone the memorial, as an actual pledge, gives meaning and reality). From the future it is temporalised as eschatological announcement ('The pledge, which the memorial sets into operation, now anticipates the future, so that the present itself occurs entirely as this anticipation concretely lived'[40]). And only finally is the eucharistic present temporalised from the present 'as dailyness and viaticum' (the eucharistic present is never possession, but always gift, to be received anew each instant, each hour, each day).[41]

This would seem highly congruent with what we have discovered about music. Musical repetition, is not, as we have seen, primarily a device whereby we in the (real) present attempt to preserve and carry forward into the unknown (and unreal) future something that otherwise might be lost in oblivion. In the midst of our fractured and distorted temporality we are given to participate in a temporality in which our past, present and future can be at peace, co-inhere. Likewise, repeated Eucharists are not a means by which the Christian community over and over again attempts to recover in its corporate memory now an ever-retreating event. Eucharistic remembering cannot be a matter of us calling to mind a nonpresence, nor is anticipation a matter of us imagining an utterly

38. Marion (1991), 166f.   39. Ibid., 170.   40. Ibid., 174.
41. Ibid., 172. Critical questions need to be asked about Marion's own version of transubstantiation, in particular whether he accords due weight to the ministry of the Holy Spirit in preserving the 'distance' between the eucharistic presence and the consciousness of the community, and in uniting us to Christ in whom the temporal modes cohere.

discontinuous and unreal future. The Eucharist is the repeated embodiment of God's summons, provoking our attention, opening us out to Christ in such a way that what Christ was, suffered and did for us is made ever and again contemporary in its completeness for us who are still 'on the way', and, moreover, in such a manner that his past is known not merely as past to us but also as future. Put another way, the Holy Spirit opens our present (and us) to Christ's past and future, and, as in the case of music, this entails not the refusal of 'our' temporality, but its healing and re-formation.

There is, of course, no pretence here that every stumbling block in eucharistic controversy evaporates in the presence of the sound of music. But enough has been outlined to show that consideration of music, through its concrete demonstration of particular kinds of temporality, not only refreshes our conceptuality but can serve to free us from some views of temporality, created and redeemed, which have disfigured the debates.

Repetition and church music

Before leaving the issue of repetition, it is worth making some brief comments about the relevance of what we have been saying to the way music is deployed in the Church. I restrict myself to some observations on musical repetition in popular culture and its relation to church music.

'It's monotonous', 'it's predictable', 'it's all the same' – comments such as these about popular music and some brands of church music (for example, the worship songs which have enjoyed huge and widespread popularity over the last few decades) echo the discussions of the mass culture theorists of the 1930s and 40s. From this point of view, repetition (within a piece of music) can be assimilated to the same category as what Adorno called 'standardisation' (as between pieces of music). Undeniably, the detractors have a point. Popular music places heavy reliance on techniques of repetition: 'if music is a syntax of equivalence, much popular music carries the principle to a highpoint'.[42] Metre is normally highly regular at every level. Related to this, even though repetitive strategies in music can function to create a sense of direction and goal-orientation, this is so only if the upper levels of metre are brought into prominence in some way. A large amount of popular music, while privileging repetition,

42. Middleton (1990), 189.

generates very few levels of metrical waves, thus subduing directionality and the sense of long-term goals. Dance music from the so-called 'rave' culture is an example, now very much alive in some Churches, paralleled in some respects by the sound-world of 'minimalist' composers (Riley, Reich, Glass).[43] It will be pointed out that this kind of musical repetition, in the hands of a burgeoning music industry, has been used to define and hold markets, to channel types of consumption, and to pre-form response. To bring these techniques into the life of the Church, especially if the music suppresses directionality (suggesting some kind of 'eternal now'), will often provoke negative reactions. Fears of manipulation, mind-numbing or even trance will often be expressed. A number of critics of some forms of music in worship are only too keen to point out the dangers.[44]

Nevertheless, while the suspicion is not always misplaced, we also need a heightened sensitivity to different forms of repetition, and to the different ways in which repetition is practised and functions within particular settings. It might be tempting to jump from the material of this chapter to the assumption that music with a very limited metrical wave structure is invariably harmful, but this would be unwise. I restrict myself to two general points. First, in virtually all contemporary popular music a high degree of repetition ensures structures which have a large measure of continuity and a relatively low incidence of disruption or radical contrast.[45] It is only very rarely acknowledged by cultural theorists (and even less in Christian denunciations of postmodern popular culture) that the multiple visual overwhelming of the video/screen culture is nearly always accompanied by music, and that the music displays very little of the fragmentation and disjointedness in the kaleidoscope of imagery which is so often attacked as harmful. There may indeed be highly eclectic 'sampling' (the bringing together of sounds from many different sources) but this is usually tied to a tight and cohesive harmonic and rhythmic structure (simple reiterated chord sequences, unvarying pace, uniform texture, and so forth). In many ways, music provides the continuity absent in the visual display. To criticise repetition too harshly in this

43. The minimalists of the 1960s, 70s and 80s would typically take tiny motifs – three or four notes – and subject them to strategies of relentless repetition, not in order to produce waves of tension and resolution but precisely to suppress them.

44. See e.g. Percy (1996), ch. 4.

45. Middleton (1990), 216f., 268ff. Most post-rock'n'roll song displays varying proportions of 'lyric' and 'epic' forms, the former marked by symmetrical and binary structures, the latter by repetition and varied repetition. What is relatively rare are structures which privilege difference and the resolution of conflict, especially on the large scale.

context may be disingenuous. Second, and this follows from the last point, the way in which musical repetition will function and be received in any particular setting depends on a vast network of constraints – acoustics, expectations, the music people are used to hearing, biological make-up, the way the music is introduced, and so forth. We can properly highlight theological resonances in musical repetition in a way that is highly instructive for theology and, by implication, for the way music is used by the Church. But this does not mean that we can instantly translate our findings into a project which outlaws some types of music and promotes others in order to guarantee a specific theological 'effect' on the hearers. Musical communication depends on a complexity of intersecting variables; any intelligent enquiry into the effects of music would do well to remember this complexity.

In the first part of this chapter, we posed the question: how can music sound so interesting when it is typically so full of repetition? How can there be novelty when there is such an incessant drive towards sameness? The chief answer, we found, lies in the manner in which repeated units of music are heard in the context of the hierarchy of metrical waves. I sought to explicate the theological fruitfulness of this with particular reference to the Eucharist. Eucharistic theology (and liturgical studies more widely?) would do well to seek wisdom from the practices of music. Not only are we given fresh means of discovering, understanding and delineating the temporality of this feast whose repetition has proved so crucial to the Church's life, but some of the most intractable dilemmas and ancient quandaries surrounding it are, to say the last, considerably eased. Moreover, we are also given partial insight into why it is that so much music has been employed in the context of the Eucharist.

However, a sense of 'newness' in music can be achieved not only through the highlighting of endlessly different metrical waves amidst repetition, but by other means also. In the next three chapters we turn to a type of music in which another kind of novelty, the novelty of the contingent, is brought into very high prominence.

III

Time to improvise

7

Boulez, Cage and freedom

[I]mprovisation on the piano is a necessity of his life. Every journey that takes him away from the instrument for some time excites a home-sickness for his piano, and when he returns he longingly caresses the keys to ease himself of the burden of the tone experiences that have mounted up in him, giving them utterance in improvisation.[1]

ALEXANDER MOSZKOWSKI, WRITING OF ALBERT EINSTEIN

[J]azz is more closely related to the realm in which music occurs – time – than is European music . . . if music – as almost all philosophies of music hold – is *the* art expressed in time, then jazz corresponds more fundamentally to the basic nature of the musical than European music.[2]

JOACHIM BERENDT

Spontaneity . . . is but the outcome of years of training and practice and thousands of experiments.[3]

STANLEY HAUERWAS

A flurry of interest in improvisation marks the current musicological landscape. Though many aspects of improvisation are only scantily understood, some major studies have established it as a serious field of enquiry.[4] This is partly because of a growing academic awareness in the West of various forms of non-Western music, whose techniques are often more dependent on improvisation than music of European provenance. Relevant also is the explosion of improvisatory practice in the arts of the twentieth century, and conversations between different types of improvising artists.

1. Moszkowski (1972), 235.   2. Berendt (1983), 182.   3. Hauerwas (1985), 52.
4. For a helpful survey of literature up to 1988, see Pressing (1988), 141–5. Especially important is the work of Dean (1989, 1993), Bailey (1992) and Berliner (1994).

The word 'improvisation' did not gain wide currency in the vocabulary of music-making until the late eighteenth and nineteenth centuries. At first it carried the relatively neutral sense of extemporisation, or of extempore performance of poetry or ballads with embellishment. By the 1850s it appears to have acquired pejorative connotations – off-hand, lacking sufficient preparation (as in 'improvised shelter', 'improvised solution'). Many musicians and musicologists continue to view it with considerable suspicion, if not disdain. For some it is synonymous with the absence of intellectual rigour. There are educationalists who see it as a distraction from authentic music-making.[5] The French composer Pierre Boulez remarks: 'with improvisations, because they are purely affective phenomena, there is not the slightest scope for anyone else to join in. Improvisation is a personal psychodrama . . . Whether we are interested or not, we cannot graft our own affective, intellectual or personal structure on to a base of that sort.'[6]

Defining improvisation is notoriously hard, partly since (like composition) it can refer to a process or a result, and sometimes both. Further difficulties arise from the cloudiness of the distinction between composition and improvisation. If, however, improvisation is taken to refer to the concurrent conception and performance of music, improvisation has played a very prominent role in the music of the Church: one only need think of early Christian adaptations of Jewish cantillation, the development of Gregorian chant, organ improvisation, the congregational improvisation in Scottish Presbyterian chapels.

It may well be that one of the main reasons for the prominence of improvisation in the Church is its strong theological resonances, which have been pointed out by a number of writers,[7] and some of which we explore here. In keeping with the focus of the book, I concentrate mainly on the potential of improvisation for deepening our grasp of theological issues relating to time and temporality. Although much improvised music exhibits all of the temporal processes we have considered so far, it can also throw into relief very particular features of musical temporality in striking ways. In this chapter and the next we ask what improvisation can contribute to a theological account of human freedom. In chapter 9 we examine the process of gift exchange in improvisation as a way of addressing the doctrine of election and ecclesiology.

5. For discussion, see Peggie (1985).   6. Boulez (1976), 65.
7. E.g. Peacocke (1993), 175ff.

Preliminary matters

Two preliminary matters need addressing. The first concerns the pervasiveness of improvisation. It is in fact present in one form or another in the music of virtually all cultures. Musicians schooled in the modern Western tradition will tend to treat improvisation not only as separate from but relatively marginal to composing and performing strictly notated music. By far the bulk of academic music history in the West has been commentary on written scores. This is not surprising, given the difficulty of reconstructing non-written music before recording was invented. But it encourages a distorted picture of the history of musical practices, and a highly parochial one, for by far the majority of non-Western music is not notated. Indeed, much of it is improvised as well. Further, as E. T. Ferand observes in his magisterial study of improvisation, 'there is scarcely a single field in music that has remained unaffected by improvisation, scarcely a single musical technique or form of composition that did not originate in improvisatory practice or was not essentially influenced by it'.[8] Even in the Western tonal tradition, after notation was developed we find, for example, that improvisation in the baroque era was prevalent and highly regarded. The keyboard player improvised over a 'figured' bass. He was free, and often expected to amplify the harmony according to circumstances. C. P. E. Bach could write:

> Variation when passages are repeated is indispensable today. It is expected of every performer. The public demands that practically every idea be constantly altered, sometimes without investigating whether the structure of the piece or the skill of the performer permits such alteration . . . One no longer has the patience to play the written notes [even] for the first time.[9]

Composers such as J. S. Bach, Handel, Domenico Scarlatti, Mozart and Beethoven were as well known in some circles as improvisers as they were as composers. With the elevation of concerts to a new and unprecedented status in the eighteenth and nineteenth centuries, improvisation began to play less of a critical role in performance, the performer's latitude being further curbed by a growing sophistication in notation. Improvisation typically became the occasion for the display of individual talent. The soloist's cadenza in a concerto is the obvious example. Even this became

---

8. As quoted in Bailey (1992), ixf.   9. As quoted in Horsley et al. (1980), 40.

increasingly prepared and was often written down in part or in whole. The eventual result was that improvisation was largely abandoned in 'high' art but retained in 'popular' folk-music traditions, receiving a massive impetus with the advent of the spirituals and jazz. Having said that, today, even in the case of music which is notated and prepared in detail, latitude in performance is usually both tolerated and encouraged according to the style and to the circumstances of the occasion – an improvisatory element is nearly always present to some degree.

All this suggests that the customary picture of improvisation as a discrete and relatively frivolous activity on the fringes of music-making might need to be replaced by one which accords it a more serious and central place. Instead of regarding thoroughly notated and planned music as the norm and improvisation as an unfortunate epiphenomenon or even aberration, it might be wiser to recall the pervasiveness of improvisation and ask whether it might be able to reveal fundamental aspects of musical creativity easily forgotten in traditions bound predominantly to extensive notation and rehearsal.

The second preliminary matter concerns how we distinguish improvisation and composition.[10] It might be thought that one is entirely spontaneous and unprepared, the other entirely calculated and protracted. But this overlooks the significant amount of pre-set material entailed in most improvisation, and the flexibility which most composers allow to, and expect of performers.

Some point to a supposed lack of intellectual rigour in improvisation compared to composition. The composer Luciano Berio (b. 1925) believes that music should involve musical 'thought', and that such thought is constituted by deliberate formal patterning concurrently operating at a number of levels: 'by musical thought I mean above all the discovery of a coherent discourse that unfolds and develops simultaneously on different levels'.[11] Improvisation, he assumes, disallows this. Along similar lines, Boulez speaks of improvisation capitulating to the crude dynamics of emotional reaction:

> Improvisation, and especially improvisation where there is a degree of sympathy between the individual members, always follows the same curve of invention: excitement – relaxation – excitement – relaxation. In so-called primitive societies a similar situation exists in religious ceremonies whose relatively simple form involves a building up of psychological tension followed by relaxation.[12]

10. On this, see Dean (1989), Nettl (1974), Prévost (1985) and Sloboda (1993), 138ff.
11. Berio (1985), 84.   12. Boulez (1976), 114.

True, much improvisation may indeed lack intellectual thoroughness. And many of the more intellectually demanding structural techniques characteristic of much composition (in particular, the moulding and perfecting of material over a considerable period of time) seem to have been slow to find their way into improvisation. But we should be careful not to overplay the point, for studies have shown that improvisation can often demand an intellectual activity at least as demanding and disciplined.[13]

Alternatively, we might point to notation as the critical difference. Composition relies on notation, the latter does not. But it seems odd to claim that composition only happens when musicians write music down. Moreover, much improvisation relies on written music: written 'arrangements' are frequently used by jazz players.

A more promising way forward is to take composition to refer to all the activity which precedes the sounding of the entire piece of music, everything which is involved in conceiving and organising the parts or elements which make up the pattern or design of the musical whole; and improvisation to mean the concurrent conception and performance of a piece of music, which is complete when the sound finishes. This lines up well with the way the words 'improvisation' and 'composition' are actually used in common speech. Christopher Small suggests that Western composed music is like a journey made by a composer who goes out, comes back from 'out there' and tells us something, as best he can, of what it was like.

> The journey may have been a long, arduous and fascinating one, and we may be excited, moved, and even amused by it, but we cannot enter fully into the experience with him because the experience was over and he was safely home before we came to hear of it . . . In improvising, on the other hand, the musician takes us with him on his journey of exploration.[14]

The distinction as understood cannot be pressed too far. The music which results from composition and improvisation may not differ radically.[15]

---

13. See e.g. Pressing (1988).

14. Small (1977), 176. If this is so, then a clear difference between composition and improvisation concerns the application of 'problem-solving' techniques. In the compositional approach, in general, problem-solving is complete before the performance. Success is judged, in large part at least, by how well the performance represents a perfect execution of ideas and interpretation. In improvisation, problem-solving is undertaken within the performance itself: 'the emphasis is upon the creative, investigative approach to an unformulated musical situation' (Prévost 1985, 181).

15. In music which is said to be improvised 'a number of compositional techniques and devices at the microcompositional level appear to be characteristic. Among them are repetition, simple variation of short phrases, melodic sequence, the tendency to start two successive sections with the same motive, the tendency to increase the length of sections as the performance progresses, and perhaps others . . . all these techniques are also present in the "set" or "fixed" compositions of certain cultures' (Nettl 1974, 9f).

Often in improvisation much is formulated in advance of performance. And the distinction might be too closely linked to an associated one between compositional and performative stages of music-making. Although familiar enough in Western aesthetics, the distinction is not as neat as it might at first seem.[16] Performance seems to entail at least some elements of composition – calculating what the music is going to sound like in advance. And sometimes a composition may include a performance of the piece in its entirety; many composers have entertained some imaginative construction of music 'in the mind's ear'. Nevertheless, we can still say with some confidence that in improvisation, conception and performance are interwoven to a very high degree, certainly to a greater extent than in music which involves an extended period of shaping material prior to performance. Whatever else improvisation is, it is 'performance music' through and through: the stress will be on process rather than product, activity rather than result.

Contingency and given constraint

A sense of contingency seems to be an important part of the perception of most music. I am using the word 'contingency' here in the broad sense of 'non-necessity'; contingent things do not have to be and contingent events do not have to happen.[17] Applied to musical experience, along with regularity and consistency, we sense (even if we do not articulate) that much of what we hear *might have been otherwise*, and the psychological force of this contingency is *newness*. This is promoted by two factors in particular. First, there is the setting up of multiple possibilities for the listener. Rarely does there seem to be only *one* possible way forward. Second, some musical events do not seem to be implied by antecedent events. There is surprise. Sometimes this surprise will follow the strong arousal of an expectation of some other musical event.[18]

---

16. See Alperson (1984).

17. The word can be used in a number of senses, the other principal one being a thing or event's dependence on some other thing or event. Of course, determinists contend that there is no such thing as ontological or cosmological contingency. Everything (including the course of a piece of music) necessarily is and everything that happens necessarily happens. For the present, I can only register my conviction that this is a deeply flawed position to hold; an adequate rebuttal would take us far beyond the scope of this book.

18. The language of expectation and implication owes much to the work of Leonard Meyer, but his approach is not without its drawbacks. See above, p. 100, n. 2.

It is almost impossible not to mention Beethoven in this connection, for 'he enlarged the number of possible futures that the past and the self could evoke and shape. His music expanded its listeners' sense of what could follow a given past without falling into chaos.

One of the things which characterises much musical improvisation is a relatively high degree of unpreparedness compared to many other forms of music, and hence a heightened sense of contingency, especially for the performers and often for non-performing listeners too (if there are any). It ought to be borne in mind that there are different degrees of openness in improvised music. Much jazz is a good deal less 'free' than is often thought, including so-called 'free jazz'![19] In fact, as with any music, improvisation is bound by a host of constraints. What is typical of much improvisation, and, arguably a key to the pleasure it affords, is, first, a strong *contrast* between the contingent and the non-negotiable 'given' constraints, between 'non-order' and order;[20] second, an *interplay* between them; and third, a *mutual enhancement* as they interact – they not only engage with, but also highlight and magnify each other. This kind of dynamic – contrast, interplay and mutual enhancement – is a familiar one in the sciences. It has been explored extensively through the category of play, and applied to a number of theological loci – creation, hermeneutics, worship, for instance – often with reference to the interaction of Word and Spirit.[21]

Our main interest in this and the next chapter is human freedom. As is often pointed out, it is all too easy to align human freedom with the utterly contingent (non-determined) and then regard the constraints of our lives as somehow inherently threatening to that freedom. Limitation is

And his music prepared and arrived at events that *were radically new* in the sense that his predecessors could not and, without his achievements, his contemporaries would not have imagined them' (Greene 1982, 53. My italics).

19. This was a major element in Theodor Adorno's fierce (and controversial) attack on jazz. Reviewing some fifty years of jazz he claimed that it operates with rigid formulae successfully repeated with only superficial change over a long period, in a diversity of pretentiously differentiated 'styles'. It is in fact not liberating but induces 'psychological regression'. See e.g. Adorno (1982). For measured assessments of Adorno on jazz and popular music, see Paddison (1993), 205ff.; Middleton (1990), 34–63.

As well as different degrees of openness, there are also different *forms*, and a cluster of associated terms to describe them. Three stand out. (a) 'Indeterminacy' speaks of the way in which a piece may be *performed* in substantially different ways – the performer is given a variety of unique ways to sing or play it. In this sense, J. S. Bach's *Art of Fugue* is indeterminate, in that the instrumentation and dynamics are not given but must be decided by the performer(s). The term 'indeterminacy' was much used in the 1950s to refer to music in which the composer left one or more parameter open to the performer: pitch, note-duration, form, sound material, etc. (b) The term 'chance' is especially associated with John Cage, whose work we discuss below. He first used the term to refer to some sort of random procedure in the act of *composition*, throwing dice for example. In due course, he elevated chance to a principle of performance. (c) Related to these two terms is the term 'aleatory', which is often used very widely to describe any music with relatively fluid determinants, but which can also mean, more narrowly, *music in which the elements are well defined but used in random combinations.*   20. See Hardy and Ford (1984), 96–9.
21. See e.g. Suurmond (1994), 37ff. *et passim.*

then seen as a curse and burden. The Christian tradition assumes that freedom is realised through and in relation to constraint. If improvisation contributes in any way to our freedom (and our conceptualising of freedom), it will be more than anything else because it invites us to enjoy a liberating engagement of contingency and constraint. Improvisation can clarify, articulate and embody the contention that constraints are not intrinsically inimical to our freedom but are required for its actualisation. This I hope to show in what follows, bringing into prominence the temporal aspects of this freedom-in-relation-to-constraint.

Boulez and Cage

I propose to open up the theological issues at stake by examining an engrossing encounter between two leading composers of the twentieth century, the Frenchman Pierre Boulez (b. 1925) and the American John Cage (1912–92). From the early 1950s, Boulez and Cage came to represent two radically opposed streams of post-war music: Boulez the arch-priest of strict musical organisation, Cage of chance, where everything and anything seems to be able to count as music. The two men came to take a keen interest in each other's work and engaged in a number of exchanges, especially by letter between 1949 and 1954. The vigorous dialogue they enjoyed during these years (and we will concentrate on this period only) reveals not only the roots of what were later to be extreme differences between them, but also striking similarities. Moreover, theological matters are only just below the surface at a number of points.

Pierre Boulez came into prominence in the 1940s and 50s as a practitioner of what came to be known as 'total serialism' – a compositional method involving the rigorous organisation of music according to mathematical patterns. Its twentieth-century antecedents lie principally in the work of Arnold Schoenberg, Anton Webern and others, who advanced techniques which involved taking the twelve notes of a chromatic scale – the notes that fill an octave on a piano – arranging them in a particular order or series and then deriving a piece of music from various permutations of that series. This scheme applied mainly to note pitches. That was not enough for Boulez. He wanted *every* musical dimension to answer to the same mathematical consistency, as evinced in the dense and ferociously complex *Structure Ia* (1952). Two years later Boulez roundly declared: 'Webern only organised pitch; we organise rhythm, timbre, dynamics;

everything is grist to this monstrous all-purpose mill.'[22] Gerald Bennett, writing in 1986, comments: 'Boulez's composition represents one of the great adventures of the music this century: the restructuring of the language by imposing on it relations of absolute logical consistency.'[23]

Propelling this scheme was a passionate belief that post-war music could only advance if there was a purging of musical memory. The language of purification abounds.[24] Boulez could even liken himself to a twentieth-century musical Descartes, fashioning a new and ruthlessly consistent compositional method from first principles.[25] Not only the memory of past musical pieces but even memory *within* a piece of music was to be suppressed. We find a ruthless evasion of features which would seek to stimulate the memory, especially repetition and clarity of theme or motif. Not surprisingly, he rebelled against any trace of the tonal system with its implicatory, directional logic of tensions and resolutions.

No one was as perceptive as Boulez himself about the dangers and drawbacks of this exacting project. The first and most obvious was that it seemed to remove a large degree of responsibility not only from the performer but from the composer too. How could the wilfulness of the composer's imagination be squared with such apparently all-embracing mathematical necessity? In a sense these pieces composed themselves. Establish the formula and much of the music would unwind effortlessly. Boulez speaks of 'a way of writing that begins with something which eliminates personal invention'.[26] For Boulez, the notion of a composer making his or her singular 'mark' on the music was beside the point; logical consistency was paramount, not the unique imprint of a particular intellect or intention, still less the composer's personality.

Acutely aware of the problems inherent in this apparent erasure of personal involvement, later Boulez relaxed his metallic rigour slightly, allowing some measure of choice to the performer.

> In his Third Piano Sonata (begun in 1955), the performer is given a kind of a map of musical routes, any of which he or she can pursue. In the

---

22. Boulez (1991), 16. My italics.   23. Bennett (1986), 84.
24. Hence Boulez's infamous criticism of Schoenberg in 1952 ('Schoenberg is Dead'). For Boulez, Schoenberg was too bridled to the principles of tonal music. See Nattiez (1993), 13; Jameux (1991), 55ff. Reginald Smith Brindle highlights the desire on the part of the total serialists to escape the musical heritage of the past: 'Total organisation was, at that time, the only way to create the *tabula rasa* on which completely new edifices could be constructed. Furthermore, it was always evident that what troubled these composers most was their fear of conventional *rhythmic* configurations. Familiar rhythmic shapes are the most difficult of all to root out of our subconscious memories' (Brindle 1987, 23).
25. As in Butler (1980), 163; cf. Peyser (1977), 63.   26. Boulez (1976), 56.

two sections, 'Parenthèse' and 'Commentaire', there are optional and obligatory structures; the order of the sonata's four movements can also be varied. The composer (like the map-maker) has explored all those possible routes in advance, but the performer can choose which to follow – Boulez calls this 'directed chance'.[27] So the piece can assume more than one shape, like a familiar view seen from different positions.[28]

The second drawback was a paradoxical lack of variety and compelling interest. With every element in a constant state of variation, without repetition, theme or any sense of development, the music quickly generates a curious and debilitating sense of monotony. Many years later, Boulez could speak of the 'academicism' of total serialism: 'there was no sonic imagination, but simply an accumulation of numerical transcriptions quite devoid of any aesthetic character'.[29]

The third deficiency relates to the last, and is put *in nuce* by Boulez himself. There was in this music, he reminisces, 'a surfeit of order being equivalent to disorder'.[30] Boulez's point was principally about perception: though the music may have been radically organised it was virtually impossible to hear it as such, even if one was aware of the formal principles supporting it. Although a piece of music does not have to yield all its meaning in perception, a modicum of perceptual intelligibility would appear to be necessary to apprehend it *as music*. Total serialism seemed to engender a kind of 'entropic' anarchy. Boulez came to describe his *Livre pour Quatuor* as an 'accumulation that springs from a very simple principle, to end in a chaotic situation because it is engendered by material that turns in on itself and becomes so complex that it loses its individual shape and becomes part of a vast chaos'.[31] The irony again, and Boulez saw it clearly, is that the music can sound remarkably similar to that of John Cage, the pioneer of 'chance'. The prescriptive determinacies of notation coincide with sonorous effects which are largely indeterminate.

In fact, Boulez developed his all-encompassing serialism during a friendship with Cage. Their letters reveal shared concerns: they were both questioning received acoustical notions (their interest was less in pure sounds than in sound complexes); Cage's concern for the rhythmic

27. Boulez (1991), 31.
28. Part of the inspiration for this came from reading some notes by Mallarmé on a projected book (Nattiez 1993, 19). Boulez writes: 'my idea is not to change the work at every turn nor to make it look like a complete novelty, but rather to change the viewpoints and perspectives from which it is seen while leaving its basic meaning unaltered' (Boulez 1976, 82).   29. Boulez (1976), 64.   30. Ibid., 57.   31. Ibid., 51.

structuring of sound-aggregates strongly appealed to Boulez; in the late 1940s Cage himself was experimenting with twelve-tone techniques of a kind not dissimilar to Boulez; and Boulez was fascinated by the reduction of the composer to anonymous personality which found realisation in Cage's use of mathematical schemata.[32]

Where, then, did they differ? The crucial point of separation, which was eventually to lead to alienation, concerned the role of chance. Cage was deeply attracted to chance procedures and was later to initiate something of a craze for 'openness' and 'indeterminacy' in which ideological and political factors were interlaced with musical and aesthetic matters. Chance grew from the status of being a compositional method to becoming a principle of performance, and would in time transform a piece of music from a 'work' into a 'happening'. Despite the opacity of Cage's philosophising, compounded by the eclecticism which feeds it, clear at least is that for him chance became pivotal principally because of his desire to let sounds have their own integrity. Sounds were seen not merely as supportive and subservient to structure and form but as significant in their own right. Composing is a matter not of making an expressive continuity but of letting 'individual sounds 'find their own expressiveness within a blank canvas of empty time'.[33] 'Where people had felt the necessity to stick sounds together to make a continuity, we . . . felt the opposite necessity to get rid of the glue so that sounds would be themselves.'[34] Cage's goal, then, was to let sounds be themselves, unimpeded by service to any abstraction, so that, as Griffiths puts it, 'the work [is], in the Zen spirit, a vehicle not of thoughts but only events'.[35] Composition is about *accepting* rather than *making*. This means exploring freely the infinite space of musical possibilities, and for that, chance assumes an essential and central place. Past musical experience prohibits all but a small range of possibilities, so the mind must be purged of thoughts which inhibit an alertness to sounds being themselves: 'chance effectively blocks the exercise of one's accumulated knowledge and prejudices'.[36]

> In *Music for Changes* (1951), coins (or marked sticks) are thrown for chance numbers, hexagrams of thirty-two or sixty-four numbers are formed, and from these the various musical elements are determined.

32. See Nattiez (1993), 8ff.   33. Pritchett (1993), 74.
34. As quoted in Brindle (1987), 126.
35. Griffiths (1981), 27. Cage later spoke of the purpose of music as being 'to sober and quiet the mind, thus making one susceptible to divine influence' (as quoted in Fleming and Duckworth 1989, 23; he uses the same phrase earlier in the interview (21)).
36. Pritchett (1993), 76.

> According to this approach, therefore, the occurrence of any particular
> sound was not the result of imposing a melodic or harmonic idea 'but
> was now the result of nothing at all but geometry: the sounds simply
> "happened."'[37]

This conception of emerging sound Cage dubbed 'no-continuity', where
the ordering of events had nothing to do with any perceived or composed
relations between them. Each sound is just itself, and any relations
among the sounds happen of themselves, not because the composer's
intellect imposes them. Continuity is the product of the artist's mind, an
abstraction; in the case of 'no-continuity' the sounds simply happen. In a
letter to Boulez, Cage describes composition as 'throwing sounds into
silence'.[38] Later, he could say: 'in this new music nothing takes place but
sounds: those that are notated and those that are not. Those that are not
notated appear in the written music as silences, opening the doors of the
music to the sounds that happen to be in the environment.'[39] We need not
fear about the future of music, he continues,

> But this fearlessness only follows if . . . where it is realised that sounds
> occur whether intended or not, one turns in the direction of those he
> does not intend. This turning is psychological and seems at first to be a
> giving up of everything that belongs to humanity – for a musician, the
> giving up of music. This psychological turning leads to the world of
> nature, where, gradually or suddenly, one sees that humanity and
> nature, not separate, are in this world together.[40]

Contrast Boulez: 'By temperament I cannot toss a coin . . . Chance must be
very well controlled. *Il y a suffisamment d'inconnu.* ("There is already
enough unknown.")'[41] Although Boulez was to enjoy his own forays into
'directed chance', and although he went on to experiment with a variety
of compositional strategies, many of them allowing a much greater
degree of invention on the part of composer and performer than his early
work, and though he was later to view total serialism as something of a
dead end, chance could never be allowed to 'rule' in the manner of Cage
but needed to be carefully circumscribed so that one could maintain the
necessary 'dialectic between order and choice'.[42] In 1951, Boulez writes to
Cage: 'The only thing, forgive me, which I am not happy with, is the
method of absolute chance (*by tossing the coins*) . . . I believe that chance

37. Ibid., 66. Interestingly, Boulez approved of *Music of Changes* but this was because of its
structuration through complex charts, not its 'chance' character. See Nattiez (1993), 10f.
38. Nattiez (1993), 78.   39. Cage (1973), 7f.   40. Ibid., 8.
41. As quoted in Peyser (1977), 82.   42. As quoted in Heyworth (1986), 19.

must be extremely controlled.'[43] With more invective, Boulez later mocked: 'To claim to be creating a musical "environment" to which one need pay no attention until it becomes of greater interest is an excuse for total laziness: laziness of planning, laziness of thought, and even laziness in performance.'[44] 'It is the acceptance of a passive attitude towards what exists: it is an idea of surrender' which opens the way to manipulation and even fascism:[45]

> The anti-social overtones of such a position seem to me so obvious that at this stage you are ripe for the sort of fascist society which barely allows you a corner to play in ... It is a highly dangerous position, even from the political point of view, because a certain kind of society will accord you the privilege of being court jester on condition that you accept the position and don't try to step outside it ... [T]his desire to be the court jester, the jester of society, and to give that society a pretext to be a closed society with fascist tendencies, is an altogether repulsive and abject state of mind.[46]

We have only examined one very short period of these composers' output. However, standing back from this intercourse between two such seminal characters, both of them audacious and sophisticated, we are led to ask whether their respective projects and their engagement with each other during these years can be read most fruitfully as exemplifying a deep suspicion of three constraints with which any composer works – corporate tradition, the physical world, and the temporalities of the physical world. For both Boulez and Cage, all three would seem to be inherently problematic as media of beneficial interaction.

First, it is clear that *both attempt to evade the constraints of tradition*, that is, the constraints of corporate musical memory, the conventions, strategies, stylistic devices and so forth of the past. We find the thoroughly modernist passion to cleanse music of the last vestiges of its debilitating history. Cage wrote in 1952 that 'It is ... possible to make a musical composition the continuity of which is free of individual taste and memory (psychology) and also of the literature and "traditions" of the art.'[47] Not only possible, for Cage it was obligatory. Similarly, for Boulez in the 1940s and 50s, discontinuity with tradition was necessary to liberate music for a fresh future. He later mused: 'I momentarily suppressed inheritance. I started

---

43. As quoted in Nattiez (1993), 112.   44. Boulez (1976), 84.   45. Ibid., 85.
46. Ibid.
47. As quoted in Brindle (1987), 75. '[W]e will certainly listen to this other music – this totally determined music or Beethoven, or whatever, but we'll never again take it seriously' (Cage, as quoted in Kostelanetz 1974, 11).

off from the fact that I was thinking, and went on to see how one might construct a musical language from scratch.'[48] 'For me it was an experiment in what one might call Cartesian doubt, to bring everything into question again, make a clear sweep of one's heritage, and start all over again from scratch, to see how it might be possible to reconstitute a way of writing that began with something which eliminates personal invention.'[49] Ever since it has always been part of Boulez's creed that composers must move music in 'new' directions; his admiration for past composers is reserved especially for those who altered the direction of music in some fundamental way. Many of Boulez's pronouncements about history are pungent with the modernist aroma. For example: 'Strong, expanding civilisations have no memory: they reject, they forget the past.'[50]

The difference between the Frenchman and the American here lies in the purpose of this mental purgation. For Boulez, the mind is to be cleared for the purpose of the effective intellectual mastery of sound, for Cage, in order to let nature 'be herself'. Boulez's suspicion of chance in music was in large part because of what he felt to be its proclivity to fall back on musical clichés: 'Much was – and is – spoken of freedom; whilst this so-called freedom is nothing but a perfumed subjection to memory.'[51] Only persistent intellectual cleansing can ensure authentic musical freedom. For Cage the mind is to be expurgated of the grids which impose links between sounds and impede them being truly themselves.

This leads us to a second similarity. Both would appear to share *a distinct unease about the relation of the composer to the constraint of nature*. The problematic is a familiar one in modernity and is frequently grounded in an ancient hesitancy about the goodness and order of the material world, leading to a suspicion about whether the non-human physical world is an environment with which we can interact closely in a way that will engender freedom. Two extremes typically result. The one is a denial of our rootedness in the material universe, the other a denial of any kind of active transcendence over it. Boulez tends to line up with the first, Cage with the second.

<hr/>

48. As quoted in Heyworth (1986), 13.   49. As quoted in Butler (1980), 163.
50. Boulez (1976), 33. 'The more I grow, the more I detach myself from other composers, not only from the distant past but also from the recent past and even from the present. Conducting has forced me to absorb a great deal of history, so much so, in fact, that history seems more than ever to me a great burden. In my opinion we must get rid of it once for all' (as quoted in Peyser 1977, 19). 'The fight,' he says, 'is a bigger one than getting the audience to cheer. The dilemma of music is the dilemma of our civilisation. We have to fight the past to survive' (ibid., 20). 'History as it is made by great composers is not a history of conservation but of destruction – even while cherishing what is destroyed' (Boulez 1976, 21).   51. Nattiez (1993), 24.

Boulez exemplifies most clearly the arch-modernist view of the artist whose sovereign constructive intellect brings order and meaning to the sonic world.[52] Admittedly this was a particular type of mastery, in that the intellectual system mattered more than the particular mind which chose to shape sound through it, but it is intellectual mastery nevertheless. The question inevitably arises: to what extent does Boulez's 'computerised passion'[53] do violence to the materials of sound? To what extent are the 'systems' which determine the music consonant with the properties and intrinsic interrelationships of sounds themselves?[54] As we noted, at this stage in his career Boulez himself was well aware that his music was complex to the point of perceptual incoherence. In an important article on Boulez's early works, Gerald Bennett observes that increasingly during the 1940s, the material Boulez uses begins to resist his rigorous structuring. As ever more elaborate and higher levels of abstraction are attained, he tends to obscure his primary musical lines and forms, and new structures begin to direct the course of the music's development. (To counter this, in at least one piece Boulez inserts a kind of shadow of the (hidden) musical lines on the surface level of the music, but this shadow 'loses its structural function and becomes merely decorative . . . it is now only embellishment.'[55] 'Intricately delicate structure becomes shimmering surface, surface masquerades as structure. The two become indistinguishable, which means the ultimate abrogation and annulment of structure itself.'[56] Bennett likens this to a half-timbered house where the framework has been covered up by repeated restoration and the new owners have painted on timbers to resemble a timbered house.[57]) Bennett declares that 'A struggle of the highest drama – and of the greatest importance – is being enacted here.' Boulez loses control over the material through the imposition of ever stricter control. It is 'one of the most important confrontations in the music of our time – that of a composer determined to force material to obey his complex structural demands on the one hand, on the other the musical material itself, increasingly reluctant to submit gracefully to these demands'.[58] Bennett concludes: 'the adventure of Boulez's music is *an examination of the very foundations of composition itself*'.[59]

52. For a sensitive situating of Boulez in relation to post-war modernist painters and writers, see Stacey (1987).   53. Jameux's phrase (Jameux 1991, 54).
54. Boulez may speak of the composition of *Structure Ia* as 'purely automatic' (Boulez 1976, 56), and the material as a kind of 'given' with a self-generated life of its own, but the 'material' of which he speaks, which is allowed to control aspects of the music, has in fact already been intellectually shaped in a highly intricate way.   55. Bennett (1986), 77.
56. Ibid., 84.   57. Ibid., 77.   58. Ibid., 41.   59. Ibid., 84. My italics.

It is not hard to correlate these remarks with a classically modernist conception of humanity's relation to the non-human environment: through ever stricter control we lose control of our God-given home, with catastrophic results. Speaking in 1975 of the composition of *Structures*, Boulez remarks that he was aware of the '*contrast*, which to my mind is necessary to composition, between *the will to make something out of the material and what the material suggests to one.*'[60] Here we could well cite Ernst Kris's (undoubtedly exaggerated) claim that in artistic modernism, 'the artist does not "render" nature, nor does he "imitate" it, but creates it anew. He controls the world through his work ... The unconscious meaning is *control at the price of destruction.*'[61] The phrase 'control at the price of destruction' links up with Boulez's phrase 'excess of order being equivalent to disorder', and could well stand as the sad motto over many of the results of the twentieth century's disrespect for the integrity of the non-human realm, all too often fuelled by questionable theologies of divine and human freedom.

Initially Cage would seem to be more promising. According to him, we must relinquish the desire to control, and 'let sounds be themselves rather than vehicles for man-made theories or expressions of human sentiments'.[62] This does not mean complete passivity, for one composes the individual sounds which become the material of the composition, but this composing is only to provide 'opportunities for experience'. Cage's interest is not in expressing, limiting or shaping, still less in 'conveying a message'. 'Until that time', Cage tells us, 'my music had been based on the idea that you had to say something. The charts [of the music of the early fifties] gave me the indication of the possibility of saying nothing.'[63] To be sure, here music is 'freed', in a sense, but the cost is an evacuation (or near evacuation) of the notion of music as constructive, of the idea that human shaping could be fruitful and enriching. The dialectic between human will and nature's constraint is thus effectively dissolved. Speaking of Cage, Edward Lippman comments: 'What clearly is at stake here is the elimination of any distinction between art and nature (or between artistic experience and ordinary experience).'[64] That is probably going too far, but it indicates the direction Cage travels, and it is a direction few have been willing to follow since (despite Cage's predictions about the dissolution of the boundary between noise and music). It is one thing to spurn

---

60. Boulez (1976), 56. My italics.   61. As quoted in Taylor (1987), 36f. My italics.
62. Cage (1973), 10.   63. As quoted in Griffiths (1981), 24.   64. Lippman (1992), 436.

the worst of humanity's aggressive imposition on the natural order, it is quite another to suppress any conception of human forming altogether. Further, we might add, Cage's stress is very much on the 'randomness' of the extra-human world, not on its inherent order.

Underlying and supporting both these two similarities, I would suggest, is a third, an unease with *temporal constraint*, or, to be more accurate, particular kinds of temporal constraint. This may be of a piece with these composers' inability to present a convincing dialectic between human embeddedness and otherness in relation to the non-human world, with associated doubts about nature possessing its own distinctive integrity (which includes a temporal integrity). In any case, their mistrust of tradition indicates the main form of musical temporality they wish to discard: directional temporal continuity. As with many of their contemporaries, any goal-oriented, teleological dynamic (so characteristic of tonal music) is not only avoided but subverted – tensions and resolutions, clearly marked out sections, development, opening and ending frames, and so forth. More than this, Boulez sought to abolish any sense of metre or rhythmic regularity either in the large scale or in the smallest details.[65] Cage's music of this period and much of his later work is perhaps best understood as a variety of what Jonathan Kramer terms 'vertical time music', which we have spoken about already.[66] Common to vertical time music is the restraint (or evasion) of temporal differentiation within the entirety of a piece of music. Cage is not prepared to see sounds as participants in some kind of progression from beginning to closure, because for him each instant is equally related to each other instant. No event can be any more significant or valuable than any other. Mertens explains:

> Any sound can be the beginning, the continuation, or the end, and no sound is more important than the next. The exclusive musical perspective found in dialectical teleology has been replaced by a randomly selected perspective, a phenomenon Cage called 'interpenetration.' By this he meant that every musical element in time and space is related to every other musical element, has an equal value, and works in all directions at the same time, without the existence of cause-and-effect relationships. The fact that each sound has the same

65. Even on those occasions in his early works where there is regularity of beat (as in his First Piano Sonata), there is no grouping of these beats at any higher level into metre. For a sensitive account of Boulez's musical engagement with time, especially of the variety of temporalities Boulez was later to explore, see Gable (1990).
66. J. Kramer (1988), 384ff. See above, p. 143.

value implies equally that each sound has no value. Cage sees sound only as a fragment in the time-continuum.[67]

Listening to such homogeneous music entails abandoning the urge to project implications and progressions, functional or articulative relationships between events (the temporal configurations, in other words, of teleological music). Here events are linked not by virtue of some purpose or 'argument', but instead by schemes originally produced by chance procedures, or (as in some of his later works) by an 'openness' to what 'happens' in performance.

As far as Boulez is concerned, though he would distance himself from much in Cage's metaphysics, and though his music of the late 1940s and early 1950s does not generally come close to vertical time music, we witness the same elision of goal-oriented temporality, thematic development, implicative harmonic relationships and so forth. Edward Cone draws out the likeness:

> When chance plays the major role in the writing of a work, as in Cage's *Music for Piano 21–52* (1955), logic . . . can take only an accidental part. The same is true of music written according to a strictly predetermined constructivistic scheme, such as Boulez's *Structures* (1952). In neither case can any musical event be linked organically with those that precede and those that follow; it can be explained only by referring to an external structure – in the one case the laws of chance and in the other the predetermined plan. *The connections are mechanistic rather than teleological: no event has any purpose – each is there only because it has to be there.*[68]

'Mechanistic rather than teleological' – curiously, despite Cage's highly charged rhetoric of chance, speaking of his music, as with Boulez, one often has recourse to the language of necessity. The irony should not be missed: the struggle to be free of a supposedly oppressive teleological system (such as tonality) would seem to come close to resulting in two kinds of (oppressive?) necessity, the one the necessity of a particular mathematical system, the other the somewhat bland necessity of 'the way things happen'.[69] This goes hand in hand with excluding evidence of personal intention, to which they both subscribed, albeit for different reasons.[70]

---

67. Mertens (1983), 107.   68. Cone (1960), 38. My italics.
69. Speaking of *Music of Changes*, Cage writes: 'Value judgements are not in the nature of this work as regards either composition, performance, or listening . . . A "mistake" is beside the point, for once anything happens it authentically is' (Cage 1973, 59).
70. We have already spoken of this in connection with Boulez. Cage says of his *Music of Changes* that it 'is an *object more inhuman than human*, since chance operations brought it into

This leads to a further reflection on the character of temporal constraint. A significant part of the problematic of the Boulez–Cage outlook (at least in the years we are considering) is a neglect of the possibility that the universe, with its sounds, is marked by contingent order – that is, open to proliferating possibilities, yet proportioned and configured. Such a picture is confirmed in the physical sciences, it would seem, by the behaviour of complex dynamical systems, which exhibit a supple interplay of stability and unpredictability, suggesting a cosmos characterised by an orderly yet abundant allowance of space, time and energy through which further abundance can emerge. The world's temporality, for all its complexity, is hard to accommodate within 'block-universe' or determinist conceptions. No one is accusing Boulez and Cage in 1950 of being either overt or covert determinists, or blaming them for being ignorant of the theory of dynamic instabilities. The point is whether either of them could do sufficient justice to contingency in the world at large and its interplay with structure.

In reading this conversation in the way I have, I am not claiming that Boulez or Cage were essentially young philosophers who simply turned their ideas into notes, and certainly not that they shared some carefully considered metaphysics. But I do want to contend that in certain respects, despite their marked differences, at this stage in their careers they stand very close to each other and that their similarities are as instructive as their differences. Insofar as their writings and music exhibit a pursuit of freedom in the three areas I have mentioned, it would appear to be a pursuit in line with that philosophical tradition which would regard constraint as inherently detrimental to authentic freedom. Interaction with constraint is more likely to inhibit than to enlarge freedom. Ironically, as we have seen, the concept of 'necessity' is often not far away.

In short, they are playing out, in music and word, some of the central pathologies of modernism. In response, we might be tempted to proceed directly to the standard language of systematic theology and subject the pivotal assumptions on which both composers depend to sustained criticism, replacing them with rich trinitarian doctrines of creation, humankind and so on. A more indirect but I think more illuminating way

---

being' (as quoted in Pritchett 1993, 109). My italics. Peter Heyworth remarks: 'At first sight, serial determinism and the wilder shores of aleatoric music [music such as Cage's during this period] appear as far apart as any two things can be. But both, when carried to their logical conclusions, seemed to [Boulez] to relieve the composer of much of his responsibility' (Heyworth 1986, 18).

forward is to stay in the world of music and let music do some of the theological work for us. In particular, we turn to particular forms of improvisation, which open up rather different possibilities, yielding especially valuable resources for exploring and articulating a theological account of human freedom.

Freedom and constraint

The assumption that any limitation on our self-determination, self-constitution and self-expression is necessarily hostile to freedom has been heavily questioned on many fronts (including the theological) in recent writing. By contrast, it is maintained, freedom is mediated through, and in relation to constraint. 'Constraint' here refers not essentially to 'confinement' but to 'specificity' or 'particular shape'.[71] Constraints are structures which prevent us from being indeterminate and amorphous creatures, and which give us our identity. There are constraints internal to the person – e.g. genetic makeup, physiological processes and so forth – and those external – e.g. other persons, the extra-human material universe and, supremely, God. Without such determinants we cannot be free.

That freedom is dependent on constraint is patently evident in many spheres. In cybernetics there is a principle which states that 'Where a constraint exists, advantage can usually be taken of it.'[72] In other words, if there were unlimited degrees of self-determination we could not advance beyond chaos. Organisations of energy become possible because stable limits are set on their possibility: 'Elaborate networks of constraint, running down eventually into the laws of motion, set the conditions and boundaries which allow different constructions of energy.'[73] Human beings have developed the capacity to submit to constraints deliberately in order to extend the possibilities of their interaction with the world: I can spend two hours a day learning a language (a self-imposed constraint) in order to increase my capacity to communicate in another country. Similarly, the freedom enjoyed in composing music depends on 'taking advantage' of constraints to enlarge communicative power. The composer Igor Stravinsky put it tellingly:

> I experience a sort of terror when, at the moment of setting to work and finding myself before the infinitude of possibilities that present

71. The terms are John Webster's (Webster 1995, 71).   72. Ashby (1956), 3.
73. Bowker (1991a), 2. In this chapter I am much indebted to John Bowker's discussions of constraint; see Bowker (1973), 86ff.; (1991a), 1ff.; (1995), 83f., 88, 96ff., 115ff., 168ff.

themselves, I have the feeling that everything is permissible to me. If everything is permissible to me . . . every undertaking becomes futile . . . I shall overcome my terror and shall be reassured by the thought that I have the seven notes of the scale and its chromatic intervals at my disposal . . . strong and weak accents are within my reach, and . . . in all these I possess solid and concrete elements which offer me a field of experience just as vast as the upsetting and dizzy infinitude that had just frightened me . . . What delivers me from the anguish into which an unrestricted freedom plunges me is the fact that I am always able to turn immediately to the concrete things that are here in question . . . Whatever constantly gives way to pressure, constantly renders movement impossible . . . Whatever diminishes constraint, diminishes strength.[74]

Authentic personal freedom, genuine particularity and self-realisation, can be exercised only in accordance with real possibilities and impossibilities. Constraints can of course threaten human freedom, as in epilepsy or solitary confinement. But what is dubious is the belief that we automatically augment freedom by reducing limitation and/or multiplying the number of possibilities open to us. For 'if possibilities are to be meaningful for free choice, they must be well-defined by structures of limit'.[75] To multiply possibilities indefinitely would in fact remove the competence of choice and thus of freedom.

Freedom, then, is not a thing or entity to be sought after, or a possession to be grasped. It qualifies arrangements of persons and things; it describes proper relationships and configurations between particularities: 'The functions of "free" are adjectival . . . It is not the name of our home or the description of our destiny but, at best, how we are at home and, at worst, how we may be at sea.'[76] Theologically speaking, to be free is not to enjoy some supposedly unbounded contingency, it is to be at home in the world, at peace with each other and with God.

Improvisation and constraint

And so to improvisation. Improvisation provides a powerful enactment of the truth that our freedom is enabled to flourish only by engaging with and negotiating constraints. To explore this we shall restrict ourselves mainly to one main form of improvisation, that typified by – but by no means confined to – 'traditional jazz': a broad stream of music originating

74. Stravinsky (1947), 63ff.   75. O'Donovan (1986), 107.   76. Lash (1996), 244.

in a complex fusion of styles in New Orleans in the early 1900s and practised, with significant modifications and developments, up until and including the 1950s.[77] At first sight, we might think that the only limit or constraint to consider is a musical structure or framework – a pattern of chords, a theme, or whatever. But improvisation involves large networks of constraint, interacting in highly elaborate ways. The improviser is *multiply* constrained, and as with all networks of constraint we can never exhaustively specify all the constraints. Some are purely passive, setting the boundary conditions; some are actively and directly causative; some are permissive, needing a particular happening in order to be activated; some are proximate, some distant; some are invariant and intransigent, some flexible and pliable.

The contingency of improvisation demands of the participants a peculiar kind of alertness to these constraints. Picking up Jacques Lecoq's use of the term *disponibilité*, Frost and Yarrow speak of 'armed neutrality':

> *Disponibilité* sums up in a single term the condition improvisers aspire to … having at (or in) one's fingertips, and any other part of the body, the capacity to do and say what is appropriate, and to have the confidence to make the choice. It's a kind of total awareness, a sense of being at one with the context: script, if such there be, actors, audience, theatre space, oneself and one's body.[78]

A constraint may in fact be rejected in improvisation: for instance, a musical convention may be spurned in order to pursue something that is felt to be more promising. But this is not done in the name of a 'freedom' dedicated to the escape of constraint. A constraint is normally refused after it has been taken seriously and tested. Initially, improvisers show hospitality to constraint, even if it might eventually be shown the door. Moreover, a musical constraint is often abandoned because it has failed in some way to engage with other constraints, for example, the particularities of the occasion.

Constraints relevant to improvisation may be divided into three broad and overlapping types: 'occasional', 'cultural' and 'continuous'. By occa-

---

77. This is not to suggest that traditional jazz is no longer alive. But the upheavals of jazz in the 1960s, especially 'free' jazz, marked a decisive challenge to the mainline of jazz up until that time. These developments were marked by less dependence on pre-established formulaic elements and conventions and more on the circumstances of the occasion. Examples are the jazz of John Coltrane, Cecil Taylor and Ornette Coleman, and more 'postmodernist' experiments: so-called 'Third Stream' jazz; the American and European free improvising ensembles who gave prominence to the interaction between performer, environment and listener; the 'recreators'; and the 'jazz-funk' movement.
78. Frost and Yarrow (1990), 152.

sional constraints, I mean the unique circumstances which are specific to a social, spatial or temporal situation, in the case of improvisation, those pertaining to a performance – for example, the acoustics of a concert hall, the mood of a particular audience. Cultural constraints are frameworks and patterns of action brought to an improvisation by the improvisers and listeners, constraints which have developed from interaction with others, perhaps over many years – the harmonic sequence in blues is an example. They include the whole range of skills and musical experience which inevitably shape any particular performance.[79] Continuous constraints are those which condition us by virtue of the fact that we all inhabit a 'given', physical world with its own integrity – for example, the way strings vibrate, bodily competence, etc.

The interest and attractiveness of improvisation depend in large part on the interplay between these constraints and the contingency of performance. In the next chapter, we shall consider some of the ways in which this interplay takes place, enacting the dynamics of Christian freedom.

Improvisation, freedom and time

Special attention will be given to the temporality of this interplay. The temporality of the world is, of course, a continuous constraint. I want to suggest that *improvisation, by enabling a freedom in relation to a vast array of constraints, can enable a freedom with respect to a fundamental continuous constraint which permeates them all, namely the world's temporality, and I want to suggest that the theological resonances of this are considerable.*

Improvisation involves a process whereby *cultural constraints* (especially, the given musical material and strategies which shape it) *are brought into engagement with the occasional constraints* (those constraints peculiar to the performance setting). Improvisation 'particularises' musical 'givens' *from* the past *for* a present occasion. To be sure, most musical performers do this to some extent, even when the music is thoroughly notated and prepared in advance. But, as we have said, in improvisation there is a particularly high level of contingency: the improviser has a considerable amount of room to interpret the given musical constraints such that they engage

79. Improviser Arthur Rhames says: 'I'm calling upon all the resources of all the years of my playing at once: my academic understanding of the music, my historical understanding of the music, and my technical understanding of the instrument that I'm playing. All these things are going into one concentrated effort to produce something that is indicative of what I'm feeling at the time I'm performing' (as quoted in Berliner 1994, 16).

with the particular circumstances of the occasion. Further, when this happens, new futures with hitherto unconsidered possibilities are opened up. In addition, *continuous constraints* are drawn into and promote this process.

Things are, of course, much more elaborate than this. For example, people themselves are bundles of constraint and contingency, determinacy and openness. Likewise the physical world we inhabit. Nevertheless, the particularising of the past for the present and future, enabled by the interplay of contingency and constraint, appears to lie somewhere near the heart of what is involved in improvising traditional jazz.

And, we shall maintain, it also lies near the heart of the temporality of freedom. Numerous bids for freedom have consisted of attempts to escape or defeat time in some fashion, something we have alluded to a number of times. Many modernist and contemporary accounts of freedom, theological and non-theological, have fallen captive to essentially atemporal conceptions of the self, with the result that attempts are made to appropriate a certain kind of divine freedom for the human agent. As Christoph Schwöbel puts it,

> Human responsibility is closely tied to observance of the temporality of actions . . . it seems that *the modern rhetoric of freedom suggests that we ignore this temporality systematically*, so that we are confronted with the long-term effects of our actions which occur beyond the time-span we can influence or control. There are many examples of our actions producing long-term effects that cancel out their intended short-term benefits. The legacy left to future generations by DDT spraying campaigns or by the long-lasting radiation levels of nuclear waste have brought this sharply to our attention.[80]

Schwöbel also observes that concepts of freedom as absolute, unlimited and sovereign imply 'illusory expectations' about the capacities of human beings. When these expectations are disappointed, scepticism soon arises. Our actions are no longer determined by confidence that anything can be changed for the good. The expectations paradoxically restrict our freedom to the point of incapacitating intentional action. Grandiose conceptions of the self as unlimited, which include a disregard of the temporality of our actions, can paralyse us into non-action. 'In this respect,' Schwöbel comments, 'the consequences of the modern rhetoric of absolute freedom are not very different from those of a radically deterministic picture of the world and the role of human agents in it.'[81] (The

80. Schwöbel (1995), 66. My italics.   81. Ibid., 67.

echoes of the Boulez–Cage exchange should not be missed.) Coming to terms with temporality as a fundamental condition of our lives – avoiding the illusion both of absolute indeterminacy and of slavery to time – will thus be critical to enjoying genuine freedom. It will be clear by now that music has much to offer here, for 'taking advantage' of the world's temporality in such a way that our freedom is enlarged is precisely what music at its best can do.

It is our task now to find out what musical improvisation in particular can offer. The freedom realised in the best improvisation is not an amorphous 'openness' struggling to conquer (or ignore) constraints, but a fruitful interaction between contingency and constraint. This is improvisation's distinctive contribution to learning to 'live peaceably with time', and thus to a theology of human freedom.

8

Liberating constraint

> [H]aving myself engaged in group improvisation over a period of time I can testify to its power to liberate aspects of one's musicality and sense of musical responsibility in a way that no other musical activity can achieve. I have been lucky enough to encounter musical experiences of power and beauty of an altogether different kind from that of either listening to, performing or even creating composed music; the degree of involvement is of a quite different kind, as one might expect from the exploration of one another's musical personalities in a loving way . . . Cardew does not exaggerate in describing the experience as erotic.[1]
>
> CHRISTOPHER SMALL

Occasional constraints

One of the most enjoyable things about improsivising with a group is the *frisson* which comes from knowing this is a 'one off' event, unprecedented and unrepeatable. And a large part of this comes from sensing the uniqueness of the circumstances of the occasion – the 'occasional' constraints. The improviser is generally much more alert to these than performers who are tied closely to notation and rehearsal. The poet Peter Riley calls improvisation 'the exploration of occasion'.[2] There is respect for the particularities of circumstance and an intimate engagement with them. Far from being a kind of cage which the musician at best tolerates and at worst ignores (or even contests), these constraints are normally invited into the improvisation: the occasion is brought to sound. Speaking of dramatic improvisation, Frost and Yarrow claim that at best it

---

1. Small (1977), 180.   2. As cited in Dean (1989), xvi.

'comes close to a condition of integration with the environment or context. And consequently (simultaneously) expresses that context in the most appropriate shape, making it recognisable to others, "realising" it as act.'[3]

The occasional constraints are of three main kinds. First, there is the physical space in which the improvisation occurs and its attendant sounds (e.g. the concert hall, with its buzzing heaters, traffic outside, etc.). Second, there are the other improvising participants (and we are presuming this group has not improvised together before), the music they produce, and the audience (if there is one). Third, there is the disposition of the improviser him/herself – mood, degree of nervousness and so forth. Here we concentrate on the second of these, in particular on the improviser's relationships with other improvisers, the temporal character of these relationships and the way in which freedom can be exemplified through them.

In more formalised concert and operatic performance, communication is normally interposed by an external agency, a score of some sort. With its stress on social process rather than finished text, and its high contingency, improvisation encourages a particular kind of immediacy of personal exchange. We do not need to endorse the inflated claims sometimes made about group improvisation to see that there are patterns of action, ways of being and behaviour here which would seem, at the very least, to illuminate the character of authentic human freedom.[4]

Helpful use can be made of the categories found in Alistair McFadyen's *The Call to Personhood*, where a relational account of human personhood is grounded in the creation of humankind in God's image and in the 're-creation of individuality' through the call of Christ. In 'monologue' the individual manipulates or is manipulated: one person treats the other as a means to an end, such that the other becomes self-confirmatory. The other's otherness becomes 'a repetition of a previously privately co-ordinated understanding'.[5] In 'dialogue' or 'undistorted communication', the

3. Frost and Yarrow (1990), 2.
4. See e.g. Prévost (1985), Dean (1989), Bailey (1992), Durant (1989). Much of the recent literature on improvisation has highlighted the implicit social and even political challenges it presents. Group improvisation questions many dominant procedures through which music is made, reproduced, circulated and consumed today. In particular, it disrupts conventional barriers between 'composer', 'performer' and 'audience', for an improviser is (normally) all three simultaneously. This is why Jacques Attali sees the growth of improvisation in the 1960s and 70s as heralding a new way of relating in which we are not merely passive consumers, but active contributors in open-ended personal exchange (Attali 1985).   5. McFadyen (1990), 26.

other's particularity is acknowledged such that one allows for the possibility of one's own expectations and intentions to be resisted: 'To recognise and intend the freedom of the other in response is to recognise that
the form and content of that response cannot be overdetermined by the
address.'[6] There is 'a readiness to allow the calls of others to transform us
in response'.[7] This does not mean that we assume the superiority of the
other, or quantitative equality between dialogue partners. Commenting
on McFadyen's work, Francis Watson writes: 'Something similar is suggested by the Pauline image of the church as body, where the allocation of
varying gifts and roles by the same Spirit establishes a formal [not quanti-
tative] equality . . . within a diversity of roles which allows for hierarchical
elements so long as these are understood in strictly reciprocal rather than
monological terms.'[8] Very much the same could be said of improvisation,
in which there would seem to be growth of personal particularity
through musical dialogue. All the skills which promote reciprocal 'undistorted communication' – which should characterise the Church as
persons-in-communion – are present in a very heightened form: for
example, giving 'space' to the other through alert attentiveness, listening
in patient silence, contributing to the growth of others by 'making the
best' of what is received from them such that they are encouraged to continue participating, sensitive decision-making, flexibility of response,
initiating change, role-changing, generating and benefiting from conflict. Without the mediation of a verbal text and conventional verbal communication, these skills have to be learned in musical modes and thus in a
sense re-thought and re-learned. This may well contribute to freer communication in other fields.[9]

There is much to draw upon here if we want to develop a properly
theological account of freedom which sees it as mediated by and through
the other in a process of concentrated dialogical action, where the constraint of others is experienced not as essentially oppressive but as conferring and confirming an inalienable particularity and uniqueness. Not
only are modernist conceptions of self-determined and self-constituted
individuals questioned, but also the dissolution of self-identity implicit
in some postmodernism.[10] Significantly, homogeneity of sound has little
place in jazz. 'Sound in jazz is . . . the slow, expressive vibrato of Sidney

6. Ibid., 119.   7. Ibid., 121.   8. Watson (1994), 112.
9. There are many points of overlap here with David Ford's intriguing discussion of the
notion of a 'singing self' (Ford 1999, 120ff). I am indebted in this section to Professor Ford
for numerous conversations on improvisation and related themes.
10. Watson (1994), ch. 6.

Bechet's soprano sax; the voluminous, erotic tenor sax sound of Coleman Hawkins; the earthy cornet of King Oliver; the "jungle" sound of Bubber Miley.'[11]

Temporality is closely intertwined with this understanding of freedom. When I, the improviser, come to terms with and engage with another improviser I come to terms with the other's temporality. Others are 'there' as constraints not only spatially but temporally. They are permanently there for the duration of this improvisation. They are not about to leave, they are as keen to play as I am. Their presence as co-musicians is permanent and constant. Further, I come to know their skills, dispositions, tendencies, and this means knowing the temporality of their typical 'moves' – their timing, their speed of response, the characteristic way they shape melodies over time. All this can be respected and in various ways incorporated into the music.[12] And the same applies to the other's treatment of me. In other words, part of our conferring particularity on each other is the conferring of time (I 'give time' to the other) such that the other person's distinctive temporality is allowed to engage with mine, and vice versa, to mutual benefit. Music's time-intensive involvement is especially well equipped to promote just this kind of interaction.

Intensifying the mutual attentiveness and reaction is a high degree of contingency. I enter into this improvisation, this series of musical events, in the belief that there is a large measure of openness, not only in my own contribution but in those of my companion improvisers. However well I know them and their temporal habits (and whatever my metaphysical beliefs about the flexibility of the physical world) I treat them, in effect, as 'open systems', a mixture of contingency and structure, not as predictable automata. The same should apply to the way they treat me. As we make music together, part of the freedom we enjoy comes from the complex interweaving of this contingency with the (more or less) predictable temporalities which characterise most people.

Cultural constraints

As far as cultural constraints are concerned, I shall concentrate on the specifically musical ones and on those limiting the improvisers themselves.

11. Berendt (1983), 144. The ethical implications of jazz for modelling 'desirable social relations' are explored vividly by Kathleen Marie Higgins, with particular reference to 'progressive' jazz and race relations (Higgins 1991, 170–80).
12. If I do not know this other person in advance, their temporal constitution has to be discovered in and through the improvisation, adding a further contingency to the situation.

By far the most important in traditional jazz are *metre* and *harmonic sequence* (corresponding to the two 'fields' of metre and key we spoke about in chapter 2). In a jazz band these are usually articulated by the so-called 'rhythm section' (piano and/or guitar, bass, and drums).[13] The theme or *melody* (normally played by the 'melody section' of a band – clarinet, saxophone or whatever), either in its entirety or in its component motifs, may be used as material for improvisation. But usually the melody is of secondary structural importance compared to metre and harmony. Metre, harmony and melody are normally shaped according to an *idiom* – such as blues, bebop, or whatever.

Metre

Virtually all that we have said about metre applies to improvised jazz. But especially characteristic of jazz is the engagement between metre on the one hand – usually strongly articulated, predictable and regular, and rhythm on the other – marked out by the improvised notes, largely unpredictable, much less repetitive and more irregular. Further, metre assumes a more fundamental role in traditional jazz than in virtually any other Western music. It is generally played by the rhythm section and rarely changes in pace.[14] 'Swing' comes from a particular kind of conversation between this steady metre and rhythm; tensions and resolutions are generated by displacing rhythmic over metrical accent.

> Syncopation involves the transformation-through-subversion of regular patterns of metrical beats – e.g. the accenting of the second and fourth beats of a four-beat bar (Example 8.1).

Example 8.1 Syncopation

> This can occur at any metrical level. One of the characteristics of swing is the 'swing eighth note' – an accent on the third note of an implied triplet within a beat (Example 8.2).

Example 8.2 Syncopation: accent on quaver

13. A rhythm section may sometimes take over 'melody section' roles, and vice versa.
14. There can be rubato ('robbing the time' of one part of a phrase to allow for the elongation of another), and slowing or speeding up from time to time, but major changes of tempo, common in composed music, are relatively rare in traditional jazz.

The tension set up through syncopation, between metrical beats and off-beat accents, can be generated in many different ways: between a bass note and a melody note, between a steady bass drum beat and melodic notes, between the different strokes of a drummer, within a rhythm section, and so on. Syncopation may be brought into relief through the presence of a drummer, but a drummer is by no means necessary.

In fact, even the players in a rhythm section rarely play strictly 'on the beat', and this is in order, usually quite unconsciously, to highlight metrical waves. Some speak of playing in three different parts of the beat. The drummer or bass player, for example, can play ahead, behind, or right 'on' the beat.[15] Fred Hersch claims that in a performance

there should be ten, fifteen different kinds of time. There's a kind which has an edge on it for a while and then lays back for a while. Sometimes it rolls over the bar, and sometimes it sits more on the beats. That's what makes it interesting . . . That's what makes it come alive. People are human, and rhythmic energy has an ebb and flow.[16]

Even here, however, what is being *assumed* is a steady, regular metre, whatever the drummer and bass player may actually play.

This dependence on metre is not a sign of laziness or lack of musical imagination. The appeal of jazz depends on it. Much hangs on the close interplay between these contrasting, incongruous elements – the relatively regular predictability of metrical waves, and the relatively irregular unpredictability of the improvised music. The two interanimate and enrich each other. Not only does the metre act as a foundation for us to enjoy the improvised rhythm; the metrical waves are, as it were, thrown into relief by the rhythm. Zuckerkandl's vivid depiction of rhythm riding the metrical waves could easily apply to traditional jazz:

The tones may be distributed over the measure regularly or irregularly; may fill the measure in rapid succession or leave it empty for long stretches; at one place crowd close together, at another spread thin; may follow the pattern of the measure with their accents or run contrary to it. This freedom of distribution and arrangement makes it possible for the tones to give the constant basic form of the wave a changing, perpetually different profile. In accordance with the will of the tones, the wave will display contours now soft and rounded, now sharp and jagged; will beat softly and calmly or with ever-increasing impact; will heave, topple, break against resistances. This *playing with the wave by the tones*, this shaping of the substance of the wave; the

15. Berliner (1994), 150ff.   16. Ibid., 151.

conjunction and opposition of two components, their mutual tension and continuous adjustment to each other – this, in music, we experience as rhythm.[17]

Therefore, not only are the rhythmic irregularity and unpredictable novelty of the improvised music enhanced by the metre, such that the musically contingent is enabled to unfold in its own way, but the metrical wave is enhanced by the improvised lines as they 'play with' the wave. Metre magnifies improvised rhythm and improvised rhythm magnifies metre.

It should be clear that in this mutually enhancing contrast-through-interplay we are given a remarkable sonic embodiment of a freedom which comes through and in relation to constraint. Metrical waves and beats are not viciously restrictive but enable the contingent particularity of the melodies to shine. And the particularity of the metrical constraint in its temporal configuration is itself enhanced, revealed not as value-free limit, but as interesting and valuable in its own right.

Harmonic sequence

A similar interplay can be seen on the large scale, in the overall structure of a piece, the 'blueprint' or 'skeleton' for improvisation. In traditional jazz this structure is normally determined by a repeated harmonic sequence, a series of chords articulated by the rhythm section. By far the most pervasive large-scale form in traditional jazz is 'theme and variations'. Though the variations might be on a given theme or melody, much more critical for shaping the large-scale structure of a piece is the chord sequence. Chord sequences are generally unadventurous compared to much composed music.[18] But again this does not imply musical incompetence. The chord sequence may be elaborated and embellished, 'voiced' in different ways (leaving the fundamental character of a chord the same but altering some of its notes), or even have some of its chords altered.[19] But, more important, as with metre and rhythm, the strength and subtlety of the music owes much to a mutually enhancing contrast-through-interplay between the pre-set harmonic constraint,[20] with its repetitive, regular predictability, and the improvised music sung or played with it, with

17. Zuckerkandl (1956), 172. My italics.
18. Even the simplest modulations – moves to new key centres – are relatively uncommon, and the elements from which the chords are built up are drawn from the basic repertoire of European tonal music. It is not surprising that 'free jazz' and its offshoots should explore harmony of greater range and variety.   19. Berliner (1994), 82ff.
20. Even if subtly modified and varied, the constraint is still 'there' and intuited as a constraint.

its relatively unrepetitive, irregular unpredictability. Once again, the constraint is the means of liberation and is itself enhanced by the improvised material.

Melody

Metre and harmony are generally used as frames to be 'filled', even though they may be enhanced in various ways and heard differently as a result of the improvisation. Melodies too can be treated like this. A melody can be *ornamented* or *embellished* (Example 8.3).

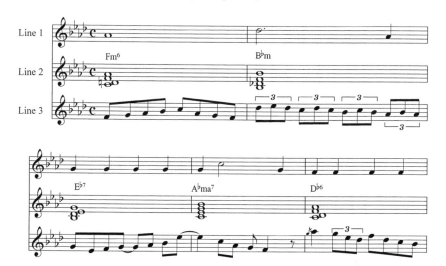

Example 8.3 Jerome Kern, 'All the Things You Are'

Example 8.3 is a transcription from a recording by the Max Roach Quintet. The melody – Jerome Kern's 'All the Things You Are' – is written in line (1), its harmonies in line (2). A riff theme is improvised – an embellishment of line (1) – by the trumpeter and tenor saxophonist (line (3)).

The decorative, embellishing paraphrase was the main improvisatory device of many of the older jazz forms (e.g. in New Orleans jazz). Here the underlying harmony is not simply a ground or supporting foundation; the melody often intensifies the momentum of the harmony. As we have seen, melody is normally laden with harmonic tension and resolution by virtue of its placement in a dynamic field of key. In jazz, it will likely augment the sense of progression already possessed by the sequence of chords.

There is an interesting parallel to this in baroque music, where, far from being merely decoration on a tree, ornamentation was regarded as playing a more fundamental role. 'The musical ornamentation of the first half of the eighteenth century was an essential element in the achievement of continuity: the decoration not only covered the underlying musical structure but kept it always flowing. The High Baroque in music had a horror of the void, and the *agréments* fill what empty space there was.'[21] The improvised elements are not simply held by the constraints but reinforce the dynamism of those very constraints. Once again: mutual enhancement through interplay.

The interlacing of melody and harmony can be much more complex and intricate than this. Jazz musicians have not remained content with decoration and embellishment. There can be *motivic improvisation* of the melody where fragments or motifs from the melody are subject to permutations of numerous kinds; for instance, they can be transferred in pitch, turned upside down, sung or played backwards. It was not long before there developed the practice of *improvising radically new melodic lines* – the 'chorus-phrase' – and this has become the chief means of melodic improvisation in modern jazz. Here, the improvisation is on the harmonic progression underlying the melody, not the melody itself: the melody is no longer a direct constraint.

> Sometimes, in older jazz especially, this means taking the chords of the harmony apart: the constituent notes of a chord are strung out in some manner. In modern jazz it is more common for a new and independent melody to be created.
>
> So, in the recording of Kern's 'All the Things You Are' just cited, a melody is improvised (line (4)) which bears virtually no relation to the original theme, only to the harmony (Example 8.4).

In some cases the principal melody never appears, a phenomenon labelled by Frank Tirro 'the *silent theme* tradition'.[22] Often a theme will be played in its entirety and return at the end of the piece, but in jazz emerging in the 1940s and 50s – for example, in 'bebop' – we find many instances of pieces in which the theme is never played at all. The original melody is implied through the harmony and other improvised melodies. The constraint is known in its absence.

> In the recording of Kern's 'All the Things You Are' (Example 8.4), although I have written the melody as line (1), in the recording this original theme is never in fact played.

---

21. Rosen (1971), 107f.   22. Tirro (1967).

Example 8.4 Jerome Kern, 'All the Things You Are'

Further, the *new improvised melodies or choruses themselves can become 'original' themes in their own right*, repeated at many performances and part of the stock-in-trade of player and audience alike: 'Many choruses become so famous that the listener would be disappointed if the musician who made them up were suddenly to play something different.'[23] And, in turn *these very melodic lines become the material for further improvisations*. Furthermore, these new basic melodies can suggest new or at least adapted harmonies.

> So, in the recording under consideration, line (4) suggested the modified chords of line (5) (Example 8.5).

And these new melodies-with-harmonies can become new songs with their own names.

> So 'Groovin' High' was derived from 'Whispering', 'Scrapple from the Apple' from 'Honeysuckle Rose', and 'Anthropology' from 'I Got Rhythm.'

23. Berendt (1983), 150; Berliner (1994), 90.

Example 8.5 Jerome Kern, 'All the Things You Are'

And in time, the melodies too might come to be performed only implicitly through implication and suggestion.

Idiom

The elements we have just been examining – metre, harmony and melody – together with all the other musical constraints, are improvised according to an idiom, a set of musical conventions or strategies. Traditional jazz is itself an idiom, and divisible into many sub-idioms. People who consciously improvise within an idiom tend not to say 'I improvise'; they use the word of the idiom: 'I play blues', 'I play hard bop.' Idioms, limiting and defining possibilities for musical creation and reception, are inextricably bound up with social meanings and codes, and sometimes with large-scale interpretative frameworks.[24]

Tradition and improvisation

We can now stand back a little and try to delineate something of the relation between occasional and cultural constraints, and bring what we have found to bear on theology. In improvisation, *cultural constraints are particularised in relation to occasional constraints.* The musical elements supplied by the culture (we have highlighted metre, harmony and melody) and the idiom which combines and shapes them are interpreted in a manner that engages with the constraints of a particular occasion. To some degree every musical performer does this, insofar as the 'givens' give her latitude. But in improvised music the increased contingency obliges the musician to work much harder at 'bringing alive' the musical constraint in a way that 'hooks into' this unique combination of occasional constraints: she plays 'for them', in this place at this time. Along with this, *the occasional constraints are themselves 'particularised'*, in the sense of magnified, developed, enabled in some manner to be more fully themselves: the particularity of other improvisers advances, we come to sense and appreciate the ambience of the setting, the acoustics of the building, and so on.

In terms of its temporality, improvisation can share with many other types of music the interweaving of the temporal modes we have spoken about in previous chapters. But improvisation foregrounds the *contingent* element of this process acutely. There is a vivid sense that we are in the realm not of a tight, closed and necessarily unfolding temporality but of a flexible responsiveness. The music's past engages with the particularities of the present occasion in such a way that the music is intuited as strongly undetermined, especially if the borrowed musical constraint appears initially to have little to do with the present occasion. And, moreover, the music's past, by being particularised in the present, opens up new futures for both cultural and occasional constraints: a range of unforeseen and inherently unpredictable possibilities can burst forth. More than this, though the piece ends, there is often a sense that this by no means exhausts the possibilities, that what has been witnessed here could have continued. There can be an awareness of the inexhaustible resources of

---

24. Durant (1989), 263ff. The word 'style' is sometimes used to refer to what we mean by idiom.

both sets of constraints, generating a confidence in a limitlessly abundant, contingent (yet structured) future. The logic of improvisation is the logic of *surplus*, non-equilibrium, propelled by contingency and constraints in interplay.

What happens if all this is interwoven with a theological theme in which matters of freedom are crucial? We take as an example the issue of Church tradition. First, improvisation is especially apt to do justice to notions of process, particularity and contingency which are so basic to a theology of tradition. 'Tradition', of course, is a notoriously ambiguous word. It is commonplace to speak of *the* tradition: the apostolic Gospel of Jesus Christ, the foundational memories of the Church which anchor its ongoing life in its founding events. In addition a distinction can made between tradition as process and tradition as the results ('deposits') of the process. Much discussion of tradition has focused on the latter, shaped by a concern to separate orthodoxy from heresy, to find universal and permanently normative expressions of tradition. While this is understandable, it has sometimes meant the Church has been insensitive to what is involved in tradition-formation. Certain assumptions about doctrinal development have not helped, especially those which see normative tradition growing like a 'coral reef'.[25] It would not be hard to illustrate how this has often been the enemy of freedom in the Church. This is why some prefer to speak of tradition as primarily a *hermeneutical process*: 'the process by which the Gospel takes *particular* form in the various times and places of the church's history.'[26] Trinitarian doctrine, for example, was the outcome of a process of particularising the Gospel for a specific context in the early Church, and has shown remarkable fruitfulness to enrich the lives of Christians in a vast range of different contexts. One writer suggests that tradition is in effect 'a series of local theologies' closely allied to and responding to a variety of cultural conditions.[27] What we have discovered about musical improvisation would seem to have much to offer in understanding and describing the dynamics of this contextualisation, especially when the related debates may have been over-dependent on theories which do scant justice to process and specific, contextual circumstance.

Second, the informal ways in which jazz has been gathered, passed on, improvised and re-improvised can remind us of a similar process in the

---

25. Hanson (1981), 26; see Bauckham (1988), 129f.   26. Bauckham (1988), 130.
27. Schreiter (1985), 12–15.

development of tradition, and of the dangers of unduly restrictive ways in which the Church has understood the sources of 'valid' themes for improvisation. It is interesting that in the Roman Catholic Church the kind of dichotomy expressed in the distinction between *Ecclesia docens* and the *Ecclesia discens*, which was inclined to identify true tradition with the teaching of the magisterium, has been widely questioned in post-Vatican II theology.[28] What of paintings, missionary activity, the testimonies of prisoners, Bible-study groups in remote churches? These improvisations are potentially as fruitful and liberating as anything issuing from a committee of priests, and they themselves will often prove their worth by repeated particularisation in radically different situations. (It is worth recalling the emergence of jazz from black slave roots.)

Third, we have seen that in jazz what is taken as a 'fundamental' theme can in fact itself be the crystallisation of a particularisation. An improvisation for a specific time and season becomes the new constraint. It has been a repeated temptation in the Church to overlook a tradition's relation to a specific context and confer on it the status of universal and permanent validity in ways which stifle freedom. In contemporary hermeneutics it is often urged that the Church's most beloved strategies and 'findings' in biblical hermeneutics, for example, should not automatically be assumed to be universally valid norms: 'In the churches of the Third World the imposition of supposedly universal norms, developed in the western Christian tradition, looks like just another form of western cultural imperialism, mistaking, according to western intellectual habit, its own particularity for universality.'[29]

Fourth, improvisation reminds us powerfully of the futility of searching for a tradition-free environment of creativity. Traditional jazz falls to bits without interacting deeply with tradition. There can be no *tabula rasa*, no producing which is not a re-producing. Even so-called 'free jazz' and 'free improvisation' are rarely as free from the inheritance of the past as its supporters would like to think.[30] The intelligibility of any music depends on indwelling proven traditions of practice, interpretation and belief, ranging from the small-scale to the corporate memories which form the large-scale interpretative grids of a cultural group. George

---

28. See Bauckham (1988), 131f.   29. Ibid., 130.
30. Durant (1989), 265ff. Durant observes that 'novelty exists only in situationally specific relationships of transgression and transformation of existing codes, rather than as some "pure" alternative to them: there is no new musical realm to discover that isn't at the same time a restructuring or reconstruction of the old' (ibid., 273).

Steiner remarks that art can develop only 'via reflection of and on preceding art, where "reflection" signifies both a "mirroring", however drastic the perceptual dislocation, and a "re-thinking". It is through this internalised "re-production" of and amendment to previous representations that an artist will articulate what might appear to have been even the most spontaneous, the most realistic of his sightings.'[31] A certain naiveté marks the quasi-Cartesian purgation of memory advocated by Boulez in the 1940s and 50s, and in a different way by Cage. Their music is no less dependent on traditions than any other, even if largely by negation, and philosophically they are especially dependent on dominant streams within modernism.

Fifth, the practice of improvisation reminds us that it is not only futile but also potentially damaging to attempt, in the name of freedom, an evasion of what Boulez called the 'great burden' of history. In Micheal O'Siadhail's words,

> Freedom. We sang of freedom
> (travel lightly, anything goes)
> and somehow became strangers
> to each other, like gabblers
> at cross purposes, builders
>   of Babel.
>
> Slowly I relearn a *lingua*,
> shared overlays of rule,
> lattice of memory and meaning,
> our latent images, a tongue
> at large in an endlessness
>   of sentences unsaid.[32]

This is one of the converging points of much sociology of knowledge, the philosophical hermeneutics of Gadamer and Michael Polanyi's philosophy of science: only through a body of corporate knowledge and a tacit 'fiduciary framework' of basic attitudes (O'Siadhail's 'latent images') are we are able to come to terms with the world we inhabit. The improviser knows this better than many. Responding to the occasional constraints amidst the high contingency of improvised performance is a

---

31. Steiner (1989), 17. Especially illuminating in this connection is Roger Lundin's discussion of the grateful receptivity which he believes should characterise a Christian posture towards tradition (and which he finds in the mature work of W. H. Auden), in contrast to the 'transcendental pretence' of the 'expansive self' evident in, for example, the tradition of Emerson (Lundin 1993, 126ff).   32. O'Siadhail (1992), 111.

hard-won skill, and there is no more effective way of learning a skill than by being an apprentice to another, indwelling the corporate tradition represented by the teacher – strategies, devices, themes and so forth. The improviser discovers in sound a *'lingua, / shared overlays of rule, / lattice of memory and meaning'*. She finds that traditions which survive and traditions which are resurrected are frequently marked by their capacity to respond to a diversity of challenges, to penetrate and explore a variety of constraints. A jazz trumpeter learns the conventions and idioms of his art precisely *in order* that he can relate to the particularities of this occasion. In the Church, as with any social grouping, past tradition frees us from a tyranny of the present, from the damaging immunity to anything which might criticise and subvert this context, from distorting perceptions which prevent us coming to terms with contemporary reality, from becoming 'strangers/to each other, like gabblers at cross purposes'. We are freed *for* an appropriate and fruitful response to our own context.

Certainly, the improviser may deliberately reject a constraint – a musical idiom, for example. In the Church, development by 'expansion' needs supplementing by development through 'pruning'.[33] But, as we also said, this cannot happen without due attention to what is refused. What we question in Boulez and Cage is not that there may be some traditions which are antagonistic to our freedom but the assumption that past tradition is inevitably of this character.

Notions of originality and novelty need to be re-cast in this light. In temporal terms, pursuing originality directly is the attempt to grasp pure contingency, to attain the singular event, unrelated to its past or future, and hence our own past or future. This can only mean the very antithesis of freedom. The eventual paralysis and dissolution is well captured by the theatrical improviser, Keith Johnstone. Reflecting on Mozart's purported claim that 'I really do not study or aim at originality', Johnstone poses the question:

> Suppose Mozart *had* tried to be original? It would have been like a man at the North Pole trying to walk north, and this is true of all the rest of us. Striving after originality takes you far away from your true self, and makes your work mediocre.[34]

Improvisation teaches us that the contingent moment arrives only in relation to webs of temporal constraint embodied in tradition, that tradition

33. Lash (1973), 145f.   34. Johnstone (1979), 88.

can point us beyond itself only insofar as we are prepared to trust and inhabit it.[35]

Sixth, improvisation alerts us to the fact that the appropriation of tradition is not simply concerned with a past impinging on a present but with generating a novel and fruitful future. Particularising in improvisation is not merely adaptation, matching up the given material with the present moment, as if 'our own time' was an autonomous, self-contained sphere whose concerns must claim normative and exclusive attention. In this 'temporal solipsism'[36] our present need becomes a kind of hermeneutical magnet which selects only those data from the past which can immediately answer to current specificities. Past *and future* are subsumed into an inflexible field of meaning ('relevance'). (As in: 'Only "X" is relevant for *my* future.') Anthony Thiselton engages in a sustained polemic against this tendency in recent pastoral theology.[37] Equally one could point to certain forms of spirituality which too easily identify the locus of Christ's encounter with us as the 'now' of our own, immediate (private) 'space', purportedly situated in a 'space of time' between the (non-existent) past and future. An improviser testifies to the fact that the borrowed musical material can expose an extensive range of fresh, unconsidered possibilities in the improvising context and in the material itself, sometimes *especially* when the material seems distinctly at odds with the present context. So it is that the best church traditions often respond to present concerns by showing us that the concerns are not absolute and may not even be appropriate, by opening up and drawing us into futures not determined by our present (or the past we have subsumed into our present), and this can happen most powerfully when the traditions seem

---

35. Back in 1919, T. S. Eliot explored this theme with singular insight in his essay 'Tradition and the Individual Talent' (Eliot 1932). He notes the tendency of the critic to 'insist, when we praise a poet, upon those aspects of his work in which he least resembles anyone else. In these aspects or parts of his work we pretend to find what is individual, what is the peculiar essence of the man.' (An interesting parallel is the New Testament critic who will only accept as authentic those teachings of Jesus which can be shown to have no parallel in contemporary or Old Testament literature.) Yet 'we shall often find that not only the best, but the most individual parts of [a writer's] work may be those in which the dead poets, his ancestors, assert their immortality most vigorously'. Eliot argues for a strenuous engagement with tradition, for an 'historical sense' in the writer which involves 'a perception, not only of the pastness of the past, but of its presence' and which 'compels a man to write not merely with his own generation in his bones, but with a feeling that the whole of the literature of Europe from Homer and within it the whole of the literature of his own country has a simultaneous existence and composes a simultaneous order'. It is just this 'historical sense' 'which makes a writer most acutely conscious of his place in time, of his own contemporaneity' (ibid., 14).

36. We have already spoken of this in chapter 2; see above, p. 63, n. 86.

37. Thiselton (1992), 604ff.

most foreign and unpromising. A tradition's deepest dissent from the interests of the present may be precisely the location of its deepest relevance.

Furthermore, just as improvisation encourages a sense of the inexhaustibility of both occasional and cultural constraints, and thus a confidence in future musical possibilities, so the very fact that traditions have lived on in the Christian community and unlocked unforeseen initiatives in an enormous variety of occasional constraints can produce a confident expectation of their potential fruitfulness in the Church's future. Improvisation can instruct us in what J. B. Metz calls a 'productive non-contemporaneity', an engagement of our past with our present for the sake of a future that is not strictly determined by either.[38]

Improvisation as a model does of course have its limitations here. The question of criteria of control cannot be side-stepped: the particularisation of tradition is always shaped by some convictions about non-negotiable tradition, some kind of *cantus firmus*. Nevertheless, improvisation, we have sought to show, is especially well suited to elucidating the dynamics of church tradition, so that deeper understanding of these dynamics is made possible. It provides a highly effective enactment of the truth that the constraints of tradition, far from being inherently threatening to the Church's freedom, are in fact a condition of it.

Improvisation in advance

Earlier I mentioned the 'silent theme' tradition, when the theme is improvised without ever being played. As a way of conceiving the process of evangelism, for example, this has obvious resonances. But there is another related and more subtle phenomenon, which, though not to my knowledge found in traditional jazz, provides an illuminating interaction of cultural and occasional constraint: 'improvisation in advance'. In the 1960s, Derek Bailey, a leading promoter of improvised music, explored a number of innovative techniques, among them improvising not on the chord currently sounding but on the next chord, yet to be heard.[39] Melody thus 'grates' because it is set over the wrong harmony. The result can be highly compelling.

Similar devices can be found in non-improvised music. We have seen how Beethoven can set melodic resolution against as yet unresolved and insecure harmony, or introduce an 'ending' in a 'beginning' context.[40]

38. Metz (1984), 169–77.   39. Bailey (1992), 87.   40. See above, pp. 101ff., 114ff.

Brahms can put harmonic closure in the midst of metrical tension.[41] The result is both disturbing and compelling. What makes improvisation in advance so interesting is that it involves a strong incongruity between what is highly contingent and an underlying constraint, and that the contingent element heralds a constraint yet to come.

In Acts 2, the crowd on the day of Pentecost are enticed not initially by the *kerygma* itself but by the manifestations of the Spirit amongst the disciples, most of all, by being able to hear the disciples speak in their own languages (vv. 6, 11). They are 'amazed' (7, 12). The experience is both disturbing and attractive. It is disturbing not only in being intrinsically implausible but in being apparently incongruous with the Jews' tradition. They put what is clearly a religious happening against the background harmony of their own tradition, and it makes little sense. At the same time, the new-found ability to communicate across cultural barriers is attractive. Here the Spirit improvises in advance in two senses. First, the *Spirit is improvising on music the crowd have yet to hear from Peter*, and, moreover, in a manner which explores the particularities of the occasion (throngs assembled in Jerusalem for Pentecost). They ask 'What does this mean?' (12). Peter directs them to the harmony and theme which has produced the improvisation, the story of Jesus, the one accredited by God, crucified and now exalted as Lord and Messiah. The remarkable togetherness (*koinonia*) they have heard through their ears is what the Spirit has improvised out of what has happened in Jesus Christ, and in such a way that their particularity flourishes. The crowd is not content to live with the incongruity between the improvisation and their own tradition's harmony. In due course, they are baptised into this new liberating constraint, and this releases a stream of new, unpredictable, improvisations – witness the narrative of Acts. Interestingly, this has been the dynamic of conversion for countless people. Most take their first major step into faith not by hearing the Christian message directly but by experiencing an improvisation on it in advance, and one which is often disturbing (in that it is incongruous

41. In the second movement of his Second Symphony (op. 73), for example, this occurs many times, contributing to one of the most drawn out instances of generating expectation and delaying gratification ever devised. The opening bars are highly ambiguous harmonically, and this is only partially resolved in bar 3 – the tonic root position is on the metrically weak beats of the bar. The cadence at the end of bar 4 reaches towards the tonic of B major, but (as with bar 6) the 'cellos are left entirely alone on the downbeat of the fifth bar, and in bar 6 the tonic expectation is subverted by the mediant, D sharp minor. The cadence at the end of bar 9 should resolve into F sharp major but we are side-tracked into D major (itself rendered unsteady by the appearance of B flat!). And the D major resolutions of bars 10, 11 and 12 are all on metrically weak beats. The only unequivocal alignment of stable harmony and metrically strong beats comes at the very end of the movement.

with the world they know and demands some kind of explanation) and attractive in that it is felt to be beneficial and enjoyable, liberating. Very often this comes through experiencing a new kind of friendship, or perhaps an enticing act of worship. And when this happens, the Spirit is 'hooking into' the constraints of people's 'occasions', not so as to be totally determined by them but to liberate people in their particularity. Second, Acts 2 is about improvisation in advance in that the whole episode, from dramatic manifestations to mass baptisms, *is an anticipation of the end-times – the Holy Spirit is the Spirit of the last days who brings about in the present the condition of the 'age to come'*. Through the Spirit – the first fruits of the final harvest (Rom. 8:23), the down-payment (2 Cor. 1:22; 5:5; Eph. 1:14), the seal (1 Cor. 1:21–22; Eph. 1:13; 4:30) of what is to come – the Church already enjoys a foretaste of the end. Though there may be alignment of improvisation and underlying harmony, that alignment is never complete this side of the eschaton – the Spirit's improvisations in our midst will always direct us ahead by pre-figuring what is yet to appear.

Particularisation and freedom

To pull together the material of the chapter so far: we have seen, first, that the primary interplay undergirding the 'particularisation' in improvisation is that between contingency on the one hand, and the given musical constraints on the other (both the cultural constraints and the constraints peculiar to the occasion itself). The intertwining of contingency and constraint lies at the heart of a theological understanding of freedom, a freedom not constituted by boundless openness or self-willed indeterminacy (O'Siadhail's 'travel lightly, anything goes') but discovered through, and in proper relation to compounds of constraint. Second, the contingent and the constraints mutually enhance one another, they mutually establish each other's particularity. This marks the freedom of the Christian: our contingency is enhanced in and through our interaction with constraint; and the constraints are enhanced in and through our (contingent) interaction with them. Third, in all this we have been speaking of temporal contingency, and intrinsic to human freedom is being in an appropriate and fruitful relation to the temporality of the world. As with many other forms of music, improvisation carries the capacity for participation in the 're-configuration of the times' which marks salvation, yet its increased contingency lends it a quality which is particularly suited to coming to terms with the interplay between constraints in their established, invariant temporality on the one hand, and the non-determinist relation between past and future and the abundance of possibilities in and through time on the other. The freedom generated through sharing in Christ displays just this interplay. We have just examined this freedom in relation to constraint with respect to the dynamics of Church tradition and the work of the Spirit as 'improviser in advance'.

Continuous constraints

And how are continuous constraints drawn into this process, those which condition us by virtue of the fact that we all inhabit a 'given', physical world with its own integrity? Here we comment on two of the most important, our bodies and the 'sonic order'.

Embodiment

Nowhere has the role of the body in improvisation been more perceptively and graphically described than in David Sudnow's extraordinary study *Ways of the Hand*, an account of the struggle of a classically trained pianist to play jazz. In his first stumbling attempts, Sudnow quickly found that particular configurations ('constellations') of the left hand would produce typical jazz chords, and in time he learned to string these together in sequences commonly found in jazz songs. This required a tactile knowledge of the shape and layout of the keyboard. The hands had to 'get to know' the keys. At first he needed to use his eyes to make sure the hands landed in the right place. Soon this became unnecessary; the body's own 'appreciative structures' could find 'a place to go'.[42] And over these chords he added standard non-improvised melodies.

However, the aim was to *improvise* melodies over a chord sequence. Where does one find material? He needed to find 'particular places to take' his fingers, and 'formulas' or strategies which would enable the hand to go to the places and play appropriate notes.

> The hand had to be motivated to particular next keys to depress, and when there was nowhere for it to go it became totally immobilised, stumbled around, and *between 'me' and 'it' there was a rather alienated relationship*.[43]

His teacher gave him 'places to go' and pathways between them, the formulas, scales, motifs, arpeggios and so on characteristic of jazz. But he sensed a large gap between his playing and real jazz. When he started to

---

42. Sudnow (1993), 13.   43. Ibid., 18. My italics.

play with bass and drums, he experienced acute problems. Significantly, he writes of it as an experience of *rush*:

> The pacing of the chord productions would itself become jagged . . . and I tended to rush the time, changing the chords a trifle before they were due, or missing a beat here and there, occasionally having one too many, and really sweating it out all the way, trying to get some lines down nicely . . . charging around in the swarm of the music, trying to 'hold on to the time,' wishing things would suddenly stop for a moment so that I could catch a breath.[44]

He adds: 'The music was not mine';[45] it was 'without humour'.[46] It was like being in traffic in Mexico City: 'The music was literally *out of hand*.'[47]

A breakthrough came in the form of what Sudnow calls 'going for the sounds'. He had always been interested in sounds and their qualities but now he became aware that he needed to aim intentionally for particular notes. Up until that time only broad parameters had received motivated determination – e.g. where to start a run of notes, which run to choose, how fast to play it. Now he found himself 'entering melodically' into the production, learning to aim for specific notes and then do something interesting with them. Vital to this search for melodicality was the *hand's relationship to the physical peculiarities of the keyboard*. He found that his hand 'had ways' with the keys that opened up a variety of manoeuvres, that 'going for the sounds' 'involved coping with the topography of the terrain by the hand as a negotiative organ with various potentials and limitations'.[48] The hand would treat the keyboard as a terrain to be engaged, relating its contours, for example, to the contours of different keys ('securing "sorts of places" in which "sorts of actions" could be taken'[49]). Knowing what the next note or next notes would sound like was more to do with hand sensations than visual inspection of the keyboard:

> When I say I know what a note will sound like, I mean that I am engaged in a *course that provides for that note's sound*, that I have a way of moving to the upcoming notes in such a fashion that the handful context of moving to them makes them upcoming notes that will have known sounds. *I do not know a note's sound apart from the context of a handful course in which its sound will figure.*[50]

> the 'major triad' is not a collection of isolatable notes with their sounds. It is an arena at hand for configurationally distanced manoeuvres.[51]

---

44. Ibid., 31f.   45. Ibid., 33.   46. Ibid., 30.   47. Ibid. My italics.   48. Ibid., 47.
49. Ibid., 53.   50. Ibid., 69. The second group of italicisations is my own.   51. Ibid., 75.

Hence sounds are not to be understood primarily in terms of what can be registered on an oscilloscope. From the point of view of piano improvisation, listening is as much to do with the hand as with the ear. 'To leave the hands out of the "hearing" enterprise at the piano is to leave music as a production unexamined.'[52] He claims:

> we must explore their relevance, and description as 'real worldly sounds,' within a bodily system of essentially organised movements and distancing configurations. It is from such a perspective that a theory of 'listening' might be developed, that the work of an 'ear' in such a 'system' might be productionally conceived.[53]

It is not surprising, therefore, to find Sudnow speaking of the 'alienated' relationship between him and his hand being healed. The hand 'had ways' with the keyboard which opened up potentialities of sound not readily discoverable in any other way.

> For some time he had known a 'chromatic way' of engaging with the keyboard: the hand assuming a posture in which the fingers are bunched up into a particular configuration. This became a useful device for playing non-chromatic music, but also for much freer forms of chromaticism (Example 8.6).

Example 8.6

> I would come down chromatically, and then play a course of notes that was only 'essentially chromatic,' not following the strict path that prescribes every adjacent key, but one that had that sort of bunchedness to it. A course followed not each and every note on the chromatic scale, but had a generalised 'chromaticality,' with, for example, whole steps interspersed with a 'correct' chromatic passage, so that this way would pass over a set of places like this.[54]

Sudnow speaks of learning to trust the hand, of the hand almost as a discrete agency:

> I began to employ the melodic hand in ways to let it . . . speak to me about the sort of shaping it was in, the sort of stance over the sector being adopted. I could take directions from the fingers about ways of moving and where to move.[55]

52. Ibid., 43.   53. Ibid., 74.   54. Ibid., 59f.
55. Ibid., 95. Sudnow is not alone in describing improvising this way. In his giant study of jazz improvisation compiled from hundreds of interviews, Paul Berliner found that improvisers quickly reach the point where, as George Duvivier puts it, 'my fingers can pick out the chords without my always thinking of them'. Improvisers liken this transition to learning a new route in the physical world (Berliner 1994, 92).

For our purposes, what is of note is the way in which these insights are related to time. The ways of the hand (and body) discovered in keyboard improvisation are understood as bound up inextricably with both the temporality of the music and the temporality of the body. Learning how to improvise successfully depends on allowing the hand (and to a significant extent other parts of the body) to shape and bring forth the temporality of the piece. The hand cannot be treated as simply an instrument to get the fingers to a place 'on time', a time pre-determined quite apart from the hand. Indeed, Sudnow found that much could be gained from suppressing the desire to take the hand to a new place, and instead allowing the hand to 'linger' and use the notes which lay under it.

> I began to see that . . . note choices could be made anywhere, that there
> was no need to lunge, that usable notes for any chord lay just at hand,
> that there was no need to find a path, image one up ahead to get ready
> in advance for a blurting out . . . Good notes were everywhere at hand,
> right beneath the fingers . . . I could *take my time* in going for a long
> run, could linger, finding right beneath a nonventuring hand all sorts
> of melodying possibilities, if I lingered there in the right ways. And
> when doing venturing [moving the arm and hand up and down the
> keyboard] in the right ways *I could move fast and take my time both
> together*.[56]

The rush and hurry of the early jazz experiments began to disappear, all that desperate grasping and grabbing at the 'out of hand' trio session. The hand found its own time, its own pace and duration, which, as the above passage makes clear, may be fast or slow, and this became integral to the temporality of the music.

This was especially evident when Sudnow was faced with keeping left and right hand together. As we have noted, in traditional jazz the melodic line is spun out over a metrically based chord-structure, the former usually played by the right hand and the latter by the left. Sudnow often struggled to line up the two. A section of melody would be played over one chord but when he wanted to repeat that section over the next chord and thus in a different harmonic context, he would often run into trouble because different hand shapes were required to play those notes in their new setting, or because he might start the repeated section slightly late. He would be hard pushed to squeeze all the 'right' notes into the allotted time for the next chord change. The balance between left and right hand was thrown out of kilter. This 'grabbing for the destination by the right

56. Sudnow (1993), 94f. My italics.

time' produced 'a course of movements with temporal disarray through-out.' The fingers and hands had to negotiate particular terrains – 'places' – but the 'places were prechosen without respect for the singable-at-handness-of-so-many-by-then'.[57]

How did he get out of this dilemma? First he had to 'get the beat into the fingers' of the right hand. The fingers themselves had in some sense to 'know the time', the accentual nodes, the arrival points, the 'prospective beatings' (i.e. metrical beats).[58] Second, relying on this 'fingerly' metrical awareness, the hand had to be allowed to find an appropriate pace of notes which would fit these metrical beats, and this meant not only getting to required destinations 'on time' but highlighting and bringing into relief, through differing speeds of notes, the varying strength of metrical beats. In all this, third, he needed to realise that the pace of notes was closely tied up with the physical possibilities of the hands and fingers in relation to the keyboard. This meant not knowing an 'absolute' speed but 'an *order* of fastness', so that 'for example, entering this diminished C way bunching [sic] with such a digitally configurated unfolding, going *up or down* could be done within a known range of rapidity'.[59]

So 'taking time' now meant the hand finding a pace of notes appropri-ate to the beat it feels and to the physical particularities of the keyboard. Playing became much more relaxed. Chords would suggest typical melodic formulae, but a formula might spill over on to the next chord, stimulating the hand to play some relaxed 'melodying' and take time to introduce the next formula. Further, there was room for 'nonstuttering and nontripping disengagements from the terrain when a saying was not at hand, disengagements that would not make the music stop but would be silences of the music'.[60] Sudnow also found that the metrical beats had to be sensed not only by the hand but also by the whole body. Watching the pianist Jimmy Rowles, he noticed how virtually his entire body was enveloped in the performing action.[61] 'He was never in a hurry . . . the song would take its time.'[62] Sudnow himself found that bodily motion of various kinds became incorporated into his improvisation rather than merely accompaniments to it. The sounds become 'in-corporated',

57. Ibid., 102.
58. Sudnow rightly sees that the metrical beats of jazz are not uniform beats on a flat time line but beats of varying intensity; the constituent notes of an improvised melody in jazz will bring into relief these patterns of intensity. An arrival point is not simply a point on a line but a point of intensity to be prepared for and followed in particular ways (ibid., 106ff). This of course links up with what we have said many times about metre.   59. Ibid., 132.
60. Ibid., 104.   61. Ibid., 81ff.   62. Ibid., 81.

embodied. This is a well-known phenomenon in jazz and highlights the very close relationship between body movement, dance and rhythmic conception.[63] The body must 'feel the beat':

> instead of keeping a beat as one may tap with rigid up-and-down finger-confined moves on the table, I began to count off the time with the finger-snapping, head-bobbing, arm-and-shoulder rotating courses having little elliptical shapings.[64]

It comes as no surprise to find that 'error' took on a new significance. When mistakes slipped in, fruitful possibilities always lay 'at hand'. Instead of stumbling around to correct the fault, the error could be incorporated, exploited. It could be drawn into the improvisation such that 'a new practice was . . . added to the hand's repertoire of ways . . . A hand was developing that was possessed of mobile ways with the topography, ways permitting the attempt, at least, *to make the best of things*.'[65] This did not make Sudnow less aware of making mistakes, but transformed his attitude to them. As John Sloboda explains (speaking of Sudnow), 'We see . . . an increasing understanding of the potentialities of almost *any* note to be used to effect in jazz . . . The improviser is relaxed and unhurried because he knows that, wherever he lands up, there are a dozen different ways of getting from there to the next place . . . The jazz improviser can enjoy his improvisation because he knows that there will always be *something* he can play.'[66] (To underline the obvious, in musical improvisation an error cannot be removed (unlike an improvised painting, for instance). Rectification has to be retrospective and cannot be erasive – all actions of the producer, in some way, must be(come) part of the work.)

As important as anything else in this new-found jazz was *singing*. Sudnow tells us that his 'central instruction' to would-be jazz players is: 'sing while you are playing'.[67] It is not entirely clear what Sudnow intends by this phrase, though many jazz players, of course, do sing while they play. In any case, he does not seem to mean merely 'sing along as you play'. It is more a case of singing as a way of interacting with the hands: Sudnow says 'I sing with my fingers', and speaks of a 'mutual jurisdiction' between voice and hand, a 'joint knowing of voice and fingers', 'a single voice at the tips of the fingers'.[68]

What Sudnow explicates in relation to jazz piano improvisation could doubtless be applied to other improvisatory music. But for us the obvious observation to make is that Sudnow's whole journey was about *discovering*

63. See Berliner (1994), 152f.   **64.** Sudnow (1993), 104.   **65.** Ibid., 55. My italics.
66. Sloboda (1993), 148f.   **67.** Ibid., 149.   **68.** Ibid., 87, 95, 150, 152.

a fresh freedom through the exploration of constraints (not their refusal or defeat), *the constraints of the body in relation to those of the keyboard and the world of sound*.

The constraint of the body, far from being treated as prison to be escaped or obstacle to be fought, became integral to the realisation of freedom: 'this jazz music *is* ways of moving from place to place as singings with my fingers. To *define* jazz . . . is to *describe* the body's ways.'[69] Granted, bodily constraints limit and foreclose possibilities – there are some things a hand will never be able to do at a keyboard which I may wish that it could do. And there is a very wide range of relevant bodily temporal processes at work in music-making.[70] But the central point holds: the body is not seen primarily as negative confinement but is drawn into a process such that its own peculiarities, specific capabilities and so forth are employed as a resource of channels of sensitivity and response, intelligence and insight, expression and articulation. In short, in and through our bodies we become free, free for interacting more fruitfully with realities beyond ourselves. *Ways of the Hand* was written, the author tells us, 'on the way toward the closer study of the human body and its works'.[71]

For any who want to develop theological conceptions of personhood which are concerned with elucidating the character of freedom and which seek to be faithful to the huge stress in the Bible on our embodiedness, there is rich material for the taking here.[72] For here is a construal of free personal being in which the particularities of the body are regarded as intrinsic to human identity and its formation, in which the body is viewed as a field of dynamic processes of exchange in our commerce with the world, in which the senses are not treated as inherently passive and in need of compensation by the active mind, and in which bodily action is not viewed merely as the outward (or even optional) consequence of some 'inner state' or intention.[73] Likewise there is much here for those at work

---

69. Ibid., 146.   70. See above, pp. 26ff., 35ff.   71. Sudnow (1993), xiii.

72. Sudnow is also far from certain postmodern conceptions of the body which would regard it as entirely constructed by social determinants.

73. For a recent theological approach to the field, see Pannenberg (1992), 181–202. It is significant that Miroslav Volf, in his seminal book *Exclusion and Embrace*, in addressing the multiple problematic of hatred and social exclusion, chooses to cast his theological response by sketching a 'phenomenology of embrace' as a way of thinking about personal and social identity under the conditions of enmity (Volf 1996, 140ff). This has considerable advantages over alternatives which would rely merely on, say, attitudes, intentions, or on conceptions of 'communion' considered without bodily involvement. Interestingly, the outline of Volf's phenomenology of embrace could be expounded very effectively in terms of group improvisation – his stress on 'undetermination' of outcome and 'risk' (147) is especially suggestive of improvisation.

in theological epistemology who urge that we become less dependent on controlling paradigms which ignore our embodiedness and our active participation as God's physical creatures in a God-given physical world.[74] It is also possible that there is material here for a Christology which would want to take the embodiedness of Jesus with due seriousness.

Further, in the case of the jazz player, such somatically realised freedom necessarily involves an exploration of the keyboard, a respectful interaction with its physical peculiarities which coheres in significant ways with a theological ecology respectful of the non-human physical world.[75] For the instrumental musician, in addition to the sounds received through the ear, the reality with which she has the most immediate bodily contact is her musical *instrument*. And it is well established that for the instrumental improviser, with the text and the analytical step of reading music often removed, the tactile relation between the performer and the instrument becomes especially close and sensitive.[76]

In any case, the dominant tradition of composed music in the West has generally regarded the creation of music as a separate activity from playing an instrument, such that the instrument is often seen as no more than a tool for carrying out the purposes of the mind or emotions, either to be disregarded as far as possible or even to be seen as some kind of enemy. Views differ among jazz improvisers about the instrument and its role. Some see it as an intruder between the player and the music. But far commoner among improvisers of all types is to regard it as materially intrinsic to the creation of the music: 'The instrument – that's the matter – the stuff – your subject.'[77] Significantly, composing away from an instrument is

74. For example, to over-rely on visual paradigms in epistemology can lead one to assume some kind of logically primary 'distance' or disengagement between self and world, which is then assumed to be a 'problem' which it is the task of epistemology to tackle. The literature on this is vast, but in relation to Michael Polanyi, who stands out by his resistance to this tendency, and the theological ramifications of his views, see e.g. A. J. Torrance (1996), ch. 5, esp. 347ff.; Begbie (1991b), 201f.; Patterson (1993).

75. I could have spoken about instruments under the heading of cultural constraints, but it seems more appropriate to do so here since instruments are so closely bound up with the embodied character of improvisation.

76. See Bailey (1992), 98ff. We might think this is especially so in the case of a singer: the physicality of sound is known in an immediate way through vocal cords and breathing. But instrumental improvisation has generally been much more ambitious than vocal. One reason is that words confine vocal music: 'A sung melody can be embellished only at the expense of directness of word communication. The "basic" folk melody usually has only one note for each syllable. If more notes are added, then words must be repeated, or new syllables be created, or existing syllables lengthened and sung to several notes' (Sloboda 1993, 142). Another reason is that the feedback necessary to improvisation is especially hard for the solo singer, with only hearing and proprioception available: it is in many cases easier to listen when playing an instrument than when singing.

77. Steve Lacey, as quoted in Bailey (1992), 99.

virtually unheard of among jazz instrumentalists. Rather than being a hindrance to expression, an obstacle to an idea, it becomes, through bodily engagement, part of the expressivity. 'Composers in the European tradition conceive a phrase by itself and then make it fit the requirements of a given instrument. *The jazz improviser creates only in terms of the instrument he plays*. In extreme instances of assimilation, the instrument becomes in some way a part of him'.[78] A jazz melody, therefore, properly exists in concrete relation to an instrument: attack, vibrato, accentuation and so forth are integral to the melody. But similar things have been said quite outside the jazz world. Consider this account of Chopin improvising:

> The other day I heard Chopin improvise at George Sand's house. It is marvellous to hear Chopin compose in this way: his inspiration is so immediate and complete that he plays without hesitation as if it could not be otherwise. But when it comes to writing it down, and capturing the original thought in all its details, he spends days of nervous strain and almost terrible despair.[79]

In cases like this, it is clear that the instrument in improvisation is no mere tool or implement to make pre-conceived sounds. Its own properties, characteristics and features are explored, honoured and incorporated into the music. The sonic properties of the instrument are investigated – timbral characteristics, its possibilities for multiphonics, microtonal effects, percussive use, etc.[80] The instrument is allowed to 'have its say'. This attitude is redolent with theological resonances of honouring the contours and characteristics of the physical world in which we have been given to participate, in marked contrast to subsuming the natural world under pragmatic, utilitarian categories.

Highly significant here is that integral to Sudnow's new-found freedom through bodily engagement with an instrument was a fertile *temporality*. The metrical structure articulated by the chord sequence needed to be sensed physically and to be highlighted in the right hand's melody. In addition, the hand's own temporal constraints were to be respectfully negotiated (a hand can accomplish only a limited number of things in a given duration, and in certain temporal configurations). And in addition to these, that very same right hand also improvises – it is part of a body which is, to an extent, undetermined, contingent. (The hand's indetermi-

78. André Hodeir, as cited in Berendt (1983), 182. My italics.   79. Hedley, et al. (1980), 298. 80. See e.g. Berliner (1994), 114ff. I am not thinking here of the 'extensions' to instruments sometimes made by players – extra strings, 'preparations' for piano, electronic treatment, and so forth, though this too may be a form of the kind of exploration we have in mind.

nacy, Sudnow certainly implies, plays a role in the improvisation.) Those frantic, 'never-having-enough-time' experiences of Sudnow's early experiments came when he failed to respect the music's metre and the body's temporal constraints. It would appear that from the point of view of temporality, true jazz emerges when, among other things, the temporal constraints of the pre-established metre, felt in the body, and the temporal constraints of the body itself come into fruitful and mutually enhancing interplay with the temporal contingency of the improvised lines of music and of the body itself. This clearly links up with many of the theological themes in previous chapters of this book, and chimes in well with our repeated emphasis on the ability of music to help us come to 'live peaceably' with time.

Sonic order

Sudnow's freedom was also discovered in relation to the order of sound itself. Body and keyboard were indwelt tacitly to explore the sonic order, and this order itself was being tacitly indwelt in order to improvise music. Improvisation's contingency stimulates a high level of aural attentiveness, a constant monitoring of the sound one is making (and the sound of others, if there are others). Add to this the absence of a text (presuming there is none) and of procedures necessary to text-processing, and it is not surprising if improvisers speak of their work as the exploration of sound. Cornelius Cardew's words are representative of many: 'We are *searching* for sounds and for the responses that attach to them, rather than thinking them up, preparing them and producing them. The search is conducted through the medium of sound and the musician himself is at the heart of that experiment.'[81] The idea of imposing thought patterns on acoustic phenomena is wide of the mark. Better is the notion of 'thinking in' notes, rhythms and so on – not thinking 'on' to them or simply 'through' them but thinking *in* them in such a way that their own integrity becomes intrinsic to the process.

    At a number of points in this book we have found ourselves resisting the tendency of some musical aesthetics to abstract music from materiality (our own materiality, and that of the non-human world). We have already spoken about the way in which the order of sound is intrinsic to the being and meaning of music, and of the grounding of this order in physical features of the non-human world as well as in universal characteristics of our

---

81. Cardew (1971), xviii.

own constitution.[82] True, words like 'universal' are potentially dangerous; much writing on musical meaning has rightly cautioned against too
quickly ascribing universal status to particular musical strategies. Music
'means' by being mediated through multiple constraints, interacting in
manifold ways. Nonetheless, as we have also said, a plausible case could be
made for holding that the derivation of some musical procedures and our
response to them can be traced not only to trans-cultural (even universally
shared) features of humanity but also to invariant features of the behaviour of physical entities distinct from humanity.[83] And, as we have repeatedly stressed, the sonic order, as part of the fabric and condition of the
created universe, is integrally a temporal order; the integrity of the sonic
order is a dynamic one. Even before sounds have become notes and tones,
they have their own temporality, and when taken up into metrical and
harmonic patterns, they further engage with other temporalities of the
world.

Improvisation, then, involves the courteous, responsive 'investigation
of sound' – in Sudnow's case, the vibration of strings and their resonance
with each other. And the improviser's investigation of sound, is, as much
as anything else, an investigation of the temporality of sound, or temporality through sound. The freedom which is so celebrated and enjoyed in
improvisation would seem to come not from an attempt to escape the limits and specificities of the physical but through a particularly attentive
attunement to living sound: a courteous interaction with a rich and mul-
tivalent physical sonic order with its own characteristic temporalities.
The theological matter at stake here concerns the limits and *therefore* the
possibilities of our commerce with the material world and its temporalities, and of our vocation to form and shape it in fresh ways. The radically
constructive 'freedom' of the modernist ego, exemplified in Boulez's total
serialist project, all too easily links with a belief that the non-human
world could never be our home, that it is essentially an impediment, at
worst an enemy. The traditional jazz improviser articulates a freedom
constituted neither by intellectual imposition, where it might be
assumed that we bring value and significance to a materiality whose value
and meaning are constantly under suspicion, nor by a somewhat sterile
passivity in the face of 'what happens' (Cage), but by a respectful shaping
of the energetic arrangements of the material world (the sonic order). The
integrity of this constraint calls forth a careful, patient welcoming of its

82. See above, pp. 51ff.   83. See above, pp. 52f.

sensed reality, such that the otherness of sound's forms is acknowledged, but also, through a vast variety of musical shapings, its dynamic configurations are enabled to take on further, and, one would hope, richer meaningful forms. This, we would maintain, points to a theological account of an authentically free relation of humankind to the physical world we inhabit, and finds its Christological grounding in the materiality of the Son's incarnation in Jesus Christ, in whom creation's integrity – including its temporal integrity – is neither disregarded nor overridden but vindicated and renewed.

Freedom, creativity and God

The fruitfulness of this conception of freedom-with-constraint which we have opened up through improvisation can be further drawn out by reference to George Steiner's work *Real Presences*.[84] Not only will we be given to see more clearly the character of Christian freedom, but, in turn, the argument can double back on itself and we can see more clearly the character of artistic creativity, in music and wider afield. Moreover, we will find that we are pushed deep into questions about the character of God.

When considering artistic creativity in relation to God, issues of freedom quickly surface. One of the most persistent forms of the attempt to link God and art has been to regard art as a bid for freedom in relation to God, an act of counter-construction, a wrestling with the Maker and the stubborn priority of his 'let there be'. George Steiner shows himself deeply sympathetic to this tradition when enquiring as to the character of human creativity, in particular the artistic generation of meaning. In *Real Presences*, he points to the predominance in our age of secondary discourse – texts about texts – and traces this to a disconnection of logos and cosmos, a 'break of the covenant between word and world', and proceeds to speak of the character of art in terms of immediacy, 'encounter' and epiphany. Here we find the necessity and inevitability of art traced unashamedly to theological considerations: 'there is aesthetic creation because there is *creation*. There is formal construction because we have been made form.'[85] Freedom is essential to Steiner's argument: the crucial difference between the primary art text and the secondary commentary on it is that 'The primary text – the poem, picture, piece of music – is a phenomenon *of freedom*.'[86] Steiner distinguishes two categories of

84. Steiner (1989).   85. Ibid., 201.   86. Ibid., 151.

freedom, that belonging to the art work and that realised in our encounter with the art work. The art work is free in the sense that it need not have come into existence: 'The poem, the sonata, the painting, could very well *not* be.'[87] And 'we are utterly free not to receive, not to meet with authentic aesthetic modes at all'.[88] When these two freedoms meet, freedom in its profoundest form is realised:

> Where seriousness meets with seriousness, exigence with exigence, in the ontological and ethical spaces of the disinterested, where art and poetics, imperatively contingent in their own coming into being and intelligible form, meet the receptive potential of a free spirit, *there takes place the nearest we can know of the existential realisation of freedom*.[89]

Steiner can go as far as claiming that in the aesthetic sphere, 'to be is to be at liberty'.[90] 'Only in the aesthetic is there the absolute freedom "not to have come into being". Paradoxically, it is that possibility of absence which gives autonomous force to the presence of the work.'[91] Accordingly, the aesthetic act is 'an *imitatio*, a replication on its own scale, of the inaccessible first *fiat*'.[92] Of course, every artist knows that her artistic work is not *ex nihilo*, it is always 'after' the first. 'Whatever its seeming novelty ... the verbal fiction, the painting, the sculpture, are ultimately mimetic ... The obstinate "thereness" of things ... the inference of immanence, seek out even the most extreme of verbal fantastications.'[93] Despite this, art constantly reaches beyond empirical exactitude, reproductive fidelity. Why? Because artistic creation is at root a bid for freedom:

> I believe that the making into being by the poet, artist and ... by the composer, is *counter*-creation ... It is radically agonistic. It is rival. In all substantive art-acts there beats an angry gaiety. The source is that of loving rage. The human maker rages at his coming *after*, at being, forever, second to the original and originating mystery of the forming of form.[94]

Here – and this is something which seems to be ignored by most theological commentary on *Real Presences* – music comes to occupy an outstanding place. Why? Although all the arts exemplify the gratuitous 'coming into being', and thus the unaccountability which is 'the essence of freedom',[95] music exemplifies freedom more than any other art. This is because music, though 'brimful of meanings'[96] (i.e. not arbitrary or chaotic) is the least obviously mimetic art, least dependent on the 'first' creation. It is

---

87. Ibid., 152.   88. Ibid., 153.   89. Ibid., 154. My italics.   90. Ibid., 153.
91. Ibid., 155.   92. Ibid., 201.   93. Ibid., 202.   94. Ibid., 203f.
95. Ibid., 164.   96. Ibid., 217.

the least amenable to empirical seizure, to analytic circumscription, the art more than any other 'which transcends the sayable, which outstrips the analysable'.[97] In music, stubborn otherness is embodied most potently, freedom is most fully actualised amongst the arts. Significantly, Steiner sees part of music's essential freedom as lying in the fact 'that it liberates us from the enforcing beat of biological and physical-mathematical clocks. The time which music "takes", and which it gives as we perform or experience it, is the only *free time* granted us prior to death.'[98] And because music enacts this intense, free, resistant otherness, because it is least dependent on the 'other', Steiner can conclude that in the making and reception of music there is a 'presumption of presence', a transcendent postulate.[99] 'It is counter-creation and counter-love, as these are embodied in the aesthetic and in our reception of formed meaning, which put us in sane touch with that which transcends, with matters "undreamt of" in our materiality.'[100]

Even this crude summary of Steiner's nuanced contentions will raise some fairly pointed questions. Brian Horne begins a powerful critique of Steiner with what he considers to be a theologian's 'contradiction' of Steiner's position. Steiner fails to take account of the ineradicable distinction between God's 'absolute' freedom not to create, which God alone possesses, and the freedom proper to the human creature, who 'by contrast and logical definition possesses only relative freedom and is subject to the necessity of creation ... Our impulse to creation ... arises out of our status as creatures endowed with relative freedom.'[101] But to be fair, this is hardly a 'contradiction' of Steiner. Though Steiner undoubtedly slips into hyperbole in speaking of humanity's 'absolute freedom' not to create and of the 'absolute gratuitousness' of the art work,[102] his whole argument seems to hinge on a fairly pointed contrast between absolute divine freedom and relative human freedom. The impulse to create, though for Steiner entailing an irreducible element of non-necessity, also involves a painful awareness that we 'come after' God, and can *only* come after him, constrained as we are by 'the forming of form' which God has already achieved. Further, Steiner stresses that art collapses without the 'felt

---

97. Ibid., 218.
98. Ibid., 196f. This, I presume, is what he means by his earlier assertion that 'music is, indeed, time made free of temporality' (ibid., 27).
99. See ibid., especially 216ff. '[Music] reinsures what I sense to be or, rather, search for in the transcendental. That is to say it demonstrates to me the reality of a presence, of a factual 'thereness', which defies either analytic or empirical circumscription' (Steiner 1997, 75).   100. Steiner (1989), 227.   101. Horne (1995), 85f.   102. Steiner (1989), 155, 153.

continuities' between what has been created and what we create.[103] The creation of art may indeed contain 'the dream of an absolute leap out of nothingness' but it is a dream only, a 'thrust towards a rivalling totality', a 'wrestling for primacy'.[104] Our freedom is not absolute, and Steiner is only too well aware of the fact.

Constraints would seem, in one sense at least, to be taken with great seriousness in Steiner's scheme. Nevertheless, and here we are at one with Horne, there is something deeply problematic about where Steiner seems to locate the essence of freedom, and the way he relates human and divine freedom. In the first place, Steiner's understanding of freedom, in the aesthetic realm at any rate, clearly centres on the notion of non-necessity, and, as expressed by persons, tends towards an ideal of unconstrained self-determination. Someone of Steiner's erudition and historical sensitivity is of course aware just how pernicious such ideas have sometimes been. Nonetheless, we need to press Steiner as to where the pivot of his understanding of freedom is being placed. It is the oppositional, 'over-against' character of the artistic act in relation to what is given which receives the strongest accent, even though he believes strongly that artistic freedom involves exercising 'courtesy' (*cortesia*) in relation to a work of art,[105] and even though he would strenuously resist the idea that an artist could or should attempt to create without regard to the traditions of the past. Freedom appears to be manifested most powerfully insofar as the artistic agent manages to be un-bound by constraint (even if that encounter with constraint may indeed be the occasion for human freedom to be realised). The production of an art work 'is liberality in essence and, rigorously considered, a wholly unpredictable choice not to be'.[106] To be sure, Steiner speaks of aesthetic freedom emerging out of the encounter between two artistic freedoms ('an exchange of liberties'[107]) – the freedom of the artist not to create and of us to refuse the work of art – but this is a resonance between two forms of essentially the same freedom, the power *not* to be and *not* to do. While quite properly bringing to the fore the contingent (i.e. unpredictable, non-necessary) aspect of artistic creation, what nevertheless seems to be lacking is the recognition that an appropriate, reciprocal and ongoing relation to constraints – to the art work, the created order, and to God – might actually be intrinsic to *constituting* our freedom.

103. Ibid., 212f.   104. Ibid., 202, 204, 205.   105. Ibid., 147ff., 155ff.   106. Ibid., 153.
107. Ibid., 154.

Second, to this conception of the free aesthetic agent there corresponds a conception of God as undifferentiated being. Horne rightly argues that a unitarian concept of God, as some kind of undifferentiated transcendent reality, cannot provide the kind of divine underwriting of art which Steiner seeks.[108] What does a trinitarian conceptuality bring, by contrast? Here Horne is especially telling. The world was brought into being not simply by the fiat of a monad, whose act the artist unconsciously or consciously counters in some kind of defiance. (Ironically, in this picture, the plausibility of pleading the cause of 'real presence' in art recedes rather than advances.) Rather, 'It is not by any other than a Trinitarian action that the world is brought into and sustained in being. The answer the creatures make is, like prayer, not so much a reply to God – our dialogue with him – but a participation in a dialogue which already exists – the eternal conversation of God himself.'[109] What then is the trinitarian shape of artistic creation? Horne suggests that 'the possibility, or potentiality, of artistic creation is lodged in the doctrine of the image';[110] to be created in the image of God is to be created in the image of the *triune* God, whose life is a life of 'exchanged love, absolute relatedness and creative energy', a life

> in which there is the eternal self-expression of the Father in his Son or Word and the eternal self-knowledge received in the flowing out and returning of the Spirit. In the human being there is the same drive to move out of the self in order to find the self, the compulsion to self-expression and self-knowledge.[111]

The propriety of artistic creation, Horne argues, is in the doctrine of the incarnation, in which the eternal dialogue between Father and Son is carried into the material of the created order; the Son of the Father through whom all things were created becomes physical, tangible flesh, one with the creation. And the necessity and inevitability of artistic creation is lodged in the doctrine of the Spirit, 'who appropriates and expropriates through human persons, materials of creation to bring into being secondary worlds'.[112] That the Spirit of God might, as it were, come to our side and generate within us the necessity and inevitability of artistic creation is not a possibility considered by Steiner, nor that in so doing the Spirit is drawing us up into that creative and redemptive movement of exchange within God's own life. The dominance of the notion of 'counter-creation' as a bid for absolute freedom effectively excludes this alternative vision.

---

108. Horne (1995), 86ff.   109. Ibid., 88.   110. Ibid., 89f.   111. Ibid., 87.
112. Ibid., 90.

In short, the freedom of the artist requires God's as well as our own agency, the agency of the Spirit who brings about that particularity-in-relation which constitutes our freedom and which has already been actualised in the Son.

Horne's contention, then, is not that Steiner is wrong to suppose that the creation and reception of art are best expounded through the categories of freedom and *cortesia* but that these categories can only begin to find their rightful place within a trinitarian milieu. It is not our place here to consider in detail the trinitarian dimensions of artistic creation. The key point to register here is that Steiner's position is rendered problematic through operating with a particular conception of the free artist, as 'agonistic' counter-creator, whose freedom is realised most potently in so far as he or she is not constrained by 'what is' or 'what has been'. And Steiner is by no means alone in working with this kind of model, or the only one to bring it into play with theological themes.

Once again, improvisation emerges as a powerful resource to refresh and re-orientate this whole field. Improvisation helps us avoid doctrines of freedom which have hampered the development of a fully trinitarian conception of artistic creativity. No improviser has to my knowledge ever talked or thought about their work as 'counter-creation', for reciprocity and gift-exchange are intrinsic to the way improvisation operates. Freedom is constituted not simply by the assertion of a supposedly bare novelty against constraint but by the interplay and exchange between what is given and what is made, and in such a way that what is given is received as inherently valuable and potentially beneficial (not merely as a means to the realisation of a boundless self-determined act), and that what is created or returned is unpredictably different, passed back/passed on in unpredictable ways at unpredictable times, yet is consonant with the gift. This is the kind of interplay in which freedom in the world is actualised, and, the theologian will go on to say, it is grounded in the divine, triune life in whose reciprocal life we are given to share. (Steiner would perhaps have fared better if he had followed through more thoroughly the implications of his praise of composers who skilfully re-work the music of others – a practice characteristic of most improvisation.[113])

Again, the temporal aspects of this need to be highlighted. It is probable that at least some of Steiner's difficulties arise from an inadequate recognition of the temporality of artistic endeavour. Steiner's stress on the

---

113. See Steiner (1989), 20f.

distinctiveness of musical temporality, on music's supposed otherness from the day to day times of life, is highly significant. As we have seen, it is unwise to assume that music's temporal freedom is best characterised primarily in terms of its difference from and independence of 'our' day-to-day times; we would do better to understand it as arising from an intensive and respectful engagement with the temporalities integral to the world. I noted earlier that many modernist and contemporary accounts of freedom have fallen prey to atemporal conceptions of the self (standing 'above time'). These are sometimes linked to unitarian concepts of divine freedom and downplay or overlook the time-embeddedness of all human action.[114] We must ask whether Steiner himself, at least in the musical aesthetics of *Real Presences*, has successfully avoided just this kind of tendency. Again, musical improvisation can come into its own here, contributing a proper recognition of the temporality which is arguably crucial to all felicitous artistic making, the temporality of the constraints with which all artistic endeavour deals.

Spirit and particularity, trust and risk

The contention that constraints are the condition of Christian freedom is hardly original but it is an important one in a climate where the characteristically modern idea of freedom as autonomy has 'been absolutised and thus proved pregnant with fresh forms of tyranny and inhumanity'.[115] We have sought to propound it through musical improvisation, which has proved singularly apt for the purpose.

We may press matters further with regard to two areas very closely linked to issues of freedom. The first concerns the work of the *Holy Spirit*. Bearing in mind that in the New Testament the tie between freedom and the Holy Spirit is very close, we would suggest that there are significant resources in improvisation for the development of a doctrine of the Spirit, especially one which would accord human freedom a key place in relation to temporality. I have touched on this a number of times, not least in this chapter. Here, I want to draw attention especially to the Spirit's particularising role. Who is the Spirit, if not the 'particulariser', the one who frees us by particularising the cultural constraints for the occasional constraints? And who is the Spirit, if not the one who 'explores the occasion', bringing freedom by drawing out the potential of singular circumstances?

114. See above, pp. 202f.   115. Lash (1996), 244.

Much recent writing in pneumatology has urged that we avoid the common inclination to ignore the particularity of the Spirit's action in favour of the Spirit's general, universal or timeless presence to the world. For example, with respect to Christology, the Spirit is the personal 'other' who maintained and empowered Christ's humanity in a way which respected and 'explored' a range of discrete historical circumstances in his earthly life.[116] In this way, our humanity, in the person of the Son, was freed from its sinful distortions to serve the Father and others. If we require a Spirit-Christology which keeps clear of Apollinarianism on the one hand (the over-determination of the humanity of Christ by the divine Word) and adoptionism on the other (which erases the incarnation of the Word), and if a key failing of much Christology has been the inability to take proper account of historical particularity, then it would seem that improvisation has much to offer.

With respect to salvation and anthropology, something similar can be said about the work of the Spirit amidst occasional constraints. The Spirit makes possible improvisatory dialogical interrelations in which personal uniqueness and singularity is affirmed and enabled to flourish through an adoption into a web of relationships. Here there is unity not despite variety but precisely in and through it (1 Cor. 12). The improvising of tradition in the Church is also, at best, the work of the Spirit. We have already seen how 'improvisation in advance' provides a remarkable way of elucidating the Spirit's particularising role in Acts 2. (It is worth underlining that the crowds did not speak the same language but heard the disciples in their *own* particular languages.) And the physical, bodily exploration of sound which marks improvisation resonates richly with a pneumatology which would seek to evade opposing Spirit and bodily 'flesh', seeing the Spirit rather as releasing bodily capacities in relation to specific constraints.

With respect to creation at large, if the Son or Word through whom all things are created is associated with the dynamic stability of reality, the Spirit is active 'to enable new possibilities, to empower freedom to live in the abundance that is given'. Speaking of the three 'modes' of God (Father, Son and Spirit), Daniel Hardy and David Ford go on to write that 'The second mode sets the pattern and ideal, and this third mode [the Spirit] is the inspiration and means of achieving and participating in

---

116. For fuller discussion and defence of this approach, see e.g. Smail (1988), Congar (1983), Spence (1990), Gunton (1993).

it.'[117] This resonates with a theme in the tradition of Basil the Great, for whom the Holy Spirit is creation's 'perfecter', bringing to particular fulfilments what has been secured in Jesus Christ, the first-born of the new creation.[118] Again, improvisation comes into its own by embodying just this dynamic.

The second area concerns *trust and risk*. Fundamental to the improviser's attitude to constraint is patient trust. And the more the trust, the more the constraints prove themselves trustworthy, which in turn produces greater trust. And so on. Trust means having the confidence that the improvisation is going to be worth the time it takes, that something is going to 'come out of it', that time will deliver something felicitous.

This trust enables risk. The greater the contingency, the more the risk of failure. The conventional performer, though she might go wrong, does have the opportunity for rehearsal, usually needing to make only minor adjustments in performance. For the improviser the risk factor is normally much higher, much more being left to the performance itself.

Despite this, as we saw in Sudnow, there is a relatively relaxed attitude to error, and this would seem to derive from at least three factors. First, error can be incorporated into the work, woven into the musical texture. The improviser usually has a flexible repertoire of devices which 'take up' the error immediately and fluently into some kind of coherent flow, such that it need not even be recognised *as* error. Second, constraints give you space to fail without complete disaster. The constraints – I am thinking especially here of cultural constraints – will carry one through. This is sensed very acutely by the composer-cum-improviser: 'The improviser can . . . dispense with much of the composer's habitual decision making concerning structure and direction.'[119] Most important, third, space to fail seems *necessary* for a superlative performance:

> we make allowances for fluffs, interruptions, squawks, and all sorts of distracting concomitants that we assume to be no part of the performance. But we also allow for his forgetting what he was doing, trying to do two things at once, changing his mind about where he is

117. Hardy and Ford (1985), 119f. It is not surprising that some have sought to use improvisation as a model in the context of integrating theological and contemporary scientific concerns with respect to the doctrine of creation. See e.g. Peacocke (1993), 175ff. The physical world is characterised by an irreducible 'contingent order', an order open to proliferating possibilities, yet proportioned and configured. It is at least arguable that this interplay between predictability and unpredictability, as a feature of the physical world as a whole, was not taken seriously by either Cage or Boulez during their exchange in the 1940s and 50s. See above, p. 197.   118. See Sherry (1992), ch. 7.
119. Sloboda (1993), 139.

going, starting more hares than he can chase at once, picking up where
he thought he had left off but resuming what was not quite there in
the first place, discovering and pursuing tendencies in what he has
done that would have taken a rather different form if he had thought
of them at the time, and so on. These are all part of his performance
tied together in a single web of intention.[120]

Why this allowance, this hospitality to blunders? Frost and Yarrow, in
their book on improvised drama, write of the juggling teacher:

Some teachers of juggling begin by giving the pupil three balls and
getting the student to throw them up in the air. The tendency is to
clutch reflexively, to tighten up, to panic and to try desperately to catch
the balls. The teacher will smile, shake his or her head, and make the
beginner throw the balls again, this time making no effort to catch.
When the balls hit the ground the teacher will nod, 'That's *supposed* to
happen.' The right to fail, to make a hash of it, is affirmed from the
beginning. The student learns to get out of the life-conditioned reflex
of trying to 'make it happen'. Then the teacher gives the relaxed student
one ball to be thrown gently from hand to hand. Then two, helping the
student to overcome the convulsive clutching which prevents the
second ball from being thrown up as the first descends. 'Don't try to
catch it, concentrate on throwing, on *emptying* the hand – make it ready
to receive the descending ball.' Finally, as the gentle rhythm of juggling
is learned, the third ball is easy to master. The hardest thing to learn is
not 'how to juggle', but how to let the balls drop.[121]

The authors continue: 'The hardest thing to learn is that failure doesn't
matter. It doesn't have to be brilliant every time – it can't be . . . What matters is to listen, to watch, to add to what is happening rather than subtract
from it.'[122] In other words, to 'clutch reflexively' at safety so that nothing
is 'thrown up', to withdraw from risk by a panic retreat into cliché means
that nothing new is learned. The music lapses into lifeless monotony.
First-rate improvisation is marked by a restful restlessness. We are freed
from the anxiety of having to create structure from scratch, forms which
will give meaning to the improvisation – *we* don't have to 'make it happen' we can entrust ourselves to the given. At the same time (or rather,
with and through time!) we are freed *by* these very structures *for* music-
making with endlessly fruitful possibilities.

We are speaking here of the shape of Christian freedom – a restful restlessness. By being given in Christ the firm stability of divine grace, the

'gentle rhythm' to be learned and endlessly re-learned, we are freed from having to 'make it happen', from that 'convulsive clutching' at 'getting it right' which prevents us from throwing anything into the air, freed from having to fabricate authentic human being. And yet this very gift liberates us for a life of joyful (not anxious) restlessness, a perilous 'emptying of our hands' for the sake of music of limitless interest and variety, in the knowledge that failure has in a sense already been accounted for and future error will in some manner be taken up. To discover that the risk 'was worth it' generates more trust, which in turn generates more fruitful risk-taking – such is Christian liberty.

In speaking of constraints in this chapter we have very often used the term 'given'. It is time now to see what it might mean.

9

Giving and giving back

In this chapter, we stay with the improvisers but allow them to move us on from human freedom to different but related theological ground. As we have found, in speaking of constraints it is quite natural to use the word 'given'. And in the world of improvisation it is hard *not* to use 'gift' language (a 'given' harmonic progression, a 'given' melody). But, as many studies have underlined, the 'gift' word-group is highly ambiguous, and instructively so.

Brute given and beneficial gift

The first ambiguity ties in with the discussion of freedom in the last chapter. In the English language, the word 'given' can denote a bare *a priori*, without purpose (beneficial or otherwise), carrying connotations of a somewhat cold, impersonal indifference – as in 'it is a given fact' or 'we can take it as given that. . . .' Alternatively, it may carry notions of inherently valuable entities and beneficial deliberation, as in: 'this meal was given to me by my beloved'. The kind of theology of freedom we were elaborating through improvisation in the last chapter clearly comes into its own when constraints are viewed fundamentally in this second, positive sense. It was just this sense of 'given' which was missing in Boulez and Cage.

Moreover, it would appear that issues about *time* are closely bound up with this double sense of gift. Why is the word 'given' still deployed in its starkly objective sense? Part of it may be that 'nothing simply and eternally *is*, but always first arrives or *arises*, if not through space, then at least through time'.[1] Things 'give themselves' (or appear to give themselves) to

1. Milbank (1995), 120.

our perception; to say that I am perceiving some thing is to assume that in some manner the thing has been involved in some kind of temporal transference such that I can now perceive it. The notions of 'gift for us', temporal limitation, and presence are thus closely intertwined. There is more than a hint of this in the English language: the word 'present' can mean 'gift' (with the associated verb 'to give' or 'to offer'), but it can also denote 'now' as distinct from past and future, and also 'here' rather than 'not here'.

In any case, the theological issues at stake can be quickly indicated by referring to the theology of creation. A scientist may talk of the givenness of the laws of nature in the sense of brute objectivity, while the theologian may speak of those same laws as given in the sense of conferred graciously by God for the freedom of his creatures and for his glory. The latter wants to say that the cosmos is the unnecessary gift of God, non-eternal and temporal through and through, 'here', among other things, for our freedom. And the world's temporality – not only 'the present moment' – is intrinsically part of what is given with creation. It should be clear from the previous chapters that music can embody a sonic demonstration of this conception of creation as 'temporal gift for our freedom'. But it should also be clear from the last chapter that musical improvisation can offer a heightened form of it, because of the way it regards continuous constraints (such as the vibrations of sound, or our bodily constitution), which can so easily be thought of as no more than stark, non-negotiable facts. As we have seen, these are not effaced or erased but engaged with in such a way as to give rise to something enriching. 'Bare given' is treated and manifested as clothed gift. And this includes the temporality of the constraints in question.

Gifts, exchange and improvisation

In addition to the fact–value ambiguity, there is ambiguity in the concept of gift with respect to the notion of exchange, or 'taking' and 'giving back'. This is not only a linguistic matter; as John Milbank observes, it points to aspects of a 'universal human condition'.[2] Many practices which may seem like pure, unilateral gift are in fact imbued with mutuality – human generosity belongs within the context of prior attachments or making such attachments. A retirement present is 'in recognition' of

2. Ibid., 122.

service to the company, part of the intention of giving flowers to our beloved is to strengthen the relationship, and so on. And it would seem that a good gift usually is aimed at receiving something back, even if only the pleasure that we have sought to benefit another. This need not lead to cynicism, to the conclusion that there is no such thing as a gift which is not entirely controlled by the self-seeking interests of coercive power.[3] Taking his cue from Pierre Bourdieu, Milbank suggests that authentic *gratuity* can characterise gift, provided, first, that there is a *delay* of return, a delay of unpredictable, indeterminate duration – to give a return gift straight away implies the discharge of some kind of debt – and second, that there is a relation of '*non-identical repetition*' between gift and counter-gift – the counter-gift cannot be the same object (without insult). And it will not necessarily be given to the original donor (though it may): a gift correctly used will invariably involve a 'giving back' to the wider social context of the donee, such that there is always a 'passing on', some kind of continuation of the original generosity. This 'passing on' contains an irreducibly unpredictable dimension – it will happen not only at unpredictable times, but also in unpredictably different circumstances, and to an unpredictable number and variety of people. It is therefore, potentially at least, limitless.

Other dimensions of giving emerge in this light. For example, there is *dedication*, that is, attention to the other(s), a determination to find a suitable gift (even though it may not be used in the way the giver expects), to find the appropriate time to surprise and delight the recipient(s) so that the gift really is received as a gift by the other(s). Further, *purity of intention is not essential* to this understanding of gift. Inappropriate motives do not necessarily prevent the gift being a gift; what is more critical is that the gift is fitting for this or that person. In addition, *the desire to receive back need not be a form of crude selfishness*, but a recognition that we are inevitably in relation with others and that some relationships are beneficial and deserve to be furthered. There can also be *joy* in giving, not the joy of self-affirmation, but the joy of going beyond oneself, finding enrichment in outgoing. To receive the other in receiving that gift demands that the *distance of the other remains in place* – delay and non-identical repetition assume the irreducible free otherness of the donor such that we do not forget that this gift came from this other person to me. The gift always carries with it

3. See the argument advanced against Derrida, for example, by Loughlin (1996b), 125ff.; Milbank (1995), 129ff.

the character of having been given by this other. Thus, it cannot be totally owned without losing its character as gift. 'To try to possess the other and his gifts, to receive them as exactly due rewards, or as things we do not need to *go on* receiving, would be simply to obliterate them.'[4] The gift remains a gift, and will never become a mere commodity, if and only if it is always regarded as *from* the other *to* me, continually seen in that mode of transferral, and consequently goes on being given through time. However, it is important to add that precisely because the gift is to be regarded as existing only *as* given by an other, something of the giver is given in the gift. To be more precise, what a giver gives reflects, bears witness to and becomes ineluctably associated with the giver, such that we may speak of the self-giving of the donor in the gift.[5]

The reader will notice how closely this accords with much of what we have been saying about traditional jazz improvisation in groups, not least its temporality. (In fact, we have implicitly spoken of delay and non-identical repetition a number of times in previous chapters.) There is delay – predictable, knee-jerk, immediate responses sound dull and destroy authentic jazz. The 'return' has to be appropriately timed, a skill often developed to a higher degree in improvisers than traditional performers owing to the increased contingency. And you do not return exactly what you receive. Though there is consistency and reliability, the temporality of improvisatory exchange is an open temporality; the sense of contingency and unpredictability is acute and innate to the process. The improviser receives the 'given' constraint – metre, harmony, melody, idiom – and 'returns' an equivalent but different gift. The giving back here usually includes passing it on in an equivalent but different (and unpredictable) form to an audience of some sort, who themselves (unpredictably) receive it in countlessly different (and unpredictable) ways, and who themselves pass it on unpredictably (perhaps in no other form than an increase of joy in their lives). Alternatively, the improvisation may be taken up by other musicians on subsequent occasions. As we have seen, in traditional jazz the improvisation itself (relying on its underlying, prior gift of harmonic progression) can function as the subject of further (unpredictable) improvisation, resulting in improvisation on improvisation. And the same expanding process can occur between improvisers in an ensemble – the melody of one leads to the new melody of another; gift leads to counter-gift, unpredictable as to content, timing and who is going to offer it.

---

4. Milbank (1995), 132f.   5. Ibid., 133ff.

'Dedication' is pivotal to this musical proliferation: in ensemble improvisation there will be acute listening (there may be visual contact too) in order to find the proper delay which ensures the appropriate surprise (and thus pleasure). The desire for a musical 'return' from the other is more often than not a desire to continue and deepen relationships which are enriching for both parties, not necessarily evidence of being possessive or merely self-serving. And, insofar as improvisation demands an attentive 'ecstatic' attitude towards and discovery of the other, there can be a joy which is the opposite of indulgent, self-enclosed pleasure.

Parallels and confirmations in other forms of improvisation are not hard to find. Keith Johnstone, founder of the improvisatory theatrical company 'Theatre Machine',[6] calls anything an actor does an 'offer'. The offer can be 'accepted' or 'blocked'. To block an offer means to prevent it developing.[7] As such it is a form of 'aggression'. 'Accepting', on the other hand, means welcoming the offer, and good improvisers, according to Johnstone, 'accept all offers made – which is something no "normal" person would do. Also they may accept offers which weren't really intended.'[8] (We recall what we have just said about purity of intention.) 'I tell my actors never to think up an offer, but instead to assume that one has already been made.'[9] In other words, you always regard yourself as a recipient. A striking expression of this posture is what Johnstone calls 'overaccepting'. Instead of concentrating on making the thing *you give* interesting,

> The trick is to make the thing you are *given* as interesting as possible. You want to 'overaccept' the offer . . . When the actor concentrates on making the thing he *gives* interesting, each actor seems in competition, and feels it. When they concentrate on making the gift they *receive* interesting, then they generate warmth between them. *We have strong resistances to being overwhelmed by gifts*, even when they're just being mimed. You have to get the class enthusiastic enough to go over the 'hump'. Then suddenly *great joy and energy are released*.[10]

This joyful, hospitable demeanour of gratitude in which gift and counter-gift are endlessly given and received should not be sentimentalised. The gift to be received is not necessarily regarded as totally good, or wholly to be affirmed. (And there may be rare cases when the gift does need to be

<hr/>

6. Johnstone (1979). In this section I am much indebted to Samuel Wells's illuminating discussion of improvisation and ethics (Wells 1996).
7. Johnstone (1979), 94ff. Blocking is not equivalent to saying 'no', because this might actually continue an action – if, for instance, I have been asked to leave and I refuse to do so.   8. Ibid., 99.   9. Ibid.   10. Ibid., 101. My italics.

rejected outright for the sake of good improvisation; although even this is only after it has been considered carefully.) Neither does 'overacceptance' imply total passivity, dissolving the initiative entirely on to others. Rather it means being willing to treat the gift as fundamentally something from which fruit can come, as an inherently valuable constraint ('as interesting as possible') from which a novelty (a counter-gift) can be generated which is consistent with the 'story' of the drama, and which in turn will provoke further novelty, and so on. The hospitality entailed in giving the other 'space' is not analogous to the evacuation of physical space, not a form of absence, but a way of being present with others in grateful recognition of their autonomy-within-relationship of gift-exchange.

What we said about 'distance' – that receiving a gift as gift demands that the irreducible otherness (and therefore freedom) of the donor remains secure – would also likely find ready agreement from the improviser. He is acutely aware of acting in this distance established by giving. This is because in improvisation there is normally a marked contrast between given and non-given (owing to the large measure of contingency). Two examples from musical improvisation illustrate the point. First, a musician improvising on a given harmony senses the radical disparity between the framework and the improvised music she gives back, the heart of the contrast being not so much that these usually sound very different (though that may be so), but that the latter is relatively undetermined. Indeed, it will be clear by now that any attempt to blur or downplay this contrast will likely enervate the jazz. The improviser is especially conscious that the given has come *from* beyond herself, and will, so to speak, always retain that status. Second, we can think of someone improvising on music provided by another player in a group. Here the given and the returned gift may sound much more alike. But successful improvisation still depends on avoiding identical repetition. More importantly, at any moment the improviser knows very sharply the contrast between the character of what has been played (which cannot be erased) and the character of what he is about to play (still largely to be formed). Again, there is at least a tacit awareness that the gift received and its giver can never come under his ownership if the improvisation is to continue in an effective way – which is also to say that the particularity and freedom of the other is not violated. To press the point, if our improviser tries to 'take over' the other player musically, or receive the music as some kind of 'expected' and 'proper' answer to something he has himself played (as a kind of due reward), or if he plays as if to suggest he has nothing more to receive from the other, then the improvisation quickly degenerates. Further, just as something of the giver 'abides' in what is received, the same will be true here: one is bound to receive something of the character of the other musician. This is especially so in jazz-group improvisation compared to a group like a symphony orchestra, given the heightened contingency typical of the former, and (usually) the absence of any score.

Milbank contends that what the New Testament denotes by *agape* is 'purified gift-exchange', and that the 'absolute gratuity' and 'absolute exchange' integral to authentic gift are not opposed to each other. On the contrary, they find their congruence in God and in his activity in the world, and together they provide the environment in which Christian freedom flourishes. Let us now unfold something of what this might mean, in conversation with the improviser.

Improvisational gift-exchange, God and humankind

God establishes a creation which is itself a 'return' to him, brought into being to praise its Creator. And God establishes creatures whose very existence is to voice creation's praise, to focus the song of creation on creation's Maker, to be 'secretaries' of praise (Herbert).[11] Humankind finds its true being in improvising on the givenness of the created world with the others who are given to us, never treating givens as something to be owned or enclosed in finality, but 'over-accepting' them in such a way that they are regarded as intrinsically interesting, and rendered more fully felicitous for a potentially enormous number of fresh melodies, harmonies and metres.

Along with this gift-exchange, God's absolute gratuity is preserved, in that he does not 'need' this return in order to be God. There is there is no internal lack which provokes God's gift:

> Not that Thou hast not still above
> Much better tunes than grones can make,
> But that these countrey-aires Thy love
>   Did take.[12]

And this return of praise is never fully paid back – the series of improvisations is potentially unlimited, endlessly repeated.

Sin is an inexplicable, absurd assault on God's freedom to give and thus a refusal to sing God's praise.[13] It is thus a denial of our being as

---

11. See Begbie (1991b).   12. Herbert (1947), 112.   13. McFadyen (1995).

God's 'return'. It is to 'block' the music of creation as gift. It is the refusal to improvise, to 'make the best' of what is given and pass on the movement of generosity. In the language of Romans 1, it is the refusal to honour God and give him thanks (v. 21). Such refusal robs the improviser of freedom to do anything for anybody, for she is alienated from the environment of gratuitous exchange which alone is the condition of her freedom. It is thus the failure not only to give but also to receive. The music of sinful humankind is marked by empty gestures of pseudo-freedom; by identical repetition – if not the attempted exact repetition of phrases, melodies or whatever (obsessive traditionalism), then the mere shuffling of musical elements, change without novelty (the 'ticking over' of a Church); spun out phrases which lead not to the expanding resonance of reciprocal gift but to fruitless dead-ends (the screaming of the prophets of Baal); grand overtures which quickly degenerate into stuttering cadences (Babel).

The dynamic of salvation brings giving and reception into extraordinarily close conjunction, and the theme of delay is prevalent throughout. In Christ, God receives us by giving a gift which *includes* a return. In Christ's own life, the Son of God in our midst, receiving and giving are inseparable. His gift to others involves his reception of others. However, there needs to be a dealing directly and finally with the persistent refusal which is sin, which we cannot eradicate. At Golgotha, God's greatest gift to us is fundamentally his reception of us – which means his acceptance (and absorption) of our refusal and at the same time his acceptance of Christ as the true 'return' God has longed for from us. On Easter day, God refuses to close down the conversation, by accepting Christ he confirms his refusal to accept our refusal of him.

Christ, then, *is* both God's gift and human return in one person. The giving of God in Christ is at one and the same time the giving of the Father's own Son to us, *and* the return or counter-gift of the perfect human self-offering on our behalf, without sin, vindicated in the resurrection. Exchange is thus integral to God's gift in Christ, before any response of ours. Now, God receives us by giving again – this time the Spirit who (as the giving gift) gives us the possibility of receiving the risen and ascended Christ. We are received by the Father, but only by virtue of, and by sharing in, the perfect return already given to us in Christ, now accessible through the Spirit.

So, the Church receives God's gift, but this means the reception of a return already made in Jesus Christ, in which we participate now by the

Spirit. This is a far cry from a model of divine unilateral self-giving designed to secure a continuing bondage of devotion and respect. But it is also far from a model of human freedom as an equally poised ability to accept or reject God's gift. That God's gift *includes* a giving 'from our side' is something often neglected in theologies of response. We 'participate in an event of communion conceived in terms of the bilateral, reciprocal giving which is realised in Christ's relationship with the Father in the Spirit and in which we are liberated to participate . . . by the Spirit'.[14] Free response is to be understood in this context. 'What is "given" in and through God's Self-communication is not a "Gift" to which we choose to respond (or not), but a "giving" in and through which we are "given" to participate within a triune matrix of dynamic and relational freedom – a being "set free" from self-bondage to "be".'[15] I, the improviser, am not thrown back on myself to make my own music, or establish some self-sustained musical space or capacity of my own. I am not confronted by a half-finished theme to which I then have to summon up resources to provide the necessary answer. *The theme which God has longed for has been played in our midst*, and we are now invited to be drawn into the improvisational duo of Father and Son, performed in the Spirit. To pick up Johnstone's words: 'I tell my actors never to think up an offer, but instead *to assume that one has already been made.*'[16]

Precisely because it is grounded in Christ's own faithfulness, and enabled by the Spirit – and is thus *sola gratia* – our return gift of faith is not a strictly contractual obligation, nor automatic (though it may be fitting and appropriate). It is rather, in a word, improvised. Delay is intrinsic to it – it is not the immediate and necessary discharge of a debt, but is unpredictable with regard to content and timing. Although this counter-gift is given back to the donor, it is limitless in scope – it is not a matter of paying off a finite debt to God. To share in God's own gratuitous exchange in faith is to be caught up in a non-identical repetition propelled by the Spirit, to be implicated in a continuing and endless 'giving back' to God in joyful, ecstatic gratitude, an improvisational process which always involves giving and receiving, which can never be finished, and which is endlessly different and continually unpredictable. And this gratuitous gift-exchange, enacted in the economy of God and overflowing through us to others, is ultimately rooted in the intra-divine trinitarian love. To participate, through the Spirit, in what Christ has done and is doing for

---

14. A. J. Torrance (1997a), 23; see A. J. Torrance (1996), *passim*, but especially 307ff.
15. A. J. Torrance (1997a), 23.   16. Johnstone (1979), 99. My italics.

us in relation to the Father, is to participate in God's gratuitousness and his inner life of exchange.

Through exploring the temporal shape of gift-exchange in improvisation, we have elucidated in very broad terms something of the temporal shape of the ever-expanding abundance of giving and receiving which God promotes and which involvement with the triune God involves. We can now be more specific. Drawing on what we have found, I propose to open up two closely related theological fields: election and ecclesial ethics.

Improvisation and the dynamic of election: Romans 9–11

It hardly needs to be said that the doctrine of election has been one of the most controversial in Christian history. Interestingly, issues concerning time have often been very near the centre of the debates. Many have argued, as I would, that there has been a persistent tendency for the theme of election to lose touch with the history narrated in Scripture, and become part of conceptual and philosophical/theological schemes elaborated apart from the economy of salvation, in such a way that election's dynamic is obscured rather than illuminated. In particular the doctrine has fallen prey to individualism, pride (individual and national), notions of an arbitrary God, and the metaphysics of iron necessity. Improvisation is perhaps the last thing anyone would think about in relation to election, yet I would suggest that it is in fact deeply instructive, especially for those who are concerned to release the theology of election from frames of thinking which distort its shape and momentum.

One of the passages most often discussed in connection with election is Romans 9–11 where Paul wrestles over the agony of the Jewish rejection of the Messiah. I submit that a legitimate way of reading these chapters is as a sustained attempt on the part of Paul to introduce the Roman Church to the improvising strategies of God, and to convince them that coming to terms with God's time and God's timing is integral to being caught up in God's electing purposes.

This is not to accord improvisation any kind of ultimate hermeneutical control. In the discussion which follows, I am indebted to many commentaries on this passage, whose conclusions I cannot here adequately justify but only assume.[17] Improvisation cannot act as a substitute for

---

17. A vast array of exegetical matters will have to be left to one side. The literature I have found most helpful includes Wright (1991), ch. 13; Dunn (1988); Fitzmyer (1993); Klein (1990); Newbigin (1989), ch. 10.

this kind of exegetical, textual work. However, I am suggesting that in the midst of exegesis, the practice of improvisation, by offering the instantiation of a particular kind of interpersonal dynamic, can serve to disclose and articulate the theological currents of these chapters very powerfully, especially the reciprocal movement which God's gracious election sets in motion. Moreover, I am suggesting that improvisation can do this more adequately than many of the more common doctrinal frames of reference which, whether consciously or unconsciously, are often quickly assumed to be appropriate for elucidating Paul's argument.

This passage, I suggest, involves improvisations of four kinds. First, the whole argument is itself an extremely ingenious improvisation on Paul's part, in that various strands of tradition are taken up, harmonised, set in counterpoint in ways which are unpredictable, novel, sometimes rough-edged but nonetheless convincing, and all for the sake of addressing a particular situation facing the Roman Church. Second, there are the improvisations which God himself has undertaken, improvisations on a fundamental theme. Third, there are improvisations which the communities concerned have undertaken. Fourth, there is a call to the Romans to improvise in a manner consistent with God's improvisations and their originating theme. The first form of improvisation I leave to one side. Our concern is mainly with the third and fourth (but this cannot be grasped without also considering at length the second).

Nothing less than God's consistency is at stake. Paul's discussion here is part of a much longer exposition of how the covenant God of Israel has demonstrated his faithfulness, how he has been true to the promises made to Abraham to fashion a community in whom and through whom the world's root difficulty will be tackled. The problem Paul addresses here is the Jewish rejection of the Gospel. The main theme – the covenant promises of God to create a worldwide family, which have found their climax in Christ – is now being improvised by God in the form of the expansion of the Church. But the Jews refuse to join in. Paul's agony is that his own flesh and blood, the people of the Messiah with all their privileges, have spurned the Messiah (9:1–5). How can anyone claim *both* that Abraham's own seed rejected the Messiah *and* that Abraham the Jew was the first of God's worldwide people? At the deepest level, the integrity of God himself is in question.

Paul's reply – and he is writing to a mixed but largely Gentile congregation – consists of a demonstration of how God's electing purpose actually operates in history. Israel's refusal in fact *serves* the ongoing improvisation of the great theme. And this improvisation works through gift-exchange, with delay and non-identical repetition. God's strategy is to promote gift-exchange, and human refusal is taken into that strategy.

This begins to be spelt out from 9:6. From very near the beginning, we are told that, after the theme was announced and improvisations began, there was human refusal, and thus two Israels (Israel 'according to the flesh' and the 'true' Israel). God never promised that all Abraham's physical offspring would be saved (9:6–13). In order that the sin and evil of the world could be dealt with, there had to be a process in which some would stand under judgement (with 'hardened hearts'). Far from being unjust (14), this actually serves God's justice, for through it God is able to share his mercy, eventually, with all. Thoroughly in line with the Jewish notions of divine righteousness, in vv. 19–29 Paul explains that God will judge and save a people for glory, but at present he is patient, restraining his proper and righteous wrath in order that more will be saved. (In apocalyptic thought, 'hardening of heart' was the prelude to final judgement.) Israel is now a 'vessel of wrath' (22), pending a final judgement. This is backed up with Old Testament imagery (25ff.) to show that what God is now doing with Israel is consistent with the way he has always acted.

The pattern is further spelt out in 9.30–10.21. *There is a movement of giving from Jew to Gentile.* Israel's refusal to improvise is the means through which the Gentiles have been brought into the covenant people of God. Interestingly, Israel's refusal is itself an improvisation, of a bizarre and destructive kind. For Israel's rejection of the Messiah is an improvisation on her rejection of the Torah, and her rejection of the Torah is an improvisation on the primary theme of the sin of Adam. The way in which God has engaged with these improvisations (and its primary theme) is dealt with from 9:30. Israel has misused the law and hence is missing out on what the Gentiles have obtained (9:30–3). That is, they have used the law to exclude non-Jews, to restrict grace to one race. Into this situation Christ steps – he is 'the end of the law' (10:4). Perhaps the least problematic reading of that highly controversial phrase is that Paul is arguing that the Torah is a good thing, holy and good, whose job is done because of what has happened in Christ. Israel's rejection of Jesus as Messiah is probably to be understood as the outworking of her misuse of the Torah, her attempt to use it as a charter of national privilege, excluding Gentiles. If Israel's abuse of the Torah reached its climax in her rejection of the Messiah, the cross brings to an end the misuse of the Torah to exclude Gentiles, and within this, the process of concentrating sin in Israel as the 'vessel of wrath'. In this sense the law has been brought to an end. Yet the law has also been vindicated in Christ on the cross – in that as the law 'tripped' Israel up, enticing her into national righteousness, so Christ has become 'the stumbling stone' (9:33) on whom the sin of the world is concentrated, the one who fully bears the sin of Adam. And, consequently, this is the way God's purposes for non-Jews are effected. Accordingly, in 10:14–18 Paul can affirm that when Christ is preached and received, a Gentile mission is unleashed (even though this carries with it the recalcitrance of the Jews (19–21)). Regardless of whether we are Jew or Gentile, through faith in this crucified and risen Messiah we are made members of the one covenant family of God (10:9–13).

The upshot is that through the death and resurrection of the Messiah, Israel's unbelief is taken up into the strategy of grace, to serve God's missionary improvisation, the inclusion of the Gentiles. Therefore, Israel's refusal becomes the means whereby the theme and its improvisations are transferred to the Gentiles such that *they* can now improvise. The Gentiles have received the Gospel from the Jews, not only in the obvious sense that the gift was actually brought to the Gentiles by (Christian) Jews but in the subtler sense that it is through (non-Christian) Jewish refusal that the gift has been made available to them.

However, not only is there giving from Jew to Gentile, *there is a movement from Gentile to Jew*. God will welcome back the Jews by means of the Gentiles. The Gentiles' improvisation will set off Jewish improvisation. In Romans 11:1–10, the question posed is: 'can *any* Jews be saved?' The answer, of course, is yes, and in reply Paul refers to himself as one of them, one of a remnant chosen by grace, not race or 'works.' But 'the rest' are 'hardened' (7ff.). The question now becomes: is the hardening of hearts permanent? Can any *more* Jews be saved? Paul reminds them that Israel's rejection is the means by which the world has been saved (11, 12, 15); more specifically, it has enabled the Gospel to be given to them, the Gentiles. But it is Paul's hope that the improvisation on the main theme of the covenant and its traditions which God has enabled among the Gentiles will provoke envy and jealousy among the Jews (11; cf. 10:19) – the Jews will hear their theme and its hugely enjoyable primary improvisations (their 'privileges' (9:4f.)) will be taken up by the Gentiles. This opens up the possibility that the Jews, provided they do not persist in unbelief (11:23), will join the Gentiles' improvisation, receiving salvation back again from the Gentiles, and joining the family of God. God, therefore, is not inconsistent. He has not permanently turned his back on his own people; that is unthinkable (11:1). Rather, he has allowed among some of them a period of hardening prior to an ultimate judgement in order that salvation can spread to others (so that the Gentiles 'come in') (25b). And, in this way, 'all Israel will be saved' (26).[18] For Gentiles to exclude *this* possibility would be tantamount to an upside-down form of the Jewish error of 'national righteousness', only this time excluding Jewish Christians.

The overall pattern Paul has been building up is drawn together in 11:28–32. The Gentiles have received mercy as a result of Israel's disobedience. But now as a result of God's mercy to the Gentiles, the Gospel can be received back again by the Jews: 'Just as you who were at one time disobedient to God [rebelling against the Creator, as spelt out in 1: 18–21] have now received mercy as a result of their disobedience, so they too have now become disobedient in order that they too may now receive mercy as a result of God's mercy to you' (30–1). God has not abandoned his people: the main theme (God's 'call' – 29) is irrevocable and stands as the basis of all the improvisations. The overall purpose of the theme and improvisations has been to create a family without racial exclusion, saved solely on the basis of God's grace.

All the principal characteristics of gratuitous gift-exchange as exemplified in improvisation are here. God's purpose as outlined in Romans 9–11 is to set in motion an ongoing process of gift-exchange between Jewish and Gentile communities. We find both the exchange and the gratuity characteristic of *agape*. Taking *exchange* first, we are not speaking of pure unilateral giving between Jew and Gentile, but a giving directed towards exchange. The Gentiles have received the great theme together with numerous improvisations in Jewish tradition, and the opportunity to improvise themselves. They have received this from the Jews, specifically because of their refusal of the Messiah. However, they have received it not only for themselves, but for the sake of 'passing it on', 'returning' it, which in these chapters means giving back both to the original donor group, paradoxically, to those whose very rejection enabled them to hear the message. Their improvised music is passed back to those who brought them the theme and its improvisations, and to those who quit the performance. So Paul, implicitly, is urging the Gentile Christians to learn to give ('return') as well as receive, not to cling to *their* improvisation, but to play it out in the hope that its attractiveness will render the (non-Christian)

---

18. We cannot here enter into the detailed debate over the vexed question of the reference of 'all Israel' (26). Perhaps the most likely option is that Paul is referring to a large but unspecified number of Jews.

Jews jealous, rekindling memories of the great themes and improvisations they had too easily forgotten, in such a way that they sense they
must join in and improvise themselves. (Direct preaching and witness is
not mentioned, though they might well have been meant.) There is evidence to suggest that some Gentile Christians at Rome were tending to
write off ethnic Jews as second-class citizens not only *within* the Church,
but also beyond reach *outside* the Church[19] in which case Paul is, among
other things, attempting to correct attitudes which would prevent the
Gospel going to Jews beyond the present boundaries of the Church.

This exchange pattern is grounded in, and is a sharing in, the
exchange enacted by God in Christ on our behalf. This is not spelt out in
detail in Romans 9–11, but is certainly present in chapters 1–8, and very
near the surface in 9:30–10:4. God's own gift of the Gospel includes a
reception of the refusal rooted in Adam's sin – the sin which worked its
way out in the misuse of the Torah and ultimately in the crucifixion of
Jesus. At the same time, Christ is the 'return', confirmed in the resurrection, the perfect return to God in a human being, the return which God
always longed for from his people. The divine gift therefore contains
within it a gift-and-return. The gift as return is of course geared towards
our return, a return which is enabled rather than simply demanded. To
share in the life of the New Adam, through the Spirit, therefore, is to
share, by grace, in an exchange which has already been enacted in him,
and to go on sharing in the dynamic of that exchange.[20]

As far as *gratuity* is concerned, the Gentile Christians are reminded
forcefully that there was no 'must' about receiving the gift and the opportunity to improvise upon it. We are not in the realm of automatic reward
or desert. There is no necessity or obligation laid upon God, nothing
which could give them any cause for presumption (11:17–24). Likewise,
their return gift to the Jews, though it may be appropriate, is not part of
any tight contract of equivalence or strict obligation. And this gratuitousness is grounded, and a means of sharing in, the absolute gratuity of God's
electing *agape*. The gratuitous exchange between Jew and Gentile communities is part of their ongoing 'return' to God. Not only is God's initial

---

19. Wright (1991), 234.
20. In line with this, there are those who would argue that a major *leitmotif* in Romans is
that God's faithfulness is demonstrated supremely in *the faithfulness of Christ*. Accordingly,
the righteousness of God is not manifest in a unilateral gift which now 'demands' (as if
contractually) a (self-generated?) 'response', but demonstrated supremely in the gift of
Christ's 'Yes' to God on our behalf. On this, see e.g. Longenecker (1998), 95–107; Campbell
(1992).

gift to the Jews *sola gratia*, so also is his gift to the Gentiles through the Jews. The Gentiles are told to banish any kind of presumption on God which would take God's 'kindness' for granted (11:22); they are grafted in by grace alone ('Do not be arrogant, but be afraid' – v. 20). And likewise the later drawing in of the Jews in chapter 11 is traced to God's electing grace – 'they will be grafted in, for God is able to graft them in again' (11:23). Paul's repeated desire is to exclude the idea of God being bound by necessity to something or someone external. He wants to undercut any claim which might be advanced on the basis of which special privileges can be sought from God. God is the gracious God of the covenant. In chapter 9, divine gratuitousness emerges strongly in Paul's discussion of God's freedom (especially in 14ff.; '[God] has mercy on whom he wants to have mercy' – v. 18; 'who indeed are you, a human being, to argue with God?' – v. 20). Contrary to exegesis which would support notions of 'the absolute power of God' (*potentia Dei absoluta*), of an utterly inscrutable and essentially unloving divine will, we must stress that here (14ff.) Paul is not using a rhetorical sledgehammer to suppress all questioning of a God who seems to choose some individuals and condemn others without any perceivable point or logic. He is concerned to show that God's electing grace is full of sense and justice, fully consistent with his promises announced to Abraham to create a covenant community for the sake of the world. There is choice, and hardening of hearts, in order that God may have mercy on all, Jew and Gentile (11:32). It is *this* logic, flowing entirely from God's unconstrained mercy (9:16), which is to be accepted rather than argued against, not some 'unseen plan'.

This gratuity is evinced, as we might expect, by *delay* and *non-identical repetition* between gift and counter-gift. And it is here that the temporal dimensions of the multiple improvisations are especially evident. Indeed, all three chapters could be read as Paul trying to enable the Romans to take God's time and God's timing seriously. *Delay* is clearly hugely important in these chapters. The crucial problem facing Paul is that of God's delay: when (if at all) are the Jews going to turn from their refusal of the Messiah? And Paul's plea to the Romans is as much as anything else a plea to recognise that delay is part of God's strategy (thoroughly in keeping with his ways in the past). The counter-gift from Gentile to Jew needs its proper and appropriate time in the improvisation initiated by God. It is not only unpredictable in timing but unpredictable in content – the relation between gift and counter-gift is clearly that of *non-identical repetition*. The Gentiles' improvisation, though consonant with the gift (and equivalent with respect to salvific power), was not identical with the gift received and had sprung up in unpredictably different circumstances among unpredictably various recipients. And, presumably, Paul would expect the same in the case of the Jews who would receive the Gospel as a result of their envy of the Gentiles. The process, of course, shares in the potentially limitless character of non-identical repetition – this mission-in-exchange must go on until God's purposes for humankind and creation are complete.

With this movement of gratuity and exchange so deeply embedded in Paul's argument, it is not surprising to find many of the associated aspects of gift-exchange in musical improvisation come to the fore. *Dedication* – attentiveness to the other – is obviously important. Also, Paul manifestly *wants the Gentiles to desire a 'return' from the Jews* to whom they are to give the Gospel – they will be part of the community. What we noted about *'distance'* is also focused sharply here. As we have just seen, Paul urges that the largely Gentile Church never forget that the gift carries the character of having been given by the Jew (11:17–22). The temptation to build a 'national righteousness' is precisely the temptation to treat the gift as 'now ours', under 'our' ownership. This curtails God's improvisation. We are never in a position to say we 'have' the gift, such that no further giving or receiving is necessary. Hence we find Paul attempting to curb any attitude which would allow the Gentiles to forget their Jewish roots ('You do not support the root, but the root supports you' – 11:18). The Gentile continually needs to receive from the Jewish faith – the 'sap' from the olive root into which they have be grafted (10:17). 'A church which is not drawing upon the sustenance of its Jewish inheritance . . . would be a contradiction in terms for Paul.'[21] Correspondingly, the Jewish Christians in Rome (including the new converts) will need to go on receiving from the Gentiles – this is not clear in Romans 9–11, but it comes to the surface in Romans 14 and 15, as we will soon see.

It is beyond our scope to trace all the improvisatory elements in Paul's argument here. But enough has been said to show that musical improvisation can throw into sharp relief the profoundest currents of the electing purposes and actions of God. With respect to the way the doctrine of election has often been handled in the Church, four comments may be made.

First, any student of these chapters knows that there has been a tendency (especially drawing on chapter 9) to interpret Paul as assuming a

---

21. Dunn (1988), 662.

predestining divine decree, individual and particular, proceeding from an essentially singular God. It is as if Paul's primary concern were the means by which a (non-trinitarian) God executes a decision which he has made from all eternity with regard to the future of human beings considered as isolated agents – some for salvation, some for eternal death. Salvation is thus conceived *a priori* in atomistic and monadic terms, with regard to both human beings and God himself. The musical equivalent would be a composer composing a piece of music, choosing from a list of performers a restricted number of recipients (simultaneously rejecting the rest), and then sending the music out to the chosen few for them to play. We have seen, using musical improvisation in an attempt to allow the text to speak clearly, that Paul's interests are rather different. For he writes of an election to salvation mediated through a process of receiving from, and passing on to others. The orientation of Romans as a whole (including Romans 9) is not towards solitary recipients of a decree but towards communities who already know the interrelatedness basic to salvation and the mission of God's people. Salvation comes, and can only come, within this mutual relatedness. The individual is of course crucially significant, but only within this mutuality. To put it differently, God gives abundantly in order to promote more giving, to generate an overflowing reciprocity, and salvation occurs within this ecology of giving. Moreover – here we move beyond what Paul says explicitly in these chapters – this is a reciprocity which reflects and shares in the eternal relatedness-in-love of the Trinity.[22] This is the momentum which the group improviser learns: to receive music from others, improvise upon it, pass it back and on to others, and all this in such a way that others are drawn in, and they in turn become the new improvisers. The Composer, we might say, comes to be known only in and through the process of passing the music on, and we find that the original music was composed in mutuality, through an infinitely abundant exchange (between Father and Son) into which we are now being caught up.

Second, it would appear that Paul is combating anything which would lead either Jew or Gentile to think they have a claim upon God, anything which would suggest that election confers privileged status, that God's covenant is a contract, that human faith is itself some kind of autonomous self-originating effort which obliges God to respond favourably.

---

22. In Ephesians 1, we recall, election is traced not to a God who is a radically singular agent, but to the Father who loves the Son, his elect one (1:4ff.).

Understood through the categories of corporate improvisation, we can go some way towards freeing the doctrine of election from the kind of conceptualities which have encouraged these misunderstandings, and do more justice to the movement of *sola gratia* which Paul is so concerned to declare to the Romans. As we have seen, improvisation at its best operates not by laying others under contractual obligations, but through gratuitous gift-exchange.

Third, good improvisation in traditional jazz has consistency and sense. It is the very opposite of arbitrary or whimsical. We mentioned earlier the danger of misreading the question 'who are you, O man, to talk back to God?' (9:20) as an implicit appeal to a bare and inaccessible divine will, entirely beyond understanding. This is a misexegesis which has been used to support highly questionable doctrines of election. Hearing these chapters through improvisation, which at its best is attractively coherent, can serve to remind us of just this danger and of the way in which Paul, far from suggesting God's ways cannot be understood at all and must be accepted without question, is at great pains in these chapters (and in other parts of Romans) to trace the momentum of his covenant love so that we perceive it clearly.

Fourth – and this pulls us closer to our concern with time – coherence is not the same as necessity. The doctrine of election has often been plagued by a metaphysics which would dissolve contingency into inexorable necessity: 'because this happened, it *had to happen* this way'. So, for example, the doctrine of predestination has been taken out of the realm of salvation, where in Paul's thought it belongs (predestination vocabulary is not used of eternal destruction). Instead of assuring Christians that their salvation springs out of the eternal love between Father and Son, it is wrongly assimilated to the doctrine of providence, and treated as an instance of the sovereign Creator's plan for, and total control over, all the events of the world. As such, it is typically set in an uneasy opposition to contingency: witness the sophisticated and somewhat sterile debates about the nature of divine causality in relation to human agency in the seventeenth century.[23] By contrast, in Romans 9 predestination is raised in connection with the character and operation of divine salvation (22f.),

---

23. See Oliver O'Donovan's exceptionally clear discussion, in O'Donovan (1986), 82ff. With this often goes a 'logico-causal' relation between the atoning death of Christ and the forgiveness of sins. See T. F. Torrance (1991), 246ff. Of course, it is still open to the exegete to claim that whatever the 'open-ended' language of Romans 9–11, a deterministic God of some sort still lurks. But one would be hard pressed to argue that this was Paul's view.

through Israel for the sake of the world. It is not part of a general theistic conception of how a transcendent God directs the cosmos at large. Accordingly, though Paul does not hesitate for a moment to ground salvation in the covenant God and affirm God's constancy and reliability, the entire three chapters (9–11) breathe a strong sense that things do not *have* to happen this way: there is coherence but there is also contingency and openness. This is the metaphysics of grace, not determinism. Improvisation's coherent patterns of open-ended give and take, imbibed with a high degree of contingency, can go a long way to challenging discussions which are tempted too easily to resort to the categories of necessitarianism, while at the same time helping us to evade any downplaying of God's consistency.

Improvisation in the Church: Romans 14:1–15:13

If patterns of mutual gift-exchange are to be seen on the macro-scale *between* communities, it is not surprising if we find Paul recommending something similar for life *within* the Christian community. The goal of God's giving is a community that responds to giving with further giving, not only beyond itself but within its own life. Hence the correspondence between the inter-community missiology of Romans 9–11 and the intra-ecclesial ethics of Romans 12–15. Every beginner in New Testament studies is told that the ethics of Romans 12–15 derive from the previous chapters. And so they do. The Church is the improvising community, living out of the expanding and limitless movement of gracious exchange which God has set in motion. This is the only way in which it, in turn, will 'give' to the world as the missionary people of God.

Here we have space to comment only on the most crucial passage for our purposes, 14:1–15:13, where Paul addresses a particular problem reflecting the clash of Jewish and Gentile Christians.[24] The former retained aspects of their Jewish heritage, the latter emphasised freedom from the law. The 'strong' are exhorted to bear with the 'weak in faith' (14:1). The 'weak' are probably predominantly Jewish converts who lack assurance that they no longer need to observe certain dietary and calendrical customs in order to please God. The majority of the Roman Christians are Gentiles, however, and the 'strong' are probably a group of

---

24. I am especially grateful to my colleague, Dr Michael Thompson, for helpful conversations about this passage, and for his own fine study (Thompson 1991).

Gentiles who pride themselves on the strength of their faith and consider the Jewish customs absurd. The 'weak', in turn, believe that the so-called 'strong' are not properly obeying God.

As Michael Thompson points out, 'Paul's overall concern in this section is . . . about the *reception* of currently separated Christians into fellowship; his desire is to promote unity among divided factions.'[25] This reception, interestingly, works both ways. Mutuality is built into the whole section. The climax of Paul's appeal is 15:7–13, which begins: 'Therefore receive (προσλαμβάνεσθε – receive/welcome/accept) one another as Christ has received you.' Content has already been given to this reception in the preceding chapter, and it may be that Paul has in mind not only those inside a particular community but all of his readers scattered across Rome. The word has strong connotations of hospitality – receiving or accepting someone into one's society, home, circle of acquaintances. The ultimate aim of this reception of one another is mutual edification (14:19), and through this, the good of the community as a single body. In other words, reception of the other *is* a way of giving to the other. We recall Johnstone's notion of 'acceptance' in dramatic improvisation. And what Johnstone describes as 'blocking', the absolute refusal of the other's contribution (and the other), is just what Paul goes on to attack.

In more detail: the strong are to 'Receive (προσλαμβάνεσθε) the one whose faith is weak' (14:1), not to impose their views on the weak, or look down upon them dismissively. The same generosity is to characterise the weak. They are not to condemn the strong, or judge them. Only Christ is the ultimate judge, before whom both parties must finally answer. Both groups must recognise the integrity of others as Christians, those whom God has received, and the improvisations they bring (which are, in this case, legitimate improvisations on the theme). They are to allow each other strength of conviction before the face of God. They are to remember that no one lives (or dies) to himself alone – one cannot claim freedom for oneself without allowing freedom to the other (14:1–12). The strong are not to put any offence ('stumbling-block' – 14:13; the term Paul used in 9:33 to speak of the Torah and Christ) in the way of the weak: this may cause him ruin. *The* stumbling-block (Christ) has already been laid in order to free God's people; there is no need for another. The strong must 'bear with' the weak: this does not mean condoning weak faith as such, but (as with Christ) patiently identifying with those who are weak so that

---

25. Thompson (1991), 162. My italics.

the weaknesses become theirs in the day-day-day experience of living for one another. And, presumably, this is not simply in order to satisfy the weak but is for the good of the community as a whole (14:19–21). Only in the weakness of interdependence as members of one body of Christ – Jew and Gentile – is there the full strength of grace. That this reception involves more than mere toleration of differences is brought out in Paul's speaking of the duty of the strong to work actively for peace. The aim is not simply absence of friction, or withdrawal from one another, but positive action geared towards the well-being of the body as a whole: mutual edification (14:19). This means the strong are going to be more dependent on the weak than they might like to imagine. (This is the opposite of the attitude referred to in 1 Cor. 12:21 – 'I don't need you!') Rom. 11:7–13 encapsulates the heart of the section in a way which links up with chapters 9–11. Paul reminds the Gentiles that it is through the Jews that they are called; he reminds the Jews that they received the Gospel for the sake of the Gentiles. The Gentiles must not forget that Christ became a Jew to save them, the Jews that Christ came among them in order that all the families of the earth would be blessed. Both together must realise that the aim of the whole is to glorify God.

Thompson has explored thoroughly the grounding of the ethics of Romans 12–15 in the example and teaching of Christ. The allusions to and echoes of Christ's teaching, and (more importantly for Paul) the appeal (implicit and explicit) to Christ's example lead Thompson to conclude that 'Paul's goal for his hearers is that individually and collectively they should be transformed progressively into the image of the person of Jesus Christ, the last Adam, and so reflect the character of God, as he did.'[26] Christ provides the key to improvising on the grace of God. The receiving/giving which is to mark the Christian community is linked to Christ's own receiving/giving – for example, in his burden-bearing (15:1), his bearing reproach (15:3), his endurance (15:4; 12:12), his reception of sinners/outsiders (15:7) and his service of others (15:8). The accent here is firmly (though not exclusively) on what was manifest on the cross. And, significantly, the fundamental action – acceptance – is traced back to God himself in 14:3: 'God has accepted' the person the strong are tempted to despise.

We have, then, in Romans 14:1–15:13 the working out in ecclesial terms of the temporal patterns of exchange found in the mission of the Church

26. Ibid., 238.

as expounded in chapters 9–11. Indeed, it could be said that the missionary dynamic of relatedness-in-mutuality of Romans 9–11 cannot properly operate *unless* the Church community is living out this ethical movement. As with the large-scale communities in the mission of the Church, so the ethics of the community must involve exchange and gratuity. There is to be mutual acceptance: they are to give to and receive from each other, and the most important thing they can give to each other is precisely the reception of each other, the hospitable love which welcomes before anything else. This *agape* springs from a sharing in Jesus Christ, whose greatest gift to them is his hospitable acceptance of them, which in turn leads them to give themselves to him and then to one another. Though not spelt out explicitly in these chapters, this mutuality between persons is made possible by the exchange already established in Christ, supremely on the cross, and the whole pattern of giving and receiving finds its source in the trinitarian exchange at the heart of God's being. Put the other way round, the mutual exchange of God's love has been established in our humanity in Jesus Christ, and now spills out in interpersonal relations within the Church.

All this is propelled by God's absolute gratuity. As far as the members of the Church are concerned, there is, of course, a sense of obligation – towards God and others – and indeed, the language of debt is used a little earlier (where the debt consists of loving one another – 13:8). We are not speaking of ethical acts of a purely formal nature, as utterly non-compulsory, indifferent to preceding circumstances or end. There is a sense in which everything Paul recommends is highly appropriate, fitting, and he is unashamed in speaking about the 'ends' of ethical action (which here means mutual edification and the good of the community). 'To be a Christian is *not* as piety supposes, spontaneously and freely to love, of one's own originality and without necessarily seeking any communion.'[27] On the other hand, we are not speaking of predictable obligation, a generosity with calculable and 'due' limits, exactly equivalent debts which can be finally discharged (13:8 makes it clear the debt to love one another is never 'paid off'). In other words, we are speaking not of contract but of covenant, and the non-identical repetition which flows from it. Consequently, the obligations Paul outlines are not heavy but a joy ('joy in the Holy Spirit' – 14:17), a characteristic mark of gratuitous gift-exchange. It is no accident that Paul ends this section (as he did Romans 11) on a high note of joy,

27. Milbank (1995), 150.

as the improvisatory dynamic sings into eternity. Paul's closing prayer displays uninhibited and uncontainable devotion, a sure and ecstatic hope that God will completely fulfil his original purpose in creation in the call of Jew and Gentile, and in the mutual exchange which can take place between them.

Reading the community ethics of Romans through the lens of improvisation has, we believe, allowed some of its strongest theological currents to be brought to the forefront, currents which are often forgotten or obscured in ethical discussion. Gratuity and non-necessity are highlighted. Any idea that the Church is a voluntary conglomeration of individuals who have opted into a club is ruled out, for with improvisation we are speaking about a practice which, even when undertaken by one person in front of an audience, intrinsically entails a dynamic of giving and receiving. More specifically, matters concerning ethics and time are helpfully brought to the fore. There is a faithfulness amongst the community to what has been given and played out by God in the past. The interweaving of contingency with consistency, so crucial to Christian ethics, can be underlined, working against the tendency to assimilate ethical obligation to the categories of conditional (predictable) contracts. ('I will give you X if you give me Y' is foreign to improvisation. Much more basic is something akin to what Miroslav Volf calls the 'will to embrace', which he argues should characterise authentic Christian community.[28]) We are given an especially apt way of understanding and speaking about the expansive joy of Christian corporate living, against views which would see the essence of the Christian life as avoiding error ('playing safe'). And intertwined with all of these is an atmosphere of attraction: as with improvisation, authentic Christian fellowship will draw others into its momentum.

In the last three chapters, I have sought to bring the practice of improvisation into close conversation with the theology of freedom, election and ecclesiology. The freedom for which improvisation is frequently lauded arises from the interplay and contrast between contingency and constraints, and a mutual enhancement of the two, and this is an interplay in which temporal factors are intensively involved. The contingency of improvisation is brought into play with occasional and cultural constraints: cultural constraints are particularised or contextualised for the

28. Volf (1996).

occasional constraints. And the continuous constraints are drawn into the process. Through enabling a freedom in relation to a huge range of constraints, improvisation can contribute towards enabling a freedom in relation to the world's temporality. I argued that the theological resonances of this are considerable. In chapter 8, through improvisation we explored the dynamics of Church tradition. I outlined some ways in which improvisation helps us to elaborate a trinitarian, Christologically sensitive doctrine of the Spirit which closely interweaves freedom, time and particularity. Through examining the way in which the human body is implicated in improvisation and the 'sonic order' negotiated, we found that improvisation held rich possibilities for developing a trinitarian theology of creativity, one in which the notion of freedom as bare autonomy is deeply challenged and in which the notion of freedom as realised through felicitous interaction with the world's constraints, including the world's temporality, is encouraged. In chapter 9, by opening up the dynamics of gift exchange – which are basic to improvisation – we found a means of elucidating and articulating the doctrine of election (as found in Romans 9–11) and ecclesial ethics (as in Romans 14 and 15).

In all this, we have been discovering the potential of music to elicit invaluable resources for the theologian, which not only refresh theology but serve to deliver it from distorting and confusing patterns of thinking. Moreover, because improvisation is not primarily a conceptuality but a rich and multi-faceted *practice*, through uncovering the theological resonances of improvisation we have in the process probably been uncovering some of the reasons why improvisation, through God's grace, has been so prevalent in one form or another in the Church.

10

———————

Conclusion

This book has been designed to show that music can enable theology to do its job better. When music takes us on its temporal adventures, we enjoy a rich and distinctive involvement with time. Because of this, music can greatly enrich our understanding of the character of time and our time-embeddedness. More than this, it can enrich our *theological* wisdom about time – time as intrinsic to God's creation, and what it means to 'live peaceably' with time by being caught up in the redeemed temporality of Jesus Christ.

I have sought to open up these matters in a few areas only, and in limited ways. For reasons explained in the introduction, with the exception of John Tavener, I have focused on music which has no obvious or overt theological links and associations. Even with this restriction, there are many forms of music I have not considered. And I have stayed largely within systematic theology: I have tried to show the benefits of music for exploring and articulating some central doctrinal loci. But rather than attempt to be comprehensive, as I indicated at the start, I have concentrated on a few specific areas in the hope that others will be stimulated to take 'theology through music' into other fields of theology and other types of musical expression.

It remains for us to stand back and reflect on the different ways in which music has functioned in this study, and what our findings might imply about the contribution of music to theology in the future.

We have found that examining the temporality of music has elicited conceptual tools – ways of thinking, models, frameworks, metaphors – for exploring, clarifying and re-conceiving the dynamics of God's world and his ways with the world. We have seen that in so doing, music can serve to release us from some common 'default' patterns of thought which have done more harm than good, and to which theology has so often resolutely clung. Music, in other words, can purge theology of some of its worst bad habits. So, to take one of numerous examples, in chapter 4 we found that the temporal wave-patterns of music not only provide a singularly powerful resource to uncover and understand the multi-levelled momentum of promise and fulfilment in the biblical narrative (pp. 106–10), they also deliver us from pernicious single-levelled, single-line models of temporality which obscure this momentum. In chapter 9, I argued that the extraordinary interplay between musical improvisers furnishes theology with a highly fruitful way of eliciting the dynamic of God's election (pp. 255–65), and that this is arguably far more appropriate to what is involved than many of the doctrinal grids so commonly employed.

Throughout, I have been at pains to stress that with music we are not reckoning with an intellectual activity extrinsically related to practical engagement with sound (although of course strenuous intellectual effort is often part of making and hearing music). We are dealing with practices, interactions with sounds, concrete encounters with the physical world, drawing on many facets of our human make-up. This means we should resist the temptation – common in many periods of theorising about music – to treat music as if it were essentially a mental construct or abstract form, which happens (unfortunately?) to get played and sung from time to time. Certainly, musical activity can generate conceptuality for the theologian, but it does so in and through being just that, an activity.

Music, to put it another way, is 'performative' through and through. This links up with our focus on temporality. I have tried to show that music entails sharing in and shaping the temporality of the world. The most fruitful conceptuality for the theologian will arise out of attending to, indeed participating in, this sharing and shaping. For the theologian wanting to explore time and God's involvement with time, music offers enrichment through enactment. In short, music *performs possibilities for theology*. It situates us in particular kinds of temporal environment and *thereby* provides theological illumination and understanding. So, for example, in chapter 3, I was concerned to show that music, *by virtue of what it enacts*, has the potential to offer highly effective ways of developing, and removing obstacles to, a theology of creation which seeks to give due weight to Christology and pneumatology. Another example: in chapter 7, we saw that the Boulez–Cage impasse concerning freedom and time can be annulled by *musical demonstration in sound*, specifically through the improvisation of traditional jazz.

Because of music's particular kind of time-involvement, an underlying current in much of what we have said (explicit in a number of places) is that music has the capacity to play a unique and positive role in the formation of Christian identity. It follows that although music can be drawn into quite conscious and focused engagement with theology (in the manner of this book), it can also operate by moulding our lives in a range of unconscious and tacit ways, thus indirectly feeding theology. It can 'inform' theology by 'forming' the theologian. When Bonhoeffer, living out his last months in prison, finds that he has music constantly on his mind, and that he resorts to the language of polyphony to do his theology,[1] is this not because his life has been significantly shaped by music, both as a listener and as a practising musician of considerable skill? With regard to time, music can do much to help cultivate 'temporal virtues' such as faithfulness, vigilance and patience. In chapter 3 we spoke about the ability of music to help us live '*with* the [temporal] grain of things, to work in the stream of God's wisdom' (Williams) (pp. 71–97). In chapters 3 and 4 we spoke much about music's ability to imbibe a certain kind of patience, one with strong Christian resonances (pp. 86–89, 103–6). In chapter 8, we saw how improvisation can be a means of developing ways of interacting with each other that are intrinsic to any Christian account of coming to terms with the 'time' of others: attending to the other, listening in silence, responding flexibly etc. (pp. 205–7). In other words, music, perhaps more than we like to admit, can potentially affect the 'shape' of Christian living,[2] and because of this, inevitably, the shape of our theology. Related to this – and this has emerged at a number of points in our argument – when we trace the theological potential of music, we will very likely be tracing some of the factors which have given music such a prominent place in the life of Christians, in worship and mission in particular. (Of course, there is a negative aspect to all this. Music may be able to shape us, but for *ill* as well as good. There needs to be an alertness to this, especially since music is the 'hidden persuader' *par excellence*. As Nicholas Cook reminds us, time and time again music 'effaces its own agency; you hear the advertiser's message, but you don't realise how much of it is coming from the music'. That is why, he continues, we need 'to understand [music's] working, its charms, both to protect ourselves

1. Bonhoeffer (1972), 302.   2. Ford (1997).

against them and, paradoxically, to enjoy them to the full. And in order to do that, we need to be able not just to hear music but to *read* it too ... for its significance as an intrinsic part of culture, of society, of you and me.'³)

A further service rendered to theology by music, evident in some sections of this book, lies in its ability to grant a heightened sensitivity to currents of social and cultural thought and practice, and to their theological dimensions. We saw, for example, how the exchange between Boulez and Cage compellingly exemplified some of the pathologies of modernity, and the theological matters implicated (pp. 186–97). I made some tentative comments about Tavener's music in relation to a current postmodern unease with time, and again, drew out some of the associated theological issues (pp. 128–46).

Related to this, on a wider front, our study would seem to show that the culture of modernity has, at least to some extent, preserved a certain theological wisdom. Concentrating mainly on music which has emerged from the seventeenth century onwards, we have discovered forms of temporality which do seem to be highly congruent with some of the temporalities of which the Christian Gospel speaks. This, of course, will hardly be good news to those who are prone to see only theological darkness in the modern West, or the corruption of long-forgotten better days (a view by no means absent in the theological scene today). It will also not be good news to those who are determined to construe music in the West as hopelessly infected by the worst of modernity, as no more than the 'product' of its damaging forces. But it is unwise to treat a culture or a culture's music in anything like such simple and monolithic terms. While there would be no point in trying to absolve Euro-centric culture or its music of all complicity in error or evil, and while opposing any idea that modern Western music possesses a kind of intrinsic theological superiority to all other types of music, we have seen enough to conclude that, even though it may be doubtless compromised in all sorts of ways, much of the music of modernity is far from being wholly captive to modernity's worst catastrophes. Perhaps some of it may be showing us a way *through* modernity.⁴

Some might infer from the foregoing pages that I have been practising and recommending a form of 'natural theology', a theology that does not 'begin' with particular revelation, divine acts, God-given texts or whatever, but proceeds from the side of creation, 'from below' – in this case, from

3. Cook (1998b), 131, 132.   4. I owe this last suggestion to Professor David Ford.

music. This perceived orientation will be highly attractive to some, especially to those concerned that music (along with other art forms) has been
sidelined for too long as a potential contributor to, rather than merely
receiver of, theological wisdom; to those wearied by theologies which
seem to be 'downloaded from above' without due regard for the integrity
of the world and our commerce with it; to those eager to find new forms of
apologetics to commend Christianity to those of little or no faith; to those
suspicious of what they see as the divisiveness of truth-claims advanced
on the basis of specific divine revelation; and to those convinced that the
development of sorely needed doctrines of creation, culture and creativity
was badly hampered in the twentieth century by Karl Barth's famous and
uncompromising opposition to natural theology, with its supposedly
negative view of human nature and creation.

Massive issues are at stake here and they are often over-simplified. In
any case, the term 'natural theology' is highly ambiguous and slippery.
However, it is worth trying to gain at least a measure of clarity about some
of the substantive matters at stake. If natural theology refers to 'every . . .
formulation of a system which claims to be theological, i.e. to interpret
divine revelation, whose *subject*, however, differs fundamentally from the
divine revelation in Jesus Christ and whose *method* therefore differs equally from the exposition of Holy Scripture',[5] then it would be inappropriate
to characterise this study as an attempt at natural theology, since there
has been a desire to avoid presupposing theological criteria more ultimate than the reconciling self-disclosure of God in and through the incarnate Son, testified in Scripture, recognised and affirmed through the
transforming presence and activity of the Spirit. Throughout I have tried
to resist giving ultimacy to factors extrinsic to, and thus potentially at
odds with, the dynamic of knowing established through the self-giving of
the triune God.

Again, this provokes immense questions which cannot be dealt with
adequately here. However, two broad issues may be briefly addressed.
First, there is the matter of whether Christian theology can ever afford to
side-step recognition of our epistemic alienation from God and of the
intrinsic relationship between revelation and atonement, and to seek a
place for theological enquiry in a supposedly neutral, sin-free territory. It
might be easy to assume that in doing theology with the musician and
musicologist, we are pulling theology into 'safe' territory, exempt from

5. Barth (1946), 74f.

the need for reconciliation and repentance, intellectual or otherwise. But this would be disingenuous. As we have said repeatedly, music does not exist in the abstract; it is a set of practices. Music is not an 'object' existing in some zone immune to the effects of human corruption. It is a thoroughly human interaction with the natural world, and as such is open to all the distortions as well as the felicities of such interactions, capable of extraordinary harm as well as extraordinary glory. Approaches to music which treat it as supremely exemplified in purportedly asocial, ahistorical 'works' can easily lead us to overlook this, as can the quick appropriation of religious language when speaking of music. (Significantly, musicologists today are increasingly sensitive to the entanglements of music in destructive ideologies: witness the music of the Third Reich, or the way in which music's rhythmic powers are taken up by sectarian groups in Northern Ireland to fuel hatred and division.)

The second broad issue is whether theology is wise to seek its determinative criteria in assumed correspondences between the dynamic structure of creaturely realities on the one hand and the dynamic forms of God's interactions with the world on the other. Of course, we may properly speak of universal configurations of meaning within the created world, laws of natures, and so forth. And to some extent music is always reliant on these, given that it employs physical bodies which will vibrate in some ways and not others, and is processed by human beings who are constituted in some ways and not others. Music is capable of highlighting and instantiating this order: basic to this book is the conviction that in its intertwining with the world's temporality, music to some degree discloses that temporality. Further, it is axiomatic for any Christian theology that the order of the cosmos is God-given, that God is in ceaseless interaction with all he has made, that creaturely reality participates in the rationality of God. None of this is at issue.

But more debatable is the extent to which a 'theology through music' – or indeed any theology – can legitimately proceed *on the basis of* assumed 'parallelisms' between its patterns of sound and the dynamics of God's involvement with the world. There are at least three matters of concern here.

(a) The first we have just mentioned. There is no reason to believe that music occupies a field unaffected by the 'fall-out' from human sinfulness; even if we were to presume intrinsic parallelisms between created and divine activity, we are still left with the problem of proper discernment, and that in turn drives us back to questions about the need for intellectual re-formation and *metanoia*, which in turn drives us back, ultimately, to matters of salvation.

(b) The second matter concerns the danger of deifying the dynamic patterns of creation and culture. At an early stage in writing, I considered calling this book 'The Sound of God'. I quickly grew dissatisfied with that title. For if the creaturely rationality of music is to be given due weight, it is more accurate to speak of music, at its best, as *the sound of the created order praising God*, in its contingency, finitude and non-divinity. (This, as we have seen, was the heart of Barth's theological appropriation of Mozart – see above, pp. 95f.) To say this is not to question either the reality or the created goodness of the world, or its power to glorify God; precisely the opposite, it is an attempt to 'allow room' for created reality to perform its true vocation in praising the Creator, refusing to assimilate what is properly creaturely to the divine.

(c) The third matter can be approached by asking the question: how appropriate or useful is it to characterise what we have highlighted in music as *vestigia Dei* – 'traces', 'reflections', 'echoes' or 'parallels' of God? Can music praise God so directly that we may speak of *integral* connections between God and musical phenomena? In response: on theological grounds, it would be quite wrong to preclude the possibility *a priori* of such connections, and, indeed, somewhat bizarre to do so, especially in the light of what we have found in this book. We may take as an example our multi-levelled metrical waves, which, we observed, bear striking resemblance to the patterns of God's activity for the world's salvation. It would seem quite appropriate to regard these as 'traces' of the Creator, to propose that God has fostered the development of these temporalities, that they have functioned and will continue to function as media of his saving activity. It would seem equally appropriate to propose that improvisation's peculiar interplay of constraint and contingency is one of the means through which God brings his faithful yet endlessly novel life to the world. And similar things could be said, to varying degrees, of the other musical phenomena we have noted. (Indeed, I have suggested that by examining such phenomena carefully we may find clues as to why certain forms of music have found such a ready place in the Christian Church.) My whole approach in this book has naturally leant in the direction of raising the possibility of links of this sort. I have presented music as a dynamic into which we are drawn, at best a healing dynamic. Given the participatory, time-embedded and healing character of the Christian Gospel, it is not surprising if we are pressed to speak about integral relations with musical processes. However, what I believe is much more questionable is the attempt to ground these divine 'marks' or 'traces' in some supposed *necessity* of created rationality to resemble uncreated rationality, and resemble it in particular ways, rather than in what God makes possible by virtue of his gracious, dynamic presence to the world. For is it not God who, in his freedom, enables creation to respond and correspond to him in ways which are true both to its integrities and to his own activity? In addition, equally questionable is the attempt to discern purported parallels in any other light than that which has been enacted in Jesus Christ, if creation has indeed found its true end and fulfilment in him. If we are not careful on these fronts, I would suggest, we risk 'reading into' God's actions features peculiar to musical dynamics (including potentially harmful ones) which are inappropriate to divine dynamics.[6]

Put differently, my intention throughout has been to allow the ultimate 'pressure of interpretation'[7] to come not from musical practice considered in and of itself (as some kind of autonomous, normative arbiter), but from a focus on the activity of the triune God, definitively disclosed in Jesus Christ, whose purpose is the participation of the world – including music – in his own triune life.

There are those who will be instinctively uneasy with this theological outlook, perhaps believing that it prematurely closes options which ought to be left open, and prevents music from exercising a broader theological role. I cannot here justify the incarnational and trinitarian orientation within which I have sought to work – and it is an orientation around a *cantus firmus*, not a closed system[8] – but I believe it has been important at least to indicate it, and the methodological repercussions which I believe it entails. (In any case, theological vacuums are not an option: all who bring music into play with theology have to come to terms with the matter of determinative criteria sooner or later, and, presumably, if consistency matters, follow them through.) For this author at any rate, pursuing 'theology through music' in this way has not only released

---

6. There may, however, be ways of construing 'natural theology' which take account of these dangers, for example, as that aspect of the theology of creation in which realms of created being and meaning, such as music, are explored with due respect to their integrity, with a view to bringing out their relatedness to the being and acts of the trinitarian God of Jesus Christ. For myself, I would prefer to speak of this as part of the task of a theology of creation rather than 'natural theology'. For discussions of 'revised' or 'transformed' natural theology, see e.g. T. F. Torrance (1985), ch. 2; Gunton (1997a); Polkinghorne (1998), 69ff.
7. A. J. Torrance (1996), 201; Torrance here borrows the concept from Daniel Hardy.
8. The image is Bonhoeffer's, taken up recently by David Ford (Ford 1999, ch. 10).

a fresh sense of the sheer inexhaustibility of theology, it has had the reciprocal effect of making music far more intriguing and enthralling.

There are others who will have the opposite problem, who will see the kind of enterprise we have undertaken as too risk-laden to be worth the trouble, too charitable in its estimation of music – in short, too close to idolatry for comfort. Given that music is so emotionally powerful and such a semantically fluid art form, to bring it into such close conversation with theology is too perilous to be worthwhile. To this I can only reply that no theology will ever be free of the risk of idolatry, since it is always mediated through creaturely thought-forms, activities and so on. The critical question to ask is: what does the risk yield? All good theology is done on the cliff-edge – one step too far and you tumble into idolatry, one step back and the view is never so good. The reader will have to judge whether we have occasionally stumbled over the precipice, and when we have not, whether the view has justified the risk.

I said in the introduction that this book was designed as a contribution to the re-vitalising of theology for the future. This was meant in the material sense, in that specific doctrinal areas have been addressed and, I hope, opened out in fresh ways. And in the process, wider topics of theological interest have been explored, again, I hope, in stimulating ways: the formation of Christian identity, the worship of the Church, cultural concerns, etc.

But my hope is that the book might also contribute to the refreshing of theology with regard to the *way* theology is done, the modes in which it is practised – in the academy, Church, college, school or wherever. It would be presumptuous of me to offer any kind of analysis of the current state of theology, either in the academy or elsewhere. However, it is undoubtedly true that, for many, an activity we might expect to be marked by a certain exhilaration and joy often turns out to be shrouded in a certain malaise. Among the factors which are sometimes mentioned in this connection are: an intellectualism, in which thought is effectively severed from other aspects of our humanity; a reluctance to believe that disciplines other than the well-tried and tested ones could have anything serious to offer to theology; a certain blinkered vision, resulting in an inability to come to terms at any depth with the vibrancies of contemporary culture, not least in the arts; a malaise concerning education in the Church, one aspect of which is that unfamiliar modes of teaching and learning, such as music, are never properly explored; and, with regard to the theology–arts conversation, a common assumption that theology's only serious gains will come from dialogue with the visual and literary arts. We have seen enough, I think, to suppose that music goes at least part of the way in addressing all of these factors.

If music *is* allowed room as a welcome and serious dialogue-partner in theology in the future, then clearly, some of theology's most embedded ways of working will be questioned. One of the most obvious challenges music will present is to ask theology if it is prepared to integrate a 'performative' mode into its work. To repeat: music bears its theological fruits most potently by being practised, by enacting possibilities. It is my experience that performed music integrated into theological research, teaching and communication bears inestimable benefits. In response to those who would see this leading inevitably to a slackening of intellectual rigour, I would suggest that potentially the effect is just the opposite: an intensification and refinement of intellectual life which can be far more responsible to God and his distinctive ways with us than much traditional theology. But to pursue these matters properly would require at least another book.

Music shows no sign of dying out. Chants will be sung, strings bowed, synthesisers programmed probably more than ever before. Music saturates our culture, holding out to the theologian sizeable opportunities which are at present woefully underdeveloped. It remains to be seen how far theologians, academic or otherwise, will avail themselves of these opportunities. But if they do, it will not be long before we will be wondering how it is that so much theology has managed to do with so little music.

Bibliography

Adair, Gilbert 1994, 'A Perfectly Composed Picture', *The Sunday Times* 11 September, 6.

Adam, Barbara 1990, *Time and Social Theory*, Cambridge: Polity Press.

    1995, *Timewatch: The Social Analysis of Time*, Cambridge: Polity Press.

Adorno, Theodor 1941, 'On Popular Music', *Studies in Philosophy and Social Sciences* 9: 17–48.

    1973, *Philosophy of Modern Music*, London: Sheed and Ward.

    1982, 'Perennial Fashion – Jazz', in *Prisms*, trans. Samuel and Shierry Weber, Cambridge, Mass.: MIT Press, 121–32.

    1984, *Aesthetic Theory*, London: Routledge and Kegan Paul.

Alison, James 1997, *Living in the End Times: The Last Things Re-Imagined*, London: SPCK.

Alperson, P. J. 1984, 'On Musical Improvisation', *Journal of Aesthetics and Art Criticism* 43: 17–29.

    1987 (ed.), *What is Music? An Introduction to the Philosophy of Music*, University Park: Pennsylvania State University Press.

Anscombe, G. E. M. 1963, *Intention*, Oxford: Blackwell.

Arnheim, Rudolf 1984, 'Perceptual Dynamics in Music Expression', *The Musical Quarterly* 70/3: 295–309.

Ashby, W. R. 1956, *An Introduction to Cybernetics*, London: Chapman and Hall.

Attali, Jacques 1985, *Noise*, trans. Brian Massumi, Manchester: Manchester University Press.

Atton, Christopher 1988, 'Improvised Music: Some Answers to Some Questions', *Contact* 33: 13–17.

Aveni, Anthony F. 1990, *Empires of Time: Calendars, Clocks and Cultures*, London: Tauris.

Bailey, D. 1992, *Improvisation: Its Nature and Practice in Music*, London: British Library.

Bailey, Kenneth E. 1995, 'Informal Controlled Oral Tradition and the Synoptic Gospels', *Themelios* 20/2: 4–11.

Baker, D. 1969, *Jazz Improvisation*, Chicago: Maher.

Ballantine, Christopher 1984, *Music and its Social Meanings*, New York: Gordon and Breach.

Balthasar, Hans Urs von 1987, *Truth is Symphonic: Aspects of Christian Pluralism*, trans. Graham Harrison, San Francisco: Ignatius Press.

Banks, Robert 1983, *The Tyranny of Time*, Exeter: Paternoster Press.

Barr, James 1962, *Biblical Words for Time*, Studies in Biblical Theology 33, London: SCM.

    1993, *Biblical Faith and Natural Theology*, Oxford: Clarendon Press.

Barry, Barbara 1990, *Musical Time: The Sense of Order*, Stuyvesant: Pendragon Press.

Barry, Malcolm 1985, 'Improvisation: The State of the Art', *British Journal of Music Education* 2/2: 171–5.

Barth, Karl 1946, *Natural Theology*, trans. Peter Frankel, London: Centenary Press.

 1956, *Church Dogmatics*, translation edited by G. W. Bromiley and T. F. Torrance, vol. I/2.

 1957, *Church Dogmatics*, translation edited by G. W. Bromiley and T. F. Torrance, vol. II/1.

 1960a, *Church Dogmatics*, translation edited by G. W. Bromiley and T. F. Torrance, vol. III/2.

 1960b, *Church Dogmatics*, translation edited by G. W. Bromiley and T. F. Torrance, vol. III/3.

 1986, *Wolfgang Amadeus Mozart*, trans. Clarence K. Pott, Grand Rapids, Mich.: Eerdmans.

Barthes, Roland 1977, *Image, Music, Text*, trans. Stephen Heath, London: Fontana.

 1985, 'Rasch', in *The Responsibility of Forms: Critical Essays on Music, Art and Representation*, trans. Richard Howard, New York: Hill and Wang, 299–312.

Barton, Stephen 1997, *Invitation to the Bible*, London: SPCK.

 1999, 'New Testament Interpretation as Performance', *Scottish Journal of Theology* 52/2: 179–208.

Barzun, Jacques 1954, *Pleasures of Music*, London: Michael Joseph.

Bauckham, Richard 1980, 'The Delay of the Parousia', *Tyndale Bulletin* 31: 3–36.

 1988, 'Tradition in Relation to Scripture and Reason', in Benjamin Drewery and Richard J. Bauckham (eds.), *Scripture, Tradition and Reason: A Study in the Criteria of Christian Doctrine*, Edinburgh: T. & T. Clark, 117–45.

 1993, *The Theology of the Book of Revelation*, Cambridge: Cambridge University Press.

 1999, 'Time and Eternity', in *God Will Be All in All: The Eschatology of Jürgen Moltmann*, Edinburgh: T. & T. Clark, 155–226.

Beardsley, Monroe C. 1966, *Aesthetics from Classical Greece to the Present*, Tuscaloosa: University of Alabama Press.

 1981, 'Understanding Music', in Kingsley Price (ed.), *On Criticizing Music: Five Philosophical Perspectives*, Baltimore: Johns Hopkins University Press, 55–73.

Beck, Guy 1993, *Sonic Theology: Hinduism and Sacred Sound*, Columbia: University of South Carolina Press.

Begbie, Jeremy S. 1989, *Music in God's Purposes*, Edinburgh: Handsel Press.

 1991a, 'The Spirituality of Renewal Music: A Preliminary Exploration', *Anvil* 8/3: 227–39.

 1991b, *Voicing Creation's Praise: Towards a Theology of the Arts*, Edinburgh: T. & T. Clark.

 1992, 'The Gospel, the Arts and Our Culture', in Hugh Montefiore (ed.), *The Gospel and Contemporary Culture*, London: Mowbray, 58–83.

 1995, 'The Ambivalent Rainbow: Forsyth, Art and Creation', in Trevor Hart (ed.) *Justice the True and Only Mercy*, Edinburgh: T. & T. Clark, 197–219.

 1996, 'Theology through Music: Tavener, Time and Eternity', in D. Ford and D. Stamps (eds.), *Essentials of Christian Community*, Edinburgh: T. & T. Clark, 3–34.

 1997, 'Theology and Music', in David Ford (ed.), *The Modern Theologians*, Oxford: Blackwell, 686–99.

 1998, 'Notes From the Celestial City', *Third Way* 21/10: 18–21.

Benjamin, William E. 1984, 'A Theory of Musical Meter', *Music Perception* 1: 355–413.

Bennett, Gerald 1986, 'The Early Works', in William Glock (ed.), *Pierre Boulez: A Symposium*, London: Eulenburg, 41–84.

Berendt, Joachim E. 1983, *The Jazz Book: From New Orleans to Jazz Rock and Beyond,* London: Granada Publishing.

Berger, Peter 1984, *And our Faces, My Heart, Brief as Photos*, London: Writers and Readers.

Berio, Luciano 1985, *Two Interviews*, trans. and ed. David Osmond-Smith, London and New York: Boyars.

Berleant, Arnold 1987, 'Musical De-Composition', in P. J. Alperson (ed.), *What is Music? An Introduction to the Philosophy of Music*, University Park: Pennsylvania State University Press, 241–54.

Berliner, Paul F. 1994, *Thinking in Jazz: The Infinite Art of Improvisation*, Chicago: University of Chicago Press.

Bernstein, Leonard 1976, *The Unanswered Question: Six Talks at Harvard*, Cambridge, Mass.: Harvard University Press.

Berry, Wallace 1976, *Structural Functions in Music*, Englewood Cliffs, NJ: Prentice-Hall.
    1980, 'On Structural Levels in Music', *Music Theory Spectrum* 2: 19–45.
    1985, 'Metric and Rhythmic Articulation in Music', *Music Theory Spectrum* 7: 7–33.

Best, David 1985, *Feeling and Reason in the Arts*, London: Allen & Unwin.

Best, Harold M. 1993, *Music Through the Eyes of Faith*, San Francisco: Harper.

Bierwisch, M. 1979, 'Musik und Sprache: Überlegungen zu ihrer Struktur und Funktionweise', in E. Klemm (ed.), *Jahrbuch Peters 1978*, Leipzig: Edition Peters, 9–102.

Black, Max 1962, 'The "Direction" of Time', in *Models and Metaphors*, Ithaca: Cornell University Press, 182–93.

Blacking, John 1973, *How Musical is Man?* Seattle: University of Washington Press.

Blasius, Leslie David 1996, *Schenker's Arguments and the Claims of Music Theory*, Cambridge: Cambridge University Press.

Bloch, Ernst 1974, *Essays on the Philosophy of Music*, Cambridge: Cambridge University Press.

Blomberg, Craig 1998, 'Eschatology and the Church: Some New Testament Perspectives', *Themelios* 23/3: 3–26.

Bockmuehl, Markus 1994, *This Jesus: Martyr, Lord, Messiah*, Edinburgh: T. & T. Clark, 1994.

Bonhoeffer, Dietrich 1972, *Letters and Papers from Prison*, ed. Eberhard Bethge, New York: Macmillan.

Boulez, Pierre 1976, *Conversations with Célestin Deliège*, London: Eulenburg.
    1981, *Points de Repère*, Paris: Christian Bourgois.
    1991, *Stocktakings from an Apprenticeship*, Oxford: Oxford University Press.

Bourdieu, Pierre 1984, *Distinction: A Social Critique of the Judgement of Taste*, trans. Richard Nice, London: Routledge and Kegan Paul.

Bowie, Andrew 1990, *Aesthetics and Subjectivity: From Kant to Nietzsche*, Manchester and New York: Manchester University Press.

Bowker, John 1973, *The Sense of God*, Oxford: Clarendon Press.
    1991a, *A Year to Live*, London: SPCK.
    1991b, *The Meanings of Death*, Cambridge: Cambridge University Press.
    1995, *Is God a Virus?* London: SPCK.

Bowman, Wayne D. 1998, *Philosophical Perspectives on Music*, Oxford: Oxford University Press.

Bracken, James 1991, *Society and Spirit: A Trinitarian Cosmology*, Selinsgrove, Pa.: Susquehanna University Press.

Braine, David 1988, *The Reality of Time and the Existence of God: The Project of Proving God's Existence*, Oxford: Clarendon Press.

Brendel, Alfred 1976, *Musical Thoughts and Afterthoughts*, London: Robson.

Briggs, N. L. 1986, 'Creative Improvisation: A Musical Dialogue', Ph. D. thesis, San Diego, University of California.

Bright, W. 1963, 'Language and Music: Areas for Co-operation', *Ethnomusicology* 7/1: 6–32.

Brindle, Reginald Smith 1987, *The New Music: The Avant-Garde Since 1945*, Oxford: Oxford University Press.

Brown, Calvin 1987, *Music and Literature: A Comparison of the Arts*, Hanover, NH and London: University Press of New England.

Brown, Harold Mayer 1988, 'Pedantry or Liberation? A Sketch of the Historical Performance Movement', in Nicholas Kenyon (ed.), *Authenticity and Early Music*, Oxford: Oxford University Press, 27–56.

Brown, Harold Mayer and Sadie, Stanley 1989 (eds.), *Performance Practice*, London: Macmillan.

Broyles, Michael 1980, 'Organic Form and the Binary Repeat', *The Musical Quarterly* 66/3: 339–60.

Brueggemann, Walter 1987, *Hope Within History*, Atlanta: John Knox Press.
    1988, *Israel's Praise: Doxology against Idolatry and Ideology*, Philadelphia: Fortress Press.

Budd, Malcolm 1985, *Music and the Emotions*, London: Routledge and Kegan Paul.
    1995, *Values of Art*, London: Penguin.

Busch, Eberhard 1976, *Karl Barth: his Life from Letters and Autobiographical Texts*, London: SCM.

Busoni, Ferruccio 1962, *Sketch of a New Esthetic of Music*, New York: Dover.

Butler, Christopher 1980, *After the Wake: An Essay on the Contemporary Avant-Garde*, Oxford: Oxford University Press.

Butt, John 1991, 'Improvised Vocal Ornamentation and German Baroque Compositional Theory – An Approach to "Historical Performance Practice"', *Journal of the Royal Musical Association* 116/1: 41–62.

Byrnside, Ronald 1975, 'The Performer as Creator: Jazz Improvisation', in C. Hamm, B. Nettl and R. Byrnside (eds.), *Contemporary Music and Music Cultures*, Englewood Cliffs, NJ: Prentice-Hall, 223–51.

Cage, John 1973, *Silence*, London: Calder and Boyars.

Cahill, Lisa Sowle 1996, *Sex, Gender and Christian Ethics*, Cambridge: Cambridge University Press.

Calvin, John 1961, *Institutes of the Christian Religion*, ed. J. T. McNeill, trans. F. L. Battles, London: SCM.

Campbell, Douglas 1992, 'The Meaning of Pistis and Nomos in Paul: A Linguistic and Structural Perspective', *Journal of Biblical Literature* 111/1: 91–103.

Campling, Christopher R. 1997, *The Food of Love: Reflections on Music and Faith*, London: SCM.

Capek, M. 1961, *The Philosophical Impact of Contemporary Physics*, Princeton: Van Nostrand.
    1991, *The New Aspects of Time: Its Continuities and Novelties*, Dordrecht, Boston and London: Kluwer Academic Publishers.

Caputo, John D. 1987, *Radical Hermeneutics: Repetition, Deconstruction and the Hermeneutic Project*, Bloomington and Indianapolis: Indiana University Press.

Cardew, Cornelius 1971, *Treatise Handbook*, London: Edition Peters.

Carpenter, Patricia 1967, 'The Musical Object', *Current Musicology* 5: 56–86.

Carr, David 1986, *Time, Narrative and History*, Bloomington and Indianapolis: Indiana University Press.

Carruthers, Mary J., 1990, *The Book of Memory: A Study of Memory in Medieval Culture*, Cambridge: Cambridge University Press.

Chadwick, Henry 1994, 'Why Music in the Church?' in *Tradition and Exploration: Collected Papers on Theology and the Church*, Norwich: Canterbury Press, 203–16.

Chafe, Eric 1991, *Tonal Allegory in the Vocal Music of J. S. Bach*, Berkeley: University of California Press.

Chesnau, J. 1992, *Brave New World: The Prospects for Survival*, trans. D. Johnstone, K. Bowie and F. Garvie, London: Thames & Hudson.

Childs, Brevard S. 1962, *Memory and Tradition in Ancient Israel*, London: SCM.

Childs, Barney 1977, 'Time and Music: A Composer's View', *Perspectives of New Music* 15: 194–219.

Childs, B. and Hobbs, C. 1982/83 (eds.), 'Forum: Improvisation', *Perspectives of New Music* 21: 26–111.

Chua, Daniel K. L. 1995, *The 'Galitzin' Quartets of Beethoven*, Princeton: Princeton University Press.

Clark, Ronald W. 1973, *Einstein: the Life and Times*, London: Hodder & Stoughton.

Clifton, Thomas 1983, *Music as Heard: A Study in Applied Phenomenology*, New Haven: Yale University Press.

Clines, David J. A. 1994, *The Theme of the Pentateuch*, Sheffield: Sheffield Academic Press.

Coker, W. 1972, *Music and Meaning: A Theoretical Introduction to Musical Aesthetics*, New York: Free Press.

Cone, Edward T. 1960, 'Analysis Today', in Paul Henry Láng (ed.), *Problems of Modern Music*, New York: Norton, 34–50.

1968, *Musical Form and Musical Performance*, New York: Norton.

Congar, Yves 1983, *I Believe in the Holy Spirit*, vol. III, London: Chapman.

Connor, Steven 1997, *Postmodernist Culture: An Introduction to Theories of the Contemporary*, Oxford: Blackwell.

Cook, Nicholas 1990, *Music, Imagination and Culture*, Oxford: Clarendon Press.

1998a, *Analysing Musical Multimedia*, Oxford: Clarendon Press.

1998b, *Music: A Very Short Introduction*, Oxford: Oxford University Press.

Cooke, Deryck 1959, *The Language of Music*, New York: Oxford University Press.

Coveney, Peter and Highfield, Roger 1990, *The Arrow of Time: A Voyage through Science to Solve Time's Greatest Mystery*, London: Allen.

Craig, William Lane 1978, 'God, Time, and Eternity', *Religious Studies* 14: 497–503.

Cranfield, C. E. B. 1982, 'Thoughts on New Testament Eschatology', *Scottish Journal of Theology* 35: 497–512.

Cullmann, Oscar 1951, *Christ and Time: The Primitive Christian Conception of Time and History*, London: SCM.

Cunningham, David S. 1998, *These Three Are One: The Practice of Trinitarian Theology*, Oxford: Blackwell.

Dahlhaus, Carl 1982, *Esthetics of Music*, trans. William W. Austin, Cambridge: Cambridge University Press.

1983, *Foundations of Music History*, trans. J. B. Robinson, Cambridge: Cambridge University Press.

1989, *Idea of Absolute Music*, trans. R. Lustig, Chicago: University of Chicago Press.

David, Hans and Mendel, Arthur 1966 (eds.), *The Bach Reader*, New York: Norton.

Davies, P. C. W. 1974, *The Physics of Time Symmetry*, Berkeley: University of California Press.

1983, *God and the New Physics*, New York: Simon & Schuster.

1987, *The Cosmic Blueprint*, London: Heinemann.

1995, *About Time*, New York: Simon & Schuster.

Davies, Stephen 1987, 'Authenticity in Musical Performance', *British Journal of Aesthetics* 27/1: 39–50.

1988, 'Transcription, Authenticity and Performance', *British Journal of Aesthetics* 28/3: 216–27.

1994, *Musical Meaning and Expression*, Ithaca and London: Cornell University Press.

Dean, Roger 1989, *Creative Improvisation*, Milton Keynes: Open University Press.

1993, *New Structures in Improvised Music, 1960–1980*, Milton Keynes: Open University Press.

Delamont. S. and Galton, M. 1986, *Inside the Secondary Classroom*, London: Routledge and Kegan Paul.

Deleuze, G. 1969, *Difference and Repetition*, trans. Paul Patton, London: Athlone Press.

Derrida, Jacques 1976, *Of Grammatology*, trans. Spivak, Gayatri Chakravorty, Baltimore: Johns Hopkins University Press.

De Selincourt, Basil 1958, 'Music and Duration', trans. Susanne Langer, in Susanne Langer (ed.), *Reflections on Art*, London: Oxford University Press, 152–60.

De Sousa, R., *The Rationality of Emotion*, Cambridge, Mass. and London: MIT Press, 1987.

DeVries, Simon, 1975, *Yesterday, Today and Tomorrow: Time and History in the Old Testament*, Grand Rapids, Michigan: Eerdmans.

Docherty, Thomas 1990, *After Theory*, Edinburgh: Edinburgh University Press.

Dolmetsch, Arnold 1915, *The Interpretation of Music of the 17th and 18th Centuries*, London: Novello.

Donington, Robert 1989, *The Interpretation of Early Music*, London: Faber.

Drees, Willem 1990, *Beyond the Big Bang,* La Salle, Illinois: Open Court.

Driver, Paul 1994, 'Spirits are lifted high by the end', *The Sunday Times* 21 August: 21.

Dunn, James 1988, *Romans 9–16*, Dallas: Word Books.

Dunnett, Roderic 1992, 'Eternal Truths Set to Music', *Church Times* 7 August, 20.

Durant, Alan 1989, 'Improvisation in the Political Economy of Music', in Christopher Norris (ed.), *Music and the Politics of Culture*, London: Lawrence and Wishart, 252–82.

Eagleton, Terry 1990, *The Ideology of the Aesthetic*, Oxford: Blackwell.

Eaton, J. H. 1981, *Vision in Worship: The Relation of Prophecy and Liturgy in the Old Testament*, London: SPCK.

Elias, N. 1992, *Time: An Essay*, Oxford: Blackwell.

Elliott, Charles 1995, *Memory and Salvation*, London: Darton, Longman and Todd.

Eliot, T. S. 1932, 'Tradition and the Individual Talent', in *Selected Essays*, London: Faber and Faber, 13–22.

Epstein, David 1981, 'On Musical Continuity', in J. T. Fraser, N. Lawrence, and D. Park (eds.), *The Study of Time*, vol. IV, New York: Springer-Verlag, 180–97.

Everson, A. Joseph 1974, 'The Days of Yahweh', *Journal of Biblical Literature* 93: 329–37.

Fabian, Johannes 1983, *Time and the Other: How Anthropology Makes its Object*, New York: Columbia University Press, 1983.

Falkenroth, U. and Brown, C. 1978, 'Patience, Steadfastness, Endurance', in *The New International Dictionary of the New Testament*, vol. II, Exeter: Paternoster, 764–76.

Fenn, Richard K. 1995, *The Persistence of Purgatory*, Cambridge: Cambridge University Press.

Ferand, Ernst 1961, *Improvisation in Nine Centuries of Western Music*, Cologne: Arno Volk Verlag.

Fétis, F.-J. 1879, *Traité complet de la théorie et de la pratique de l'harmonie contenant la doctrine de la science et de l'art*, Paris: Brandus.

Fiddes, Paul 1991, *Freedom and Limit: A Dialogue between Literature and Christian Doctrine*, London: Macmillan.

Fitzmyer, Joseph A. 1993, *Romans*, London: Chapman.

Fleming, Richard and Duckworth, William 1989 (eds.), *John Cage at Seventy-Five*, Lewisburg, Pa.: Bucknell University Press, and London and Toronto: Associated University Press.

Foley, Edward 1993, 'Toward a Sound Theology', *Studia Liturgica* 23/2: 121–39.

Ford, David F. and Stamps, Dennis 1996 (eds.), *Essentials of Christian Community*, Edinburgh: T. & T. Clark.

Ford, David F. 1997, *The Shape of Living*, London: Fount.

1999, *Self and Salvation: Being Transformed*, Cambridge: Cambridge University Press.

Forte, Allen and Gilbert, Steven 1982, *Introduction to Schenkerian Analysis*, New York: Norton.

Fraser, J. T. 1987, *Time the Familiar Stranger*, Amherst: University of Massachusetts Press.

Fraser, J. T. and Lawrence, N. 1975 (eds.), *The Study of Time*, vol. II, Berlin, Heidelberg and New York: Springer-Verlag.

Frith, Simon 1996, *Performing Rites: On the Value of Popular Music*, Oxford: Oxford University Press.

Frost, Anthony and Yarrow, Ralph 1990, *Improvisation in Drama*, London: Macmillan.

Fubini, Enrico 1990, *A History of Music Aesthetics*, trans. Michael Hatwell, London: Macmillan.

Gable, David 1990, 'Boulez's Two Cultures: The Post-War European Synthesis and Tradition', *Journal of the American Musicological Society* 43: 426–56.

Garfield, Darren 1992, 'The Music of John Tavener and his Changing Religious Affiliations', dissertation for Theology and Religious Studies Tripos, University of Cambridge.

George, Graham 1970, *Tonality and Musical Structure*, New York and Washington: Praeger.

Giddens, A. 1995, *A Contemporary Critique of Historical Materialism: Power, Property and the State*, Basingstoke: Macmillan.

Gill, Theodore A. 1986, 'Barth and Mozart', *Theology Today* 43: 403–11.

Glock, William 1986 (ed.), *Pierre Boulez: A Symposium*, London: Eulenburg.

Goldingay, John 1990, *Approaches to Old Testament Interpretation*, Leicester: Apollos.

Gooddy, William 1969, 'Outside Time and Inside Time', *Perspectives in Biology and Medicine*, 12/2: 239–53.

1977, 'The Timing and Time of Musicians', in Macdonald Critchley and R. A. Henson (eds.), *Music and the Brain*, London: Heinemann, 131–40.

Goodman, Nelson 1976, *Languages of Art: An Approach to a Theory of Symbols*, Indianapolis: Hackett Publishing.

Graham, Gordon 1997, *Philosophy and the Arts*, London: Routledge.

Greene, David B. 1982, *Temporal Processes in Beethoven's Music*, New York: Gordon and Breach.

Griffin, David R. 1986 (ed.), *Physics and the Ultimate Significance of Time*, Albany: State University of New York Press.

Griffiths, Paul 1974, 'Tavener and the Ultimos Ritos', *Musical Times* 115: 468–71.

    1981, *Cage*, Oxford: Oxford University Press.

    1985a, *New Sounds, New Personalities: British Composers of the 1980s in Conversation with Paul Griffiths*, London: Faber.

    1985b, *Olivier Messiaen and the Music of Time*, London: Faber and Faber.

Grigson, Lionel 1985, 'Harmony + Improvisation = Jazz', *British Journal of Music Education* 2/2: 187–94.

Guhrt, J. and Hahn, H.-C. 1978, 'Time', in *The New International Dictionary of the New Testament*, vol. III, Exeter: Paternoster, 826–50.

Gunton, Colin 1985, 'Creation and Re-Creation: An Exploration of Some Themes in Aesthetics and Theology', *Modern Theology* 2/1: 1–19.

    1991a, 'Mozart the Theologian', *Theology* 94: 346–9.

    1991b, 'The Spirit in the Trinity', in Alasdair Heron (ed.), *The Forgotten Trinity*, vol. III, London: BCC/CCBI, 123–35.

    1993, *The One, the Three and the Many: God, Creation and the Culture of Modernity*, Cambridge: Cambridge University Press.

    1995a, *A Brief Theology of Revelation*, Edinburgh: T. & T. Clark.

    1995b, 'God, Grace and Freedom', in Colin E. Gunton (ed.), *God and Freedom: Essays in Historical and Systematic Theology*, Edinburgh: T. & T. Clark, 119–33.

    1997a, 'The Trinity, Natural Theology, and a Theology of Nature', in Kevin J. Vanhoozer (ed.), *The Trinity in a Pluralistic Age: Theological Essays on Culture and Religion*, Grand Rapids, Mich.: Eerdmans, 88–103.

    1997b, 'Between Allegory and Myth: The Legacy of the Spiritualising of Genesis', in Colin E. Gunton (ed.), *The Doctrine of Creation*, Edinburgh: T. & T. Clark, 47–62.

    1997c, *Yesterday and Today: A Study of Continuities in Christology*, London: SPCK.

    1998, *The Triune Creator: A Historical and Systematic Study*, Edinburgh: Edinburgh University Press.

Guthrie, Steven 1998, 'Arnold Schoenberg and the Cold Transparency of Clear Cut Ideas', unpublished paper delivered to The Theological Research Seminar, St Mary's College, University of St Andrews.

Gurvitch, G. 1963, 'Social Structure and the Multiplicity of Times', in E. A. Toryakin (ed.), *Sociological Theory, Values, and Sociocultural Change*, London: Free Press of Glencoe, 171–85.

Hamm, Charles 1995, *Putting Popular Music in its Place*, Cambridge: Cambridge University Press.

Hanslick, Eduard 1957, *The Beautiful in Music*, trans. Gustav Cohen, Indianapolis: Bobbs-Merrill.

Hanson, Richard 1981, *The Continuity of Christian Doctrine*, New York: Seabury Press.

Happel, Stephen 1993, 'Metaphors and Time Asymmetry: Cosmologies and Christian Meanings', in Robert John Russell, Nancey Murphy and C. J. Isham (eds.), *Quantum Cosmology and the Laws of Nature: Scientific Perspectives on Divine Action*, Rome: Vatican Observatory Publications and Berkeley: The Center for Theology and the Natural Sciences, 103–34.

Hardy, Daniel W. 1995, 'The Logic of Interdisciplinary Studies and the Coherence of Theology: The Director's Report for 1994', Princeton: Center of Theological Inquiry.

1996, *God's Ways With the World: Thinking and Practising Christian Faith*, Edinburgh: T. & T. Clark.

Hardy, Daniel W. and Ford, David F. 1984, *Jubilate. Theology in Praise*, London: Darton, Longman and Todd.

Hargreaves, D. 1986, *The Developmental Psychology of Music*, Cambridge: Cambridge University Press.

Hargreaves, D. and North, Adrian C. 1997, *The Social Psychology of Music*, Oxford: Oxford University Press.

Harrison, Carol 1992, *Beauty and Revelation in the Thought of Saint Augustine*, Oxford: Clarendon.

Harvey, David 1990a, 'Looking Back on Postmodernism', in Andreas C. Papadakis (ed.), *Post-Modernism on Trial*, London: Academy Editions, 10–12.

1990b, *The Condition of Postmodernity. An Enquiry into the Origins of Cultural Change*, Oxford: Blackwell.

Harwood, Dale 1976, 'Universals in Music: A Perspective from Cognitive Psychology', *Ethnomusicology* 20/3: 521–33.

Hasty, Christopher F. 1981, 'Rhythm in Post-Tonal Music: Preliminary Questions of Duration and Motion', *Journal of Music Theory* 25: 183–216.

1986, 'Succession and Continuity in Twentieth-Century Music', *Music Theory Spectrum* 8: 58–74.

Hauck, F. 1979, 'ὑπομένω, ὑπομονή', in *Theological Dictionary of the New Testament*, ed. G. Kittel, trans. and ed. G. Bromiley, vol. IV, Grand Rapids, Mich.: Eerdmans, 581–8.

Hauerwas, Stanley 1981, *A Community of Character*, Notre Dame: University of Notre Dame Press.

1985, *Against the Nations*, Minneapolis: Harper and Row.

1989, *Resident Aliens*, Nashville: Abingdon.

Hawking, Stephen 1998, *A Brief History of Time: from the Big Bang to Black Holes*, London: Bantam Press.

Haydon, Geoffrey 1995, *John Tavener: Glimpses of Paradise*, London: Gollancz.

Hedley Arthur, Brown, Maurice, Temperley, Nicholas and Michalowski, Kornel 1980, 'Chopin, Fryderyk Franciszek', in S. Sadie (ed), *The New Grove Dictionary of Music and Musicians*, vol. IV, London: Macmillan, 292–312.

Heelas, Peter, with Lash, Scott and Morris, Paul 1996 (eds.), *Detraditionalization: Critical Reflections on Authority and Identity*, Cambridge, Mass. and Oxford: Blackwell.

Heikenheimo, Seppo 1972, *The Electronic Music of Karlheinz Stockhausen*, trans. Brad Absetz, Helsinki: Suomen Musikkitieteellinen Seura.

Helm, Paul 1988, *Eternal God: A Study of God Without Time*, Oxford: Clarendon Press.

1997, 'Eternal Creation: The Doctrine of the Two Standpoints', in Colin E. Gunton (ed.), *The Doctrine of Creation*, Edinburgh: T. & T. Clark, 29–46.

Hepburn, R. W. 1976, 'Time-Transcendence and Some Related Phenomena in the Arts', in H. D. Lewis (ed.), *Contemporary British Philosophy: Personal Statements*, London: Allen and Unwin, 152–73.

Herbert, George 1947, *The Poems of George Herbert*, with an introduction by Arthur Waugh, Oxford: Oxford University Press.

Heron, Alasdair 1979, 'The Time of God', paper presented at the Annual Conference of The Society for the Study of Theology.

1983, *Table and Tradition*, Edinburgh: Handsel Press.

Heyworth, Peter 1986, 'The First Fifty Years', in William Glock (ed.), *Pierre Boulez: A Symposium*, London: Eulenburg, 3–39.

Higgins, Kathleen Marie 1991, *The Music of Our Lives*, Philadelphia: Temple University Press.

Hilton, Julian 1988 (ed.), *Performance*, London: Macmillan.

Hindemith, Paul 1961, *A Composer's World: Horizons and Limitations*, New York: Anchor Books.

Hodges, John Mason 1995, 'Windows into Heaven: The Music of John Tavener', *Image* 10: 88–94.

Hodgson, J. and Richards, E. 1974, *Improvisation: Discovery and Creativity in Drama*, London: Methuen.

Hogan, T. Wayne 1975, 'Time Perception and Stimulus Preference as a Function of Stimulus Complexity', *Journal of Personality and Social Psychology* 31/3: 32–5.

Hohn, H.-W. 1984, *Die Zerstörung der Zeit: Wie aus einem göttlichen Gut eine Handelsware wurde*, Frankfurt: Fischer Alternativ.

Holman. C. L. 1996, *Till Jesus Comes: Origins of Christian Apocalyptic Expectation*, Peabody, Mass.: Hendrickson.

Hooker, Morna 1990, *From Adam to Christ: Essays on Paul*, Cambridge: Cambridge University Press.

Horne, Brian 1995, 'Art: A Trinitarian Imperative?' in Christoph Schwöbel (ed.), *Trinitarian Theology Today*, Edinburgh: T. & T. Clark, 8–91.

Horsley, Imogen, Collins, Michael, Badura-Skoda, Eva and Libby, Dennis 1980, 'Improvisation: I. Western Art Music', in S. Sadie (ed), *The New Grove Dictionary of Music and Musicians*, vol. IX, London: Macmillan, 31–52.

Hughes, Graham 1979, *Hebrews and Hermeneutics*, Cambridge: Cambridge University Press.

Hull, John M. 1990, *Touching the Rock: An Experience of Blindness*, London: SPCK.

Hunsinger, George 1991, *How to Read Karl Barth: The Shape of his Theology*, Oxford: Oxford University Press.

Ihde, Don 1970, 'Studies in the Phenomenology of Sound: I. Listening, II. On Perceiving Persons, III. God and Sound', in *International Philosophical Quarterly* 10/2: 232–51.

Ingarden, R. 1986, trans. Adam Czerniawski, *The Work of Music and the Problems of its Identity*, Basingstoke: Macmillan.

Isham, Christopher and Polkinghorne, John 1993, 'The Debate Over the Block Universe', in Robert J. Russell, Nancey Murphy and C. J. Isham (eds.), *Quantum Cosmology and the Laws of Nature: Scientific Perspectives on Divine Action*, Rome: Vatican Observatory Publications and Berkeley: The Center for Theology and the Natural Sciences, 135–44.

Jackson, Roland 1975, '*Leitmotive* and Form in the *Tristan* Prelude', *Music Review* 36: 42–53.

Jaffé, Daniel 1999, 'High Priest of Music', *Classic CD* 111: 28–31.

James, Jamie 1995, *The Music of the Spheres: Music, Science, and the Natural Order of the Universe*, New York: Copernicus Press.

Jameux, Dominique 1991, *Pierre Boulez*, trans. Susan Bradshaw, London: Faber.

Jenner, Brian 1989, 'Music to the Sinner's Ear?', *Epworth Review* 16: 35–38.

Jenson, Robert W. 1969, *God after God*, Indianapolis: Bobbs-Merril.

1982, *The Triune Identity*, Philadelphia: Fortress Press.

1988, *America's Theologian: A Recommendation of Jonathan Edwards*, New York and Oxford: Oxford University Press.

1991, 'Does God have Time? The Doctrine of the Trinity and the Concept of Time in the Physical Sciences', *CTNS Bulletin* 11/1: 1–6.

1992, *Unbaptized God: The Basic Flaw in Ecumenical Theology*, Minneapolis: Fortress Press.

Johnson, Robert Sherlaw 1989, *Messiaen*, London: Dent.

Johnstone, Keith 1979, *Impro: Improvisation and the Theatre*, London: Faber.

Jones, Ivor H. 1989, *Music: A Joy for Ever*, London: Epworth Press.

Jüngel, Eberhard 1995, 'The Emergence of the New', in *Theological Essays*, vol. II, ed. John Webster, trans. A. Neufeldt-Fast and John Webster, Edinburgh: T. & T. Clark, 35–58.

Kant, Immanuel 1996, *Critique of Pure Reason*, trans. Werner S. Pluhar, Indianapolis: Hackett Publishing.

Keller, Hans 1994, *Essays on Music*, ed. Christopher Wintle, Bayan Northcott and Irene Samuel, Cambridge, Mass.: Cambridge University Press.

Kerman, J. 1985, *Contemplating Music: Challenges to Musicology*, Cambridge, Mass. Harvard University Press.

Kermode, Frank 1967, *The Sense of an Ending: Studies in the Theory of Fiction,* Oxford: Oxford University Press.

Kern, Stephen 1983, *The Culture of Time and Space, 1880–1918*, Cambridge, Mass.: Harvard University Press.

Kirby, W. J. Torrance 1997, 'Praise as the Soul's Overcoming of Time in the *Confessions* of St. Augustine', *Pro Ecclesia* 6: 333–50.

Kirk, Andrew 1998, *The Meaning of Freedom: A Study of Secular, Muslim and Christian Views*, Carlisle: Paternoster Press.

Kirwan, Christopher 1989, *Augustine*, London: Routledge and Kegan Paul.

Kivy, Peter 1984, *Sound and Semblance: Reflections on Musical Representation*, Princeton: Princeton University Press.

1990, *Music Alone: Philosophical Reflections on the Purely Musical Experience*, Ithaca: Cornell University Press.

1993, *The Fine Art of Repetition: Essays in the Philosophy of Music*, Cambridge: Cambridge University Press.

Klein, W. W. 1990, *The New Chosen People: A Corporate View of Election*, Grand Rapids, Mich.: Zondervan.

König, Adrio 1989, *The Eclipse of Christ in Eschatology: Toward a Christ-Centred Approach*, Grand Rapids, Mich.: Eerdmans and London: Marshal, Morgan & Scott.

Kostelanetz, Richard 1974 (ed.), *John Cage*, Harmondsworth: Penguin Books.

1989, *Conversing with Cage*, London: Omnibus.

Kramer, Jonathan D. 1981, 'New Temporalities in Music', *Critical Inquiry* 7: 539–56.

1988, *The Time of Music*, New York: Schirmer.

Kramer, L. 1990, *Music as Cultural Practice 1800–1900*, Berkeley and London: University of California Press.

1995, *Classical Music and Postmodern Knowledge*, Berkeley and London: University of California Press.

Kraus, Hans-Joachim 1966, *Worship in Israel*, Oxford: Blackwell.

Kristeva, J. 1989, *Language the Unknown: An Initiation into Linguistics*, trans. Anne M. Menke, New York: Columbia University Press.

Küng, Hans 1992, *Mozart: Traces of Transcendence*, London: SCM.

Lacugna, Catherine Mowry 1993, *God for Us: The Trinity and Christian Life*, San Francisco: Harper Collins.

Lancelot, James 1995, 'Music as a Sacrament', in David Brown and Ann Loades (eds.), *The Sense of the Sacramental: Movement and Measure in Art and Music, Place and Time*, London: SPCK, 179–85.

Landes, D. S. 1983, *Revolution in Time: Clocks and the Making of the Modern World*, Cambridge, Mass.: Belknap Press of Harvard University Press, 1983.

Langer, Susanne 1953, *Feeling and Form*, New York: Scribner's.

   1957, *Philosophy in a New Key*, Cambridge, Mass.: Harvard University Press.

Langford, Michael J. 1981, *Providence*, London: SCM.

   1994, 'The Trinity and Time's Flow', *Dialog* 33/1: 62–70.

Lash, Nicholas 1973, *Change in Focus*, London: Sheed and Ward.

   1986, 'Performing the Scriptures', in *Theology on the Way to Emmaus*, London: SCM, 37–46.

   1996, *The Beginning and the End of 'Religion'*, Cambridge: Cambridge University Press.

Lauer, Robert H. 1981, *Temporal Man: The Meaning and Uses of Social Time*, New York: Praeger Publishing.

Lawrence, N. 1975, 'Temporal Passage and Spatial Metaphor', in J. T. Fraser and N. Lawrence (eds.), *The Study of Time*, vol. II, Berlin, Heidelberg and New York: Springer-Verlag, 196–205.

Leftow, Brian 1991, *Time and Eternity*, Ithaca and London: Cornell University Press.

Le Huray, Peter G. 1990, *Authenticity in Performance: Eighteenth-Century Case Studies*, Cambridge: Cambridge University Press.

Leppard, Raymond 1988, *Authenticity in Music*, London: Faber.

Lerdahl, Fred and Jackendoff, Ray 1983, *A Generative Theory of Tonal Music*, Cambridge, Mass. and London: MIT Press.

Lester, Joel 1986, *The Rhythms of Tonal Music*, Carbondale: Southern Illinois University Press.

Levy, Kenneth 1990, 'On Gregorian Orality', *Journal of the American Musicological Society* 43: 185–227.

Lippman, Edward 1992, *A History of Western Musical Aesthetics*, Lincoln and London: University of Nebraska Press.

Litweiler, J., *The Freedom Principle*, New York: Morrow & Co., 1984.

Lochhead, Judith 1979, 'The Temporal in Beethoven's Opus 135: When Are Endings Beginnings?' *In Theory Only* 4/6: 3–30.

Longenecker, Bruce 1998, *The Triumph of Abraham's God: The Transformation of Identity in Galatians*, Edinburgh: T. & T. Clark.

Loughlin, Gerard 1996a, *Telling God's Story: Bible, Church and Narrative Theology*, Cambridge: Cambridge University Press.

   1996b, 'Transubstantiation: Eucharist as Pure Gift', in David Brown and Ann Loades (eds.), *Christ: The Sacramental Word*, London: SPCK, 123–41.

Lucas, John 1973, *A Treatise on Time and Space*, London: Methuen.

   1993, 'The Temporality of God', in Robert John Russell, Nancey Murphy and C. J. Isham (eds.), *Quantum Cosmology and the Laws of Nature: Scientific Perspectives on Divine Action*, Rome: Vatican Observatory Publications and Berkeley: The Center for Theology and the Natural Sciences, 235–62.

Lundin, Roger 1993, *The Culture of Interpretation: Christian Faith and the Postmodern World*, Grand Rapids, Mich.: Eerdmans.

McCabe, Herbert 1987, *God Matters*, London: Chapman.

McClary, Susan 1991, *Feminine Endings: Music, Gender, and Sexuality*, Minneapolis: University of Minnesota Press.

McFadyen, Alistair 1990, *The Call to Personhood: A Christian Theory of the Individual in Social Relationships*, Cambridge: Cambridge University Press.

    1995, 'Sins of Praise: The Assault on God's Freedom', in Colin E. Gunton (ed.), *God and Freedom: Essays in Historical and Systematic Theology*, Edinburgh: T. & T. Clark, 32–56.

Mackenzie, Iain 1994, *The Anachronism of Time: A Theological Study into the Nature of Time*, Norwich: Canterbury Press.

Maconie, Robin 1990, *The Concept of Music*, Oxford: Oxford University Press, 1990.

McTaggart, J. M. E. 1908, 'The Unreality of Time', *Mind* 17: 457–74.

Maddocks, Fiona 1992, 'For the Love of God and the Right Note', *Observer* 14 June, 63.

Margolis, Joseph 1980, *Art and Philosophy*, Brighton: Harvester Press.

Marion, Jean-Luc 1991, *God Without Being: Hors-Texte*, trans. Thomas A. Carlson, Chicago and London: University of Chicago Press.

Marshall, Bruce D. 1993, 'Review of Richard H. Roberts, *A Theology on Its Way? Essays on Karl Barth*', *Journal of Theological Studies* 44: 453–8.

Martland, S. 1989, *Extreme Conditions, Extreme Responses: New Music*, Oxford: Oxford University Press.

Meade, Robert D., 1977, 'Time Estimates as Affected by Motivational Level, Goal Distance, and Rate of Progress', *Journal of Experimental Psychology* 58: 275–79.

Mellers, Wilfrid 1980, *Bach and the Dance of God*, London: Faber.

    1983, *Beethoven and the Voice of God*, London: Faber.

Mellor, Hugh 1981, *Real Time*, Cambridge: Cambridge University Press.

Mertens, Wim 1983, *American Minimal Music*, trans. J. Hautkeit, New York: Alexander Broude.

Messiaen, Olivier 1994, *Music and Color: Conversations with Claude Samuel*, trans. E. Thomas Glasgow, Portland, Oreg.: Amadeus Press.

Metz, J. B. 1984, 'Productive Noncontemporaneity', in J. Habermas (ed.), *Observations on 'The Spiritual Situation of the Age': Contemporary German Perspectives*, Cambridge, Mass. and London: MIT Press, 169–77.

Meyer, Leonard B. 1959, 'Some Remarks on Value and Greatness in Music', *Journal of Aesthetics and Art Criticism* 18: 486–500.

    1970, *Emotion and Meaning in Music*, Chicago: University of Chicago Press.

    1973, *Explaining Music: Essays and Explorations*, Berkeley: University of California Press.

Michon, John A. 1978, 'The Making of the Present: A Tutorial Review', in Jean Requin (ed.), *Attention and Performance*, vol. VII, Hillsdale, NJ: Erlbaum, 90–2.

    1985, 'The Compleat Time Experiencer', in John A. Michon and Janet L. Jackson (eds.), *Time, Mind, and Behaviour*, New York: Springer-Verlag, 20–52.

Middleton, Richard 1983, '"Play it again Sam"': Some Notes on the Productivity of Repetition in Popular Music', in Richard Middleton and David Horn (eds.), *Popular Music*, vol. III, Cambridge: Cambridge University Press, 235–70.

    1990, *Studying Popular Music*, Milton Keynes: Open University Press.

Milbank, John 1990, *Theology and Social Theory: Beyond Secular Reason*, Oxford: Blackwell.
   1995, 'Can a Gift be Given? Prolegomena to a Future Trinitarian Metaphysic', *Modern Theology* 11/1: 119–61.
Minear, Paul S. 1987, *Death Set to Music*, Atlanta: John Knox Press.
Mitchell, Jolyon 1999, 'Sound of Heart', *Third Way* 22/5: 18–21.
Moltmann, Jürgen 1967, *Theology of Hope*, London: SCM.
   1985, *God in Creation: A New Theology of Creation and the Spirit of God*, London: SCM.
   1990, *The Way of Jesus Christ: Christology in Messianic Dimensions*, London: SCM.
   1996, *The Coming of God*, London: SCM.
Moody, Ivan and Phillips, Peter 1987, 'John Tavener's Music for the Church', *Composer* 91: 11–18.
Morgan, Robert P. 1977, 'Spatial Form in Ives', in H. Wiley Hitchcock and Vivian Perlis (eds.), *An Ives Celebration*, Urbana: University of Illinois Press, 145–58.
   1980, 'Musical Time/Musical Space', *Critical Inquiry* 6/3: 527–38.
   1988, 'Tradition, Anxiety and the Current Musical Scene', in Nicholas Kenyon (ed.), *Authenticity and Early Music*, Oxford: Oxford University Press, 57–82.
Moszkowski, Alexander 1972, *Conversations with Einstein*, London: Sidgwick and Jackson.
Mowinckel, Sigmund 1962, *The Psalms in Israel's Worship*, Nashville: Abingdon Press and Oxford: Blackwell & Mott.
Narmour, E. 1977, *Beyond Schenkerism: the Need for Alternatives in Music Analysis*, Chicago: University of Chicago Press.
Nattiez, Jean-Jacques 1990, *Music and Discourse: Toward a Semiology of Music*, trans. Carolyn Abbate, Princeton: Princeton University Press.
   1993, *The Boulez–Cage Correspondence*, trans. Robert Samuels, Cambridge: Cambridge University Press.
Nettl, Bruno 1974, 'Thoughts on Improvisation: A Comparative Approach', *Musical Quarterly* 60: 1–19.
Neumann, Frederick 1989, *New Essays in Performance Practice*, Ann Arbor: UMI Research Press.
Neumann, Gerhard 1994, 'The "Masters of Emptiness" and the Myth of Creativity: George Steiner's *Real Presences*', in Nathan A. Scott and Ronald A. Sharp (eds.), *Reading George Steiner*, Baltimore: Johns Hopkins University Press, 246–61.
Neville, Robert Cummings 1993, *Eternity and Time's Flow*, Albany, NY: State University of New York Press.
Newbigin, Lesslie 1989, *The Gospel in a Pluralist Society*, London: SPCK
Newlin, Dika 1980, *Schoenberg Remembered: Diaries and Recollections (1938–76)*, New York: Pendragon Press.
Newton, Isaac 1962, *The Mathematical Principles of Natural Philosophy*, vol. I, trans. A. Motte, Berkeley: University of California Press.
Newton-Smith, W. H. 1980, *The Structure of Time*, London: Routledge and Kegan Paul.
Norris, Christopher 1985, *Contest of Faculties: Philosophy and Theory After Deconstruction*, London: Methuen.
   1989, *Music and the Politics of Culture*, London: Lawrence and Wishart.
Norton, Richard 1984, *Tonality in Western Culture: A Critical and Historical Perspective*, University Park and London: Pennsylvania State University Press.
Nowotny, H. 1994, *Time: The Modern and Postmodern Experience*, Cambridge: Polity Press.

O'Connell, Robert, 1978, *Art and the Christian Intelligence in St Augustine*, Oxford: Blackwell.

O'Daly, Gerard 1977, 'Time as *Distentio* and St. Augustine's Exegesis of *Philippians* 3,12–14', *Revue des Etudes Augustiniennes* 23: 265–71.

    1987, *Augustine's Philosophy of Mind*, San Diego: University of California Press.

O'Donnell, John 1983, *Trinity and Temporality*, Oxford: Oxford University Press.

O'Donovan, Oliver 1986, *Resurrection and Moral Order: An Outline for Evangelical Ethics*, Grand Rapids, Mich.: Eerdmans.

    1986, *On the Thirty Nine Articles: A Conversation with Tudor Christianity*, Exeter: Paternoster.

O'Siadhail, Micheal 1992, *Hail! Madam Jazz: New and Selected Poems*, Newcastle upon Tyne: Bloodaxe.

    1995, *A Fragile City*, Newcastle upon Tyne: Bloodaxe.

    1996, 'Crosslight', in D. Ford and D. Stamps (eds.), *Essentials of Christian Community*, Edinburgh: T. & T. Clark, 49–60.

Ostransky, Leroy 1960, *The Anatomy of Jazz*, Seattle: University of Washington Press.

Owens, Jessie Ann 1997, *Composers at Work*, Oxford University Press.

Paddison, Max 1993, *Adorno's Aesthetics of Music*, Cambridge: Cambridge University Press.

Padgett, A. G. 1992, *God, Eternity and the Nature of Time*, New York: St. Martin's Press.

Pannenberg, Wolfhart 1991, *Systematic Theology*, vol. I, trans. Geoffrey W. Bromiley, Grand Rapids, Mich.: Eerdmans.

    1992, *Systematic Theology*, vol. II, trans. Geoffrey W. Bromiley, Edinburgh: T. & T. Clark.

Patterson, Sue 1993, 'Janet Martin Soskice, Metaphor and a Theology of Grace', *Scottish Journal of Theology* 46: 1–26.

Peacocke, Arthur, 1979, *Creation and the World of Science: The Bampton Lectures 1978*, Oxford: Clarendon Press.

    1980, 'The Theory of Relativity and Our World View', in *Einstein: The First Hundred Years*, M. Goldsmith, A. Mackay and J. Woudhuysen (eds.), Oxford: Pergamon Press, 73–91.

    1984, *Intimations of Reality: Critical Realism in Science and Religion*, Notre Dame: University of Notre Dame Press.

    1993, *Theology for a Scientific Age*, London: SCM.

Peggie, Andrew 1985, 'The Place of Improvisation in Music Education', *British Journal of Music Education* 2/2: 167–9.

Pelikan, Jaroslav 1986a, *Bach Among the Theologians*, Philadelphia: Fortress Press.

    1986b, *The Mystery of Continuity: Time, and History, Memory and Eternity in the Thought of Saint Augustine*, Charlottesville: University Press of Virginia.

    1988, *The Melody of Theology*, Cambridge, Mass.: Harvard University Press.

Percy, Martyn 1996, *Words, Wonders and Power*, London: SPCK.

Peters, Ted 1993a, *God as Trinity: Relationality and Temporality in Divine Life*, Louisville, Ky.: Westminster/John Knox Press.

    1993b, 'The Trinity in and Beyond Time', in Robert John Russell, Nancey Murphy and C. J. Isham (eds.), *Quantum Cosmology and the Laws of Nature: Scientific Perspectives on Divine Action*, Rome: Vatican Observatory Publications and Berkeley: The Center for Theology and the Natural Sciences, 263–91.

Peyser, Joan 1977, *Boulez*, London: Cassell.

Phillips, Peter 1983, 'The Ritual Music of John Tavener', *Contact* 26: 29–30.

Pickstock, Catherine 1999, 'Soul, City and Cosmos after Augustine', in John Milbank,
    Catherine Pickstock and Graham Ward (eds.), *Radical Orthodoxy*, London and
    New York: Routledge, 243–77.
Pike, Nelson 1970, *God and Timelessness*, London: Routledge and Kegan Paul.
Platten, Stephen and Pattison, George 1996, *Spirit and Tradition: An Essay on Change*,
    Norwich: Canterbury Press.
Polkinghorne, John 1989, *Science and Providence*, London: SPCK.
    1991, *Reason and Reality*, London: SPCK.
    1995, 'Temporality in Relation to Divine Action', unpublished paper delivered at the
    Center of Theological Inquiry, Princeton.
    1998, *Science and Theology: An Introduction*, London: SPCK.
Pople, Anothony 1994 (ed.), *Theory, Analysis and Meaning in Music*, Cambridge: Cambridge
    University Press.
Pressing, J., 1984a, 'A History of Musical Improvisation 1600–1900', *Keyboard*, 10/11:
    64–68.
    1984b, 'A History of Musical Improvisation to 1600', *Keyboard*, 10/12, 59–67.
    1984c, 'Cognitive processes in improvisation', in W. R. Crozier and A. J. Chapman
    (eds.), *Cognitive Processes in the Perception of Art*, Amsterdam: North Holland, 1984,
    345–63.
    1988, 'Improvisation: methods and models', in J. A. Sloboda (ed.), *Generative Processes
    in Music: The Psychology of Performance, Improvisation and Composition*, Oxford:
    Oxford University Press, 128–78.
Prévost, E. 1982, 'The Aesthetic Priority of Improvisation', *Contact* 25: 32–37.
    1985, 'Improvisation: Music for an Occasion', *British Journal of Music Education* 2/2:
    177–86.
Prigogine, Ilya 1980, *From Being to Becoming: Time and Complexity in the Physical Sciences*, San
    Francisco: W. H. Freeman.
Prigogine, I. and Stengers, I. 1984, *Order out of Chaos: Man's New Dialogue with Nature*,
    London: Fontana.
Pritchett, James 1993, *The Music of John Cage*, Cambridge: Cambridge University Press.
Quinn, John 1965, *The Concept of Time in St. Augustine*, Rome: Studia Augustiniana.
Rad, Gerhard von 1962, *Old Testament Theology*, vol. I, trans. D. M. G. Stalker, New York:
    Harper & Row.
    1965, *Old Testament Theology*, vol. II, trans. D. M. G. Stalker, New York: Harper &
    Row.
Rahner, Karl 1966, *Theological Investigations*, vol. IV, London: Darton, Longman and
    Todd.
Ramsey, B. 1989, 'Lost Paradise: John Tavener in Discussion with Basil Ramsey', *Music
    and Musicians International* 38/4: 7–10.
Ricoeur, Paul 1984, *Time and Narrative*, vol. I, Chicago and London: University of Chicago
    Press.
    1988, *Time and Narrative*, vol. III, Chicago and London: University of Chicago Press.
    1995, *Figuring the Sacred: Religion, Narrative, and Imagination*, ed. Mark I. Wallace, trans.
    David Pellauer, Minneapolis: Fortress Press.
Rist, John M. 1994, *Augustine*, Cambridge: Cambridge University Press.
Roberts, Richard 1979, 'Barth's Doctrine of Time: Its Nature and Implications', in S. W.
    Sykes (ed.), *Karl Barth: Studies of His Theological Method*, Oxford: Clarendon Press,
    88–146.

Robinson, Gillian 1993, *Rethinking Imagination: Culture and Creativity*, London: Routledge and Kegan Paul.

Rochberg, George 1984, 'The Concepts of Musical Time and Space', in *The Aesthetics of Survival: A Composer's View of Twentieth-Century Music*, Ann Arbor: University of Michigan Press, 78–136.

Rosen, Charles 1971, *The Classical Style: Haydn, Mozart, Beethoven*, London: Faber and Faber.

1986, 'The Piano Music', in William Glock (ed.), *Pierre Boulez: A Symposium*, London: Eulenburg, 85–97.

Rothstein, Edward 1995, *Emblems of Mind: The Inner Life of Music and Mathematics*, New York: Avon Books.

Rowell, Lewis 1981, 'The Creation of Audible Time: How Musics Begin', in J. T. Fraser, N. Lawrence and D. Park (eds.), *The Study of Time*, vol. IV, New York: Springer-Verlag, 198–210.

1983, *Thinking About Music*, Amherst: University of Massachusetts Press.

1985, 'The Temporal Spectrum', *Music Theory Spectrum* 7: 1–6.

Rowland, Christopher 1982, *The Open Heaven: A Study of Apocalyptic in Judaism and Early Christianity*, London: SPCK, 1982.

1985, *Christian Origins*, London: SPCK.

1995, 'Eucharist as Liberation from the Present', in David Brown and Ann Loades (eds.), *The Sense of the Sacramental: Movement and Measure in Art and Music, Place and Time*, London: SPCK, 200–15.

Russell, Robert John 1991, 'Is the Triune God the Basis for Physical Time?' *CTNS Bulletin* 11/1, 7–19.

1993, 'Finite Creation Without a Beginning: The Doctrine of Creation in Relation to Big Bang and Quantum Cosmologies', in Robert John Russell, Nancey Murphy and C. J. Isham (eds.), *Quantum Cosmology and the Laws of Nature: Scientific Perspectives on Divine Action*, Rome: Vatican Observatory Publications and Berkeley: The Center for Theology and the Natural Sciences, 293–329.

Russell, Robert John, Murphy, Nancey and Isham, C. J. 1993 (eds.), *Quantum Cosmology and the Laws of Nature: Scientific Perspectives on Divine Action*, Rome: Vatican Observatory Publications and Berkeley: The Center for Theology and the Natural Sciences.

Russell, Robert J., Stoeger William R. and Coyne, George V. 1988 (eds.), *Physics, Philosophy, and Theology: A Common Quest for Understanding*, Rome: Vatican Observatory Publications.

Ruwet, Nicholas 1987, 'Methods of analysis in musicology', *Music Analysis* 6: 1–2, 3–9, 11–36.

Sachs, Curt 1953, *Rhythm and Tempo: A Study in Music History*, New York: Norton.

Said, Edward 1991, *Musical Elaborations*, New York: Columbia University Press.

Sandberger, Jörg V. 1991, 'Theologische Existenz angesichts der Grenze und auf der Grenze. Karl Barth über Mozart und Paul Tillich über Bildende Kunst', *Theologische Zeitschrift* 47: 66–86.

Saussure, Ferdinand de 1966, *Course in General Linguistics*, trans. Wade Baskin, New York: McGraw Hill.

Sayers, Dorothy 1941, *The Mind of the Maker*, London: Methuen.

Schenker, Heinrich 1954, *Harmony*, trans. Elizabeth Mann Borghese, ed. Oswald Jonas, Chicago and London: University of Chicago Press.

Scher, Paul (ed.), 1992, *Music and Text: Critical Inquiries*, Cambridge: Cambridge University Press.

Scherchen, Hermann, *The Nature of Music*, trans. William Mann, London: Dennis Dobson, 1950.

Schleiermacher, Friedrich 1967, *Christmas Eve: Dialogue on Incarnation*, trans. Terrence N. Tice, Richmond, Va.: John Knox Press.

Schoenberg, Arnold 1975, 'Composition with Twelve Tones (I) 1941', in Leonard Stein (ed.), *Style and Idea: Selected Writings of Arnold Schoenberg*, London: Faber and Faber, 214–45.

Schreiter, R. J. 1985, *Constructing Local Theologies*, London: SCM.

Schuldt, Agnes Crawford 1976, 'The Voices of Time in Music', *American Scholar* 45: 549–59.

Schulenberg, David 1995, 'Composition and Improvisation in the School of J. S. Bach', in Russell Stevenson (ed.), *Bach Perspectives*, vol. I, Lincoln, Nebr. and London: University of Nebraska Press, 1–42.

Schwartz, E. and Childs, Barney 1967 (eds.), *Contemporary Composers on Contemporary Music*, New York: Da Capo Press.

Schwöbel, Christoph 1995, 'Imago Libertatis: Human and Divine Freedom', in Colin E. Gunton (ed.), *God and Freedom: Essays in Historical and Systematic Theology*, Edinburgh: T. & T. Clark, 57–81.

Scruton, Roger 1983, *The Aesthetic Understanding*, London: Methuen.
    1997, *The Aesthetics of Music*, Oxford: Clarendon.

Sessions, Roger 1971, *The Musical Experience of Composer, Performer, Listener*, Princeton: Princeton University Press.

Shakespeare, William 1978, *Shakespeare's Sonnets*, ed. S. C. Campbell, London: Bell and Hyman and Totowa, NJ: Rowman and Littlefield.

Shepherd, John and Wicke, Peter 1997, *Music and Cultural Theory*, Cambridge: Polity Press.

Sherry, Patrick 1992, *Spirit and Beauty: An Introduction to Theological Aesthetics*, Oxford: Clarendon.

Shove, Patrick and Repp, Bruno, H. 1995, 'Musical Motion and Performance: Theoretical and Empirical Perspectives', in John Rink (ed.), *The Practice of Performance: Studies in Musical Interpretation*, Cambridge: Cambridge University Press, 55–83.

Siegel, H., *Schenker Studies*, Cambridge: Cambridge University Press.

Sirota, Victoria R. 1994, 'An Exploration of Music as Theology', *Theological Education* 31/1: 165–73.

Skaife, A. M. 1967, 'The Role of Complexity and Deviation in Changing Musical Taste', Ph.D. thesis, University of Oregon.

Sloboda, John 1988 (ed.), *Generative Processes in Music*, Oxford: Oxford University Press.
    1993, *The Musical Mind*, Oxford: Oxford University Press.

Smail, Tom 1988, *The Giving Gift*, London: Hodder & Stoughton.

Small, C., 1977, *Music–Society–Education*, London: John Calder.
    1987, *Music of the Common Tongue*, London: John Calder.

Smart, J. J. C., 1972, 'Time', in Paul Edwards (ed.), *The Encyclopaedia of Philosophy*, vol. VII, New York and London: Macmillan, 126–34.
    1980, 'Time and Becoming', in P. Van Inwagen (ed.), *Time and Cause,* Dordrecht and London: Reidel, 3–15.

Smith, F. Joseph, *The Experiencing of Musical Sound: Prelude to a Phenomenology of Music*, New York, London and Paris: Gordon and Breach, 1979.

Solomon, L. 1985/86, 'Improvisation II', *Perspectives of New Music* 24: 224–35.

Sorabji, Richard 1983, *Time, Creation and the Continuum: Theories in Antiquity and the Early Middle Ages*, Ithaca: Cornell University Press.

Sparshott, Francis 1982, *The Theory of the Arts*, Princeton: Princeton University Press.

1987, 'Aesthetics of Music: Limits and Grounds', in P. J. Alperson (ed.), *What is Music? An Introduction to the Philosophy of Music*, University Park: Pennsylvania State University Press, 33–98.

Spence, Alan 1990, 'John Owen and Trinitarian Agency', *Scottish Journal of Theology* 43/2: 157–73.

Spencer, Jon Michael 1991, *Theological Music: Introduction to Theomusicology*, New York, Westport, Conn. and London: Greenwoood Press.

1994 (ed.), *Theomusicology*, Durham, NC: Duke University Press.

Spufford, Margaret 1989, *Celebration*, London: Fount.

Stacey, David 1990, *Prophetic Drama in the Old Testament*, London: Epworth.

Stacey, Peter F. 1987, *Boulez and the Modern Concept*, Aldershot: Scholar Press.

Stannard, Russell 1993, *Doing Away with God? Creation and the Big Bang*, London: Marshall Pickering.

Stedman, Preston 1979, *The Symphony*, Englewood Cliffs, NJ: Prentice-Hall.

Steiner, George 1989, *Real Presences. Is There Anything in What We Say?* London: Faber and Faber.

1997, *Errata: An Examined Life*, London: Phoenix.

Steinitz, Richard 1994, 'John Tavener', in *John Tavener*, Chester Music, no date.

Stockhausen, Karlheinz 1959, ' . . . how time passes . . .', trans. Cornelius Cardew, *Die Reihe* 3: 10–40.

Stravinsky, Igor 1947, *Poetics of Music in the Form of Six Lessons*, trans. Arthur Knodel and Ingolf Dahl, Cambridge, Mass.: Harvard University Press.

Stravinsky, Igor and Craft, Robert 1968, *Dialogues and a Diary*, London: Faber & Faber.

Sturch, R. L. 1974, 'The Problem of Divine Eternity', *Religious Studies* 10: 487–93.

Sudnow, David 1993, *Ways of the Hand: The Organisation of Improvised Conduct*, Cambridge, Mass. and London: MIT Press.

Suurmond, Jean-Jacques 1994, *Word and Spirit at Play: Towards a Charismatic Theology*, London: SCM.

Swinburne, Richard 1994, *The Christian God*, Oxford: Clarendon Press, 1994.

Sykes, Stephen 1996, 'Ritual and the Sacrament of the Word', in David Brown and Ann Loades (eds.), *Christ: The Sacramental Word*, London: SPCK, 157–67.

Tanner, Michael 1988, 'The Pastness of the Present and the Presence of the Past', in Nicholas Kenyon (ed.), *Authenticity and Early Music*, Oxford: Oxford University Press, 137–211.

Tarasti, Eero 1994, *A Theory of Musical Semiotics*, Bloomington and Indianapolis: Indiana University Press.

Tavener, John, Mother Thekkla and Moody, Ivan 1994, *Ikons: Meditations in Words and Music*, London: Fount.

1995a, 'Art and the End-Point', unpublished lecture.

1995b, 'Towards a Sacred Art', in David Brown and Ann Loades (eds.), *The Sense of the Sacramental: Movement and Measure in Art and Music, Place and Time*, London: SPCK, 172–8.

1997, 'The Hussey Lecture', unpublished lecture.

'Sacred Music in the 20th Century', unpublished lecture, no date.

'The Sacred in Art', unpublished lecture, provided by Chester Music, source
unknown, no date.

Taylor, Brandon 1987, *Modernism, Post-Modernism, Realism: A Critical Perspective for Art*,
Winchester: Winchester School of Art Press.

Taylor, Charles 1989, *Sources of the Self: The Making of the Modern Identity*, Cambridge,
Mass.: Harvard University Press.

The Doctrine Commission of the Church of England 1995, *The Mystery of Salvation*,
London: Church House Publishing.

Thiselton, Anthony C. 1976, 'The Parousia in Modern Theology: Some Questions and
Comments', *Tyndale Bulletin* 27: 27–53.

1981, 'Knowledge, Myth, and Corporate Memory', in The Doctrine Commission of
the Church of England, *Believing in the Church: The Corporate Nature of Faith*,
London: SPCK, 45–78.

1992, *New Horizons in Hermeneutics*, London: Marshall Pickering.

1995, *Interpreting God and the Postmodern Self: On Meaning, Manipulation and Promise*,
Edinburgh: T. & T. Clark.

1998, 'Human Being, Relationality, and Time in Hebrews, 1 Corinthians and
Western Traditions', *Ex Auditu* 13: 76–95.

Thom, Paul 1990, 'Young's Critique of Authenticity in Musical Performance', *British
Journal of Aesthetics* 30/3: 273–6.

Thomas, Downing A. 1995, *Music and the Origins of Language: Theories from the French
Enlightenment*, Cambridge: Cambridge University Press.

Thomas, Ewart A. C. and Weaver, Wanda B. 1975, 'Cognitive Processing and Time
Perception', *Perception and Psychophysics* 17: 363–7.

Thompson, Michael 1991, *Clothed with Christ: The Example and Teaching of Jesus in Romans
12.1–15.13*, Sheffield: Sheffield Academic Press.

Thurian, Max 1983, 'The Eucharistic Memorial, Sacrifice of Praise and Supplication', in
Thurian, Max (ed.), *Ecumenical Perspectives on Baptism, Eucharist, and Ministry*,
Geneva: World Council of Churches, 90–103.

Tirro, F. 1967, 'The Silent Theme Tradition in Jazz', *Musical Quarterly* 53: 313–34.

Titon, Jeff Todd 1984, *World of Music: An Introduction to the Music of the World's Peoples*, New
York: Schirmer, London: Macmillan.

Torrance, Alan J. 1993, 'Response by Alan J. Torrance', in Hilary Regan and Alan J.
Torrance (eds.), *Christ and Context*, Edinburgh: T. & T. Clark.

1995, 'Demythologising Temporal Passage – Theological Reflections on D. C.
Williams' Theory of the Manifold', unpublished paper given to the Systematics
Seminar of the Faculty of Divinity, University of Cambridge.

1996, *Persons in Communion: Trinitarian Description and Human Participation*,
Edinburgh: T. & T. Clark.

1997a, 'The Self-Communication of God: Where and How does God Speak?'
unpublished paper delivered at the Annual Conference of The Society for the
Study of Theology.

1997b, '*Creatio ex Nihilo* and the Spatio-Temporal Dimensions, with Special
Reference to Jürgen Moltmann and D. C. Williams', in Colin E. Gunton (ed.), *The
Doctrine of Creation*, Edinburgh: T. & T. Clark, 82–103.

Torrance, James B. 1996, *Worship, Community and the Triune God of Grace*, Exeter:
Paternoster.

Torrance, T. F. 1969, *Space, Time and Incarnation*, Oxford: Oxford University Press.

1976, *Space, Time and Resurrection*, Edinburgh: Handsel Press.

1981a, *Divine and Contingent Order*, Oxford: Oxford University Press.

1981b (ed.), *The Incarnation*, Edinburgh: Handsel Press.

1982, *Reality and Evangelical Theology*, Philadelphia: Westminster.

1984, *Transformation and Convergence within the Frame of Knowledge. Explorations in the Interpretation of Scientific and Theological Enterprise*, Belfast: Christian Journals.

1985, *Reality and Scientific Theology*, Edinburgh: Scottish Academic Press.

1991, 'The Atonement, The Singularity of Christ and the Finality of the Cross: The Atonement and the Moral Order', in Nigel M. de S. Cameron (ed.), *Universalism and the Doctrine of Hell*, Carlisle: Paternoster and Grand Rapids, Mich.: Baker Book House, 223–56.

1995, *Divine Meaning: Studies in Patristic Hermeneutics*, Edinburgh: T. & T. Clark.

1996, *The Christian Doctrine of God, One Being Three Persons*, Edinburgh: T. & T. Clark.

Travis, Stephen 1980, *Christian Hope and the Future of Man*, Leicester: IVP.

Tumelty, Michael 1992, 'John Tavener', *Classical Music* 464: 18–19.

Valéry, Paul 1968, *Poésies*, Paris: Gallimard.

Vanhoozer, Kevin J. 1990, *Biblical Narrative in the Philosophy of Paul Ricoeur: A Study in Hermeneutics and Theology*, Cambridge: Cambridge University Press.

1998, *Is There a Meaning in the Text? The Bible, the Reader and the Morality of Literary Knowledge*, Leicester: Apollos.

Volf, Miroslav 1996, *Exclusion and Embrace: A Theological Exploration of Identity, Otherness, and Reconciliation*, Nashville: Abingdon.

Wagner, Richard 1907, 'On Franz Liszt's Symphonic Poems', in *Richard Wagner's Prose Works*, trans. William Ashton Ellis, London: William Reeves.

Walker, Andrew 1996, *Telling the Story: Gospel, Mission and Culture*, London: SPCK.

Walton, Kendall 1988, 'What is Abstract About the Art of Music?' *Journal of Aesthetics and Art Criticism* 46/3: 351–64.

Warnock, Mary 1994, *Imagination and Time*, Oxford: Blackwell.

Watts, F. and Williams, M. 1988, *The Psychology of Religious Knowing*, Cambridge: Cambridge University Press.

Watson, Francis 1994, *Text, Church and World: Biblical Interpretation in Theological Perspective*, Edinburgh: T. & T. Clark.

1995, 'Christ, Law and Freedom', in Colin E. Gunton (ed.), *God and Freedom: Essays in Historical and Systematic Theology*, Edinburgh: T. & T. Clark, 82–102.

1997, *Text and Truth: Redefining Biblical Theology*, Edinburgh: T. & T. Clark.

1998, 'Theology and Music', *Scottish Journal of Theology* 51/4: 435–63.

Webb, Stephen H. 1996, *The Gifting God: A Trinitarian Ethics of Excess*, Oxford: Oxford University Press.

Weber, Otto 1983, *Foundations of Dogmatics*, vol. II, trans. Darrell L. Guder, Grand Rapids, Mich.: Eerdmans.

Webster, John 1995, *Barth's Ethics of Reconciliation*, Cambridge: Cambridge University Press.

Weigert, Andrew J. 1981, *Sociology of Everyday Life*, London: Longman.

Weinandy, Thomas G. 1995, *The Father's Spirit of Sonship: Reconceiving the Trinity*, Edinburgh: T. & T. Clark.

Weiser, A 1962, *Psalms*, London: SCM.

Welker, Michael 1994, *God the Spirit*, Minneapolis: Fortress Press.

Wells, Samuel 1996, 'Keeping the Story Going: Improvisation and Casuistry in Christian Ethics', unpublished paper.

Wetzel, J. 1990, *Augustine and the Limits of Virtue*, Cambridge: Cambridge University Press.

Whitrow, G. J. 1972, 'Reflections on the History of the Concept of Time', in J. T. Fraser, N. Lawrence and D. Park (eds.), *The Study of Time*, vol. IV, New York: Springer-Verlag, 1–11.

1980, *The Natural Philosophy of Time*, Oxford: Clarendon Press.

1988, *Time in History*, Oxford: Oxford University Press.

Wilkinson, David A. 1993, *God, the Big Bang and Stephen Hawking*, Tunbridge Wells: Monarch.

Williams, D. C. 1951, 'The Myth of Passage', *The Journal of Philosophy* 48: 457–72.

Williams, Rowan 1989, 'Postmodern Theology and the Judgment of the World', in Frederic B. Burnham (ed.), *Postmodern Theology: Christian Faith in a Pluralist World*, New York: Harper Collins, 92–112.

1992, 'Saving Time: Thoughts on Practice, Patience and Vision', *New Blackfriars* 73: 319–26.

1994, 'Keeping Time', in *Open to Judgement: Sermons and Addresses*, London: Darton, Longman and Todd, 247–50.

Wintle, Christopher 1994 (ed.), *Hans Keller: Essays on Music*, Cambridge: Cambridge University Press.

Witkin, Robert W., 1998, *Adorno on Music*, London: Routledge.

Wolterstorff, Nicholas 1980a, *Art in Action*, Grand Rapids: Michigan: Eerdmans, 1980.

1980b, *Works and Worlds of Art*, Oxford: Clarendon Press.

1987, 'The Work of Making a Work of Music', in P. J. Alperson (ed.), *What is Music? An Introduction to the Philosophy of Music*, University Park: Pennsylvania State University Press, 103–29.

Wood, James 1992, 'Chant of the Mystic Musician', *The Guardian* July 20: 18–19.

Wright, N. T. 1991, *The Climax of the Covenant*, Edinburgh: T. & T. Clark.

1992, *The New Testament and the People of God*, London: SPCK.

Yates, Frances A. 1966, *The Art of Memory*, Chicago: University of Chicago Press.

Young, Frances 1990, *The Art of Performance: Towards a Theology of Holy Scripture*, London: Darton, Longman and Todd.

Zimmerli, Walther 1963, 'Promise and Fulfilment', in Claus Westermann (ed.), *Essays on Old Testament Interpretation*, London: SCM, 89–122.

1971, *Man and his Hope in the Old Testament*, London: SCM.

Zizioulas, John 1985, *Being as Communion*, New York: St. Vladimir's Seminary Press.

Zuckerkandl, Victor 1956, *Sound and Symbol: Music and the External World*, London: Routledge and Kegan Paul.

1959, *The Sense of Music*, Princeton: Princeton University Press.

1960, Review of Deryck Cooke's *The Language of Music*, in *Journal of Music Theory* 4/1: 104–9.

1973, *Man the Musician*, Princeton: Princeton University Press.

Index of names

Abraham 109, 110, 256, 257, 261
Adam 83, 149, 257, 258, 260, 267
Adam, Barbara 35, 36, 59, 72, 73, 86
Adorno, Theodor 155, 156, 173, 185
Alperson, P. J. 184
Ambrose of Milan 83
Aristotle 56
Ashby, W. R. 198
Astaire, Fred 40
Attali, Jacques 5, 155, 205
Auden, W. H. 129, 218
Augustine of Hippo 29, 56, 63, 64–5, **75–85**, 96, 129, 137, 148
Austen, Jane 137

Bach, C. P. E. 181
Bach, J. S. 6, 7, 95, 131, 137, 156, 157, 170, 181, 185
Bailey, Derek 179, 205, 221, 231
Ballantine, Christopher 14
Balthasar, Hans Urs von 3
Banks, Robert 72
Barry, Barbara 160
Barth, Karl 3, 60, **93–6**, 114, 148, 151, 152–3, 275, 277
Barthes, Roland 21, 28
Barton, Stephen 4
Basil the Great 243
Bauckham, Richard 119, 120, 122, 216, 217
Baudrillard, Jean 155
Bechet, Sidney 206–7
Beethoven, Ludwig van 7, 12, 43, 49, 101, 102, 114–18, 126, 150, 157–64, 166, 184, 221
Begbie, Jeremy S. 5, 13, 14, 15, 16, 34, 105, 129, 133, 146, 231, 252
Benjamin, William E. 60, 155
Bennett, Gerald 187, 193
Bentley, John 130
Berendt, Joachim E. 179, 207, 213, 232

Berger, Peter 58
Berio, Luciano 182
Berleant, Arnold 37, 50, 162
Berliner, Paul F. 179, 201, 209, 213, 226, 229, 232
Bernstein, Leonard 101, 163
Bierwisch, M. 22
Black, Max 65
Blacking, John 52
Bockmuehl, Markus 119
Bonhoeffer, Dietrich 3, 273, 278
Boulez, Pierre 180, 182, **186–97**, 203, 218, 219, 234, 243, 246, 272, 274
Bourdieu, Pierre 248
Bowker, John 91, 92, 198
Bowman, Wayne D. 20, 100, 155
Brahms, Johannes 44, 157, 222
Braine, David 32
Brindle, Reginald Smith 187, 189
Brown, Calvin 20, 104
Broyles, Michael 159
Brueggemann, Walter 167, 168
Bultmann, Rudolf 60, 122
Butler, Christopher 187, 192

Cage, John 185, **188–92**, **194–7**, 203, 218, 219, 234, 243, 246, 272, 274
Calvin, John 170
Campbell, Douglas 260
Campling, Christopher R. 44, 49
Capek, Milic 67
Cardew, Cornelius 204, 233
Chadwick, Henry 81, 84
Chafe, Eric 3
Chopin, Frederic 40–2, 160, 232
Chua, Daniel K. L. 117
Clark, Ronald W. 29
Clifton, Thomas 34
Clines, David J. 108–9

[303]

Index of biblical verses

General index